# The Modern Corporate Manager: Responsibility and Regulation

WILLIAM A. GROENING

McGRAW-HILL BOOK COMPANY

New York   St. Louis   San Francisco   Auckland   Bogotá
Hamburg   Johannesburg   London   Madrid   Mexico   Montreal   New Delhi
Panama   Paris   São Paulo   Singapore   Sydney   Tokyo   Toronto

**Library of Congress Cataloging in Publication Data**

Groening, William A., date.
The modern corporate manager.

(Regulation of American business and industry series)

Includes index.

1. Directors of corporations—Legal status, laws, etc.—United States. I. Title. II. Series.

KF1423.G76        346.73′06642        80-21829
ISBN 0-07-024940-7

1234567890 DODO 8987654321

The editors for this book were Robert A. Rosenbaum, Kathleen Tappen, and Susan Thomas; the designer was Elliot Epstein; and the production supervisor was Paul A. Malchow. It was set in Palatino by The Heffernan Press Inc.

Printed and bound by R. R. Donnelley & Sons Company.

*To Virginia*

# Contents

CHAPTER TWELVE

## Self-Regulation by Managers: Compliance, Circumspection, and Cognizance

# Preface

---

This book is for corporate managers and their counsel. It is concerned with the responsibilities and liabilities of managers at all levels, not just directors and chief executives but also functional and line managers whose daily efforts keep America's corporations running. It is not an exhaustive treatment of the law, but it presents to both manager and lawyer some of the more important federal statutes regulating business conduct and their impact upon the manager personally.

In the lively debates on the role of the corporation in modern society, critics frequently assert that the corporation is "faceless," concerned only with making money, oblivious to the public welfare, and immune from restraints on its conduct.

In my forty years of corporate experience I have found the American corporation to be not faceless, but rather an aggregation of many faces—of people having hopes, fears, and ambitions of their own but generally conscious of the rights and proper concerns of others. Far from being immune from restraints upon its conduct, the corporation is subjected to an incredible maze of laws and regulations affecting almost every aspect of its daily business operations. Failure to comply strictly with the rules can result in serious penalties not only for the corporation but also for the individual manager. It is my belief that the legal responsibility of managerial personnel has not received sufficient attention either within or outside the corporation. Managers often do not learn of the potentialities of their personal liability until it is too late.

This book, therefore, brings together some of these potentialities. Beginning with the early days of corporate history, it traces the development of managerial responsibility for the acts of the corporation in its relations with third parties, as well as the relationship of the manager to the corporation and its stockholders under state corporation laws. Moving then into the arena of federal regulation of business, it examines the personal liability features of the principal federal statutes pertaining to business, including the enforcement policies of the government. It is concerned with laws relating to transportation, antitrust, health, safety and the environment, employee relations, securities, and some aspects of international trade. Space does not permit coverage of all the federal laws that might have been described. Attention has, however, been directed to those federal statutes that are believed to be of interest to the broadest segment of managers of industrial and mercantile corporations.

The history of the federal regulatory laws, their interpretation, and their enforcement has shown that exposure to liability has steadily increased, that the pace of public and private enforcement has accelerated, and that penalties have been made larger and are more frequently imposed. The past decade has witnessed a particularly strong upward trend in subjecting the corporate manager to personal liability.

Despite this background of the most extensive governmental regulation of business in the nation's history, there are critics of corporate conduct who demand much greater regulation. Their efforts are directed primarily to the structural nature and governance of the large corporation. The traditional concept of the corporation is attacked by those who see it not as a private business but as a public institution approaching that of a political entity. They want it governed by representatives of government or of various interest groups. Other, less severe critics would impose less severe reforms. Still others, in government as well as private sectors, urge greater voluntary attention by management to the quality of corporate governance and the recognition of the various segments of society upon which the corporation may have an impact or by which it may be impacted.

Of all the proposals, those that look to voluntary efforts have the best of the argument. Wresting control of the corporation from its management and politicizing it to satisfy vague and undefinable public needs will benefit neither the corporation nor the public it serves. This does not mean, however, that corporate managers can afford to be complacent. They must recognize the temper of the times. As responsible citizens, they should make certain that the laws are obeyed. Without sacrificing attention to the business and financial needs of their corporation, managers should evaluate the public interest aspects of their activities to assure that their actions and attitudes of today are the best for the welfare of the corporation and its stockholders tomorrow.

WILLIAM A. GROENING

Midland, Michigan

# CHAPTER ONE

# Introduction

---

As we enter the last decades of the twentieth century, we find American business going through a period that is one of the most complicated, perplexing, and frustrating that it has yet experienced.

Immense as were the problems of the Great Depression of the 1930s, they were no more challenging or baffling than those facing the corporate executive of the 1980s. The executive of fifty years ago faced economic problems almost entirely: loss of sales, loss of profits, the necessity of releasing employees, and, in many cases, personal financial ruin.

Today there still are economic problems, but they are more apt to be the problems of inflation and energy and their consequences. In addition, the corporate executive today is confronted with a myriad of governmental regulations covering almost every conceivable aspect of business operations. They may vary in nature, scope, and severity with the size of the company or the nature of its business, but no executive is free of them. The laws and regulations governing business in the 1980s are much more extensive than anyone in business or the government could have possibly anticipated a half-century ago. Nor is that all.

The very reason for a company's existence may be seriously challenged today. If its operations pollute the water or the atmosphere, it not only may be in violation of law and be required to abate the offending pollution, but there even may be a demand that it go out of business completely, or that it cease manufacturing an offending product. If a company shuts down an operation to abate pollution, it may mean the end of jobs, thus wreaking havoc in the community in which the factory is located, and the executive may be accused of being callous to the needs of employees and their families.[1]

Executives may be called upon by the authorities to right social injustices of the past, whether or not they contributed to them in any manner, by increasing employment of minority-group members at the expense of other, possibly better qualified, candidates. Compliance may result in criticism for reverse discrimination or for being indifferent to the needs of still other minorities. If the same standard of performance is demanded from new minority employees that the employer has demanded of other employees, there may be accusations of discrimination for not having adequately taken cultural differences into account in personnel evaluations. If the employer does not demand the same standard of performance, there may be criticism and resistance by other employees, and perhaps by stockholders, if they perceive that efficiency and profits are thereby reduced.

The foregoing are just a few simple examples of the dilemmas faced by today's business executives. Daily they confront problems of compliance with the antitrust laws; securities laws; laws regulating health, safety, and the environment; laws regulating all phases of the employer-employee relationship; and other federal and state laws too numerous to mention. In addition, there are those who would impose upon the corporate manager responsibilities for curing the social ills of the world. Some urge the company to get out of South Africa, or Chile, or some other country whose regime a particular group of critics does not like. Others urge the company to support or to oppose Israel in its long-standing feud with the Arabs. Some may want companies to take measures to conserve energy, to preserve the environment, to employ and promote minorities, not only in accordance with legal requirements, but often considerably beyond such requirements. Some are not content to leave such measures or compliance with the law or ethical standards to the good faith efforts of management or to the monitoring of such efforts by authorized government agencies. Often critics do not trust either the management or the government agencies. So they wish to install "watchers" to make sure that management does its job the way they, the critics, wish it done. If the managers are concerned with profits, they are greedy. If they try to comply with social objectives, they are careless with the stockholders' money.

All this hue and cry, whether by members of Congress, academics, consumerists, or other activist groups, generally is directed at the largest corporations, which constitute the upper tier of those whose stock is traded on the New York Stock Exchange.[2] Corporations, their critics say, are faceless and responsible to no one. But then some faces *are* found—the faces of corporate managers, to whom the criticism is then directed. Management is said by critics to be responsible to no one except itself—not to the stockholders, not to employees, not to the government, not to customers, not to the public.[3]

Based upon first-hand observation and the experience of four decades of corporate law practice, it is my opinion that the charges of lack of responsibility so commonly leveled at the management of large corporations are greatly exaggerated and usually without solid foundation. My experience may suggest a bias toward the corporate point of view. I readily admit a measure of bias, but also plead that mine is an

"objective bias." Be that as it may, this book will show that there is an immense body of law imposing personal responsibilities, personal liabilities, and personal penalties upon corporate managers, and that these responsibilities are awesome and the attendant liabilities and penalties severe and real. This does not mean that the laws are always obeyed. But the laws and the potential liabilities are there, whether the corporation be large or small. Managers do indeed face serious personal risks in the performance of their management functions.

The title of this book highlights the modern corporate manager. That manager is, of course, the book's central character. What do I mean by a "manager"? First, I use the term "manager" to include any person who has a management function in a modern American corporation.[4] At the top of the corporate pyramid is the board of directors. One may question whether a director *qua* director is really a manager. One might say, more exactly, that a director is one of a collegial group to whom top management reports. But most state corporation laws specify that a corporation "shall be managed by its board of directors." Only recently (1974) has the Delaware corporation code been amended to provide that a corporation "shall be managed by or *under the direction* of its board of directors"[5] [emphasis supplied], and a few other states are now making a similar amendment. So directors are managers, and their responsibilities, their exposure, and their regulation will be discussed.

The chairman of the board is by definition a director, is also generally involved in active day-to-day management, and often is the chief executive officer. The president, whether chief executive officer or chief operating officer, is also nearly always a member of the board. In most corporations one or more vice presidents or other officers are also directors. These full-time officer-directors are called "inside directors," a term that will be used frequently in this book.

Directors not serving the corporation fulltime are generally called "outside directors," but in the semantics of recent discourses on the subject, their "outsideness" may be questioned if they are lawyers, investment bankers, or other professionals serving the corporation, or if they are retired officers of the corporation or executives of companies that are important customers or suppliers. The responsibilities and liabilities of inside directors and outside directors may not always be the same, as we shall see.

Another category of manager must also be considered. That is the officer who is not a director. The number of officers who are not directors in large American corporations exceeds the number of those who are directors. They, too, have very real legal responsibilities and exposures and are subject to much regulation.

Finally, there is the vast number of managerial personnel who do not have officer rank, but who have important day-to-day responsibilities for making an enterprise work. They are factory managers, research managers, sales managers, chief accountants, purchasing agents, traffic managers—people holding every conceivable kind of job title imaginable, tens of thousands of people who in their daily occupations face the task of "front-line" compliance with our laws and regulations, and who face personal liabilities, personal penalties, and probably loss of employment if they do not comply satisfactorily.

So we are going to be looking at the responsibilities, liabilities, and regulation of corporate managers of varying ranks.

Traditionally, corporate managers have been men. But we live in an era when traditions are being broken. With the increasing number of women pursuing business careers and rising in the corporate hierarchy, the modern corporate manager may be a man or a woman. In this book, therefore, when masculine nouns and pronouns are occasionally used for simplicity, they are intended to refer to both male and female managers unless the context clearly indicates the contrary.

We will begin our exploration of the subject with a brief review of corporate origins. We will examine the liability of corporate managers under laws fashioned by the courts and under various state statutes. This is a highly technical legal subject. The cases are legion and much has been written about it. I will not attempt to analyze all the cases in the fashion of a scholarly legal text, but the end-of-chapter notes will tell you where such texts can be found, if you wish to pursue the subject in more depth.

Primary attention will be devoted to the personal liabilities and civil and criminal sanctions imposed upon corporate managers at all levels by the increasing number of statutes enacted by the Congress of the United States in its efforts to regulate a wide range of business operations. Where appropriate, we also will look at some selected state statutes on these subjects. We will see that the traditional concepts of management responsibility that exist under the state corporation laws and in the court decisions based upon them and upon common-law concepts are only a very small portion of the exposures that the modern corporate manager faces.

Laws governing business activities have been increasing in volume and intensity as time progresses. While the first of those laws is now approaching its centennial, the rate of their enactment, the standards of responsibility, and the severity of the sanctions they impose have increased from decade to decade. The result is that today it is difficult to find any phase of business activity not subject to substantial regulation and exposure of the manager who deliberately or inadvertently fails to comply.

As pervasive as modern regulation appears, there still seems to exist, on the part of critics of corporations in and out of government, a desire for yet more laws and more regulation, directed primarily at the large corporations and their managers. The corporations and their managers have a bad press. Being low in public esteem and relatively high in material wealth, they make inviting targets for those who want to correct the ills of modern society, actual or imagined. We will examine these criticisms and some of the proposals for corporate reform as they

affect the manager, and evaluate the proposals not only from the viewpoint of business people and their lawyers, but from that of the general
public as well.

I do not perceive, however, that I will have finished my task merely
by describing the law and the potentialities and evaluating current
proposals for reform. As one who has been in the fray, I think I may also
have some worthwhile observations about what corporate managers
can do in their daily operations to assure compliance, to demonstrate
responsible corporate conduct, to reduce exposure to liability, to reduce
unwarranted criticism of business corporations, and, it is hoped, to
slow the steady trend toward overregulation.

## NOTES

1. The problems caused by the closing of the Youngstown Sheet and Tube steel
   plant at Youngstown, Ohio, constitute an outstanding example. See "A
   Huge Pink Slip for an Ohio City," *Bus. Week*, Oct. 3, 1977, pp. 39–40; "Who
   the Hell Wants to Catch Trout in the Mahoning?" *Ind. Week*, Oct. 10, 1979,
   p. 19.

2. The classic source cited for the lack of corporate democracy is Berle & Means,
   *The Modern Corporation and Private Property* (rev. ed. Harcourt, Brace &
   World, 1968; first published, 1932), a study of the 200 largest corporations.
   Eisenberg contends that shareholder governance is effective in some smaller,
   publicly held corporations. Eisenberg, *The Structure and Governance of the
   Corporation* (Little, Brown & Co., 1976) 64–68. Conard maintains that corporate democracy does exist in several thousands of other publicly traded
   corporations. Conard, *Corporations in Perspective* (The Foundation Press,
   1976) 338.

3. This is the central theme of Stone, *Where the Law Ends: The Social Rule of
   Corporate Behavior* (Harper & Row, 1975); and Nader, Green & Seligman,
   *Taming the Giant Corporation* (W. W. Norton & Co., 1976).

4. I use the terms "manager" and "management" in a broader sense than the
   classic definition of the words. See, for example, Berle & Means, *The Modern
   Corporation and Private Property* 196:

   > Management may be defined as that body of men who, in law, have formally
   > assumed the duties of exercising domination over the corporate business and
   > assets. It thus derives its position from a legal title of some sort. Universally, under
   > the American system of law, managers consist of a board of directors and the senior
   > officers of the corporation.

5. See discussion of these statutory provisions in Chapter 3 at notes 1–5.

# CHAPTER TWO

# Corporate Origins: Limited Liability of Shareholders and Managers

An understanding of almost any field can be facilitated by a brief look at its historical background. So it is worthwhile to devote a few pages to corporate origins.

In early corporate history we see the separation of the corporate "personality" from that of its members. We see the rise of limited liability of stockholders and the recognition of the corporate act as distinguished from the act of its managers. At common law we see a form of limited liability on the part of managers, although the term "limited liability" seems never to have been used to describe the liability of a corporate manager.

The term "common law" generally connotes nonstatutory principles of law as developed by the courts over the centuries. In this book the term is sometimes used in the field of corporation law to describe also the application of such principles to interpretation of a state corporation statute.

Upon this foundation we will examine the statutory rules, liabilities, and penalties which, in specific areas of the law outside of corporation law per se, have been superimposed upon, and have expanded, the common-law rules of managerial responsibility.

## THE EVOLUTION OF THE CORPORATION

Although the corporation as we know it today is of fairly recent origin, the concept of a corporate body having a separate existence apart from its members goes back to ancient times. Scholars disagree whether the corporation began with the Assyrians, the Greeks, or the Romans.[1] They also disagree as to whether corporations were used for business purposes in ancient times.

Whatever may have been the status of the corporation as a business entity during ancient times, the guild of the Middle Ages developed as a commercial entity, although still not of the type we know today.[2] Alfred Conard, professor of law at the University of Michigan, credits the Italians in the fourteenth and fifteenth centuries with developing the idea of shares in the corporation which could be traded and an elected board of governors.[3]

In the seventeenth century, the separateness of a corporation from its members was described by Lord Coke in *Sutton's Hospital Case* with these words: "For a corporation aggregate of many is invisible, immortal, and rests only in intendment and consideration of the law."[4] Two hundred years later, Chief Justice John Marshall gave a similar definition in the *Dartmouth College* case: "A corporation is an artificial being, invisible and intangible, and existing only in contemplation of the law."[5]

The age of exploration was also the age of the growth of the commercial spirit, and in England corporations were chartered by the sovereign to engage in exploration and trading. One of the most significant of these corporations was the East India Company, chartered by Elizabeth I in 1600. But by 1692, only three exploration and trading companies of any importance remained. In addition to East India, there were the Royal African Company and the Hudson's Bay Company. The latter survived as a British corporation until 1970 when, on its 300th anniversary, it was changed to a Canadian corporation. At the end of the seventeenth century, more frequent chartering of corporations occurred. Each corporation was authorized by a specific act of Parliament. Among the most notable charters of this period were those of the Bank of England, which still survives, and the South Sea Company, which foundered in the first major corporate scandal, the South Sea "bubble" of 1720.

The first business corporation to be organized on American soil did not appear until 1752 with the organization of The Philadelphia Contributionship for Insuring Houses from Loss by Fire, which did not, however, receive its charter from the Pennsylvania Legislature until 1768. The second American business corporation was the Bank of North America, chartered by the Continental Congress in 1781. The Massachusetts Legislature chartered a bank in 1784 and a bridge company in 1785. In 1786, Pennsylvania chartered another insurance company and New York chartered the first American manufacturing corporation, The Associated Manufacturing Iron Company. There were somewhere between five and twenty American business corporations in existence at the time of the adoption of the Constitution in 1787.[6] At the Constitutional Convention, James Madison on two occasions proposed an article or provisions relating to federal incorporation, but the proposal was defeated each time.[7] There have, of course, been federally chartered corporations, such as national banks, savings and loan associations, credit unions, the American Red Cross and a few other special corporations, which were mainly of a nonbusiness nature, but there has never

been a federally chartered manufacturing or mercantile corporation.
Federal incorporation is an implied power that may be exercised when
"necessary and proper" to the exercise of an express power vested in
the Congress, such as the power to regulate commerce.[8] We will examine federal incorporation more thoroughly in Chapter 11.

The decade following the adoption of the Constitution saw a significant increase in the number of business corporations, all incorporated by special acts of the state legislatures. Scholars have estimated
the number existing in 1800 as between 100 and 335.[9] Generally these
corporations were bridge and turnpike companies, banks, and insurance companies. Very few were engaged in manufacturing or mercantile activities, but by 1830 the New England states alone had 1,900
business corporations, of which nearly 600 were engaged in manufacturing or mining.[10] Because of the proliferation of corporations, their
chartering by a special act of a legislature rapidly was becoming impractical and also subject to possible abuses, as incorporators and legislators might each seek special favors from the other.

In 1795 North Carolina became the first state to adopt a general
corporation law, by which incorporators could obtain charters by application to a state administrative official and by compliance with the
various statutory requirements for incorporation. Massachusetts followed with a general corporation statute in 1799. New York adopted its
first incorporation statute in 1811 and Connecticut enacted one in 1837.
Other states followed in quick succession. Not only did incorporation
under general law become the normal practice, but most states went a
step further by forbidding incorporation by special act of the legislature. By the end of the nineteenth century, only Connecticut, Massachusetts, and New Hampshire still permitted special acts of incorporation.[11]

Since the United States government, unlike other national governments, did not provide a general incorporation law (except for certain
types of financial institutions), business corporations were the creatures
of the states of their respective incorporation. The question was then
raised as to the power of a corporation of one state to do business in
another state. This question was eventually laid to rest by the United
States Supreme Court in 1868 in the case of *Paul v. Virginia*,[12] when it
held that a state must on a nondiscriminatory basis admit a corporation
of another state to do business within its boundaries. This decision set
the stage for nationwide business enterprises, which could establish
factories, sales offices, and warehouses wherever the exigencies of good
business practice required, by applying for a permit from the "foreign"
state and paying the required fees and taxes.

The next significant step in corporate development was the so-called
modernized corporation statute. The earlier state corporation statutes
were filled with cumbersome detail. To a large extent they were concerned with form more than with substance. New Jersey in 1875

adopted the first of the modernized statutes.[13] It permitted considerable latitude in governing the internal affairs of the corporation, strengthening the positions of the directors and officers, and moving away from the old court-made concept of *ultra vires* (beyond its powers), by which a corporation was permitted to engage only in the very narrow lines of business defined in its charter and was prohibited from doing many of the things that its management might consider necessary and proper in the furtherance of its objectives at a later date. Maine was the next state to adopt a modernized corporation statute. In 1899 Delaware adopted a new general corporation law modeled upon the New Jersey act.

The popularity of Delaware as a state of incorporation is well known. Delaware incorporation is a great convenience to business executives and their counsel. Corporations have been organized or reincorporated in Delaware to obtain a perpetual charter when other states placed a limited term of years upon corporate existence. Others have found state requirements of stockholders' preemptive rights to subscribe to additional shares to be an encumbrance to a public offering of convertible bonds or convertible preferred stock or the establishment of employee stock purchase plans or option plans. They have gone to Delaware to eliminate preemptive rights. Still other corporations have selected Delaware to obtain a charter with a broad statement of business purposes because their "home state" so severely limited the business purposes of their corporations as to make a multibusiness operation impossible without the use of subsidiaries.

Many of these restrictions have been removed in recent years by states such as Texas and Michigan, but a corporation once organized in Delaware is likely to remain there. Delaware incorporation is also a source of great controversy; there are those who find something sinister in it. This subject will be treated more fully in Chapter 11.

## SOME BASIC OBSERVATIONS

In discussing the responsibilities of corporate managers, it is well to begin with a basic understanding of what corporations we are talking about. Conard has listed four classes of corporations according to their size and diversity of ownership. At the top he places the 200 largest corporations, which he and Philip Blumberg, professor of law at Boston University, call the "megacorporations." These corporations constitute .01 percent of all American corporations. He emphasizes that their distinctive characteristic is that "they are too big for any one to take over by a tender offer; and their shareholders are too numerous to permit a revolution by proxy fight."[14]

The next group Conard calls the "available" corporations. Their shares are publicly traded, but each is small enough to be susceptible to a takeover or to a proxy revolution. He estimates their number between 15,000 and 20,000, or about 1 percent of the total active business corporations in the United States.

The third category Conard describes as the "awkward stage" corpo-
rations, of which he estimates there may be 100,000. These are the corporations that are too small to be publicly traded but too large to enjoy the advantages of close corporations—that is, those who, by contract, charter, or bylaw, restrict the transfer of shares to outsiders.

Conard's fourth category is the closely held corporation, having thirty or fewer shareholders. He points out that between 90 and 95 percent of all United States corporations fall in this category. Generally, their assets and revenues are under $1 million. Their median is probably $100,000, and typically they have three shareholders.

In discussing the legal responsibilities and liabilities of corporate managers, it should be borne in mind that, generally speaking, the legal principles are the same whether the corporation is a megacorporation or a closely held corporation. There are, however, exceptions in the application of principles, such as the responsibilities under the Securities Exchange Act of 1934, that are based upon the size of the corporation and the number of shareholders, or in the enforcement of some of the more recent environmental legislation. There also may be a number of differences in responsibilities outside the area of legal obligation. For example, activists are not apt, either as stockholders or as members of the public, to confront managers of closely held or awkward stage corporations with social-issue questions or demands.

## LIMITED LIABILITY OF SHAREHOLDERS

An outstanding characteristic of the corporation is the concept of limited liability of members or shareholders—that is, that members or shareholders have no personal liability for the debts or other obligations of the corporation. Once they have paid for their shares, their liability is satisfied. It is this feature that has made it possible to attract investors with risk capital to invest in new enterprises, and that has facilitated the ready transferability of shares and has thus in a very practical sense established the corporation as an entity apart from its shareholders. Stevens has succinctly described the separateness of the corporation from its shareholders, which inevitably leads to limited liability, with these words:

> [A]ccording to the orthodox theory which still prevails, corporate rights and obligations are not the rights and obligations of the human beings who welded themselves into one unit, but are the rights and obligations of that one which is the product of their fusion. At the root of this view is the conception, not that the associates have a corporate personality separate and distinct from their individual legal personalities, but that there is a corporate person which is separate and distinct from the individual members; they are several right and duty bearing units; it is a single additional right and duty bearing unit.[15]

Despite the logic of Stevens's summation, made near the middle of the twentieth century, limited liability of shareholders did not always exist. In 1765, Blackstone stated in his *Commentaries* that shareholders are not liable for the debts of the corporation, but the early cases were confusing on this subject.[16] The first general corporation law of New York, the Manufacturing Corporation Act of 1811, made specific reference to limited liability, stating:

> [F]or all debts which shall be due and owing by the company *at the time of its dissolution,* the persons then comprising such company shall be individually responsible to the extent of their respective shares of stock in the said company and no further.[17] [Emphasis supplied.]

The implication was that so long as the corporation is a going concern, the shareholders have no responsibility to creditors, even though they may not have paid their stock subscriptions in full, but upon dissolution, creditors can proceed against shareholders to the extent of unpaid subscriptions. This is still the law today.

Limited liability of shareholders was rapidly developed in the United States during the early nineteenth century, but Great Britain did not establish limited liability by statute until Parliament enacted the Limited Liability Act of 1855.[18]

## CORPORATE LIABILITY FOR WRONGS

Equally as uncertain as the liability of shareholders in the early development of the corporation was the liability of the corporation itself for torts or crimes. In ancient Rome, since a corporation was considered an artificial being, it was therefore incapable of committing a tort or a crime.[19]

### Tort Liability

A tort is a civil wrong, other than breach of contract, for which the wrongdoer will be held liable in a suit for damages. Not a crime, which is an offense against the state, a tort is a wrong against a person, natural or corporate. In some instances, however, the same act may result in both tort and criminal liability.

In England the question of tort liability became entangled in the rigid formal requirements of the time that were necessary for bringing actions to court.[20] But in 1774 Lord Mansfield upheld a judgment against a municipal corporation for failure to repair a watercourse so as to keep it navigable, and in 1812 Lord Ellenborough upheld an action against the Bank of England for conversion of bank notes entrusted to it.[21]

The first American case holding a corporation liable for a tort committed by its agents was decided in Massachusetts in 1807.[22] In 1830 Chief Justice Marshall held that corporate liability for tort was "well settled."[23]

# Criminal Liability

The question of criminal liability at common law seemed even more perplexing than that of tort liability. If a corporate charter did not authorize the commission of torts, it most certainly did not authorize the commission of crimes. So far as responsibility of the principal is concerned, a crime is an even more personal act than a tort. At common law, a corporation could not be guilty of a crime.[24] Many scholars have questioned the policy of holding a corporation vicariously liable for criminal acts committed by its officers and employees, but it appears to be settled law that the act of the employee, of whatever level, will be imputed to the corporation to establish criminal responsibility.[25]

## LIMITED LIABILITY OF MANAGERS

Thus we have seen that it is settled law that a stockholder as such is not liable for the debts or acts of the corporation in which he or she has invested and that the corporation itself may be held liable for the torts and crimes committed by its officers and employees in the scope of their duties.

But what of the officers and employees themselves? At common law, it appears that their liability also was, in a sense, limited. In contract situations, an agent (officer, employee, or person otherwise delegated to act) is merely the instrumentality or means by which a principal (corporate or, in some cases, individual) acts. The other party is concerned about the ability, financial, technical, or otherwise, of the principal to perform the contract. The agent may or may not be the person or one of the persons who will be performing on behalf of the principal. Therefore, in a suit for breach of contract, an agent will not be liable for the acts of the principal except in those situations where the agent has failed to disclose to the other party that he or she is acting for a principal, thereby misleading the other party as to the identity of the contracting party.[26]

In tort situations, however, the rule is quite different. A person who is guilty of tortious conduct cannot at common law defend on the ground of having acted for another. The person is liable for the consequences of her or his acts. This is readily understandable in the case of a personal act, as, for example, when an employee drove the employer's automobile negligently and collided with another, causing injury and damage. In a contract situation, the other party was promised performance by the principal, not by the agent. But in an automobile accident, as in any tort situation, the injured party was not promised anything. He was damaged in his person or his property, and it is immaterial to him whether the person who drove the other car was acting for another or on his own behalf. That the corporation may also be personally liable for the tort does not exonerate the employee. In most situations, it may make no practical difference, as probably both the corporation and the employee will be covered by the same automotive liability insurance policy, but if the corporation is insolvent and has failed to insure its automobile, it can make a big difference to the employee.

All the foregoing refers to the active participant in the tortious act. But what about the nonparticipating manager?

## Negligence

A 1973 decision of the Louisiana Supreme Court, *Canter v. Koehring Company*,[27] illustrates circumstances under which corporate managers may be held liable or not liable for the negligence of the corporation. This case was concerned with the personal liability of six corporate managers of two different companies, none of them a corporate officer. The case resulted from the death of a construction foreman, who was killed when the boom of a large crane broke while lifting a heavy tower or chemical still. The widow and children of the deceased foreman brought a wrongful death action against five engineering employees of the manufacturer for whom the still was being installed and one supervisory employee of the construction contractor by whom the deceased foreman had been employed. The manufacturer's engineers were Baker, the superintendent of engineering; Spalding, the plant construction engineer, who reported to Baker and who had general supervision over the twelve to fifteen contractors at the plant site; Smith, a construction engineer; Sach, a project or field engineer; and Stacy, the field engineer assigned to the particular job. Substantial evidence showed that the manufacturer had delegated to these five engineer defendants its "engineering responsibility to furnish adequate weight information for the lift to be accomplished safely."[28] The still alone weighed 46 tons, which was within the lifting capacity of the crane, but about 7 tons of appurtenances (insulation, ladders, piping, catwalks, etc.) had been affixed to it. The addition of the appurtenances brought the weight above the capacity of the crane and caused it to break.

The court addressed itself to the question of personal liability of a corporate officer, agent, supervisor, or employee. It held that where a corporation has a duty of care to the plaintiff and breach of that duty has caused the damage for which recovery is sought, and where the corporation has delegated that duty, there can be personal liability on the part of the delegate resulting from personal fault. The delegate is liable for failure to discharge the obligation with the degree of care required by ordinary prudence under the same or similar circumstances. But the court emphasized that, to be held liable, the delegate must have a personal duty toward the injured plaintiff. General administrative responsibilities are not sufficient grounds for basing personal liability upon a corporate manager. The court stated:

> If the defendant's general responsibility has been delegated with due care to some responsible subordinate or subordinates, he is not himself per-

sonally at fault and liable for the negligent performance of this responsibility unless he personally knows or . . . should know of its non-performance or mal-performance and has nevertheless failed to cure the risk of harm.[29]

On trial, the jury found four out of the five engineers to be guilty of personal negligence. The court found there was substantial evidence to support these findings. A review of the individual situations is useful, as it illustrates the differing kinds of responsibility of managers engaged in the same project, with differing legal consequences.

Baker, the superintendent of engineering, "personally ordered the vessel lifted into position immediately upon finding the project was behind schedule, thus depriving those involved of an opportunity to use a shorter boom and for more reflection as to the move."[30]

Smith, the construction engineer, had attended a conference with the contractor's field supervisor an hour before the fatal lift and permitted it to proceed, even though he was aware of the equipment and of the weight information.

Sach, the project or field engineer, gave the contractor erroneous weight information of 46 tons, although he knew of the actual greater weight.

Stacy, the field engineer, had the responsibility of having the correct weight information determined and should have known that the appurtenances had added weight to that shown on the equipment list, but he permitted the lifting to go ahead upon the incorrect assumption as to the weight.

The court held that each of these four was correctly found to be guilty of personal negligence.

On the other hand, the jury found Spalding, the plant construction engineer, free from personal negligence. His were general administrative responsibilities. With twelve to fifteen contractors to supervise, he necessarily had to delegate authority. There was no evidence either that he had delegated his responsibility to an incompetent subordinate or that "he should by the exercise of reasonable care have known of the breach of duty by the subordinate . . . engineers." (Baker, his superior, was held liable, not because of his higher position in the engineering hierarchy, but because of his active involvement in the lifting operation.)

The negligence of Frenzel, the contractor's job superintendent, was also before the jury. The jury held him jointly liable with the four engineers of the manufacturer in having caused the accident. Upon review, the court found substantial evidence to support this finding, stating that he was "under such notice as to the possible inaccuracy of the weight furnished as to have required him in ordinary prudence to have checked further before undertaking a lift of the magnitude involved."[31]

The practical effect of the *Canter* decision and the other decisions consistent with it is apparent. Principals are responsible for their agents, but an agent does not become responsible for the acts of sub-agents merely because of being their supervisor. A manager who has no reason to doubt the competency of subordinates is entitled to rely upon the assumption that they will satisfactorily perform their duties. But an agent (or subagent) who is *personally* negligent may be held personally liable. To hold the supervising agent liable merely because he or she is a supervisor would pose a responsibility upon supervisors that would be wholly inconsistent with the realities of the business world. On the other hand, to absolve an agent of personal liability merely because he or she is acting for a principal would be unjust both to the principal and to the injured party. Proper responsibility for corporate torts is promoted by the rules enunciated in *Canter*.

## Other Torts

Tort liability of a manager is not confined to negligence situations. If a corporation unlawfully takes (technically, converts) the property of another, the manager who participates personally in the conversion on behalf of the corporation may be held personally liable. This was the result in *Olin Mathieson Chemical Corp. v. Planters Corp.*,[32] in which a corporation received goods on consignment from another corporation under a contract providing that upon sale of the goods, the proceeds were to be held in trust for the consignor. The treasurer of the consignee, however, commingled the proceeds with the consignee's funds and used them for corporate purposes. Because of his personal participation in the misappropriation, the treasurer was held personally liable, even though he received no personal benefit from the misappropriation. In a recent case of unfair competition, a corporate president who normally directed the activities found to constitute unfair competition was held personally liable.[33]

## Directors' Liability for Corporate Torts

Directors also enjoy an immunity at common law from liability for torts of the corporation in which they have not personally participated. If, however, a corporation commits a tort upon the express direction of its board of directors, the directors voting to give the direction may be held personally liable.[34] But express direction may not be a requisite if there is a clear duty on the part of the directors to monitor performance. That apparently was the rationale of the decision of the Fifth Circuit in *Emmert v. Drake*,[35] where the directors authorized the borrowing of money by the corporation upon a promissory note containing a provision that it was to be repaid out of the proceeds of the first public sale of corporate stock. Stock was sold, but the proceeds were used for other purposes. Later, when the corporation was insolvent, the directors were held personally liable for having failed to assure themselves that the proceeds of the stock sale were used to pay off the indebtedness. In this case, then, there was no active participation in a tort. There probably was not even a tort in the usual sense of the term. The corporation

breached a contract, and the misappropriation was found to be in the nature of a tort. Whether the legal theory of the wrong is based on tort or contract law, the important point is that the directors were personally involved in the commitment as to the use of corporate funds, and had a duty to see that this commitment was fulfilled.[36]

## Mismanagement and Insolvency

Still another potential liability on the part of corporate management arises at common law when the corporation becomes insolvent and the unpaid creditors accuse the directors and top officers of neglect of duty—mismanagement of the corporation. The standards of due care required of managers have been more fully examined in the cases concerned with relations between managers and the stockholders, and this subject is dealt with in the next chapter. Suffice it to say here that directors and officers have in fact been held liable for mismanagement upon the suit of a creditor. In this type of situation, a creditor may bring a derivative action (that is an action in her or his own name but on behalf of the corporation) against the directors and officers.[37] As the creditor will usually be one of numerous unpaid creditors and the damage done to this individual is indirect, the creditor's situation is not unlike that of the shareholder who sues in a derivative action on behalf of the corporation to protect his or her interests and the interests of all the other shareholders. (Further discussion of derivative actions is reserved for Chapter 3, since such actions are more frequently brought by shareholders than by creditors.)

## Individual Liability for Corporate Crimes

At common law, the liability of the individual corporate manager for criminal acts of the corporation is similar to liability for tortious acts. The crux of the matter is personal participation. For personal criminal acts—assault, conversion of property, or other acts inherently criminal in nature—one is just as responsible for the consequences whether acting for oneself or for a corporate principal. But a manager has no responsibility for the criminal act of a subordinate unless he or she authorized it, consented to it, or in some manner participated in it. The corporation may share guilt because the act was done on its behalf and the active participant will be guilty simply because it was his or her criminal act. But the unknowing and nonparticipating manager bears none of the responsibility.[38]

## CONCLUSION

From this discussion of liability to third parties at common law, we may conclude that limited liability is not exclusively a feature of stock ownership. A certain measure of limited liability inheres in the corporate manager, although it is a different kind. The stockholder invests money in the corporation and may lose it if the enterprise fails, but that is the totality of the loss. The manager, on the other hand, takes different kinds of risks, including the risk of tort or the risk that a crime may be committed by the corporation. The manager's liability is limited to the extent that there will be no liability, either civil or criminal, unless the manager has actively participated in, consented to, or authorized the offending act. This is the common law. But we shall see in later chapters that this special kind of limited liability of the corporate manager has been diminished over the years by statutory enactments regulating various kinds of business activity, defining new statutory crimes, imposing new standards of personal conduct upon corporate managers, and providing civil and criminal penalties upon both corporations and their managers in cases of violation.[39]

## NOTES

1. Williston, writing in the *Harvard Law Review* nearly a century ago, noted Blackstone's ascription of the origin of the idea of a corporation to Numa Pompilius, the legendary second king of Rome (715 B.C.–673 B.C.). He compared this theory with that of Angell and Ames, who maintained that the corporate concept was known to the Greeks, and that the Romans borrowed it from them. Williston suggested an even earlier origin—that primitive societies may have been made up of corporate bodies, and that the family, the clan, and the tribe partook of the nature of corporations. But he stated that corporations were not used for business purposes in Roman times. Williston, "History of the Law of Business Corporations Before 1800," 2 *Harv. L. Rev.* 105 & 149 (1888). Conard, however, quotes Arthur Dewing as "finding evidence of mercantile joint venture among the Assyrians two thousand years before the embryo of legal corporateness stirred in the womb of Roman law." Conard, *Corporations in Perspective* (The Foundation Press, 1976) 129.

2. Williston, 2 *Harv. L. Rev.* 105, 108, & 149.

3. Conard, *Corporations in Perspective* 130.

4. 10 Co. Rep. 1a at 32b; 77 Eng. Rep. 937, 973 (1613). See also Conard, *Corporations in Perspective* 128.

5. Trustees of Dartmouth College v. Woodworth, 17 U.S. (4 Wheat.) 518, 636, 4 L. Ed. 629 (1819).

6. Williston, 2 *Harv. L. Rev.* 105, 149, & 165–166, places the number at five, but Conard remarks that Williston "certainly overlooked some." Conard, "Business Corporations in American Society," *Law Quadrangle Notes,* Vol. 22, No. 3, pp. 7–9 (U. of Mich., 1978). Henn has placed the number at twenty and states that during the colonial period some of the English trading companies and "a handful of native business corporations" carried on business in the colonies. Henn, *Handbook of the Law of Corporations* (2d ed., West Publishing Co., 1970) 18. See also Lattin, *The Law of Corporations* (2d ed., The Foundation Press, 1971) 170, for an additional discussion of the evolution of Anglo-American corporations.

7. Henn, *Handbook of the Law of Corporations* 18.

8. McCulloch v. Maryland, 17 U.S. (4 Wheat.) 316, 4 L. Ed. 579 (1819). See also Ballantine, *Corporations* (Callaghan & Co., 1946) 36.

9. Williston places the number of business corporations at the end of the eighteenth century at 100, of which about half were in Massachusetts, several of these being manufacturing companies. He states that there were very few manufacturing corporations in other states. Williston, 2 *Harv. L. Rev.* 105, 149, & 165. Berle and Means place the number at 335, of which only 6 were manufacturing companies and 219 were turnpike, bridge, and canal companies, 67 were banks and insurance companies, and 36 furnished water and fire protection or dock facilities. Berle & Means, *The Modern Corporation and Private Property* (rev. ed., Harcourt, Brace & World, 1968) 11.

10. Dodd, *American Business Corporations until 1860* (Harvard University Press, 1954) 8.

11. Henn, *Handbook of the Law of Corporations* 19.

12. 75 U.S. (8 Wall.) 168, 19 L. Ed. 357 (1868).

13. Henn, *Handbook of the Law of Corporations* 19.

14. Conard, *Law Quadrangle Notes*, Vol. 22, No. 3, pp. 7–9 at 8.

15. Stevens, *Private Corporations* (West Publishing Co., 1936) 8.

16. Dodd, *American Business Corporations Until 1860* 85. Ballantine states that at common law, co-ownership involved great risk of loss, even to small investors. Ballantine, *Corporations* 34.

17. N.Y. Laws, 34th Sess. 1811, c. 67; 1 N.Y. Rev. Laws 245 (1813).

18. 18, 19 Vict. c. 133.

19. Williston, 2 *Harv. L. Rev.* 123.

20. Stevens attributes early doubts about corporate responsibility for tort to two problems: (1) Vicarious responsibility for the wrongful acts of another was not a readily accepted concept; and (2) since commission of a tort was not among the activities authorized by the memorandum of association, the corporation may have lacked the capacity to commit the act. Stevens, *Private Corporations* 311.

21. Dodd, *American Business Corporations Until 1860,* p. 110 and cases cited.

22. Gray v. Portland Bank, 3 Mass. 364 (1807).

23. Fowle v. Common Council of Alexandria, 28 U.S. (3 Pet.) 398, 409 7 L. Ed. 719 (1830).

24. Williston, 2 *Harv. L. Rev.* 124.

25. *New York Central & Hudson River R.R. v. United States*, 212 U.S. 481, 53 L. Ed. 613, 29 S. Ct. 304 (1909), upholding the constitutionality of penalizing a railroad under the Elkins Act in an action against the railroad and its assistant traffic manager for granting an unlawful rebate to a shipper. For a thorough discussion of the subject, see Dolan & Rebeck, "Corporate Criminal Liability for Acts in Violation of Company Policy," 50 *Georgetown L.J.* 547 (1962). See also Edgerton, "Corporate Criminal Responsibility," 36 *Yale L.J.* 827, 837 (1927). The indictment, trial, and acquittal of Ford Motor

Company for "reckless homicide" in September 1978 (in a case concerning Pinto automobiles) is a recent and dramatic example of attempting to fix criminal liability upon a corporation for what has normally been regarded as a personal offense. See *Wall St. J.*, Sept. 14, 1978, p. 2, and March 14, 1980, p. 5.

26. Henn, *Handbook of the Law of Corporations* 447.

27. 283 So. 2d 716 (La. 1973).

28. *Id.*, 716, 726.

29. *Id.*, 716, 721.

30. *Id.*, 716, 726.

31. *Id.*, 716, 727. There are many reasons why plaintiffs may elect to sue managerial employees, rather than the corporation. For example, in an effort to circumvent the limitation of liability to the employer under workers' compensation laws, attorneys for employees killed or injured in an explosion at a Continental Grain Co. elevator have sued four of Continental's top officials. *Bus. Week,* Aug. 7, 1978, p. 81. In a matter in which I was personally involved for the defense in Louisiana in 1975, the plaintiff in a pollution-abatement suit against an out-of-state corporation attempted to avoid federal court jurisdiction by suing two Louisiana resident managers of the corporation without suing the corporation. The suit was dismissed without opinion in 1976. Caillouet v. Watkins, 18th Judicial District Ct., La., N. 20,245.

32. 236 So. C. 318, 114 S.E.2d 321 (1960).

33. Donsco Inc. v. Casper Corporation, 587 F.2d 602 (3d Cir. 1978).

34. 3A Fletcher, *Cyclopedia of Corporations* (perm. ed., Callaghan & Co., 1975) 201–203.

35. 224 F.2d 299 (5th Cir. 1955).

36. For a more detailed discussion of the cases on personal liability for corporate torts, see Feuer, *Personal Liabilities of Corporate Officers and Directors* (2d ed. Prentice Hall, Inc., 1974) 187–196. See also 3A Fletcher, *Cyclopedia of Corporations* 201–281.

37. Stevens, *Private Corporations* 595, 603; Ballantine, *Corporations* 185; Comment, "Corporations—Liability of Directors to Creditors for Negligent Management," 34 *Mich. L. Rev.* 521–524 (1936).

38. While this may appear to be a good elementary statement of the common law, we shall see that the requirement of direct knowledge or participation has been considerably eroded in recent years. See United States v. Park, 421 U.S. 658, 44 L. Ed. 2d 489, 95 S. Ct. 1903 (1975), discussed in Chapter 6 under the heading, "The *Park* Case." See also Sethi, "Who Me?" *The Wharton Magazine*, Vol. 2, No. 4, pp. 1–27 (1978). For a discussion of the rationale of holding managers responsible for corporate crime, see "Developments in the Law—Corporate Crime: Regulatory Corporate Behavior Through Criminal Sanctions," 92 *Harv. L. Rev.* 1227–1375 at 1259–1275 (1979).

39. Stevens, speaking of the relative responsibility of the corporation and its managers for corporate crime, says:

The theoretical possibility of imputing criminal responsibility is always there, but in a given case it may be more effective and better social policy to penalize the agents, including officers and directors, and not the body of innocent stockholders. On other occasions, where the corporate group has indisputably directed or failed to check illegal acts, it may prove wiser to penalize the corporation by imposing a fine or even by forfeiting the charter and to free the agent. [Stevens, *Private Corporations* 325–326.]

# CHAPTER THREE

# Directors, Officers, and Shareholders: The Traditional View

In Chapter 2 we took a brief look at the liability of corporate managers at various levels to third parties. We were concerned with situations where the corporation itself was accused of a tort or a crime, and the question was whether, and to what extent, the manager might personally be held liable or guilty. We now move into a larger field—larger from the standpoint of the volume of decided cases and from the traditional viewpoint of the potential for personal risk—that of the liability of the manager to the shareholders of the corporation.

At common law the question of liability of managers to third parties is of less importance than that of liability to shareholders, because third parties can generally recover against the corporation itself, unless it is insolvent. But if the injured party is a shareholder or the corporation itself, recovery against the corporation is not a practicable remedy, since the injured party would, in whole or in part, be paying his or her own damages. So the shareholders look to the managers personally for redress.

The subject of this chapter consists of the responsibilities of managers to shareholders at common law and under the state corporation acts. An understanding of these responsibilities will serve as a prelude to a later discussion of the federal securities laws and the vast amount of discussion of corporate responsibility that has been undertaken in recent years.

Most of the cases concerning the liability of managers involve the responsibilities of directors or of officers who are also directors. This is natural, since it is to the directors that the shareholders most often look for redress of their grievances. This is not to say, however, that nondirector officers and nonofficer managers do not have responsibilities to shareholders. They most certainly do, but where they fail in their responsibilities, it is more likely that such managers will be dealt with by the higher officers or by the directors. Therefore, as a starting point we will look at the relationship of the board of directors and the corporation.

## THE BOARD OF DIRECTORS: ITS RESPONSIBILITIES

The typical state corporation statute solemnly announces that a corporation "shall be managed by its board of directors."[1] This may have been a true statement in a bygone era and it may still be true in the third and fourth categories of corporations as described by Conard[2]—those at the "awkward stage" and those that are closely held. But for the "megacorporations" and the "available" corporations, to borrow Conard's definitions, management *by* the board of directors is impracticable. Delaware, where the greatest number of these very large corporations are incorporated,[3] recognized the practicalities of the situation and the impossibility of its own statutory language in 1974 when it amended its statute to read:

> The business and affairs of every corporation organized under this chapter shall be managed *by or under the direction of* a board of directors, except as may be otherwise provided in this chapter or in its certificate of incorporation.[4] [Emphasis supplied.]

In the same year, similar language was approved for the Model Business Corporation Act by the American Bar Association Committee on Corporate Laws. Other states have not moved rapidly to follow Delaware in amending the comparable sections of their corporation codes, but it is expected that they will do so in due time.[5] Not being the home of many very large corporations, perhaps the other states do not feel an urgent necessity.

Whatever the legal nuances of the statutory provisions of the directors' responsibility to manage, there can be no question that ultimate responsibility rests with them, whether they manage directly or by delegation to the chief executive and other officers. Their responsibility to the shareholders is twofold: They have an "internal" responsibility to direct the affairs of the corporation for the benefit of *all* the shareholders, and not just for their own benefit; and they have an "external" responsibility to direct the affairs of the corporation in its relations with third parties in a prudent and businesslike manner.

Both these responsibilities require good faith. The internal responsibility might best be described as "avoiding conflict of interest." The external responsibility might most accurately be defined as "exercising good business judgment." Occasionally these responsibilities will overlap and both may sometimes be involved in the same situation.

CONFLICT OF INTEREST

**25**

*Directors,
Officers, and
Shareholders:
The Traditional
View*

It is sometimes said that directors are fiduciaries. There is considerable and respectable authority for such a statement.[6] I do not propose to get into the arguments as to whether or not directors are really fiduciaries in the legal sense of the term. If the reader wishes to pursue this subject, there are references in the end-of-chapter notes that should be helpful. It is sufficient to say that the responsibilities of a director are very much *like* those of a fiduciary. We shall now proceed to examine some of those responsibilities in the light of practical situations that have arisen.

"Conflict of interest" is a current buzzword. Today we probably hear it more often in situations involving government employees (that is, involving relationships between a government official and an entity with which the official may have a business or personal connection inconsistent with the official's acting impartially in the government position). But it is an old expression frequently found in cases concerned with the situation in which a director or a corporate manager has an interest on both sides of a transaction.

If we go back, we find that a century ago the law on conflict of interest was much more stringent than it is today. Harold Marsh has said:

> In 1880 it could have been stated with confidence that in the United States the general rule was that any contract between a director and his corporation was voidable at the instance of the corporation or its shareholders, without regard to the fairness or unfairness of the transaction.[7]

There was no way in those days that a disinterested majority of the board could give validity to a contract in which a director had an interest. It appears that some modern critics of corporations would like to return to such a rule.[8] But the rigid rule of 1880 eroded over the next thirty years. It was based upon the concept that a corporate director was a fiduciary, and the movement away from the fiduciary rule was based on a theory that a trustee could deal with the trust property with the permission of the beneficiary of the trust.[9] This is probably a nice theory if one must proceed from the basis that a director is a fiduciary, but if it is recognized that a director is not a fiduciary in the strict sense of the term, but simply a person who has obligations *resembling* those of a fiduciary, one need not go into such legal contortions to find an exception. The exception that developed was, of course, that a contract was not voidable if it had been ratified by a disinterested majority of the board of directors. The exception, it is submitted, is a desirable one. It recognizes the realities of the business world. If boards of directors are composed entirely of so-called insiders, then perhaps the exception is not needed. A good argument could be made that inside directors should devote their entire time, energy, and resources to the affairs of their corporations and therefore should never have a contract (except, of course, an employment contract) with their corporations. But, in the modern world, inside directors are often regarded with suspicion, and outside directors are favored. With a few exceptions, outside directors, as constituted traditionally and continuing to the present time, simply cannot function if they cannot have business relations, directly or through other entities with which they are associated, with the corporations on whose boards they sit.[10]

A banker will not take a directorship in a manufacturing corporation if it means that the bank must discontinue providing banking services to the manufacturer. And a manufacturer will not accept a seat on the board of a large retailer if, as a consequence, the retailer can no longer buy and sell the consumer products produced by the manufacturer. (There is some modern thought that bankers and suppliers should not be directors, but this thought is a long way from becoming law.) Even a university president may hesitate if a directorship means that the corporation on whose board he or she has been invited to sit will, as the price of having the president's service, discontinue its long-standing research program at the university and cease contributing to its annual fund-raising campaigns.

So contracts and other business relationships between corporations and their directors or entities in which their directors have an interest may be permitted upon vote of a disinterested majority. But what is a disinterested majority? Is it a majority of a quorum? Is it a majority of the disinterested directors? Or is it a majority of the whole board? The cases are not consistent on the subject, but nearly all agree that an interested director cannot be counted in determining a quorum.[11]

But ratification by a disinterested majority was not the final answer. While a rigid prohibition of interest in a contract was unrealistic, merely allowing the contract because a disinterested majority approved was too glib a solution. The contract might be one that was unfairly favorable to the director or the entity he or she represented, and the other directors might have ratified merely because maybe next year they would like to have a similar contract. Thus the decisions evolved to a position where the court would look at the *fairness* of the contract to the corporation, with the interested director having the burden of overcoming a presumption against invalidity.[12]

It took about eighty years for the courts to progress from the rigid prohibition to the rigid exception to what is in essence a rule of reason. The history of the rule demonstrates that courts change with the times, and out of these evolutionary changes can emerge rules that are fair to all concerned, as fairness is perceived at a given time.

In 1967, the Delaware Legislature amended its corporation code to set forth specifically the conditions for resolving validity of a contract in which a director or an officer has an interest either directly or in a representative capacity: (1) disclosure to the board of the material facts of the transaction and good faith authorization by a majority of disinterested directors even though less than a quorum; *or* (2) disclosure to the stockholders of the material facts of the transaction and approval in good faith by a majority of the stockholders; *or* (3) fairness of the transaction to

the corporation as of the time it is authorized, approved, or ratified by the
directors or the stockholders.[13] The alternatives permitted by Delaware
appear to be a regression from the court decisions that premised the
validity of the transaction upon the ultimate question of fairness. It could
be argued, however, that proving fairness can be a very tricky matter,
because there is ample opportunity to examine the transaction with 20-20
hindsight.

## Other Business Interests

Having looked at the procedure for resolving conflicts of interest, at least
on the board of directors level, it is appropriate to examine some of the
typical conflict situations that can arise. The transaction between the
corporation and a director, an officer, or an entity in which the director or
officer has an interest is the situation that most readily comes to mind.
For example, there may be an underwriting contract with an investment
banking firm, one of whose directors also sits on the corporation's board.
Another may be a major supply contract between two manufacturers
who have one or more directors in common. These are substantial transactions that are capable of being analyzed and presented to the board,
together with an evaluation of competitive situations.

Another type of conflict of interest occurs where the director or officer
has a business on the side, perhaps for the sole purpose of supplying the
corporation. Probably the most publicized of that type of situation was
the discovery in the early 1960s that the president of Chrysler Corporation was the owner of a supply company that was doing an extensive
business with Chrysler to the exclusion of other qualified suppliers. That
revelation resulted in the president's forced resignation and created a
great stir among corporate executives and corporate counsel. Almost in
unison the larger corporations issued internal pronouncements against
conflicts of interest on the part of executive, administrative, and professional employees, with detailed statements as to the types of situations
that would be regarded as conflicts, the penalties for violation, and the
procedures for resolving borderline situations.[14] Most of the corporations that adopted such pronouncements in the sixties still have them in
effect and revise and republish them from time to time to remind their
employees of the rules.

## Seizure of Opportunity

Another variant of the conflict-of-interest situation is called "seizure of
corporate opportunity." The typical situation this phrase implies is
where a business opportunity is presented to the corporation but an
officer or a director takes it for personal gain. This might involve an offer
to sell a parcel of land, a patent, a distributorship, or another company, or
almost any kind of business opportunity that can be imagined.

Seizure of the opportunity can come about in a variety of ways. The chief executive or another officer may receive the offer in an official capacity and, without saying anything to the company's other executives, accept it for him- or herself or another entity in which he or she is interested. Or the matter may be taken to the board of directors with a recommendation against acceptance. The officer might even recommend that the board of directors accept, and the board might, instead, reject. Then perhaps the officer would accept the offer for him- or herself. Perhaps that officer would not accept, but another director would. The other director might be one who had voted for acceptance by the corporation or who had voted against acceptance.

It is difficult to justify personal acceptance by one who has concealed the opportunity from colleagues or who has recommended against it or who has voted against it, but the situation would appear to be quite different if the offer has been disclosed, recommended, voted upon, and rejected by the board.

But what if the recommendation or the vote against acceptance was based upon a sincere belief that the corporation lacked the financial ability to accept the offer or that the subject of the offer did not "fit" the corporation's business? Cases have gone both ways on this subject. It would appear that those who decided against the officer or director, where there was no disclosure, can be more easily supported. It would have been very easy for the officer or director to have disclosed to the directors a personal interest in accepting the offer they had rejected and to have received their approval. Such approval could probably withstand a legal contest under either the test of fairness of the transaction to the corporation or the vote of a disinterested majority.[15]

## Competition with the Corporation

Closely related to the subject of corporate opportunity is the subject of competition with the corporation. It appears that in an earlier era, directors were not held to be acting contrary to the best interests of the corporation if they were also directors of a competitor. That is not, however, the rule today. Moreover, for reasons not so much related to the conflict-of-interest problem as concerned with preservation of competition, federal statutes prohibit interlocking directors among competitors in a variety of situations, which will be discussed in Chapter 5.

The corporate manager who surreptitiously prepares to go into a competitive business while still remaining on the payroll of the corporation may be guilty of a serious breach of ethical conduct and liable to the corporation for damages caused by this breach.[16] The corporate manager who, on leaving the corporation, takes its trade secrets along and then uses them in the new position is, of course, committing the same kind of offense against the former employer as one who starts soliciting business for a new enterprise in competition with the corporation while still remaining on its payroll.

Whatever the label—seizure of corporate opportunity, competition with the corporation, or misappropriation of trade secrets—all are acts

against the corporation to which the manager owes an obligation of
loyalty. They involve a breach of duty, an appropriation of property, or
both, and the courts have, except in rare instances, enjoined them and
have awarded damages to the corporation and against the defaulting
manager.[17]

## Executive Compensation

Another field where the interests of the corporation and the manager may
be in possible conflict is that of executive compensation. It is obvious
that managers must be compensated for their services. Very few executives own such large blocks of stock in their corporations that they can
afford to work only for the dividends that their efforts may produce. Even
if an executive were so endowed, it would be unreasonable to expect
performance without compensation when other stockholders would be
receiving proportional dividends and other employees would be receiving salaries.

But who determines the compensation of the top officers? Generally
speaking, the power to determine their compensation inheres in the
board of directors. But problems can arise when a number of the directors
are officers or other insiders. There is a risk of "back-scratching"—each
officer-director supporting a generous salary for the other. Just because
this happens does not mean that there has been any impropriety. If the
salaries established by this means are reasonable, they will be immune to
attack. But there have been cases where salaries of executives have been
successfully attacked on the basis of self-dealing *and* unreasonableness.[18]
Well-managed corporations will generally avoid this problem by placing
the determination of the compensation of the chief executive and other
top officers in the hands of a committee of the board, composed of
outside directors or directors who are retired officers and therefore no
longer receiving salaries for active service.

But executive compensation does not stop with mere payment of
salaries. There may be a bonus plan, a stock option plan, deferred
compensation arrangements, and numerous other methods for attempting to make compensation correspond to good corporate earnings or to
minimize the impact of higher tax brackets. Some of these plans have had
a stormy history.

Stock option plans were frequently litigated in the 1950s when they
first came into popular usage after favorable tax treatment was provided
by the Revenue Act of 1950.[19] The thrust of the complaints against
options was that they constituted gifts of corporate property to the
optionees. Those plans, however, that placed affirmative obligations
upon the optionees, such as remaining in the employ of the corporation
for a stated period, were able to withstand such onslaughts.[20] Again,
these various special compensation plans have had a better history of
being sustained against conflict-of-interest charges when administered

by a disinterested majority of the board of directors or a disinterested committee of directors. Generally, it is also the practice to seek stockholder approval of such plans before making awards under them or to make the first awards subject to ratification by the stockholders at their next meeting. Federal statutes and regulations in the fields of taxation and securities, as well as the listing requirements of the New York Stock Exchange, have frequently established minimum ground rules which, if observed, satisfy the regulatory requirements and at the same time provide a basis of reasonableness that go a long way in protecting the compensation plan from stockholder attack.[21]

## Loans to Executives

Closely related to executive compensation is the matter of loans to executives. Such loans are most often to finance the purchase of a home upon transfer to a new location, to exercise a stock option, or to purchase stock in the open market. These loans are generally permitted by state corporation laws, although until 1967 they were forbidden to directors and officers of Delaware corporations under penalty of personal liability of those who authorized the transaction.

In an earlier era, such loans were subject to attack as a diversion of the corporation's assets from its usual business purposes. Where there is an express statutory authorization, as in Delaware,[22] the business purpose may be presumed, but the transaction is still subject to scrutiny under the disinterested majority test, the fairness test, or both. The Model Business Corporation Act formerly contained a prohibition against loans to a director but now permits such a loan with stockholder consent, and also permits a loan to an employee who is a director if the board of directors decides that the loan may benefit the corporation. Twelve states have enacted provisions comparable with, or identical to, the Model Act.[23]

## Conflict of Interest and Individual Stockholders

We have thus far been concerned with those conflict-of-interest situations where the interest of the corporation as a whole may possibly be in conflict with that of the individual manager. There are, however, other situations where the interest of an individual stockholder or a group of stockholders, as distinguished from the entire corporation, may be adverse to that of the managers. Both of these will be important subjects in the corporate practice and the jurisprudence of the 1980s. One of these subjects is insider trading and another consists of the problems of sale or defense of control.

## Insider Trading

At common law, there were no particular inhibitions against insider trading. With very few exceptions, the attitude of the courts a half-century or more ago was that a corporate manager was perfectly free to

trade in the corporation's stock upon a securities exchange with full
knowledge of good news or bad news that could affect its value, without
any obligation to disclose the news publicly. This remained "good law"
in the majority of the states up to the time of passage of the Securities
Exchange Act of 1934. Even after that, it persisted in situations where, for
some reason or other, the provisions of that Act were not applicable.[24]
The courts have now, by analogy to the Securities Exchange Act, abandoned their views of two generations ago; instead, they follow the
principles of that Act in setting forth sound common-law rules governing
the obligation of a corporate manager to the stockholders.[25] We shall
discuss insider trading further in Chapter 8, which deals with the federal
securities laws, for it is under those laws that the law of insider trading
has developed in an orderly and sometimes dramatic way.

## Sale or Defense of Control

The problems of sale or defense of control are very much with us in this
era of mergers and acquisitions, both friendly and unfriendly. Sale of
control relates to the act of selling to a third party the shares that constitute the legal or practical control of the corporation. Defense of control
relates to the resistance of efforts of persons outside the management to
unseat the management, either by an acquisition of all, or a controlling
portion of, the shares of the corporation, by a proxy contest, or by both.
Corporate managements sometimes resist offers of merger or fight tender
offers by various means—appealing to stockholders not to accept the
offer, seeking an injunction against the attempted acquisition, usually
on antitrust grounds, seeking another offerer, or invoking a state statute
designed to protect corporations from "unwanted tenders."[26]

In selling or defending control, corporate directors and officers expose
themselves to personal liability. There are bound to be some stockholders who *want* a merger or tender offer to succeed. They see themselves
making a windfall profit, since such offers are always at prices above
current market value. Some stockholders will perceive the management
of their company as interested only in protecting its own interest. If they
believe the chief executive and other top managers are interested only in
protecting their own positions, they may sue the directors and officers,
alleging conflict of interest, bad faith, and manipulations contrary to the
best interests of the stockholders.

Not all such lawsuits succeed; not all corporate managers are scoundrels interested only in their own welfare and caring naught for the
welfare of their corporation and its stockholders. Not all who make
tenderer offers are knights in white armor, seeking to rescue the fair
corporate damsel from the oppression and rapaciousness of the management. But the mere bringing of such a lawsuit can bring terror to even
the most well intentioned manager. There will likely be *something* in the
corporate files that may be found by the plaintiff during the pretrial stage

in discovery proceedings that will reveal that the chief executive *was* concerned about losing his or her position. Even though all the legal and economic bases for the executive's resistance and that of the board may be perfectly sound, the slightest suggestion that management may *also* have been interested in preserving its own position may suffice to convince a jury that it should bring in a generous verdict against the management.[27]

The reverse can also happen. The management may *favor* a merger. As an example, let us suppose that an exchange of shares is proposed and then, after the merger, the acquiring company experiences serious losses and the only profitable operation it has is the acquired corporation. The stock of the acquiring corporation plunges and the erstwhile stockholders of the acquired corporation bring a fraud claim against their erstwhile chief executive, alleging that he or she misled them into voting for the merger; they argue that the executive's chief motivation was a long-term employment contract with deferred compensation—a much more lucrative and secure arrangement than had existed with the former board of directors, which had never been notified of the new employment contract. The stockholders might have a valid claim.[28]

## A Corporation's Purchase of its Own Stock

Another situation where management and other stockholders may find themselves as adversaries involves the purchase by the corporation of its own stock. A corporation's repurchase of its own shares often occurs when there is a surplus of cash in the corporation, with no capital investment possibilities, or only limited ones. This may lead the board to decide that the best investment the corporation can make is in its own stock.

Another reason may be the need for shares to be issued in exchange for shares of other corporations to be acquired, or in connection with employee stock purchase plans, executive option plans, or bonus plans, accompanied by the desire to avoid diluting the equity of existing stockholders. Repurchases of these two types are often made by very large corporations and generally do not pose a conflict-of-interest problem.[29]

### GOING PRIVATE

If the management holds a high percentage of the shares and the number of nonmanagement stockholders is relatively small, the purchase of outstanding shares with corporate funds may tend to reduce the position of the remaining stockholders to a point where they may be frozen out by a merger with a corporation organized specifically for that purpose. This device, known as "going private," is a phenomenon of the past decade.[30] The management may or may not have legitimate reasons for wanting to "go private," but whatever management's motives, an attack by unwilling stockholders, alleging conflict of interest, is to be expected.

## Proxy Contests

Another aspect of the defense-of-control problem is the use of corporate funds in proxy contests. In a proxy contest, the insurgents are stockholders who are attempting to oust the incumbent management by use of the normal machinery for electing the board of directors. In the normal corporate annual meeting situation where there is no contest for the seats on the board, corporate funds are customarily and routinely used for the solicitation of proxies on behalf of the management. But is this a proper use of corporate funds if there is a contest? From the relatively few cases that have been decided on this subject, it appears that reimbursement is proper if there is a good faith contest concerning corporate policies, but not if the contest is merely a struggle for control for the sake of control.

If the management is entitled to expend funds to defend its position, can the insurgents demand corporate funds to attack management's position? Does it make a difference if they are successful? They have now become the management, and if it has been a good faith contest over corporate policies, there appears to be no logical reason why they should not be reimbursed.[31] There do not, however, appear to be any clear answers to these problems.

## PRUDENCE IN MANAGEMENT: AN EXTERNAL OBLIGATION

We have examined briefly the internal obligations of managers to stockholders—with a variety of situations labeled with the all-inclusive term "conflict of interest."

There is, as mentioned earlier, another type of responsibility that managers bear to stockholders: the "external" obligation. As that term is used here, it connotes the obligation of the management (*i.e.*, the officers and directors) to manage the affairs of the corporation in a reasonable and prudent manner—to earn a profit on the stockholders' investment, to avoid losses and unwarranted liabilities, to comply with the law, and in general to maintain the corporation in good, sound condition.

Sometimes questions of internal and external obligations will be intermixed in the same fact situation, but in the absence of such a mixture we will find that the obligation of the corporate manager to the stockholders at common law is not so rigid in external matters as it is in internal matters.

The difference in obligation between internal matters and external matters is logical from both a legal and a practical viewpoint. Corporate managers should conduct their personal affairs and their company's affairs in such a way that their loyalty to their corporation is unquestioned. The law is relatively clear in spelling out the boundaries, and if any question arises, legal counsel can be consulted. Or one can utilize what the mentor of my early professional days used to call the "smell test." "If it doesn't smell right," he would say, "don't do it."

When it comes to such matters as launching a new product, expanding manufacturing capacity, entering into a joint venture, or acquiring a smaller company, corporate officers and directors can make mistakes no matter how carefully they may survey the market, try to forecast economic trends, or outguess their competitors. There are very few corporate managers who have not at some time either found that the public did not really want the new product that their company placed on the market at great expense or watched with dismay as a brand-new manufacturing plant was completed and ready to go into production just at the beginning of a recession. Other managers have found that an acquired company was full of defects in production methods and marketing practices that were not apparent upon the premerger evaluation, or have found that their business principles and practices were so different from those of their joint-venture partner that the venture could not be successfully managed. All these situations can lead to losses. Some of them can be very large and have a major adverse effect upon the finances of the corporation.

What is the responsibility of the corporate manager in such a situation? Suppose the loss is $100 million? That amount is not inconceivable in today's economy.[32] Should the directors and officers be held personally liable for their poor business judgment? Merely to state the question invites the response: "Of course not!" If directors and officers are to be held personally liable for simple errors in business judgment, there are very few who would want to be a corporate director or officer. No matter how high the reward, the risk would be too great.

But it does not always follow that the corporate manager is, or should be, completely immune from liability for losses incurred by the corporation. The law says the manager should act as a "prudent man." It implies that a director or an officer will act as an "ordinarily prudent man" would in similar circumstances. In addition to having originated at a time when women were not admitted to corporate hierarchies, the term "ordinarily prudent man" is vague and incapable of precise definition. However, like its use in the law of torts, it is a term that is workable. Somehow courts and juries have been able to apply it to the fact situations that come before them and generally achieve just results.[33]

The director or officer is expected to exercise ordinary skill, care, and diligence, but is not an ensurer that the correct decision always will be made. Sometimes, in retrospect, a business decision made in good faith may seem stupid. The court should not, however, indulge in hindsight to detect all the fallacies in a manager's determination, or all the factors that were not taken into account but which, upon later reflection, now appear to be significant.

Standards of due care have evolved over decades as courts have been called upon to decide disputes between stockholders and management where corporations have incurred losses. One early twentieth-century case went so far as to absolve a director from liability on the ground that he lived so far from the board's meetingplace that it was difficult for him to attend, that he was frequently absent and hence unfamiliar with the affairs of the corporation.[34] No one could reasonably expect to arrive at such a conclusion today. But even from that ill-considered decision, we

can derive one valid observation. That is, the more the manager is involved or should be involved in the affairs of the corporation, the higher will be the standard of responsibility. The chief executive, by reason of full-time employment in, and primary responsibility for, the affairs of the corporation, must necessarily be expected to know more about them than an outside director.

Much has been written, particularly in recent years, about the necessity for an outside director to be a person of inquiring mind who will take nothing upon faith but will probe for the truth. We will examine this concept in more detail in the later chapters, but at this point it is sufficient to observe that, probe and inquire as the outside director may, he or she cannot be expected to know the affairs of the corporation with the intimate detail known to the chief executive or other top officers who may or may not be directors. This is not to say that gross negligence or willful misconduct is, or should be, the only basis upon which outside directors should be held liable for mismanagement of a corporation, but it does say that they should not be held liable merely because they did not know everything the chief executive or the other higher officers knew.

The state statutes have been rather slow to enunciate rules under which corporate managers may measure their conduct. They have lagged behind the courts in this respect. But, in recent years, state legislatures are beginning to recognize that their statutes are deficient and are either codifying existing case law from their own states or, in the absence of such law, are adopting and codifying the case law of other states. Pursuant to this trend, the following was added to Section 35 of the Model Corporation Act in 1974:

> A director shall perform his duties as a director, including his duties as a member of any committee of the board upon which he may serve, in good faith, in a manner he reasonably believes to be in the best interests of the corporation, and with such care as an ordinarily prudent person in a like position would use under similar circumstances. In performing his duties, a director shall be entitled to rely on information, opinions, reports or statements, including financial statements and other financial data, in each case prepared or presented by:
>
> (1) one or more officers or employees of the corporation whom the director believes to be reliable and competent in the matters presented,
>
> (2) counsel, public accountants or other persons as to matters which the director believes to be within such person's professional or expert competence, or
>
> (3) a committee of the board upon which he does not serve, duly designated in accordance with a provision of the articles of incorporation or the by-laws, as to matters within its designated authority, which committee the director believes to merit confidence, but he shall not be considered to be acting in good faith if he has knowledge concerning the matter in question that would cause such reliance to be unwarranted. A person who so performs his duties

shall have no liability by reason of being or having been a director of the corporation.[35]

A provision very much like that of the Model Corporation Act was adopted by New York in 1977.[36] Delaware has not adopted a general standard comparable with that of the opening sentence in the Model Act provision, but has paralleled the Model Act in setting forth affirmatively steps that directors may use to insulate their liability in arriving at business decisions. The Delaware statute reads as follows:

> A member of the board of directors of any corporation . . . or a member of any committee designated by the board of directors shall, in the performance of his duties, be fully protected in relying in good faith upon the books of account or reports made to the corporation by any of its officers, or by an independent certified public accountant, or by an appraiser selected with reasonable care by the board of directors or by any such committee, or in relying in good faith upon other records of the corporation.[37]

The Model Act and Delaware Act statements appear to be consistent with sound practice in basing reliance upon experts within the appropriate field of the expert's competence.

BUSINESS JUDGMENT

In the matter of directors' and officers' decision making, another term has acquired considerable legal significance. That term is "business judgment." In its broadest sense, it could cover the situations we have been discussing, such as due care and the ordinarily "prudent man." But in the legal literature, it has a somewhat narrower connotation. It does not seem to be concerned with the elements of "the deal going sour," as we have been discussing, but it is usually associated with the question of whether the directors and officers are making an appropriate use of the corporation's resources in a more absolute sense.

In an earlier era, for example, the authority of corporate management to make charitable contributions out of corporate funds was questioned, but that question has been clearly laid to rest and the courts recognize that charitable contributions do enhance the corporation's standing in the eyes of the public and do have a salutary effect in the promotion of its business objectives.[38]

This principle was extended in the late 1960s when Standard Oil of Indiana sold bonds in European currencies at rates higher than it would pay in the United States, when the purpose was to assist in propping up the nation's sagging balance of payments.[39] Another example, in 1970, was the case of contributions to Allegheny County made by United States Steel in lieu of local personal property taxes. This enabled the personal property tax exemption adopted by the Pennsylvania Legislature to be extended to include Allegheny County, which was heavily dependent on personal property taxes from the steel industry and would have suffered extreme hardship as a result of the exemption.[40] These cases may be of some comfort to managers who, in response to pressure to take action to achieve social objectives, may voluntarily refrain from making otherwise profitable investments in certain countries or in certain types of products, or who may hire or promote less-qualified employees in order to improve their company's racial composition.[41]

The business judgment rule has also been extended to a situation where a board of directors refrained from taking action against an officer who condoned bribery of foreign officials.[42] Now we are again coming close to the conflict-of-interest cases. Needless to say, this decision has been criticized by those who take a dim view of the morality of corporate management. The decision of the court in *Gall v. Exxon*, however, is a sound one. The determination not to sue the officer was made on behalf of the board by a special committee of disinterested directors appointed by the board and empowered to investigate, make a determination, and take appropriate action in the matter. The defaulting officer had lost his position with the corporation. The amount of the bribe was so large that he could never reimburse the corporation for anything approaching the full amount. And he was not the person who instigated or paid the bribe. Certainly the committee took all these facts into account and arrived at a decision based upon its sound judgment. There has appeared no evidence of mutual back-scratching or undercover deals, as the critics have suggested.

Business judgment must continue to be respected by the courts. Only when there has been fraud, bad faith, or gross negligence should a court try to second-guess the deliberations of boards of directors and of executive management. There is no evidence that the courts are about to retreat from this position.

## Derivative Suits

In almost all the situations that we have been discussing in this chapter, we have been concerned with an adversary relationship, either actually existing between the corporation and the manager or alleged to be existing. If all litigation on the obligation of the manager to the corporation were to be brought by the corporation itself, there would be very few cases, for in most instances the defendant-managers are still managers of the corporation. An exception, of course, occurs where a manager has been dismissed and the new management brings an action against the former manager for alleged misconduct or mismanagement. But a corporation is owned by its stockholders, and if management is dishonest or negligent in the discharge of its duties, it is the stockholders who will be the ultimate losers.

The stockholders are, in a sense, like the beneficiaries of a trust. Just as the law has long recognized the right of the beneficiary of a trust to sue a trustee for breach of trust, so the courts in the early nineteenth century granted a stockholder the right to sue the management for alleged defaults in the management of the corporation.[43] The right of the individual stockholder was, however, in common with the rights of all other stockholders, and any wrong that was committed would affect the stockholder only to the extent that it would diminish the value of his or her investment in the corporation. Therefore, an action by a stockholder against an alleged defaulting management is brought on behalf of the corporation and is called a stockholders' derivative suit.

A great deal of jurisprudence has been developed on the subject of the stockholders' derivative suit.[44] State corporation laws frequently impose conditions and procedural rules designed to prevent the derivative action's being abused. There is a concern that such actions are sometimes brought, not to further the best interests of the corporation, but to promote particular grudges of the plaintiff or to enrich the lawyers who represent the plaintiffs. A common provision is that the plaintiff must have been a stockholder at the time of the transaction upon which the suit is based.[45] The Model Corporation Act contains a provision requiring a plaintiff holding less than 5 percent of the outstanding shares to give security for costs unless the value of his or her stock in the corporation is more than $25,000. The Model Act also permits the court, upon a finding that the action was brought without reasonable cause, to require the plaintiff to pay to successful defendants the reasonable expenses, including attorneys' fees, incurred by them in the defense of the action.[46]

Provisions of this nature are, of course, very controversial and can be strongly defended or roundly criticized, depending upon one's experience and orientation. A plaintiff's lawyer would regard them as an unnecessary encumbrance designed to discourage derivative actions in all except the most flagrant and easily provable cases of management negligence or bad faith. Corporate counsel, on the other hand, regard such provisions as necessary to help slow the ever-increasing torrent of corporate litigation, much of which they earnestly believe to be commenced by irresponsible plaintiffs.[47]

## CONCLUSION

We have been skipping very rapidly over the various kinds of situations in which the corporate manager, particularly at the director and officer level, is exposed to personal liability to the corporation and its shareholders in the event that this executive acts in bad faith or is guilty of mismanagement. We have not attempted to cover all the various ramifications of the principles that have been discussed in this chapter and have, in fact, mentioned very few of the numerous court decisions in this field of the law.

The conclusion is inescapable, however, that at common law and under the corporation statutes as interpreted by the courts, corporate managers are held to a very high degree of responsibility.[48] Perhaps not every court decision has achieved justice in the eyes of those who would hold corporate managers to the very highest degree of responsibility, or

in the eyes of those who feel that corporate managers are not at all to be trusted, but I know of no field of the law where every decision that has ever been made has satisfied all the interested parties.

In later chapters we will take a look at the current criticisms of corporate managements and some proposals to make them more responsive to the public needs, but first we are going to examine some of the principal statutes, especially federal, that have, in increasing numbers, set new and higher standards of performance for corporate managers in many fields of activity and have imposed penalties, civil and criminal, for violation of the statutory standards.

To look solely to the responsibilities and liabilities of corporate managers at common law and under the state incorporation statutes and to conclude that that is the extent of their responsibilities is most unrealistic in 1980. It is essential to see how much further their responsibilities and liabilities have been expanded by statutes, such as the securities laws, that are related to the corporate field. It is also essential to become familiar with other statutes, such as those pertaining to trade regulation and to health, safety, and the environment, that are outside the field of corporation law as such, but nevertheless have a strong impact upon the decision making, performance, and liability of corporate managers.

## NOTES

1. See, for example, *Ill. Ann. Stat.*, ch. 32, § 157.33 (Smith-Hurd); *Ind. Stat. Ann.*, § 23-1 to 2-11 (Burns); *La. Rev. Stat.* §§ 12-81 (West); *Mich. Comp. Laws* § 450.13; *Mo. Ann. Stat.*, § 351.310 (Vernon); *N.J. Stat. Ann.*, § 14A; 6-1; *Tex. Civ. Stat.* Art. 2.3 (Vernon); *Wash. Rev. Code Ann.* § 23A.08.340. See also *Ohio Rev. Code Ann.*, § 1701.59 (Page) and *Pa. Stat. Ann.*, tit. 15 § 1401 (Purdon).

2. Conard, "Business Corporations in American Society," Law Quadrangle Notes, Vol. 22, No. 3, pp. 7–9 at 8 (U. of Mich., 1978).

3. Henn states that of 1,278 companies listed on the New York Stock Exchange, 452 are incorporated in Delaware and 158 in New York. Henn, *Handbook of the Law of Corporations* (2d ed. West Publishing Co., 1970) 6, § 1.

4. Delaware Corporation Law, (8 *Del. Code Ann.*) § 141(a). Massachusetts has long provided for management by the board and certain named officers. *Mass. Ann. Laws*, ch. 156, § 21.

5. Model Business Corporation Act Annotated, 1977 Supplement, § 35 (West Publishing Co. 1977). See "Report of Committee on Corporate Laws: Changes in the Model Business Corporate Act," 30 *Bus. Law.* 501 (1975). States that have followed Delaware and the Model Code in adopting the "under the direction of" language include Connecticut (1975), *Conn. Gen. Stat. Ann.*, § 33-313; Florida (1975), 18 *Fla. Stat. Ann.*, § 607.111; Iowa (1976), 28A *Iowa Code Ann.*, § 496A.34; New York (1977), *N.Y. Cons. Laws Ann.*, § 701 (McKinney).

6. Professor Dodd cites Chancellor Kent in Attorney General v. Utica Insurance Co., 2 Johns. Ch. 371 (N.Y. 1817) for an early statement of the applicability of

the principles of fiduciary law to directors and officers of business corporations. Dodd, *American Business Corporations until 1860* (Harvard University Press, 1954). 70. Henn, *Handbook of the Law of Corporations* 250, states: "[D]irectors, with their powers and responsibilities for managing the property of another, *i.e.*, the corporation . . ., are in a fiduciary relationship with the corporation." Conard, *Corporations in Perspective* (The Foundation Press, 1976) 34–35, states that, although the statutes are generally silent on the subject, judges have made directors fiduciaries. See also Garrett, "Duties and Liabilities of Corporate Directors," 22 *Bus. Law.* 29, 33 (1966), and Arsht, "Reply to Professor Cary," 31 *Bus. Law.* 1113, 1114 (1976).

Pennsylvania's Business Corporation Law declares: "Officers and directors shall be deemed to stand in a fiduciary relationship to the corporation. . . ." *Pa. Stat. Ann.* tit. 15, § 1408 (Purdon). Although state statutes, except those of Pennsylvania, generally do not use the word "fiduciary" in describing the obligations of directors or officers, there are numerous cases holding that directors occupy a fiduciary relationship to the corporation and its stockholders. See 3 Fletcher, *Cyclopedia of Corporations* (perm. ed., Callaghan & Co., 1975) 142–157 and cases cited. The American Bar Association Committee on Corporate Laws has declined to use the term "fiduciary" in the Model Business Corporation Act, because its use "presents the possibility of importing into the area of corporation law more than is appropriate of the attributes and obligations of a fiduciary as firmly established in the law of trusts." "Report of the Committee on Corporate Laws: Changes in the Model Business Corporation Act," 30 *Bus. Law.* 501, 506 (1975). An excellent overview of the concept of the term is Kaplan, "Fiduciary Responsibility in the Management of the Corporation," 31 *Bus. Law.* 883 (1976).

7. Marsh, "Are Directors Trustees?" 22 *Bus. Law.* 35, 36 (1966).

8. See Nader, Green & Seligman, *Constitutionalizing the Corporation: The Case for Federal Chartering of Giant Corporations* (The Corporate Accountability Research Group, 1976) 213.

9. Marsh, 22 *Bus. Law*, 35, 40.

10. Courts have struggled hard with the problem of how best to handle transactions between the director and his corporation and those between corporations having one or more common directors. The struggle has centered around the director's duty as a fiduciary to his corporation and his conflicting self-interest, with the recognition of a practical fact of corporate life that such transactions are frequent and often to the advantage of the corporation. Then, too, there has been the surprising disclosure in some quarters that directors, for the most part, are not bent on skullduggery. [Lattin, *The Law of Corporations* (2d ed., The Foundation Press, 1971). See also Stevens, *Private Corporations* (West Publishing Co., 1936) 565–579.]

11. Marsh, 22 *Bus. Law.* 35 at 42 and cases cited.

12. *Id.*, 35 at 44 and cases cited. Conflict-of-interest problems can also arise in transactions between a parent corporation and a partially owned subsidiary, and the fairness of the transactions may be questioned by minority stockholders. Cases in this area are concerned primarily with corporate liability, although a manager may in some cases incur personal liability, especially if holding a dominant position. See 3 Fletcher, *Cyclopedia of Corporations* 182–183.

13. Delaware Corporation Law (8 *Del. Code Ann.*) § 144.

14. The concern of yesteryear can be ascertained by a review of the American Bar Association symposium on the subject, held in 1961. See Watt, "Formalizing the Corporate Policy and Minimizing Exposure to Conflicts of Interest"; Wadmond, "Conflicts of Business Interest and Seizure of Corporate Opportunity"; and Thanhouser, "The Corporate Counsel's Viewpoint," 17 *Bus. Law.* 42, 48, 63, 79 (1961).

15. For more detail on seizure of corporate opportunity, see Wadmond, 17 *Bus. Law.* 48, and Jacobs, "Business Ethics and the Law: Obligations of a Corporate Executive," 28 *Bus. Law.* 1063 (1973). See also Carrington & McElroy, "The Doctrine of Corporate Opportunity as Applied to Officers, Directors and Stockholders of Corporations," 14 *Bus. Law.* 957 (1959).

16. Duane Jones Co. v. Burke, 306 N.Y. 172, 117 N.E. 2d 237 (1954); Craig v. Graphic Arts Studio, Inc., 166 A.2d 444 (Del. Ch. 1960); Red Top Cab Co. v. Hanchett, 48 F.2d 236 (N.D. Cal. 1931). These cases and others are discussed by Wadmond, 17 *Bus. Law.* 48 (1961).

17. Fairchild Engine & Airplane Corp. v. Cox, 50 N.Y.S. 2d 643 (S. Ct. 1944); B.F. Goodrich Co. v. Wohlgemuth, 117 Ohio App. 493, 192 N.E. 99 (1963). See also Jacobs, 28 *Bus. Law.* 1063, 1067.

18. Stratis v. Andreson, 254 Mass. 536, 150 N.E. 832 (1926); Meyer v. Fort Hill Engraving Co., 249 Mass. 302, 143 N.E. 915 (1924); Landstreet v. Meyer, 201 Miss. 826, 29 So. 2d 653 (1947). See Marsh, 22 *Bus. Law.* 35 at 59; and Feuer, *Personal Liabilities of Corporate Officers and Directors.* (2d ed., Prentice-Hall, Inc., 1974) 63.

19. Gottlieb v. Heyden Chemical Corp., 33 Del. Ch. 177, 91 A.2d 57 (1952), 33 Del. Ch. 283, 92 A.2d 594 (1952), 34 Del. Ch. 84, 99 A.2d 507 (1953); Kerbs v. Calif. E. Airways, Inc., 33 Del. Ch. 69, 90 A.2d 652 (1952).

20. Kaufman v. Schoenberg, 33 Del. Ch. 211, 91 A.2d 786 (1952); Beard v. Elster, 39 Del. Ch. 153, 160 A.2d 731 (1960); Dann v. Chrysler Corp., 41 Del. Ch. 438, 198 A.2d 185 (1963), *aff'd*, Hoffman v. Dann, 42 Del. Ch. 123, 205 A.2d 343 (1964), *cert. denied*, 380 U.S. 973 (1965), Olson Brothers Inc. v. Englehart, 42 Del. Ch. 348, 211 A.2d 610 (1965). The Delaware Legislature adopted a statutory standard in 1953: "In the absence of actual fraud in the transaction, the judgment of the directors as to the consideration for the issuance of such rights or options and the sufficiency thereof shall be conclusive." Delaware Corporation Law (8 *Del. Code Ann.*) § 157.

21. Special federal income tax treatment of executive stock options was provided before 1976 for options meeting certain requirements including stockholder approval. 26 U.S.C. § 422. The New York Stock Exchange (NYSE) requires stockholder authorization of options issued to directors, officers, or key employees as a condition for listing on the Exchange the shares issued pursuant to the option. NYSE *Company Manual,* § A-7. The Securities and Exchange Commission exempts from the short-swing provisions of the Securities Exchange Act (discussed in Chapter 8 under the heading "Section 16(b)—Trading") the grant of options pursuant to a plan that has been approved by stockholders, 17 C.F.R. § 240.16b-3.

22. Delaware authorizes loans to officers and other employees "whenever, in the judgment of the directors, such loan . . . may reasonably be expected to benefit the corporation." Delaware Corporation Law (8 *Del. Code Ann.*) § 143.

23. Model Business Corporation Act Ann. § 47 (West Publishing Co., 2d ed. 1971, and 1973 and 1977 Supps.). States having an identical or comparable provision are Arizona, California, Florida, Iowa, Kansas, Kentucky, Maryland, Michigan, New Jersey, Oregon, Rhode Island, and West Virginia. For discussions of the general principles and the cases involving loans to directors and officers, see Rich, "Corporate Loans to Officers, Directors and Shareholders," 14 *Bus. Law.* 658 (1959); Wadmond, 17 *Bus. Law.* 48, 54; Marsh, 22 *Bus. Law.* 35, 68; Feuer, *Personal Liabilities of Corporate Officers and Directors* 59–62.

24. Board of Commissioners of Tippecanoe County v. Reynolds, 44 Ind. 509, 15 Am. Rep. 245 (1873); Goodwin v. Agassiz, 283 Mass. 358, 186 N.E. 659 (1933). See discussions in Lattin, *The Law of Corporations* 294, 318; Feuer, *Personal Liability of Corporate Officers and Directors* 122–132; Stevens, *Private Corporations* 579; Comment, "Corporations—Duty of Directors to Stockholder in Stock Exchange Sales," 32 *Mich. L. Rev.* 678–685 (1934); Note, "Corporations: Right of a Director to Purchase Shares from the Stockholders: Duty of Disclosure," 19 *Cornell L.Q.* 103–108 (1933).

25. Brophy v. Cities Service, 31 Del. Ch. 241, 70 A.2d 5 (1949); Diamond v. Oreamuno, 24 N.Y. 2d 494, 248 N.E. 2d 910 (1969); discussed by Scriggins, "Developments in State Corporation Law—1969," 25 *Bus. Law.* 1691, 1697 (1970). See also Ratner, "Federal and State Roles in the Regulation of Insider Trading," 31 *Bus. Law.* 947 (1976).

26. Among the recent unsuccessful tender offers (or attempted takeovers) have been the attempt of American Express Co. to acquire McGraw-Hill, Inc. (*Wall St. J.*, Jan. 19, 1979, p. 3, & March 2, 1979, p. 4) and the attempt of Brascan, Ltd. to acquire F.W. Woolworth Co. (*Wall St. J.*, April 10, 1979, p. 3, & May 30, 1979, p. 3). Both have resulted in lawsuits by stockholders against directors and officers of the target corporations for having thwarted offers that plaintiff stockholders considered advantageous. ("McGraw-Hill," *Wall St. J.*, Feb. 1, 1979, p. 2; "Woolworth," *Wall St. J.*, April 17, 1979, p. 11.)

A number of states have enacted statutes designed to slow down the takeover process by requiring reporting to state officials. Such statutes have been criticized as being promanagement and in conflict with the Williams Act, a 1968 amendment to the Securities Exchange Act of 1934 requiring a report to be filed with the Securities and Exchange Commission by a person or group acquiring 5 percent or more of the shares of a company under SEC jurisdiction. Such a report must include, among other things, a statement of intention concerning acquisition of control. 15 U.S.C. § 78m(2)(d) & (e). A federal court in Texas held unconstitutional an Idaho statute regulating takeovers on the ground that the Williams Act had preempted the field and that Idaho had no power to legislate. The statute was, however, reinstated by the United States Supreme Court on a procedural ground that the action was commenced in the wrong court, that venue in the Texas court was improper because the locus of the claim was in Idaho, the statute in question being an Idaho statute and the regulatory action having been taken by Idaho officials. Leroy v. Great Western United Corp., 443 U.S. 173, 61 L. Ed. 2d 464, 99 S. Ct. 2710 (1979). The question of the validity of state takeover laws was not passed upon by the Supreme Court and remains unsettled. In the meanwhile, the SEC has adopted rules intended to equalize power between acquiring companies or groups and managements of target companies by requiring disclosures of specified information from both tenderers and target companies. SEC Releases 33-6158 and 34-16384 (Nov. 29, 1979); 44 Fed. Reg. 70326; 17 C.F.R. §§ 230.434b, 240.14d-1-9. For complete discussions of all the aspects of tender offers, see Fleischer, *Tender Offers: Defenses, Responses and Planning* (Law & Business, Inc., Harcourt Brace, 1978) and Lipton & Steinberger, *Takeovers and Freezeouts* (New York Law Journal Seminars-Press, Inc., 1978).

27. Marsh, in commenting upon defense of control, says: "It is impossible to command the directors in this situation to avoid any conflict of interest, since it has been unavoidably thrust upon them. And to suggest that they abdicate before every challenge would be ridiculous." Marsh, 22 *Bus. Law.* 35, 60. A discussion of the various tactics used in defense of control appears in Kaplan, 31 *Bus. Law.* 883–927 at 911. Because of the application of the business judgment rule, discussed later in this chapter under the heading "Business Judgment," there are very few cases in which managers have been held liable for acts in defense of control. In Bennett v. Propp, 41 Del. Ch. 14, 187 A.2d 405 (1962), the chairman and the president, who took affirmative steps of purchasing shares with corporate funds to maintain control, were held liable, while the directors, who ratified the transaction, were exonerated.

28. In a recent Nebraska case, the directors of a mutual insurance company recommended and submitted to policyholders for approval a transaction by which the assets and business were transferred to a new company at a price that the court found to be less than the fair value. The president of the transferring company was also the president (at a higher salary) of one of the two corporations that owned all the stock of the transferee. The president was held liable on a conflict-of-interest basis and the directors were held to have breached their duty by failure (1) to have an independent appraisal of the transaction and (2) to disclose all material facts to the policyholders. Doyle v. Union Insurance Co., 202 Neb. 599, 277 N.W. 2d 36 (1979). A related problem is that of sale of control. In a typical situation, the directors might own the controlling shares and sell them to an outside group on terms more favorable than the purchasers are willing to pay to the minority. This problem is more closely concerned with relations among various groups of stockholders than it is with a strict management responsibility. The reader desiring to pursue this problem further is directed to Kaplan, 31 *Bus. Law.* 883–927 at 907, and Feuer, *Personal Liabilities of Corporate Officers and Directors* 102–109.

29. A recent discussion of repurchases of these types, together with some other, possibly less important, reasons for repurchases, appears in *Wall St. J.*, May 3, 1979, p. 40.

30. Problems of purchase of the corporation's own shares become intermixed with those of defense of control. See Osborn, "Developments in Corporate Law, 19 *Bus. Law.* 577–591 at 579 (1964). For further discussion of "going private," see Kaplan, "Fiduciary Responsibility in the Management of the Corporation," 31 *Bus. Law.* 883–927 at 902–907 (1976); Tracy, "How Herbert Kohler Won His Bid for Privacy," *Fortune*, Feb. 12, 1979, pp. 84–85. The courts have held that, even though statutory procedures are followed, a minority may not be arbitrarily frozen out. The transaction may be enjoined in the absence of a valid business purpose and, even if such a purpose is found to exist, the minority stockholders are entitled to a hearing to deter-

mine the fairness of the price to be paid for their shares. Berkowitz v. Power/Mate Corp., 135 N.J. Super. 36, 342 A.2d 566 (1975); Tanzer v. International General Industries, Inc., 379 A.2d 1121 (Del. 1977); Singer v. Magnavox, 380 A.2d 969 (Del. 1977). In 1979 the Securities and Exchange Commission adopted a new rule requiring detailed disclosure of the terms of a "going private" transaction, including statements regarding the fairness of the transaction and the extent of participation of nonemployee directors in negotiating and approving the terms of the transaction and in preparing the report on its fairness. 17 C.F.R. § 240.13e; SEC Release 34-16075, *eff.* Sept. 7, 1979; 44 Fed. Reg. 46736.

31. For a more complete discussion of the use of corporate funds in proxy contests, see Feuer, *Personal Liabilities of Corporate Officers and Directors* 110–115; also, Eisenberg, *The Structure and Governance of the Corporation* (Little, Brown & Co., 1976) 102–110.

32. Among large corporate write-offs during the 1970s were Singer Co., $400 million, closing of business operations and certain other business lines "Singer Performs Costly Surgery," *Bus. Week,* Jan. 12, 1976, p. 30); Firestone Tire & Rubber Co., $110 million, closing of excess production capacity (Firestone: *A Report of Progress,* Richard A. Riley, Chairman, Annual Meeting of Stockholders, Jan. 27, 1979, pp. 7–8); International Telephone & Telegraph Corp., $320 million, closing of cellulose mill ("ITT to Close Mill in Quebec, Sets Charge of $320 million and Sees 3rd Quarter Loss," *Wall St. J.,* Sept. 13, 1979, p. 3); Polaroid Corp., $68 million, write-off of instant movie system ("Polaroid to Take Large Write-Off on Its Polavision," *Wall St. J.,* Sept. 13, 1979, p. 5).

33. Adkins and Janis, "Some Observations on Liabilities of Corporate Directors," 20 *Bus. Law.* 817–831 (1965); Stevens, *Private Corporations* 588–595.

34. Bowerman v. Hamner, 250 U.S. 504, 63 L. Ed. 1113, 39 S. Ct. 549 (1919). Criticized in Lattin, *The Law of Corporations* 275.

35. Model Business Corporation Act Ann., 1977 Supp. § 35.

36. *N.Y. Bus. Corp. Law,* Sec. 717 (McKinney). Provisions comparable or identical to the Model Act have also been adopted in California, Connecticut, Florida, Georgia, Iowa, Maine, Maryland, Michigan, New York, and Tennessee. See Model Business Corporation Act Ann., 1977 Supp. § 35, annotations at 271–272.

37. Delaware Corporation Law, (8. *Del. Code Ann.*) § 141(e).

38. A.P. Smith Manufacturing Co. v. Barlow, 13 N.J. 145, 98 A.2d 581, 39 *A.L.R.* 2d 1179 (1953); Union Pacific R.R. v. Trustees, Inc., 8 Utah 2d 101, 329 P.2d 398 (1958). For a comparison of these cases, see Wetzel & Winokur, "Corporations and the Public Interest—A Review of the Corporate Purpose and Business Judgment Rules," 27 *Bus. Law.* 235–242 at 237–239 (1971).

39. Sylvia Martin Foundation, Inc. v. Swearingen, 260 F. Supp. 231 (S.D.N.Y. 1966).

40. Kelly & Wyndham, Inc. v. Bell, 266 A.2d 878 (Del. S. Ct. 1970), *aff'g* 254 A.2d 62 (Del. Ch. 1969).

41. See comments on extension of the business judgment rule to new social situations in Wetzel & Winokur, 27 *Bus. Law.* 235–242 at 241. The context here

is responsibility to stockholders, but there may, of course, be a risk of charges of reverse discrimination. Charges of reverse discrimination in employment practices were, however, defeated in United Steelworkers of America v. Weber, 443 U.S. 193, 61 L. Ed.2d 480, 99 S. Ct. 2721 (1979).

42. Gall v. Exxon Corporation, 418 F. Supp. 508 (S.D.N.Y. 1976); Abbey v. Control Data Corp., 460 F. Supp. 1242 (D. Minn. 1978). For a review of the factual background of the *Exxon* case, see "To Pay or Not to Pay: How Exxon Official Agonized Over Making '71 Italian Contribution," *Wall St. J.,* July 14, 1978, p. 1.

43. Hichens v. Congreve, 4 Russ. 562, 38 Eng. Rep. 917 (Ch. 1828); Foss v. Harbottle, 2 Hare 461, 67 Eng. Rep. 189 (Ch. 1843).

44. For a more complete discussion of the law of stockholders' derivative actions, see Stevens, *Private Corporations* 666; Ballantine, *Corporations* (Callaghan & Co., 1946) 184; Lattin, *The Law of Corporations* 413; Feuer, *Personal Liabilities of Corporate Officers and Directors* 194; 3 Fletcher, *Cyclopedia of Corporations* §§ 1276, 1277, 1282; Knepper, *Liability of Corporate Officers and Directors* (3d ed. Allen Smith Company, 1978) 525–555.

45. *Cal. Corp. Codes,* § 800 (West); Delaware Corporation Law (8 *Del. Code Ann.*), § 327; *Fla. Stat. Ann.* § 607–147 (Harrison); *Ill. Ann. Stat.,* ch. 32, § 157.45 (Smith-Hurd); *Mich. Comp. Laws,* § 450.1491; *N.J. Stat. Ann.,* § 14A:3-6; *N.Y. Bus. Corp. Law,* § 626; *Pa. Stat. Ann.,* tit. 15, § 432 (Purdon); *Wash. Rev. Code Ann.,* § 23A.08.450.

46. Model Business Corporation Act, § 49. A recent decision of the United States Supreme Court was concerned with the right of disinterested directors (not defendants in the suit) to obtain dismissal of a stockholders' derivative action on the ground "that continuation of the litigation was contrary to the best interests of the company and its shareholders." The action was against a registered investment adviser and several directors of an investment company, registered under the Investment Company Act, for having allegedly made improper investments within the meaning of that Act and the Investment Advisers Act. The District Court, upon a finding that the disinterested directors were truly disinterested and independent and did not act fraudulently or corruptly, granted the motion. The Court of Appeals for the Second Circuit reversed, holding that under the Investment Company Act, disinterested directors did "not have the power to foreclose the continuance of frivolous litigation." The Supreme Court reversed the Court of Appeals and held that the Act did not deny such power to disinterested directors, but that the question of their right to a dismissal was one of state law. Burks v. Lasker, 441 U.S. 571, 60 L. Ed.2d 404, 99 S. Ct. 1831 (1979).

47. For a discussion of the pros and cons of the Model Corporation Act, Sec. 49, see the comment at 2 Model Business Corp. Act § 49, Annot. 32, and Eisenberg, "The Model Business Corporation Act and the Model Business Corporation Act Annotated," 29 *Bus. Law.* 1407–1428 at 1418 (1979). See also Conard, *Corporations in Perspective* (The Foundation Press, 1976) 399–403.

48. See Berle & Means, *The Modern Corporation and Private Property* (rev. ed.,. Harcourt, Brace & World, 1968) 197; Conard, *Corporations in Perspective* 379 at 381.

# CHAPTER FOUR

# Emergence of Penal Sanctions In Regulated Industries

A few federal statutes, some as early as 1852, established rather elementary safety standards for steamships and penalties for their violation, but that was about all in the line of federal law relating directly to business that existed prior to 1887.[1]

## THE INTERSTATE COMMERCE ACT

Federal regulation of business began on February 4, 1887, the day the Interstate Commerce Act became law.[2] In the late 1800s the railroads had achieved a position of great importance in the economy of the nation. The system of railroads, linking both coasts and reaching into cities and towns all over the country, played a large role in the nation's economic development by facilitating the movement of persons and goods. But because all the other sectors of the economy were so dependent upon the railroads, there were numerous opportunities for abuse, most of which centered on discrimination in rates, fares, and other charges, and in service among different customers. It is beyond the scope of this book to go into detail concerning the conditions of the railroad industry prevailing prior to the Interstate Commerce Act, but it is sufficient to say that the Congress was persuaded that the time had arrived for a law comprehensively regulating that industry.[3]

The Act established the Interstate Commerce Commission as the first of the innumerable administrative tribunals that were destined to play a preeminent role in the operation of the federal government and the regulation of business as we know it today. The most important substantive aspect of the Interstate Commerce Act was its regulatiom of rates, fares, and charges. It was concerned with nondiscrimination in these fields. For the first time, there were specific laws and specific rule-making power directed at business conduct, and penalties were prescribed for violation of the laws and the rules formulated thereunder. Section 10 of the Act provided that any director or officer of a carrier or any person acting for and employed by it who violated any regulation issued under the authority of the Interstate Commerce Act would be guilty of a misdemeanor and subject to a $5,000 fine.[4]

The Department of Justice lost no time in enforcing the provisions of Section 10. In *United States v. Tozer*,[5] an indictment was brought against an agent of the Missouri Pacific Railway Company for charging a shipper less than the prescribed rate. The offense was alleged to have occurred in June 1887, a mere four months after the enactment of the Act. The defendant was not an officer or a director of the carrier, but was apparently a member of middle management. Objection to the indictment was made on the ground that it did not show that the defendant had any authority to perform the acts charged. The court overruled the objection, stating that it was sufficient to show that the accused was, in fact, the agent of a railway company subject to the provisions of the Act and that the alleged wrong was committed under the color of his office or agency.

In 1889 the Interstate Commerce Act was amended to increase the severity and scope of its penalties.[6] In addition to the $5,000 fine, the Act now provided for a prison sentence of not to exceed two years, or for both fine and imprisonment, if the violation consisted of a discrimination in rates, fares, or charges. The same penalties were also prescribed for false billings or classification. The Act was also extended to penalize any shipper obtaining a lower rate by false billing or false claim, or any shipper inducing unjust discrimination by bribery or otherwise. Such a penalty could be imposed upon the shipper, whether a natural or a corporate person, and any officer or agent acting for the shipper in the matter. Again, the same penalty of a $5,000 fine, two years imprisonment, or both was imposed.

A strange anomaly of the Act, as originally enacted and as amended in 1889, was that it did not impose criminal penalties or forfeitures upon the carrier itself, but only upon its officers and agents and upon shippers and their officers and agents.[7] So, in the early years of the Interstate Commerce Act, officers and agents of railway corporations bore the sole responsibility for their corporations' violations. It was not until 1903 that violations of the Interstate Commerce Act by an officer, director, or agent of a railway corporation were made violations by the corporation itself, subjecting it to fines. This was done by enactment of the Elkins Act,[8] which also abolished imprisonment for violations. Imprisonment was restored, however, by the Hepburn Act,[9] which came three years later and has remained a feature of the penal provisions of the Interstate Commerce Act ever since. Fines and imprisonment of managers were destined to be part of numerous other federal laws that were to follow in the ever-increasing efforts of the Congress to regulate business and to legislate standards of business conduct.

There are not many reported cases under the Interstate Commerce Act and its amendments interpreting the applicability of criminal sanctions to managerial personnel, but the few there are clearly indicate that such personnel are held to strict accountability for compliance with the law. Knowingly granting a preference subjects a traffic manager or general freight agent to criminal penalties. In one early case, however, a clerical employee, having some supervisory responsibilities, encountered an unusual situation in the granting of credits and continued to grant them after inquiring of their validity and being reassured by his supervisor. Unknown to him, the supervisor was personally participating in an unlawful discrimination. The clerical employee was held not to be criminally liable.[10]

While rate and fare discrimination was the original reason for enactment of the Interstate Commerce Act and establishment of the Interstate Commerce Commission, regulation of railroad carriers did not stop there. Other requirements were embodied in the original Act, and over the years it was amended, supplementary acts were added, and the authority of the Commission was expanded so that there was extensive coverage of such matters as establishment and discontinuance of routes by so-called certificates of convenience and necessity, recordkeeping, reports, safety, hours of work, nondisclosure of business information concerning shippers, interlocking directorates, mergers and consolidation of carriers, and issuance of corporate securities by carriers, to name only a part. As these provisions were enacted, penalties and forfeitures for their violation were also prescribed.[11]

A limitation upon the liability of railroad directors and officers in the issuance of securities was established in 1944 in *Casey v. Woodruff*.[12] Under the authority of Section 20a of the Interstate Commerce Act, as amended by the Transportation Act of 1920,[13] all plans for the issuance of railroad securities were required to be submitted to the Interstate Commerce Commission for approval before issuance. Directors, officers, attorneys, or agents who participate, assent, or concur in the issue of securities without such prior approval were subject to fines of up to $10,000, imprisonment up to three years, or both. In *Casey v. Woodruff*, the directors of the Erie Railroad submitted to the Commission a plan for the sale of refinancing bonds. The plan was disapproved by the Commission after the directors and officers had gone to considerable expense in the preparation of the plan and in taking numerous preliminary steps. A stockholders' derivative action was brought against the directors and officers to recover the expenses. The court held that under Section 20a the Commission had the power to substitute its own judgment for that of the railroad's directors and officers in determining whether the issuance of securities was wise or prudent and therefore had the authority to disapprove. But disapproval by the Commission did not mean that the directors and officers were liable for negligence in the discharge of their duties. To hold otherwise, the court stated, would have

> . . . a deadening effect on the initiative of the management of the railroad if its directors could not even apply to the Commission for authority to do something which under the law required the Commission's approval except that the risk of being held personally liable if the regulatory body withheld the approval. [14]

The court also noted that holding the directors and officers liable in such a situation also could inhibit the Commission from properly exercising its discretion because of fear of subjecting the management of applicants to personal liability.

## Expansion of the Interstate Commerce Act: Other Types of Carriers

The railroads were thus the first industry to be singled out for extensive regulation by the federal government, but they were followed by other types of common carriers in the succeeding decades. Again, the purpose was to prevent discrimination. In 1906, the Hepburn Act brought interstate pipelines for "the transportation of oil or other commodity, except water and except natural or artificial gas" under the provisions of the Interstate Commerce Act. [15]

Water transportation was subjected to various federal laws from an early date, but not on a comprehensive regulatory basis. As we have seen in the opening paragraph of this chapter, there were federal statutes pertaining to shipping and imposing personal liabilities upon shipowners and masters as early as 1852. The first effort to regulate water carriers began with the Shipping Act of 1916, [16] followed by the Merchant Marine Act of 1920 [17] and the Intercoastal Shipping Act of 1933. [18] In 1940, comprehensive regulation of water carriers came with the enactment of Part III of the Interstate Commerce Act. [19] To the extent that provisions of the Shipping Act and the Intercoastal Shipping Act were inconsistent with Part III, they were repealed. Nevertheless, certain provisions of each of the acts remained in effect. [20] It is not within the scope of this book to explain the substantive differences among the various laws regulating water transportation or the jurisdictional differences of the Interstate Commerce Commission and the Federal Maritime Commission under these laws. It is sufficient to say that each of the laws imposes penalties for infractions by the carriers, their directors, officers, and other corporate managers.

Motor carriers remained free of federal regulation until 1935, when Part II of the Interstate Commerce Act was enacted. Under Part II, substantive laws, procedures, and penalties that were very much like, and in many instances identical with, those applicable to rail carriers were imposed upon motor carriers.[21] Directors, officers, and agents of motor

carriers found themselves subject to the same types of penalties that their counterparts in the railroad, pipeline, and shipping industries had experienced for decades.

## REGULATION OF PIPELINES

The jurisdiction of the Interstate Commerce Commission over oil pipelines, which had been conferred by the Hepburn Act in 1906, was terminated in 1977 by Section 306 of the Energy Reorganization Act, which transferred its functions in that field to the Secretary of Energy.[22]

Regulation of natural gas pipelines (and of the entire natural gas industry) was vested in the Federal Power Commission under the Natural Gas Act, enacted in 1938,[23] and was transferred in 1977 to the Federal Energy Regulatory Commission.[24]

Again, in the regulation of pipelines for the transportation of oil and gas, there are provisions for publication and approval of rates, certificates of convenience and necessity, nondiscrimination in service and charges, safety, and all the other substantive matters associated with the other types of transportation. An added feature of oil and gas regulation has also been regulation of the prices of the commodities themselves. The procedures and penalties for violation of the laws pertaining to pipelines and the regulations issued under them closely parallel those of the other transportation industries. Corporate managers have exposures very similar to their counterparts in such industries.

## REGULATION OF AIR CARRIERS

Another great branch of the transportation industry, the airlines industry, has also come in for its share of regulation, although not by the Interstate Commerce Commission. Airlines are regulated by the Civil Aeronautics Board under the authority of the Federal Aviation Act of 1958,[25] which repealed and superseded the Civil Aeronautics Act of 1938.[26] These acts provided standards for the regulation of fares and charges, certificates of convenience and necessity, safety, nondiscrimination, and all the other aspects of the business, very much like the statutes regulating rail, water, motor, and pipeline carriers, with generally only such differences as might be appropriate to the differences in the mode of transportation. The penalties for violation generally paralleled those existing in the other acts.

Especially significant and appropriate in the regulation of air carriers is the rigidity of enforcement of safety regulations. For example, in *United States v. Newman*,[27] a pilot who flew a commercial plane in Hawaii was fined for violating the safety regulations when he knew that the aileron turn-tab actuator assembly had been reversed during servicing so that the "Drop Left Wing" switch dropped the right wing and vice versa. It was no defense that he knew which switch to operate to get the desired result. The court noted that there had never been a court challenge to the exact meaning of the safety regulations. In another case, a supervising foreman was fined for the errors of his repair crew in improperly assembling an Electra prop in an overhaul operation.[28] The court said he was responsible for the work even though he did not actually participate in it.

The Congress has recently enunciated in its declaration of policy under the Airline Deregulation Act of 1978 that safety is "the highest priority" in air commerce.[29] The emphasis in the regulation of airlines under the new law is upon safety, competition, and economy. To that end, regulation of routes and fares is being phased out. But penalties upon the carriers and their managers for violation of the remaining laws and regulations are, of course, continued.

## REGULATION OF COMMUNICATIONS

Closely related in principle to the regulation of the various forms of transportation is the regulation of various forms of communication, such as telephone, telegraph, radio, and television. Some very elementary statements of duties of telegraph companies and their managers can be found as far back as 1888.[30] Communication by wire or wireless came under the jurisdiction of the Secretary of Commerce and Labor in 1912.[31] In order to provide for the orderly use of wavelengths, the Radio Act of 1927 provided for the licensing and regulation of radio broadcasting stations by the Federal Radio Commission.[32] With passage of the Communications Act of 1934,[33] the Federal Radio Commission was replaced by the Federal Communications Commission and the powers of the Interstate Commerce Commission in wire and wireless communication were transferred to the Communications Commission. Under the Federal Communications Act and its predecessors, directors, officers, and other managers of communication companies have found themselves subject to very much the same kinds of rules and the same kinds of liabilities as their counterparts in the transportation industries.

## RECENT LEGISLATIVE DEVELOPMENTS

There has been a great deal of discussion in recent years of the necessity of "deregulating" some of the regulated industries, particularly those engaged in the various forms of transportation. Some of this deregulation has been accomplished, particularly, as we have noted, in the relaxation of the rigidity of air-fare regulation and the requirements for certification of air-carrier routes, pursuant to the Airline Deregulation Act of 1978. This does not mean, however, that these industries are becoming "lawless" or completely unregulated. Standards of safety, nondiscrimination, conflict of interest, and other accepted norms of ethical corporate behavior remain, as do the sanctions for their violation. There is no indication that responsibility of corporate managers is being

diminished or that penalties for violations are being relaxed. Legislative
developments of recent years reaffirm this point.

As noted earlier, the new Department of Energy and the new Federal
Energy Regulatory Commission were created by the Congress in 1977,
and they were granted, among other things, the preexisting powers of
regulation over oil and gas pipelines and the natural gas industry. In
1978, the Revised Interstate Commerce Act was adopted.[34] It is a complete recodification, clarification, and modernization of the original 1887
Act and all its numerous amendments and supplementary acts. The penal
provisions remain.

## CONCLUSION

The Interstate Commerce Act almost a century ago was the prototype of a
long line of federal statutes that not only have set standards of business
conduct for specific industries and industry in general, but also have
imposed sanctions upon corporations that do not comply with them and
upon those individuals in corporations who either participate in the
noncompliance or are responsible for it. In this chapter, we have been
concerned with common carriers in transportation and communications,
and their managers. In succeeding chapters, we will trace the development of personal responsibility in corporate situations through laws
pertaining to other types of industries and to industry in general.[35]

## NOTES

1. In 1852 a federal statute prescribed civil liability upon the part of a vessel,
   its master, mate, engineer, and pilot for injury to passengers caused by
   carelessness, negligence, or willful misconduct. 10 Stat. 72; suspended in
   1871, 16 Stat. 453; 46 U.S.C. § 491. See Sherlock v. Alling, 93 U.S. 99, 23 L.
   Ed. 819 (1876). The 1871 statute also provided for inspection and certification of vessels as to maximum passenger limits and for fines and jail
   sentences for carrying passengers in excess of the limits. Both the owner
   and the master of the ship were liable for the penalties. 16 Stat. 454; 46
   U.S.C. §§ 451–452. It also prescribed fines and imprisonment for violation
   of federal standards for carrying explosives on a ship. 16 Stat. 441; 46 U.S.C.
   § 170. An 1872 statute required certain entries in a ship's logbook and
   penalized the master for omissions or false entries, 17 Stat. 276; 46 U.S.C.
   § 201.
2. 24 Stat. 384. The Interstate Commerce Act and all its amendments, including those discussed in this chapter, are codified in 49 U.S.C. §§ 11901–
   11916.

   Some states began regulation of railroads before the federal government
   entered the field. Massachusetts started in 1861, Minnesota in 1871, and
   California in 1878. As federal regulation of carriers and utilities has grown,
   there has been a concurrent growth of state regulation over the activities of
   carriers and utilities of an intrastate, as distinguished from an interstate,
   nature.
3. A concise discussion of the conditions leading up to the passage of the

Interstate Commerce Act and of its principal provisions and their significance, written only two decades after its enactment, appears in Drinker, *A Treatise on the Interstate Commerce Act* (George T. Bisel Co., 1909).

4. Drinker, at page 61 of his treatise, cited in note 3 above, states that the creation of penal and criminal liability on the part of officers of the carriers was one of the principal changes that the Act made in the common law pertaining to common carriers.

5. 37 F.635 (E.D. Mo. 1889). This case appears to be the first criminal action under the Interstate Commerce Act.

6. 25 Stat. 858. See United States v. Union Manufacturing Co., 240 U.S. 605, 60 L. Ed. 822 (1916).

7. See the court's comments *In re* Peasley, 44 F. 271, 275 (N.D. Ill. 1890).

8. 32 Stat. 847.

9. 34 Stat. 587.

10. United States v. Michigan Central R. Co., 43 F. 26 (N.D. Ill. 1890). Other cases showing various levels of middle and lower management involved in criminal proceedings for violation of the Interstate Commerce Act include New York Central and Hudson River R.R., 212 U.S. 481, 53 L. Ed. 613, 29 S. Ct. 304 (1909) (assistant traffic manager); Kennedy v. United States, 375 F. 182 (4th Cir. 1921) (car clerk); Dearing v. United States, 167 F.2d 310 (10th Cir. 1948) (conductor); Berg v. United States, 176 F.2d 122 (9th Cir. 1949) (accountant). See also Drinker, *Treatise on the Interstate Commerce Act* 477. This list of cases is not intended to be exhaustive. Most of the criminal proceedings for violation of the Interstate Commerce Act are unreported. The court in the recent case of Key Line Freight, Inc. v. United States, 570 F.2d 97 (6th Cir. 1978) commented on the "dearth of cases in the area of rebates." Although that case was concerned with the conviction of the carrier rather than of the individuals involved, it illustrates the strictness of construction applied to violations concerning discrimination, preferences, and rebates in that the carrier was held to have granted unlawful rebates in furnishing to employees of shippers expense-paid trips to the Kentucky Derby at a cost of about $150 each.

11. All the various penal provisions of the Interstate Commerce Act have recently been revised, clarified, and compiled in chapter 19 of the Revised Interstate Commerce Act, P.L. 95–473, Oct. 17, 1978; 49 U.S.C. §§ 11901–11916.

12. 49 N.Y.S. 2d 625 (1944).

13. 41 Stat. 494.

14. 49 N.Y.S. 2d 625, 640.

15. 34 Stat. 584. For background and determination of constitutionality, see The Pipe Line Cases, 234 U.S. 548, 58 L. Ed. 1459, 34 S. Ct. 956 (1913).

16. 39 Stat. 728. The surviving sections of the Shipping Act are found at 46 U.S.C. §§ 801–841.

17. 41 Stat. 988; 46 U.S.C. §§ 861–889.

18. 47 Stat. 1425. The surviving sections of the Intercoastal Shipping Act are found at 46 U.S.C. §§ 843–848.

19. 54 Stat. 929. Part III was compiled at 49 U.S.C. §§ 901–923, which has now been superseded by the Revised Interstate Commerce Act, 49 U.S.C. §§ 11901–11916.

20. An interesting feature of water-carrier regulation is the requirement that the chairman of the board, the president, the chief executive officer, and a majority of the directors of a corporation owning a vessel engaged in coastwise trade or interstate commerce be citizens of the United States. Violation of these provisions can result in civil penalties and fines for the offending corporations and their directors and officers. 46 U.S.C. §§ 802, 883–1.

21. 49 Stat. 543. Part II was compiled at 49 U.S.C. §§ 301–325, which has now been superseded by the Revised Interstate Commerce Act, 49 U.S.C. §§ 11901–11916.

22. P.L. 95-91; 91 Stat. 581; 42 U.S.C. § 7155.

23. 52 Stat. 821; 15 U.S.C. § 717–717w.

24. 91 Stat. 583; 42 U.S.C. § 7172.

25. P.L. 85-726; 72 Stat. 731; 49 U.S.C. §§ 1301–1542.

26. 52 Stat. 973.

27. 331 F. Supp. 1240 (D. Hawaii 1971).

28. United States v. Garrett, 296 F. Supp. 1302 (N.D. Ga. 1969), *aff'd*, 418 F.2d 1250 (5th Cir. 1969), *cert. denied*, 399 U.S. 927 (1970). See also United States v. Duncan, 280 F. Supp. 975 (N.D. Tex. 1968).

29. P.L. 95-504; 92 Stat. 1705; 49 U.S.C. § 1302.

30. 25 Stat. 384, which imposed upon officers and agents the duty of affording to the government and the public equal facilities and equal interchange with other telegraph companies without discrimination and to carry out orders of the Interstate Commerce Commission. Fines of $1,000 and imprisonment for six months were its penalties for violation.

31. 37 Stat. 302.

32. 44 Stat. 1162.

33. 48 Stat. 1064; 47 U.S.C. §§ 151–609.

34. P.L. 95-473; 92 Stat. 1337–1470; 49 U.S.C. §§ 10101–11916.

35. Most of the acts discussed in this chapter also have provisions concerning interlocking directors and officers. These provisions will be discussed in Chapter 5 in the context of the Clayton Act provisions concerning interlocking directors generally.

CHAPTER FIVE
# *The Antitrust Laws and Individual Responsibility*

There is probably no field of the law that has occupied more of the time, attention, and concern of corporate executives at all levels than has that of the antitrust laws. The Sherman Antitrust Act became law in 1890, and at this stage it is an active nonagenarian, showing no tendency to slow down.

Despite misgivings by some academicians and some activists as to their true effectiveness and by some lawyers and some in the business community as to their clarity, the fact remains that the antitrust laws are generally accepted by the broad spectrum of the population as a necessary and desirable part of American jurisprudence and American business life. There is never any serious consideration of weakening the antitrust laws. The only debate is the extent to which they should be strengthened.

As we shall see in this chapter, there have been considerable procedural amendments during the past decade designed to make the antitrust laws more effective. Further strengthening is a lively topic in the halls of Congress and among legal scholars, economists, practicing lawyers, and business executives. Moreover, the enforcement of the antitrust laws is consistently a matter of prime concern to every administration, be it Democratic or Republican. Each new Attorney General, each new Assistant Attorney General in charge of the Antitrust Division, each new Chairman of the Federal Trade Commission seems to try to outdo the preceding official in at least the initial vigor of that person's antitrust enforcement. It may be debatable whether each succeeds to the high degree that was promised upon taking office, but the apparent enthusiasm of each new incumbent can scarcely be questioned.

We have seen in Chapter 4 that the Interstate Commerce Act, enacted in 1887, marked the beginning of regulation of business by the federal government. That Act was directed primarily at a single industry, which the Congress in its wisdom determined was in need of specific regulation. The impact of the Interstate Commerce Act was, as we saw, not limited solely to the carriers that it regulated and to their personnel, but also affected the shippers and their personnel. Nevertheless, the main thrust of the Act was upon the carriers and their people. Generally speaking, the effect upon shippers was peripheral. The involvement of a shipper occurred usually, but not always, only when a carrier also was involved, as when a preferential rate was charged. The Sherman Antitrust Act, on the other hand, enacted just three years after the Interstate Commerce Act, had a more direct impact upon practically all industry.

Like the Interstate Commerce Act, the Sherman Act was designed to remedy what were perceived to be abuses by certain large corporations. This time Congress did not direct its attention to the members of a specific industry, but rather, to the members of any industry that might engage in anticompetitive practices. There was concern that monopoly power was being concentrated in the hands of too few corporations. Combinations of competitors could control production and prices. Or, competitors could simply merge into one large entity.

Unlike the Interstate Commerce Act, however, the Sherman Act does not provide for detailed rules and regulations. In fact, it is not considered a "regulatory" statute. There is no administrative tribunal to whom the business person must go for permission to change prices or to enter new markets or to discontinue old markets. Prices and markets very definitely are affected by the Sherman Act but in a different way. The Act lays out broad rules, so broad as to be almost constitutional, rather than statutory, in nature.

To understand this fully, it is well to take a look at the substantive provisions of the Sherman Act.[1] As originally enacted, Section 1 read:

> Every contract, combination in the form of trust or otherwise, or conspiracy, in restraint of trade or commerce among the several States, or with foreign nations, is hereby declared to be illegal. . . . Every person who shall make any contract or engage in any combination or conspiracy hereby declared to be illegal shall be deemed guilty of a misdemeanor, and, on conviction thereof, shall be punished by fine not exceeding $5,000, or by imprisonment not exceeding one year, or by both said punishments, in the discretion of the court.

Section 2 (as originally enacted) read:

> Every person who shall monopolize, or attempt to monopolize, or combine or conspire with any other person or persons, to monopolize any part of the

trade or commerce among the several States, or with foreign nations, shall be deemed guilty of a misdemeanor, and, on conviction thereof, shall be punished by fine not exceeding $5,000, or by imprisonment not exceeding one year, or by both said punishments, in the discretion of the court.

There is not a word in either Section 1 or Section 2 concerning the particular acts in restraint of trade, such as price fixing or market allocation, that have long been recognized among the principal practices prohibited by the Act. These practices and others too numerous and detailed to summarize have been found by interpretations of the courts over the past nine decades to be "in restraint of trade" within the meaning of Section 1 of the Sherman Act and, if followed in combination with others, have been held to be prohibited by it. Rather than attempt to describe in detail the various kinds of trade restraints covered by Section 1, we will be concerned with trade restraints from the viewpoint of the responsibility of the individual corporate manager, the manner in which his or her action or responsibility or liability is affected by the Act.[2] Likewise, in our observations of the corporate manager's position under Section 2, we shall not really be concerned about whether a given practice amounts to monopolization or an attempt to monopolize, but rather, we shall be interested in the relationship of the individual to the corporation in a fact situation where monopolization, attempt to monopolize, or conspiracy to monopolize is alleged.

## SCOPE OF THE CLAYTON ACT AND THE
## FEDERAL TRADE COMMISSION ACT

After two decades of experience with the Sherman Act, an interest developed in strengthening the antitrust laws to provide a means of stopping incipient violations by prohibiting practices that, if unabated, it was reasoned, would lead to restraints of trade and monopolistic practices of the magnitude proscribed by the Sherman Act. Thus, in 1914 the Congress enacted two additional statutes which, together with the Sherman Act, constitute the main fabric of our antitrust laws as we know them today. They are the Clayton Act and the Federal Trade Commission Act. Both these acts, like the Sherman Act, have been amended over the years to meet the demands of the times and to strengthen them. The main features of the Clayton Act, so far as the purposes of this chapter are concerned, are Section 2 concerning price discrimination (amended and expanded by the Robinson-Patman Act in 1936), Section 3 concerning tying contracts, Section 4 concerning treble damages, Section 7 concerning mergers and acquisitions (amended and expanded by the Celler-Kefauver Act of 1950), Sections 8 and 10 concerning interlocking directorates, and Section 14 dealing with penalties for directors, officers, and agents.[3] These sections will each be discussed in this chapter in the context of their effects upon corporate managers.

The Federal Trade Commission Act, as originally enacted, contained only one statement of substantive law:

Unfair methods of competition in commerce are declared illegal.[4]

The Act also established the Federal Trade Commission to conduct investigations, issue complaints, hold hearings, and issue orders in enforcement of the Act. This, then, was one of this country's earlier administrative tribunals, although it is a quarter-century junior to the Interstate Commerce Commission. Violations of the Sherman Act and the Clayton Act have long been recognized as unfair methods of competition within the meaning of the Federal Trade Commission Act, and thus has grown up the anomalous practice of having a Cabinet department, the Department of Justice, and an administrative tribunal, the Federal Trade Commission, enforcing the same federal statutes. In addition, many other practices, such as false or deceptive advertising and disparagement of a competitor's product, to name only two, have been held to be unfair methods of competition within the meaning of the Federal Trade Commission Act.[5]

## THE CONCEPT OF INDIVIDUAL
## RESPONSIBILITY: CRIMINAL SANCTIONS

Despite the efforts of legislators to enact what they believe to be clear statutes, it is not unusual for questions to arise as to their proper interpretation. In the case of criminal penalties for violations of the antitrust laws by officers, directors, and agents of a corporation, no question was raised, however, until the early 1960s.

It should be noted that the Sherman Act did not refer to directors, officers, or employees as such in its penal provisions. Instead, it used the inclusive term "person" without any differentiation between corporations and natural persons, except for the reference to imprisonment, which, of course, is an impossibility for a corporation. Thus, unlike the Interstate Commerce Act, which in its early stages imposed penal sanctions only upon the individuals acting for the corporation, the Sherman Act sought to penalize both the corporation and the persons acting for it. The practice from early days was to indict both the corporation and its directors and officers for antitrust violations, and no effort was made to distinguish whether these persons were acting individually or in their representative capacities.[6]

Section 14 of the Clayton Act provided that a violation of the penal provisions of the antitrust laws by a corporation should be deemed to be also a violation by the individual directors, officers, or agents who authorized, ordered, or performed any of the acts constituting the violation. The penalty upon the individual was a fine not exceeding $5,000 or imprisonment not exceeding one year, or both. These were the same penalties that were imposed by the Sherman Act. In 1955, however, the

Sherman Act was amended to increase the maximum fine from $5,000 to $50,000, but no change was made in the fine imposed by the Clayton Act. The question then arose as to whether an indictment of a director, officer, or agent acting on behalf of a corporation could be brought under the Sherman Act alone, or whether it was necessary to bring the indictment under Section 14 of the Clayton Act. In a few reported cases, the defendants argued successfully in the district court that the penal provisions of the Sherman Act applied to individuals only when they were acting in their personal capacity, but that when they were acting on behalf of a corporation, the penal provisions of the Clayton Act applied exclusively.[7] So, for a brief period, corporate directors, officers, and agents faced only a potential $5,000 fine rather than a potential $50,000 fine for antitrust violations. The distinction was, however, short-lived. In 1962 the United States Supreme Court, in *United States v. Wise*,[8] held that Section 14 of the Clayton Act was intended to be a reaffirmation of the basic penal provisions of the Sherman Act and that those provisions applied to a corporate officer participating in an antitrust violation, whether or not that officer was acting in a representative capacity. In a concurring opinion Supreme Court Justice Harlan stated:

> I think there can have been no serious doubt even as early as 1890 that officers could be punished for crimes committed for their corporations. Until well into the nineteenth century the corporation itself could not be convicted; the individuals who acted in its name of course could be. . . . However, it was recognized that corporate officers could be convicted for "representative" crimes even after the corporation's immunity was worn away . . . in line with the rule . . . that an agent might be punished for crimes committed by his principal.[9]

The decision in the *Wise* case not only clarified any possible ambiguity in the law, but it also achieved a just result in placing the responsibility for an antitrust violation where it properly belonged—upon the shoulders of the individual who authorized, ordered, or committed the violation—with no opportunity for that person to escape with a lesser penalty on the ground of just doing her or his job.[10]

## INDIVIDUAL CIVIL RESPONSIBILITY: INJUNCTIONS AND ORDERS

The matter of individual responsibility of the corporate manager in antitrust matters is not solely a question of interpreting the penal provisions of the law. There are other remedies of a civil nature for antitrust violations. The Justice Department is empowered to bring civil actions to abate antitrust violations, particularly those of a continuing nature.[11] The Federal Trade Commission is authorized to issue cease-and-desist orders against the continuance of unfair methods of competition, which, as we have seen, include antitrust violations.[12] Also, persons damaged by antitrust violations may recover treble damages from violators.[13] Each of these remedies presents questions of the extent to which relief may be granted against a corporate manager.

The injunction and the cease-and-desist order present similar problems, and the decisions on one tend to be cited as precedent for the other. Each, of course, is an order against the continuation of certain acts and courses of conduct, as well as against the resumption of such acts when once discontinued and against the performance of other acts which may have the effect of accomplishing the same purpose as the prohibited violative acts. Violation of an injunction is contempt of court, for which the violator may be fined or imprisoned. Violations of a cease-and-desist order result in monetary penalties prescribed by the Federal Trade Commission Act. The main defendants in such injunctions and orders are, of course, the corporations against whom the actions or proceedings have been brought. Generally, such orders include within their scope all directors, officers, agents, and employees acting for and on behalf of the respective corporations. Often, however, the government may seek to have such injunctions or orders read specifically upon named individuals who have acted on behalf of the corporations. At this point, the question of personal participation by the corporate managers, as well as the question of their representative capacity, becomes of paramount importance.

The leading case on the subject is *Hartford Empire Co. v. United States,* decided by the United States Supreme Court in 1945.[14] In that case, the government sought injunctions against future violations upon the part of numerous corporations in the glass industry, as well as numerous named officers and directors. The Court dismissed the action as to those individuals who had not participated in any capacity in the wrongdoing. The mere fact that they occupied high office in their respective corporations was not a sufficient basis for naming them in the injunction. If, in fact, such a person did participate in a violation of the injunction in the future, the sweeping language of the injunction to the effect that it was binding upon all directors, officers, employees, and agents would be sufficient to warrant a contempt proceeding against such an individual for the violation.

Certain officers were, however, found to have actively participated in the illegal activities. The Court allowed the injunction to stand against them but qualified it to cover them only in their capacities as officers and agents of the corporate defendants. The net result is probably no different in practical effect than if the injunction had simply applied to the defendant corporations and their directors, officers, employees, and agents without naming them. The effect on the named individuals would be mainly psychological. By being named in the injunction, they were being warned by the Court that they were persons whose future performance would be closely watched, and, of course, they had the stigma of having been found to be violators of the law.

A series of cases on Federal Trade Commission orders has, over the years, developed the circumstances under which corporate managers

might be named in cease-and-desist orders. Not all these cases involve violations of the Sherman Act or the Clayton Act, for in some cases they involve other methods of unfair competition. The principles for naming or not naming corporate managers in the order do not, however, depend upon the type of violation involved. Rather, they are determined by the participation of the individual, the individual's position in the corporation, and the possibilities of evasion if the individual is not named. The United States Supreme Court was called upon to decide some of these questions eight years before the *Hartford Empire* case. In *Federal Trade Commission v. Standard Education Society*, [15] the two corporate respondents, Standard Education Society and Standard Encyclopedia Corporation, were owned by the same three stockholders, who were also the managers of Standard Education Society. The Federal Trade Commission found that Standard Encyclopedia had been organized for the purpose of evading any order against Standard Education, and accordingly, it issued its cease-and-desist order against the two corporations and the three individuals. The Supreme Court, in reviewing the order, noted that the individuals had acted as though no corporation existed. Their action in setting up Standard Encyclopedia raised the possibility that they might organize still more corporations to evade the order. Therefore, the Court reasoned, in order for the cease-and-desist order to be fully effective, the three individuals must be included within it.

The *Standard Education* decision is easily understood because it is evident that the individuals were not actually within a corporate framework. For all practical purposes, their corporations were being operated like partnerships or sole proprietorships. Later Federal Trade Commission orders, however, appear to have gone beyond the *Standard Education* decision. *Standard Distributors Inc. v. Federal Trade Commission*, [16] decided by the United States Court of Appeals for the Second Circuit subsequent to both *Standard Education* and *Hartford Empire*, held that *Standard Education* meant that the top officer in control could be joined in a cease-and-desist order whether or not a situation existed where there might be evasion. The Fifth Circuit, a few years later, modified the cease-and-desist order in *Doyle v. Federal Trade Commission* [17] to remove from the order the names of two managerial employees who had left the respondent corporation. The court pointed out that a cease-and-desist order is like an injunction and, following *Hartford Empire*, the two individuals could not be included in the order in their personal capacity and they no longer had a representative capacity in the corporation to warrant their being named. The court found no threat of evasion, as had existed in *Standard Education*.

The conclusion from the cases is, therefore, that an injunction or a cease-and-desist order will be issued against a named corporate manager in a representative capacity only when it is established that such a manager has personally authorized, condoned, or participated in the activity that is the subject of the injunction or order. The manager will be bound by the order, however, even if not named in it. Even one who has not so authorized, condoned, or participated will be bound by the terms of the injunction or order without being specifically named. A corporate manager will not be named in an injunction or order in a personal capacity unless (1) there has been a finding of violation of law in the individual's personal, as distinguished from his or her representative, capacity, or (2) the circumstances of the relationship of the individual to the corporation are such that there is substantial risk of evasion of the order if the individual is not bound in a personal capacity.

## INDIVIDUAL CIVIL RESPONSIBILITY: DAMAGE ACTIONS

Persons who have been aggrieved by an antitrust violation by a corporation or a combination of corporations normally look to the corporate defendants for redress and sue them for treble damages under the provisions of Section 4 of the Clayton Act. Normally, they do not join as defendants the corporate managers who participated in the violation. The corporations generally have more resources than their managers, and since it is money that the plaintiffs are seeking, they see no need to sue the individuals. An exception, of course, is made when the corporate defendant is very small and the manager very wealthy, or when the corporate defendant is insolvent. Consequently, there are very few decided cases on the liability of corporate managers in treble-damage actions, although there are decisions recognizing that corporate managers can be personally liable in such actions.[18] There are no statistics on the extent to which corporate managers have been sued for treble damages for antitrust violations.

In contrast with the relative unimportance of damage actions by third parties against corporate managers for antitrust violations, there is an interesting line of cases on the subject of recovery by a corporation from its own managers for antitrust violations and the inevitable corollary of the rights of stockholders to sue such managers.

The right of a corporation to sue its managers for involving it in antitrust violations was clearly stated by the Court of Appeals for the Tenth Circuit in *Wilshire Oil Co. v. Riffe*.[19] In that case, the corporation had been indicted in two courts for price fixing, had pleaded *nolo contendere* (no contest) to one charge and not guilty to the other, but upon trial, was found guilty. It paid fines in both actions. The corporation then sued the vice president and two salesmen, who had committed the violation, for recovery of the fines. Their defense was that since the corporation was itself guilty of the offenses, recovery should be denied because it came into court with unclean hands. The court refused to recognize unclean hands as a defense and held the individuals liable, not under the antitrust laws as such, but rather, for having breached their fiduciary duty to the corporation in involving it in an antitrust violation. In its opinion, the court stated:

Here the criminal liability of the corporation is purely vicarious. It results solely from the activity of the corporate employees. To allow those employees to assert that their own unlawful conduct operates to defeat the right of their corporation to recover for the injury caused by that same conduct, is an exercise in circuitous reasoning.[19,1]

There has been some discussion by legal scholars of the difficulties of allowing a corporation to recover from its managers for antitrust violations.[20] It has been suggested that the corporation might not be able to prove damages, as it may actually have profited from the antitrust violation. It would appear, however, that inability to prove damages should not be a bar to the right of the corporation to bring the action. In an era when treble-damage actions are of increasing importance, the likelihood of a corporation's being able to retain any profits from a discovered antitrust violation is remote. It would appear to be sound public policy to permit a corporation to fasten personal liability upon those of its personnel who have caused it to violate the law, subjecting it to fines, injury to its reputation, and possible treble-damage actions. If the corporation has profited from the violation, the burden of proving this should be on the culpable individuals.

While the right of a corporation to sue its own managers for causing it to engage in an antitrust violation appears to be established, stockholders' derivative suits against such managers have generally not been successful. Decisions in the early days of the Clayton Act denied recovery by a stockholder in a derivative action for treble damages against officers who had committed an antitrust violation.[21] These decisions were premised on the ground that the stockholder's derivative action was a suit on the equity side of the court, where a jury trial was not permitted, and that a determination of damages was a question for a jury, but there was no jury. Therefore, the derivative actions were dismissed on procedural grounds. Legal scholars have pointed out that since the days of those early decisions, the Federal Rules of Civil Procedure have eliminated the archaic separation of law and equity and that there is no reason today why, in the same action, a judge cannot try the right of the stockholder to sue and a jury cannot decide the amount of damages. While the procedural principle may now be different, there appear to be no reported cases where a stockholder has succeeded in a derivative action in causing a corporate manager to reimburse the corporation for losses caused by an antitrust violation. There seems to be only one case that clearly recognized the right to bring the action; in that case, recovery was denied because the directors had previously decided against suing the individual offenders, and the court, applying the business judgment rule, found that there was no evidence of fraud or bad faith in their decision.[22] The problem is really one of state law, involving the ordinary fiduciary responsibilities of directors and their exercise of business judgment. All the aspects of these problems, as they were discussed in Chapter 3, are present in a stockholders' derivative suit for an antitrust violation. Such suits do not properly involve interpretations of the antitrust laws. Moreover, the proper interpretation of Section 4 of the Clayton Act should be that the offending corporation itself (in whose shoes the stockholder stands in a derivative action) is not within the class of persons whom the Congress was seeking to indemnify when it provided for treble-damage actions.[23]

A stockholders' derivative action of a different sort appeared in the aftermath of the electrical equipment cases, which will be discussed later in this chapter under the heading "Evolution of Severity of Criminal Penalties." In *Graham v. Allis-Chalmers Manufacturing Co.*,[24] the directors were sued for having failed to prevent antitrust violations by minor officials. The court denied recovery, holding that the law does not require directors in every case to establish an espionage system to make certain that the corporation's personnel are obeying the law. The court stated that wrongdoing by employees is not to be anticipated as a general proposition, and it is only where the facts and circumstances of an employee's wrongdoing clearly throw the onus for the results on inattentive or supine directors that the law shoulders them with the responsibility.

## WHO IS A CONSPIRATOR?

The question of the separateness of the corporate manager from the corporation is not only important from a procedural, penal, and remedial point of view, but in certain types of situations, it may go to the very essence of determining whether or not the antitrust laws have been violated. The problem arises in Sherman Act suits, usually those brought by private plaintiffs as distinguished from those brought by the government. Section 1 of the Sherman Act forbids contracts, combinations, or conspiracies in restraint of trade. It should be noted that each of these words connotes the concurrence of two or more persons. One person acting alone is incapable of violating Section 1.

The typical case that arises in this area is the complaint of a customer of the corporate defendant concerning pricing or distribution practices that the corporate defendant has adopted and pursued unilaterally. Unless the plaintiff can somehow prove a combination or conspiracy of the corporation with another party, he or she is literally unable to establish a violation of Section 1. So the plaintiff joins one or more of the corporate managers as defendants with the corporation and alleges a conspiracy between the corporation and its managers. In the leading case on the subject, *Nelson Radio and Supply Co. v. Motorola Inc.*,[25] the court held that the action of the officers and other representatives of a corporation in determining its business policies does not constitute the type of concerted activity forbidden by Section 1, as the corporation is acting through the only medium through which it can possibly act. In the words of the court:

sell its goods, the quantity it will produce, the type of customers or market to *Laws and*
be served, or the quality of goods to be produced do not result in the *Individual Responsibility*
corporation being engaged in a conspiracy in unlawful restraint of trade
under the Sherman Act.[26]

*Nelson Radio* has been cited and followed in a number of subsequent
decisions,[27] but it did not answer all the questions concerning the problem of individual liability of corporate managers in situations involving
unilateral action on the part of a corporation. Section 2 of the Sherman
Act presents some of the same problems, but because that section goes
beyond Section 1, the results can sometimes be different. While Section 1
prohibits concerted action, Section 2 prohibits not only *concerted* action
to monopolize but also prohibits *unilateral* action in monopolizing or
attempting to monopolize. So, if the charge is a combination or conspiracy to monopolize as distinguished from a charge of monopolizing or
attempting to monopolize, the decision will follow *Nelson Radio* when
the only defendants are the corporation and one officer.[28] On the other
hand, if the charge is against two or more officers, there is good authority
for the position that they can be held guilty of conspiring.[29] The difference is that monopolizing is itself an illegal act. So two or more officers
may be guilty of conspiracy if they jointly decide upon a course of
conduct intended to achieve monopolization. Similarly, if one or more
officers performs an act that is calculated to achieve monopolization,
there can be liability under Section 2. Liability here is not predicated on
conspiracy, but upon the performance of an act (monopolizing or attempting to monopolize) forbidden by the statute, and such liability is
no different in nature than any other illegal act performed by a manager
on behalf of a corporation.[30] The same principle prevailed where a charge
of conspiracy by corporate officers with their corporation in violation of
Section 1 of the Sherman Act to discriminate in price was dismissed, but
the officers were continued in the case as active participants in the
alleged price discrimination as a violation of the Robinson-Patman Act.[31]

## EVOLUTION OF SEVERITY OF CRIMINAL PENALTIES

It is scarcely necessary to tell the corporate executive that the antitrust
laws impose criminal penalties for violation. That fact is well known and
has been impressed by counsel upon the executives of their corporate
clients with varying degrees of success (and sometimes, unfortunately,
failure) over many decades.

Penalties became more severe in 1974 with the passage of the Antitrust
Procedures and Penalties Act.[32] That Act changed the nature of a Sherman Act violation from a misdemeanor to a felony and sharply increased
the penalties. For the first time, the distinction between a corporation
and an individual was recognized by the words of Sections 1 and 2. Since

1955 the maximum fine for either a corporation or an individual had been $50,000. Now the penalty for a corporation was a maximum fine of $1 million and the new penalty for an individual was a maximum fine of $100,000, or imprisonment for not to exceed three years (increased from the previous one year), or both. These somewhat dramatic increases in penalties reflected an increasing impatience on the part of the Congress with the fact that after nearly eighty-five years of experience with the antitrust laws, violations continued to occur. There was testimony in the congressional hearings that "profits from antitrust violations can run into billions of dollars."[33]

The history of the application of criminal penalties to corporate managers in antitrust matters can be roughly divided into three periods. The first period began with the enactment of the Sherman Act and ended in 1960, when the electrical equipment cases flashed across the headlines, featuring imprisonment of executives of large corporations. The second period began in 1960 and ended with the Antitrust Procedures and Penalties Act of 1974. The third period began with the 1974 Act.

## The Pre-Electrical Equipment Era

During the first period, the imposition of penalties upon individuals was generally lenient. The maximum penalties imposed by the statute were relatively light and there appeared to be a reluctance to use them. In the case of individuals, the courts were concerned with such subjects as the possible uncertainties of the antitrust laws, the question whether the defendant really intended to violate, the degree of individual responsibility, the amount of benefits, if any, accruing to the accused from the violation, and cooperation with the government after indictment. Criminal actions were often settled by pleas of *nolo contendere* (no contest, the defendant neither admitting nor denying the charges). There is very little decisional law on the subject. Most of the penalties were fines. It appears that only forty-eight jail sentences were imposed during this period, half of them during the first fifty years and half during the last twenty years.[34]

A closer analysis of the penalties during this period, however, shows that jail sentences were rarely, if ever, meted out to "legitimate" business executives. The antitrust laws were often used during this period as a means of controlling and punishing economic racketeering, either by labor leaders who had strayed from their usual and accepted role of representing their membership in collective bargaining into extortion and similar questionable practices, or by outright racketeers who had obtained control of business enterprises (usually relatively small) and had used them as a base for extortion and other anticompetitive activities that fell within the literal language of the antitrust laws.[35]

Near the end of the first period, however, an event occurred that was the precursor of the second period. In 1959, a price-fixing indictment was brought in the United States District Court for the Southern District of Ohio against McDonough Co. and other corporations in the hand-tool industry and four executives of the corporations. All defendants pleaded

*nolo contendere*. Up to that time, a *nolo* plea had always been followed by a fine, with a single exception having occurred when a judge had placed a defendant on probation for one year.[36] This time, however, Judge Mell G. Underwood surprised the defendants by imposing a $5,000 fine and a ninety-day jail sentence upon each individual. The judge's position was that the statute said jail sentences should be imposed and that he was going to do what the statute said should be done.[37]

## The Electrical Equipment Cases and Their Legacy

While the *McDonough* sentences were being meted out, the Department of Justice was investigating reports of possible price fixing in the electrical equipment industry. The result was seven indictments against forty corporations and eighteen individuals handed down in the United States District Court in Philadelphia a few months after the *McDonough* sentencing. The electrical equipment cases were to become legendary. Probably no other antitrust proceedings in the history of the Sherman Act before or after that time received so much attention in the public press. The original seven indictments grew to twenty, involving thirty corporations and forty-five corporate managers on charges of price fixing, collusive bidding, and division of markets. Each indictment covered a different product line utilized in the generation, transmission, or distribution of electricity. The corporate defendants were in most instances very large companies, the dollar amounts of commerce affected by the alleged conspiracies were huge, and the agreements had been in effect for a long time and had been made and carried out systematically and clandestinely. The individuals involved held very responsible positions in their respective corporations, although not of the chief executive rank.

While the judge in *McDonough* had imposed jail sentences upon *nolo* pleas, the thinking at that time was that such an action was an aberration and that the usual practice of accepting *nolo* pleas and fining the corporations and the individuals would continue to be followed in other cases. Accordingly, *nolo* pleas were tendered in the electrical equipment cases, but Attorney General William P. Rogers urged Judge J. Cullen Ganey not to accept them. To the surprise of all parties, the judge acceded to the Attorney General's request and refused the pleas. The parties then changed their pleas to guilty, and on February 6, 1961, seven corporate executives were sentenced to prison terms of thirty days each. Twenty-two others were given suspended prison sentences and were placed on probation for five years. In addition, the court imposed fines totaling $2 million, of which $117,500 was imposed on the individuals.[38]

In the aftermath of the electrical equipment cases, corporate counsel found their executive audiences increasingly receptive to warnings concerning the dangers of overstepping the bounds in antitrust matters. It was now becoming apparent that the threat of jail sentences for antitrust violations was real and not just some imagined remote peril in the minds of overcautious corporate counsel. Courts started commenting on the need to take seriously the congressional provision for imprisonment. In *United States v. National Dairy Products Corp.*, the trial judge observed that since 1890 the sentencing records seemed to indicate that judges did not think Congress really meant its provision for jail sentences to be carried out, but he stated that he did not believe judges should read in a distinction between "ordinary crime and white collar crime" that Congress had not made.[39]

The number of prison sentences for antitrust violations did not, however, increase substantially immediately after the electrical equipment cases. In fact, during the next five years, although 62 cases involving 325 individual antitrust defendants were disposed of, only one person was sent to jail. From 1966 to the end of the second period, thirty-six defendants were sentenced to, and served in, prison. While it might be said that the second period ended with the enactment of the Antitrust Procedures and Penalties Act of 1974, the largest number of jail sentences, fines, and impositions of probation for price-fixing violations under the preexisting law came in 1977 in *United States v. Alton Box Board Co.*[40] The government urged that the sentences be imposed under the more stringent provisions of the 1974 Act. The court refused to follow this recommendation, stating that "the defendants must be tried for, found guilty of, and sentenced within the limitations of the stature as it existed at the time of their violation of the law." Of the forty-eight individual defendants in a price-fixing case before the court for sentencing, Judge James B. Parsons imposed fines on all forty-eight, placed seventeen on probation, and sentenced fifteen to jail. Eight of the fifteen were, however, given "alternative service" sentences, under which they could work with probation officers on the unemployment problems of criminal offenders on the lower end of the economic scale. The judge, in providing for alternative services, stated:

> When our laws that seek to make available to the ultimate consumers the lowest feasible prices by maintaining competition in an open and fair market place are violated by corporate executives who otherwise are charitable and law abiding citizens, such violations together with other facts about their lives often reveal an absence of empathy with people on the lower level of our economic scale. They desperately need to spend substantial time discovering and working personally with and on behalf of those who have far too little to spend for the products they consume. Carefully planned projects of alternative sentences can best provide for this compelled program of rehabilitation.[41]

Alternative service sentences have received a great deal of attention, not all favorable. The first antitrust sentence involving alternative service occurred in 1974. Eight corporate officers, who pleaded *nolo contendere* in a price-fixing case, were fined, received suspended prison sentences, and were placed on a year's probation with a requirement that they make speeches to business and civic groups on the evils of price fixing.[42] Other types of sentences have included required community service and chari-table contributions, as well as confinement in a community treatment center to help rehabilitate alcoholics and drug addicts.[43] The Department of Justice has strongly criticized the use of alternative sentences. Assistant Attorney General Donald I. Baker personally appeared before Judge Parsons in the *Alton Box Board* case to oppose them, but was unsuccessful in persuading him.[44] Since then, however, community service as an alternative to prison in antitrust convictions seems to have fallen into disuse.

## Enforcement Under the Antitrust Procedures and Penalties Act

The current period of criminal antitrust enforcement began, as I have noted, with the 1974 Act in which the status of an antitrust offense was raised from misdemeanor to felony and more severe punishment was authorized. The new Act was followed by increased militancy on the part of the Antitrust Division of the Department of Justice. In November 1976, Assistant Attorney General Baker reported that indictments of individuals had increased progressively from 24 persons in 1972 to 84 in 1974 and to more than 100 in 1976.[45] His successor, John H. Shenefeld, reported a similar level—88 personal indictments in 1977, 103 in 1978, and a total of 253 in 1977 through 1979, as compared with an average of 30 a year in the late 1960s and early 1970s.[46] So far as jail sentences were concerned, Baker reported two in 1976, totaling seventy-five days. Shenefeld reported 24 personal sentences totaling 1,561 days in 1977 and 29 personal sentences totaling 2,928 days in 1978. Shenefeld also reported that days to be spent in jail rose from 560 in 1976 to 2,360 in 1979. Fines upon individuals totaled $551,000 in 1976, $775,200 in 1977, nearly $2 million in 1978, and $2.1 million in 1979. Shenefeld did not state the number of persons fined in each of the years, but the context of his remarks to the Committee on the Judiciary of the House of Representatives indicates that the average fine was considerably higher in 1978 than in 1977.

### GUIDELINES FOR SENTENCING RECOMMENDATIONS

Baker's remarks were a prelude to his disclosure of proposed sentencing guidelines in antitrust cases. After some modification, they were issued on February 24, 1977, under the title "Justice Department Guidelines for Sentencing Recommendations in Felony Cases under the Sherman Act."[47] They contained recommended prison terms for individuals, recommended fines for individuals, and recommended fines for corporations.

With regard to prison terms, the guidelines establish a basic recommendation of eighteen months, the midpoint of the three-year sentencing range provided for by the Congress in 1974. This figure is subject to adjustment upward and downward by the application of five "factors in aggravation" and three "factors in mitigation." On the aggravation side, the Department first will take into account the amount of commerce involved. Stating that the eighteen-month base is predicated upon $50 million of affected commerce in a year, an increased amount of commerce could add from one to six months to the base. As an example, it is stated that $500 million of commerce would result in six additional months of sentence.

The next factor in aggravation is the position of the individual. The eighteen-month base is intended to apply to the average employee and a "run-of-the-mill member of the conspiracy." This statement underlines the point that a middle-management employee should be equally as concerned about complying with the antitrust laws as a top-management employee. Too often, middle-management people have failed to take the antitrust laws seriously because they think the legislation applies only to "the big guys." The guidelines emphasize, however, that the eighteen-month base will be moved upward from one to six months when the defendant is a "sales manager, vice president, president or chairman (or [in] any other position where the individual is largely giving orders rather than following directions)." Also regardless of rank, there will be upward adjustment for a person who has been the obvious leader of the conspiracy. The guidelines caution, however, that apart from the high officials and the leaders, all other offenders will be treated equally, with no effort at determining relative degrees of culpability.

The third factor in aggravation is the existence and degree of predatory or coercive conduct, the use of threats, force, or economic reprisals. Again, this can add from one to six months to the base.

The fourth factor is the duration of participation. If the violation has lasted longer than a year, the recommendation for sentence will be increased by one to six months.

Previous conviction is the fifth factor in aggravation. If the prior offense is an antitrust offense, including one where the defendant has pleaded *nolo contendere*, the maximum sentence of three years will be requested. If the prior conviction is "for a similar state or federal crime," there will be an upward adjustment of one to six months.

The first factor in mitigation is cooperation with the government. The guidelines clearly point out that "remorse that is unaccompanied by cooperation with the government is not a factor in mitigation." Similarly, withdrawal from the conspiracy is of little value in the absence of actively helping the government. The guidelines emphasize that the government "must actually *need*, receive, and accept the cooperation" in order for it to be a mitigating circumstance.

The second factor in mitigation is personal, family, or business hardship. This includes such matters as age, health, family responsibilities, and extreme business hardship. The burden is on the defendant to submit all facts in support of a request for this type of mitigation, and the defendant is warned to be prepared for investigation by medical experts, the FBI, or other experts to determine the validity of the request.

The final mitigating factor, added after the proposed guidelines were first revealed, is the involvement of relatively small amounts of commerce in a localized situation. This is the reverse of the first factor in aggravation.

The guidelines for fines for individuals are based upon the guidelines for prison terms. The Department of Justice has emphasized that it "would prefer to recommend a fine only in those circumstances . . . where a prison sentence is not always appropriate." Since, however, the court may not always follow the prison sentence recommendations or the government may occasionally find a situation where it does not consider a prison sentence appropriate, recommendations for fines will always be submitted, with the preference for imprisonment emphasized when that is the government's wish. The basic fine to be recommended is $50,000, the midpoint of the statutory range, but not to exceed 25 percent of the defendant's net worth. The factors in aggravation or mitigation described in connection with prison sentences are applied by converting months into dollars. For each month above or below the eighteen-month base, the basic fine would be subject to an adjustment of one-eighteenth of the basic dollar fine.

The guidelines have now been in effect since 1977. While there has been much discussion and wringing of the hands in prior years as to the effectiveness of antitrust enforcement, there can be little doubt that in adopting its guidelines and in pursuing them in the courts, the Justice Department has both professed and practiced a tough antitrust enforcement policy. When Baker unveiled the proposed sentencing guidelines, he commented that although the Antitrust Division was increasing its emphasis upon criminal prosecutions, he could "see no sign that our efforts have yet stemmed the tide of criminal price fixing."[48] Shenefeld has not commented on the effectiveness of the guidelines in deterring would-be violators, but he has expressed enthusiasm for the increase of personal penalties in 1978, as described above, as well as concurrent increases in the number and size of corporate fines. Summarizing these increases, Shenefeld told the House Judiciary Committee:

> This pattern reflects, I believe, an increasing sensitivity on the part of the judiciary to the underlying seriousness of antitrust violations and the policy message sent by Congress in changing criminal antitrust violations from misdemeanors to felonies in December 1974. Through our sentencing guidelines and with our recommendations for increased penalties in specific cases, we have attempted to press this point home in the courts.[49]

## INVESTIGATIONS OF ANTITRUST VIOLATIONS

With the increases in criminal penalties for antitrust violations mandated by the Antitrust Procedures and Penalties Act of 1974, accompanied by the increased vigor of antitrust enforcement, particularly in seeking substantial jail terms, the risks to corporate managers in investigatory procedures have also assumed an increasingly greater importance.

As government-initiated antitrust suits may be either criminal or civil, so also may the investigatory proceedings be either criminal or civil. The criminal investigation is conducted by the Justice Department before a grand jury impaneled in a United States district court, and a criminal indictment for an antitrust violation may not be issued without the authorization of the grand jury. No grand jury proceedings are required, or, for that matter, permitted, in an investigation having as its objective a civil suit for violation of the antitrust laws. It is not unknown, however, for the Justice Department to conduct an investigation before a grand jury in search of a criminal violation, then to determine that it does not have a strong enough evidentiary position to prove a criminal violation and to start a civil action for an injunction in lieu of a criminal action.

The Justice Department cannot, however, effectively pursue a civil action without having accumulated some evidence upon which to base its claim of an antitrust violation. It needs some sort of tool by which to gather its evidence, and this tool is called a civil investigative demand.

GRAND JURY PROCEEDINGS

A corporate manager may be called to appear before a grand jury either as an individual or in a representative capacity. The former occurs when a subpoena is issued ordering the individual to appear and testify before the grand jury concerning his or her knowledge of the matters that are the subjects under investigation or to produce documents in his or her personal possession relating to such matters. The latter occurs when a *subpoena duces tecum* is served upon a corporation commanding it to appear through a corporate officer and to produce certain documents in the corporation's files concerning the subject of the investigations. The corporate officer who appears to present the documents in response to the subpoena upon the corporation is not testifying as an individual, but is testifying on behalf of the corporation that a proper search has been made of the files and that the documents proffered to the jury are all those in the possession of the corporation that are responsive to the subpoena.

In the grand jury investigation, the position of the corporate manager under the Fifth Amendment to the United States Constitution, guaranteeing privilege against self-incrimination, becomes very important. If appearance is merely as the corporate officer identifying the documents furnished in response to a *subpoena duces tecum* served upon the corporation, the officer is not testifying as an individual but as a corporate representative, and if the documents contain information that tend to incriminate the officer, there is no basis for a claim of immunity from prosecution.[50] More than likely, the appearance of the officer under such circumstances is voluntary, as another officer could probably be sent to the grand jury to identify the documents, but that would not be of much help to the officer whose incriminating activities are disclosed in the documents.

On the other hand, the corporate manager, whether officer or nonofficer, who is served with a subpoena in a personal capacity is entitled to the protection of the Fifth Amendment. Under the provisions of federal law existing prior to December 15, 1970, an individual subpoenaed to testify before a grand jury in an antitrust investigation was granted automatic immunity. If an indictment was issued against the witness for a violation of the antitrust law based upon the transaction or transactions that were the subject of the testimony, the compulsory appearance and testimony of the individual before the grand jury was a complete defense.[51] This was called "transactional" immunity and protected the witness even though no effort was made to use against him his direct testimony before the grand jury.

In 1970, however, important changes were made with the enactment of the Organized Crime Control Act of 1970.[52] Under that Act, the immunity ceased to be automatic. The privilege must be claimed by the individual before testifying. Under the old law, in antitrust matters, the individual did not have to claim the privilege against self-incrimination but received it by the mere act of testifying pursuant to a subpoena.[53] Under the new law, if the witness refuses on Fifth Amendment grounds to give testimony, the Justice Department cannot obtain the testimony without receiving a court order. That order will grant immunity but only against the use of the witness's own testimony in a criminal proceeding brought against the witness. This is called "use immunity" and is to be distinguished from transactional immunity, which existed under the old law. In the absence of transactional immunity, the government may prosecute the witness for the offense disclosed in the compelled testimony so long as it does not use either the testimony itself "or any information directly or indirectly derived from" it or the "fruits" of the testimony. The burden is on the government to prove that its evidence against the individual is in no way derived from his or her testimony, but is from a completely independent source.[54]

## THE CIVIL INVESTIGATIVE DEMAND

While grand jury investigations have been available to discover antitrust violations and to initiate criminal proceedings for them from the beginning of the antitrust laws, the civil investigative demand is relatively new. Prior to 1962, the Justice Department had no effective means of compelling testimony and production of documents in the conduct of investigations of a civil, as distinguished from a criminal, nature. The Antitrust Civil Process Act was passed by the Congress in 1962 and its scope was considerably enlarged by the Antitrust Improvements Act of 1976.[55] Under the provisions of the 1962 Act, the Justice Department is authorized to issue and serve upon any person, natural or corporate, a civil investigative demand requiring the production of documentary material that the Justice Department believes may be in the possession of that person and may be relevant to the matter under investigation. Under the 1976 amendments, the civil investigative demand may now require written answers to interrogatories as well as personal examination under oath. The person compelled to appear for personal examination may be accompanied by counsel, but the proceeding is otherwise private. In case of refusal to answer, the Justice Department may seek an order compelling the answer and, of course, the witness would then be in contempt of court for a continued refusal to answer. If the witness claims the privilege against self-incrimination, the procedure under the Organized Crime Control Act, discussed earlier in connection with grand jury proceedings, may be invoked.

## Investigation by the Federal Trade Commission

The Federal Trade Commission also has broad investigative powers that are not limited solely to seeking out violations, as in the case of the Justice Department. Section 6 of the Federal Trade Commission Act empowers the Commission, among other things:

> (a) To gather and compile information concerning, and to investigate from time to time the organization, business, conduct, practices, and management of any person, partnership or corporation engaged in or whose business affects commerce, excepting banks and common carriers . . . and its relation to other persons, partnerships and corporations.

> (b) To require . . . persons, partnerships and corporations, engaged in or whose business affects commerce, excepting banks and common carriers . . . to file with the Commission . . . reports or answers in writing to specific questions, furnishing to the Commission such information as it may require as to the organization, business, conduct, practices, management, and relation to other corporations, partnership and individuals of the respective persons, partnerships and corporations filing such reports or answers in writing.[56]

The Commission may conduct investigative hearings and has subpoena powers to compel the attendance and testimony of witnesses. If the witness claims privilege against self-incrimination, the procedure authorized under the Organized Crime Control Act, and discussed earlier in this chapter with regard to grand jury proceedings and civil investigative demands, may be invoked, as those provisions also apply to proceedings before any agency of the United States governement.

## IMMUNITY IN PROCEEDINGS UNDER OTHER STATUTES

It is well to note at this point that, although we are discussing in this chapter the application of the provisions with regard to self-incrimination as they pertain to antitrust investigations, these provisions are not limited solely to antitrust matters. They apply to any proceeding before or ancillary to:

> (1) a court or grand jury of the United States,

(2) an agency of the United States, or

(3) either House of Congress, a joint committee of the two houses, or a committee or a subcommittee of either House. . . .[57]

In subsequent chapters we will discuss numerous other federal statutes prescribing standards of business conduct and authorizing regulations. Corporate managers may find themselves called upon to furnish information or to give testimony in numerous investigatory or administrative proceedings where they may be personally involved in an alleged or suspected violation of the statute and potentially liable for personal penalties. The applicability of the immunity provisions of the Organized Crime Control Act will not be repeated in each of the chapters, but it should be borne in mind that in investigatory or administrative proceedings under any of these statutes, the manager can be compelled to testify and give incriminating information and will not receive a complete immunity from prosecution but only an immunity from the use of the compelled testimony or information derived from it.

## INTERLOCKING DIRECTORATES

Another area in which the antitrust laws have placed personal responsibilities and liabilities upon corporate managers is in the matter of interlocking directorates. The regulation of interlocking directorates had its origin in the early part of the century. It was the result of great concern over the fact that competitors frequently had directors in common and that their presence could frustrate the purposes of the Sherman Act by having such directors take simultaneous action for two or more competitive corporations; such action, while perhaps not precisely meeting the test of combination of conspiracy by competitors under the Sherman Act, achieved the same result of concerted action. The most eloquent condemnation of this practice was made in a series of articles in *Harper's Weekly* by Louis D. Brandeis, who was later to become a justice of the United States Supreme Court.[58] Like so many acts of Congress, the regulation of corporate interlocks was a compromise and left many areas so unaffected as to cause debate on the efficacy of the law down to the present day.

## Section 8 of the Clayton Act

Regulation of interlocks was accomplished by two sections of the Clayton Act when it was made law in 1914—Section 8 and Section 10.[59] Section 8 prohibits a person from simultaneously serving as a director of any two or more corporations having capital and surplus of more than $1 million, where such corporations are competitors, "so that elimination of competition by agreement between them would constitute a violation . . . of the antitrust laws." Exceptions were made for banks, banking associations, trust companies, and common carriers subject to the Interstate Commerce Act. Section 10 makes special provisions regulating the manner in which common carriers can have business dealings with corporations with which they have interlocking directors or officers.

For the first thirty-five years of its existence, Section 8 was marked by very little enforcement effort. No case in interpretation of Section 8 reached the United States Supreme Court until 1953. In that first case, *United States v. W.T. Grant Co.*,[60] the government brought an action for an injunction against Hancock, who was serving simultaneously as a director of four retail chains. After the suit was started, he resigned from three of the boards and then moved to dismiss the action on grounds of mootness. The lower court granted the motion and the Supreme Court held that the lower court had not abused its discretion.

The Grant decision was, however, based solely upon the discretion of the trial court. In more recent years, trial courts have exercised their discretion the other way, so that it is now customary to grant injunctions against interlocking directorates even when the interlock has ceased.[61] The reasoning of the courts is that once an interlock has occurred, the offender should not escape the sanction of the law by merely resigning and then, perhaps, joining the board of another competitor in the future, or that corporations that have had interlocks should be free to resume them until such time as the government moves again to break up the interlock. An injunction will be granted so that a future violation can be punished by a contempt citation.

There have been a few cases as to the exact nature of the competition that must exist between two companies before Section 8 can be invoked. An effort was made in one case to obtain an interpretation that Section 8 be limited to only those situations where there might be a substantial lessening of competition, but the court held that since such a phrase, which appears in some other sections of the Clayton Act, was not in Section 8, it would not be read in. The sole test was whether an agreement between the two companies to eliminate competition would violate the antitrust laws.[62] Another decision held, however, that Section 8 did not apply where the amount of competition between the corporations was *de minimis*.[63] That case also held, however, that parent or subsidiary companies are not to be considered in determining whether competition exists. A more recent district court decision is in sharp disagreement, stating that to ignore parent and subsidiary corporations in deciding Section 8 questions "ignores the realities of intercorporate relationships."[64]

Cautious corporate counsel will advise their clients to avoid the uncertainties of relying upon either *de minimis* competition or competition between subsidiaries or parents of the interlocked companies as valid exceptions to Section 8.

There are a number of corporate director situations not covered by Section 8 that have been the cause of comment by legal scholars, government officials, and members of Congress. These are probably the result of the compromise nature of the section at the time of its adoption. Some efforts have been made to extend the scope of Section 8 through court

decisions and consent decrees.

One notable omission is the lack of a prohibition of a nondirector-officer's serving as a director of a competitor. The government, in a series of enforcement actions in the 1950s and 1960s, was able to obtain a substantial number of consent decrees that not only eliminated interlocking directorates among competitors and prohibited them in the future, but also prohibited the corporations' having a director, officer, or employee of one corporation serving as a director, officer, or employee of one of the other corporations.[65]

Still another omission that has been frequently criticized is that of the supplier-customer relationship. The Justice Department, in this same series of enforcement actions, proceeded against a number of corporations that were in closely related complementary businesses without being full-blown horizontal competitors and achieved consent decrees prohibiting their having interlocking directors, officers, or employees.[66]

There has also been considerable concern about interlocks through third persons, such as having two directors of the same corporation serve on the boards of second and third corporations that are competitors. This practice was challenged by the government in the early 1970s in *United States v. Cleveland Trust Company*[67] on the theory that Cleveland Trust Company was in effect a director of two competing manufacturing companies by having one of its directors on the board of one manufacturer and another of its directors (both of them executive officers of Cleveland Trust Company) on the board of the other manufacturer. The government claimed that each of the directors was the deputy of Cleveland Trust Company. The suit was settled by a consent decree, and so there is no adjudication of the legal validity of the government's position.

The exception of banks from the purview of Section 8 has also been a cause of criticism. The Federal Trade Commission has attempted to narrow this exception in its proceeding *In re Perpetual Federal Savings and Loan Association*.[68] In that case the FTC took the position that the exception for banks in Section 8 applied only when both the interlocked corporations are banks and that a savings and loan association is not a bank but is in competition with a bank. Therefore, an interlocking directorate between a bank and a savings and loan association violates the policy, if not the letter, of Section 8 and is accordingly an unfair method of competition within the meaning of the Federal Trade Commission Act.

Corporate managers serving on boards of directors of companies other than their own must be ever alert to the prohibitions of Section 8 and must also keep a watchful eye on the attitudes of the Federal Trade Commission as well as the Department of Justice with regard to those situations which might, but cannot quite literally, come within the prohibitions of the section. There have been numerous efforts in Congress in recent years to broaden the scope of Section 8, but none of them has been successful.[69]

While Section 8 of the Clayton Act exempts interlocking directorates between common carriers subject to regulation by the Interstate Commerce Commission, Section 10 of the Clayton Act places specific prohibitions and conditions upon certain types of transactions between common carriers and other corporations. That section applies specifically to transactions in securities, supplies, or other articles of commerce, and to contracts for construction or maintenance, when the aggregate amount of business between the carrier and another corporation exceeds $50,000 in any one year. If the common carrier has as a director, president, manager, purchasing or selling officer, or agent in the particular transaction, any person who is at the same time a director, manager, or purchasing or selling officer, or owner of a substantial interest in the other corporation, no such transactions or contracts will be permitted without competitive bidding under rules prescribed by the Interstate Commerce Commission. Each director, agent, manager, or officer knowingly voting for or directing such violation or aiding or abetting in it is subject to a $5,000 fine or a year in jail, or both.[70]

Section 10, like Section 8, is a part of the antitrust law, but it definitely has conflict-of-interest overtones. It has been construed as applying to secret payments from a supplier,[71] and as permitting treble-damage actions by stockholders and by fare-paying passengers, although recovery in each case was denied when the transaction was held not to be of the type prohibited by Section 10.[72]

## Other Statutes Pertaining to Interlocks

While Section 8 of the Clayton Act exempts common carriers subject to the Interstate Commerce Act from the prohibition of interlocking directorates, subsequent laws regulating carriers deal specifically with such interlocks. Generally speaking, their approach has not been absolute prohibition, but the establishment of procedures for approval or disapproval.

The Transportation Act of 1920 makes it unlawful for a person to hold the position of director or officer of more than one railroad carrier, except as specifically authorized by order of the Interstate Commerce Commission. The same section regulating interlocks prohibits a director or an officer of a railroad carrier from receiving any money or thing of value in respect of the negotiation, hypothecation, or sale of any securities to be issued by such a carrier, or to share in any of the proceeds thereof.[73] A violation of these provisions can result in a fine up to $10,000 or imprisonment up to three years, or both. Comparable provisions are found in the Federal Communications Act with regard to directors and officers of communications carriers.[74]

The intent and purpose of the Federal Aviation Act provisions relating to interlocks were examined in *Lehman v. Civil Aeronautics Board*.[75] In that case, the Civil Aeronautics Board (CAB) denied a director of Pan American Airways the authority to accept a seat on the board of United Fruit Company because that company operated steamships which, among other things, carried vacation travelers to the Caribbean. The denial was upheld by the Court of Appeals of the District of Columbia, which stated that the personal integrity of the individual was not an issue. The statute was enacted to preserve competition and should be strictly enforced. In the same case, the CAB also considered the applications of four different partners of the underwriting firm, Lehman Brothers, to serve as directors of four different airlines or aircraft manufacturers. Their applications were also denied by the CAB and the denial was upheld by the court. The court noted that the fact that the proposed directors were partners in the same firm did not automatically disqualify them from serving as directors of competing airlines or aircraft manufacturers, but since each partner would be seeking for his underwriting firm the underwriting business from the airline or aircraft manufacturer of which he was a director, each such partner would be, in effect, an agent of the other partners, in violation of the prohibitions against an officer's or director's having a representative or nominee in another carrier or in a company engaged in any phase of aeronautics.

To make certain that the statutory provisions concerning interlocking directorates in the airline industry are observed, regulations of the Civil Aeronautics Board require directors and officers of air carriers to file annual reports describing their interests in air carriers, other common carriers, companies engaged in any phase of aeronautics, or corporations that are principal stockholders or in control of any of the foregoing.[76]

In 1942, with the addition of Part IV of the Interstate Commerce Act, subjecting freight forwarders to regulation, the Congress prohibited any director, officer, employee, or agent of a railroad, pipeline, motor carrier, or water carrier subject to the provisions of the Interstate Commerce Commission from directly or indirectly owning or controlling stock in any freight forwarder. Interlocking directorates between freight forwarders and the foregoing common carriers were not, however, prohibited. To the contrary, the statute not only permitted interlocking directorates, but made a specific exception for directors' qualifying shares from the prohibition against stock ownership.[77]

## NOTES

1. 26 Stat. 209; Sections 1 and 2 in their present form appear in 15 U.S.C. §§ 1 and 2.

2. Numerous books and articles have been written on the subject of the antitrust laws. Among the recent legal texts on the subject are Austin, *Antitrust: Law, Economics, Policy* (Matthew Bender, 1976); Sullivan, *Handbook of the Law of Antitrust* (West Publishing Co., 1977); and Areeda & Turner, *Antitrust Law: An Analysis of Antitrust Principles and Their Applications* (Little, Brown & Co., 1978). For an extensive analysis of the legal and economic theories of the

antitrust laws as applied to specific substantive provisions and interpretations, see Bork, *The Antitrust Paradox: A Policy at War with Itself* (Basic Books, 1978). For books written primarily for nonlawyers, see Kintner, *An Antitrust Primer: A Guide to Antitrust and Trade Regulation Laws for the Businessman.* (2d ed., Macmillan Co., 1973); VanCise, *The Federal Antitrust Laws* (3d rev. ed., American Enterprise Institute for Public Policy Research, 1975); VanCise, *Understanding the Antitrust Laws* (Practising Law Institute, 1976); and Hancock, *Executive's Guide to Business Law* (McGraw-Hill Book Co., 1979) 7-1 to 24-18.

3. The cited sections are found in 15 U.S.C. §§ 13, 14, 15, 18, 19, 20, and 24, respectively.

4. 38 Stat. 719; this section in its present form appears in 15 U.S.C. § 45.

5. Murphy, "Keys to Unlock the Interlocks: Dealing with Interlocking Directorates," 11 *U. of Mich. J. of L. Ref.* 361–386 at 378–380 (1978) and cases cited. See also Keefe, "Dual Enforcement Has Its Problems," 65 *A.B.A.J.* 638–639 (1979).

6. Rooks, "Personal Liabilities of Officers and Directors for Antitrust Violations and Securities Transactions," 18 *Bus. Law.* 579–611 at 584 (1963), citing as leading cases United States v. Swift, 188 F.92 (N.D. Ill. 1911) and United States v. Winslow, 195 F.578 (D. Mass. 1912). At p. 583, Rooks also discusses the likelihood that many of the activities prohibited by the antitrust laws were also illegal at common law.

7. United States v. National Dairy Products Corp., 196 F. Supp. 155 (W.D. Mo. 1961); United States v. A.P. Woodson Co., 198 F. Supp. 582 (D.D.C. 1961); United States v. Milk Distributors Association, 200 F. Supp. 792 (D. Md. 1961).

8. 370 U.S. 405, 8 L. Ed.2d 590, 82 S. Ct. 1354 (1962).

9. *Id.,* 417.

10. Among the law review notes on *Wise* are those appearing in 4 *B.C. Ind. & Com. L. Rev.* 177 (1962), 31 *Fordham L. Rev.* 368 (1962), and 8 *Villanova L. Rev.* 105 (1962).

11. 15 U.S.C. § 4.

12. 15 U.S.C. § 45.

13. *Id.,* § 15.

14. 323 U.S. 386, 89 L. Ed. 322, 65 S. Ct. 373 (1945); followed in United States v. Imperial Chemical Corporation, 100 F. Supp. 504 (S.D.N.Y. 1951); United States v. Crown Zellerbach Corporation, 141 F. Supp. 118 (N.D. Ill. 1956), and Deaktor v. Fox Grocery Co., 332 F. Supp. 536 (W.D. Pa. 1971). Two years before *Hartford Empire,* the Second Circuit vacated a cease-and-desist order against a corporate officer who was also a director of a trade association upon a finding that he had never attended a directors' meeting and knew nothing about the price-fixing activities of the association. Phelps Dodge Refining Corp. v. FTC, 139 F.2d 393 (2d Cir. 1943).

15. 302 U.S. 112, 82 L. Ed. 141, 58 S. Ct. 113 (1937).

16. 211 F.2d 7 (2d Cir. 1954). Other decisions upholding orders against individuals either because of threat of evasion or top officer participation or both

include Sebrone Co. v. FTC, 135 F.2d 676 (7th Cir. 1943); Gelb v. FTC, 144

F.2d 580 (2d Cir. 1944); Steelco Stainless Steel v. FTC, 187 F.2d 693 (7th Cir. 1951); Consumer Sales v. FTC, 198 F.2d 404 (2d Cir. 1952); Tractor Training Service v. FTC, 227 F.2d 420 (9th Cir. 1955), *cert. denied*, 350 U.S. 1005 (1956); Goodman v. FTC, 244 F.2d 584 (9th Cir. 1957); Surf Sales Co. v. FTC, 259 F.2d 744 (7th Cir. 1958); Pati-Port Inc. v. FTC, 313 F.2d 103 (4th Cir. 1963); Rayex Corp. v. FTC, 317 F.2d 290 (2d Cir. 1963); Coro Inc. v. FTC, 338 F.2d 149 (1st Cir. 1964); and Benrus Watch Co. v. FTC, 352 F.2d 313 (8th Cir. 1965).

17. 356 F.2d 381 (5th Cir. 1966).

18. The leading case on the subject is Kentucky-Tennessee Light & Power Co. v. Nashville Coal Co., 37 F. Supp. 728 (W.D. Ky. 1941). See also Cott Beverage Corp. v. Canada Dry Ginger Ale, Inc., 146 F. Supp. 300 (S.D.N.Y. 1956), *aff'd*, 243 F.2d 795 (2d Cir. 1957). These cases are discussed in Rooks's article (cited in note 6) in 18 *Bus. Law.* 579 at 591; Manning, "The Antitrust Laws and the Corporate Executive's Civil Damage Liability," 18 *Vand. L. Rev.* 1938–1961 (1965); and Whiting, "Antitrust and the Corporate Executive," 47 *Va. L. Rev.* 929–987 (1961).

19. 409 F.2d 1277 (10th Cir. 1969).    19.1 *Id.*, 1283.

20. Forte, "Liabilities of Corporate Officers for Violation of Fiduciary Duties Concerning the Antitrust Laws," 40 *Ind. L.J.* 313–340 (1964); "Corporations—Liability of Employees—Corporation May Seek Indemnity for Civil or Criminal Liability Incurred by Employees' Violation of Antitrust Law Without Corporation's Knowledge or Consent," 83 *Harv. L. Rev.* 943–950 (1970).

21. Fleitman v. Welsbach Street Lighting Co., 240 U.S. 27, 60 L. Ed. 505, 36 S. Ct. 233 (1916); United Copper Securities Co. v. Amalgamated Copper Co., 244 U.S. 261, 61 L. Ed. 1119, 37 S. Ct. 509 (1917); Decorative Stone Co. v. Building Trades Council of Westchester County, 23 F.2d 426 (2d Cir. 1928), *cert. denied*, 277 U.S. 594 (1928.).

22. Simon v. Socony-Vacuum Oil Co., 179 Misc. 202, 38 N.Y.S. 2d 270 (1942), *aff'd mem.*, 267 App. Div. 890, 47 N.Y.S. 2d 589 (1944). See also Clayton v. Farish, 191 Misc. 136, 73 N.Y.S. 2d 727 (1947), which suggests that the directors may be liable only if they were disloyal to the corporation.

23. In *Kentucky-Tennessee Light,* cited in note 18, the plaintiff corporation joined its own former president as a defendant in the treble-damage action against the defendant corporation and its president. It was alleged that the defendant corporation and its president had paid an illegal brokerage commission to the plaintiff's former president in violation of the Robinson-Patman Act. It does not appear from the decision whether there was recovery from the plaintiff's former president. In this case, it appears that the former president was not violating the law on behalf of his corporation but, rather, against it. For a complete discussion on the subject of stockholder suits in antitrust situations, see Blake, "The Shareholders' Role in Antitrust Enforcement," 110 *U. of Pa. L. Rev.* 143–178 (1961).

24. 40 Del. Ch. 335, 182 A.2d 328 (1962), 41 Del. 78, 188 A.2d 125 (1963).

25. 200 F.2d 911 (5th Cir. 1952).

26. *Id.*, 914.

27. Marion County Co-op Ass'n v. Carnation Co., 114 F. Supp. 58 (W.D. Ark. 1953); Goldlawr Inc. v. Shubert, 276 F.2d 614 (3d Cir. 1960); Poller v. Columbia Broadcasting System, 284 F.2d 599 (D.C. Cir. 1960), *rev'd* on other grounds, 368 U.S. 464 (1962); Sperry Rand Corp. v. Nassau R.&D. Associates, 152 F. Supp. 91 (E.D.N.Y. 1957); George W. Warner & Co. v. Black & Decker Mfg. Co., 172 F. Supp. 221 (E.D.N.Y. 1959); Johnny Maddox Motor Co. v. Ford Motor Co., 202 F. Supp. 103 (W.D. Tex. 1960); Bergjans Farm Dairy v. Sanitary Milk Producers, 241 F. Supp. 476 (E.D. Mo. 1965); Chapman v. Rudd Paint & Varnish Co., 409 F.2d 635 (9th Cir. 1969). A corporate officer seeking dismissal of a conspiracy charge failed when there were multiple corporate defendants. While he could not conspire with his own corporation, he could conspire with another corporation. Deaktor v. Fox Grocery Co., 332 F. Supp. 536 (W.D. Pa. 1971). Closely related to the questions of conspiracy between a corporation and its personnel is the question of interdivisional conspiracy within a corporation, which has been held to be impossible for the same reasons that determined *Nelson Radio* and the above-cited cases. See Joseph E. Seagram & Sons v. Hawaiian Oke & Liquors, Ltd., 416 F.2d 71 (9th Cir. 1969).

28. Higbie v. Kopy-Kat, Inc., 391 F. Supp. 808 (E.D. Pa. 1975).

29. An early decision on this subject is Patterson v. United States, 222 F. 599 (6th Cir. 1915), *cert. denied,* 238 U.S. 635 (1915). Milton Handler cites *Patterson* in support of his statement:

> It has long been the law that when a company monopolizes an industry, the directors who authorize or participate in the challenged corporate action may be guilty of conspiracy with the corporation and each other to monopolize in violation of Section 2. There is no conceptual difficulty in such an idea, and nothing strange about holding directors liable for conspiring to commit the crime which the corporation can itself perpetrate alone. [Handler, *Twenty-Five Years of Antitrust* (Matthew Bender & Co. 1973) 702–703; *reprinted from* 76 *Yale L.J.* 92–126 at 121 (1966).]

See also Barndt, "Two Trees or One? The Problem of Intra-Enterprise Conspiracy," 23 *Mont. L. Rev.* 158–199 (1962).

30. Lorain Journal Co. v. United States, 342 U.S. 143, 96 L. Ed. 162, 72 S. Ct. 181 (1951); Tillamook Cheese & Dairy Ass'n v. Tillamook County Creamery Ass'n, 358 F.2d 115 (9th Cir. 1966); Shoenberg Farms, Inc. v. Denver Milk Producers, Inc., 231 F. Supp. 266 (D. Col. 1964). *Shoenberg* appears to be in conflict with *Patterson* (note 29) in stating that although the corporate officers may violate Section 2 by performing acts to monopolize, they cannot conspire with each other and with the corporation to monopolize in violation of Section 2.

31. Cott Beverage Corp. v. Canada Dry Ginger Ale, Inc., 146 F. Supp. 300 (S.D.N.Y. 1956), *aff'd,* 243 F.2d 795 (2d Cir. 1957). The same result was reached in a case involving an illegal tie-in in violation of Section 3 of the Clayton Act. Higbie v. Kopy-Kat, Inc., 391 F. Supp. 808 (E.D. Pa. 1975).

32. P.L. 93-528, 88 Stat. 1706.

33. H.R. Report No. 1463, 93d Cong., 2d Sess., *reprinted in* 1974 *U.S. Code Cong. & Ad. News* 6535.

34. For a more complete treatment of the statistics during the first period, as well as a portion of the second period, see Wright, "Jail Sentences in Antitrust

Cases," 37 F.R.D. 111 (1965); Flynn, "Criminal Sanctions under State and
Federal Antitrust Laws," 45 *Tex. L. Rev.* 1301–1346 (1967); Posner, "A Statistical Study of Antitrust Enforcement," 13 *J. of Law & Econ.* 365–419 (1970).

35. One of the few reported cases of this type is United States v. Shapiro, 103 F.2d
775 (2d Cir. 1939). For comment on the limited use of jail sentences during
this period, see Breit & Elzinga, "Antitrust Penalties and Attitudes Toward
Risk: An Economic Analysis," 86 *Harv. L. Rev.*, 693–713 at 695 (1973). See also
articles by Flynn and Posner cited in note 34. The remarks of the court in
United States Gulf Shrimpers & Oystermen's Association, 1957 *Trade Cases*
(CCH) ¶ 68,906 (D.C. Miss. 1957), in suspending nine-month prison sentences, are typical of the attitude toward antitrust during the first period:
"[A] large number of testimonials indicate that the defendants are not
criminals in the acceptation of that term, but were, of course, guilty of
violations of law charged to them."

36. 1977–2 *Trade Reg. Rep.* (CCH) ¶ 8,801.

37. United States v. McDonough Co., 1959 *Trade Cases* (CCH) ¶ 69,482 (S.D.
Ohio, 1959).

38. The proceedings in the electrical equipment cases and in the subsequent
treble-damage suits are described at length in Bane, *The Electrical Conspiracies: The Treble Damage Actions* (Federal Legal Publications, Inc., 1973).
The story of these cases is also described in Smith, "The Incredible Electrical
Conspiracy," *Fortune*, April 1961, pp. 132 *et seq.*, and May 1961, pp. 161 *et seq.*

39. 1964 *Trade Cases* (CCH) ¶ 71,163 (W.D. Mo. 1964). In 1965 Robert L. Wright, of
the Antitrust Division, urged the United States District Judges' Institutes on
Sentencing to treat antitrust defendants like other criminal defendants in jail
sentencing. Wright, 37 F.R.D. 111.

40. 1977-1 *Trade Cases* (CCH) ¶ 61,336 (N.D. Ill.). The statistics on jail sentences
after 1960 cited in this paragraph are found in Appendix II to this case at
p. 71,177.

41. 1977-1 *Trade Cases* (CCH) ¶ 61,336 at p. 71,769.

42. United States v. H.S. Crocker Co., 4 *Trade Reg. Rep.* (CCH) ¶ 45,074 at
p. 53,563-2 (N.D. Cal. 1974).

43. United States v. Champion International Corp., 4 *Trade Reg. Rep.* (CCH)
¶ 45,074, at p. 53,583 (D. Ore. 1974); United States v. Borden, Inc., 4 *Trade
Reg. Rep.* (CCH) ¶ 45,074, at p. 53,581 (D. Ariz. 1976).

44. Alternative service sentences are discussed at greater length in White, "Sentencing of Criminal Antitrust Offenders—Tne Need for Exercise of Judicial
Discretion in the Interest of Individual Justice," 46 *Antitrust L.J.* 513–527
(1977).

45. Text of Prepared Statement by Donald L. Baker before the Tenth New England Antitrust Conference Concerning the Sentencing of Antitrust Felons,
Nov. 20, 1976, ATRR (BNA), No. 790, D-1 (Nov. 23, 1976).

46. Statement of John H. Shenefeld before the Committee on the Judiciary,
United States House of Representatives, Concerning Department of Justice
Authorization, Fiscal Year 1980, March 21, 1979, and remarks of Shenefeld at
Thirteenth Annual New England Antitrust Conference, Nov. 16, 1979. See
ATRR (BNA), No. 940, A-16 (Nov. 22, 1979).

**47.** ATRR (BNA), No. 803, F-1 (March 1, 1977).

**48.** Baker's statement, cited in note 45.

**49.** Shenefeld's statement, cited in note 46. An example of recent severe sentences involves J. Ray McDermott & Co. which in 1979 was fined $1 million for price fixing while four of its executives were fined a total of $225,000 and given suspended sentences of twelve and thirty-six months. *Bus. Week,* June 18, 1979, p. 144. Sanford Litvack, shortly after succeeding Shenefeld as head of the Antitrust Division, reaffirmed the Justice Department's policy of seeking jail sentences for executives convicted of price fixing. "New Antitrust Chief to Seek Jail Terms in Price-Fix Cases," *Wall St. J.,* Jan. 24, 1980, p. 2.

**50.** United States v. American Radiator & Standard Supply Corp., 278 F. Supp. 608 (W.D. Pa. 1967); United States v. Globe Chemical Co., 311 F. Supp. 535 (S.D. Ohio 1969). See also *In re* Cowles Communication, Inc., 3 *Trade Reg. Rep. (CCH)* ¶ 8,831 (1971).

**51.** 32 Stat. 904 and 34 Stat. 798 (formerly 15 U.S.C. §§ 32, 33, now repealed). Also 38 Stat. 722, 15 U.S.C. § 49 (now amended by repeal of the immunity).

**52.** P.L. 91-452; 84 Stat. 922. The portions of the Act pertinent to this discussion are compiled at 18 U.S.C. §§ 6001–6005.

**53.** United States v. Monia, 317 U.S. 424, 82 L. Ed. 376, 63 S. Ct. 409 (1943).

**54.** Kastigar v. United States, 406 U.S. 441, 32 L. Ed.2d 212, 92 S. Ct. 163 (1972), *reh. denied,* 408 U.S. 931, citing Murphy v. Waterfront Commission, 378 U.S. 52, 12 L. Ed. 2d 678, 84 S. Ct. 1594 (1964). For a more complete discussion of the subject, see Withrow, "Antitrust Investigations and the Grand Jury—The Implications of the New Immunity Provisions of the Organized Crime Control Act of 1970," 28 *Bus. Law.* 887–896 (1973).

**55.** 76 Stat. 748; 90 Stat. 1383; 15 U.S.C. §§ 1311–1314.

**56.** 15 U.S.C. § 46. See also FTC Rules of Practice, 16 C.F.R. § 2.1–2.15.

**57.** 18 U.S.C. § 6002.

**58.** Brandeis, "Breaking the Money Trusts," *Harper's Weekly,* Nov. 22, 1913, to Jan. 17, 1914.

**59.** 15 U.S.C. §§ 19 & 20.

**60.** 345 U.S. 629, 97 L. Ed. 1303, 73 S. Ct. 894 (1953).

**61.** United States v. Newmont Mining Co., 1964 *Trade Cases* (CCH) ¶ 71,030, 34 F.R.D. 504 (S.D.N.Y.); Treves v. Servel, Inc., 244 F. Supp. 773 (S.D.N.Y.); SCM Corp. v. FTC, 565 F.2d 807 (2d Cir. 1977).

**62.** United States v. Sears, Roebuck & Co., 111 F. Supp. 614 (S.D.N.Y. 1953).

**63.** Paramount Pictures Corp. v. Baldwin-Montrose Chemical Co., 1966 *Trade Cases* (CCH) ¶ 71,678 (D.C.N.Y.).

**64.** Kennecott Copper Corp. v. Curtiss-Wright Corp., 449 F. Supp. 951 (S.D.N.Y.1978). See also *In re* Penn Central Securities Litigation, 367 F. Supp. 1158 (E.D. Pa. 1973).

**65.** *Trade Reg. Serv.* (CCH) ¶ 4580.20 cites fifteen such decrees, all of which are published in CCH *Trade Cases.*

66. 1 *Trade Reg. Rep.* (CCH) ¶ 4580.30 cites six such decrees, all of which are published in CCH *Trade Cases.*

67. 392 F. Supp. 699 (N.D. Ohio 1974), *aff'd mem.*, 513 F.2d 633 (6th Cir. 1975); consent decree, 1975–2 *Trade Cases* (CCH) ¶ 60,611.

68. 3 *Trade Reg. Rep.* (CCH) ¶ 21,371 (1977). See also United States v. Crocker National Corp., 422 F. Supp.686 (N.D. Cal. 1976), holding that Section 8 forbids an interlock between a bank and an insurance company.

69. For a review of the history, development, and criticisms of Section 8, see Kramer, "Interlocking Directorships and the Clayton Act after 35 Years," 59 *Yale L.J.* 1266–1275 (1950); Travers, "Interlocks in Corporate Management and the Antitrust Laws," 46 *Tex. L. Rev.* 819–864 (1968); Halverson, "Interlocking Directorates—Present Antitrust Enforcement Interest Placed in Proper Analytical Perspective," 21 *Villanova L. Rev.* 393–409 (1975–1976); Whiting, Goldman, Wilson, Turner & Halverson, "Unlocking Interlocks: The On-Again Off-Again Saga of Section 8 of the Clayton Act," 45 *Antitrust L.J.* 315–354 (1976); Murphy, "Keys to Unlock the Interlocks; Dealing with Interlocking Directorates," 11 *U. of Mich. J. of L. Ref.* 361–386 (1978).

70. 15 U.S.C. § 20.

71. United States v. Boston & Maine Railroad, 380 U.S. 157, 13 L. Ed. 2d 728, 85 S. Ct. 868 (1965).

72. Klinger v. B.& O. Ry., 432 F.2d 506 (2d Cir. 1970); Cleary v. Chalk, 488 F.2d 1315 (D.C. Cir. 1973), *cert. denied,* 416 U.S. 938 (1974).

73. 41 Stat. 494. In its present form, this section is 49 U.S.C. § 11322.

74. 48 Stat. 1074; 47 U.S.C. § 212.

75. 209 F.2d 289 (D.C. Cir. 1953), *cert. denied,* 347 U.S. 916 (1954).

76. 14 C.F.R. § 245.1.

77. 56 Stat. 293. This section in its present form is 49 U.S.C. § 1011.

# CHAPTER SIX

# The Manager and Health and Safety: Product Standards and the Environment

During the past decade no phase of regulatory activity has experienced such rapid and all-pervasive growth as that pertaining to health, safety, and the environment. Concern about water, air, and noise pollution, about product safety, about real or imagined dangers to health is expressed in the Congress, the state legislatures, in executive departments of government. Similar concern is found in schools and colleges, in labor organizations, in consumer organizations, in conservation clubs, in the churches, and in many other organizations too numerous to mention. Great impetus has been given to laws and regulations intended to make the nation a safer place in which to work and to play, to reduce the hazards, current or potential, of the food we eat, the water we drink, the clothing we wear, the houses in which we live, the vehicles in which we travel, the air we breathe, the sounds we hear, the articles we use for recreation, and all the other facets of living in late twentieth-century America. These laws and regulations have imposed responsibilities and liabilities not only upon the corporations of America, but also upon their managers, of a scope and magnitude that none would have dreamed possible a generation ago. The requirements and administration of many of these laws are controversial. While their purposes may be laudable, there has also been some overreaction by well-meaning legislators and administrators.

As complicated, far-reaching, and new as these laws are, they nevertheless have origins going back to the beginning of the century. One might even suggest that the demise of the nineteenth century was marked by the enactment of the federal government's first environmental law, the Refuse Act of 1899.[1] That statute, enacted by the Congress to facilitate navigation, was dusted off in 1970 and used for a system of industrial permits for discharges into waterways for approximately two years until it was replaced by more modern legislation.[2]

## The Food and Drug Act of 1906

As we shall see in our discussion of water-control law later in this chapter, the Refuse Act of 1899, despite its all-inclusive language, was probably not meant by the Congress to be the serious environmental law that it became in 1970. So we must go to 1906 for the real and intended beginning of federal law in the field of health, safety, and the environment. This beginning was the Food and Drug Act of 1906.[3]

The law has long been concerned with the safety of food and drugs. Early court decisions in the field of torts placed a much higher degree of responsibility upon a manufacturer of articles intended for human consumption than upon a manufacturer of other articles. This distinction has diminished in recent decades with the dramatic changes in product-liability law whereby warranties of fitness and strict liability have greatly enlarged the liability of manufacturers of almost all articles.

In the early 1900s, however, it was the feeling of the lawmakers that simply imposing liability after the fact for unsafe or defective food or drugs was not sufficient protection of the public. The very nature of the articles called for a high degree of responsibility. Some mechanism must be found for placing responsibility upon the manufacturer *before* the condition of the product caused injury. There must be a way of holding manufacturers responsible for the condition of their products and of removing them from the stream of commerce without having to prove that a person was actually harmed. This philosophy was to permeate all legislation relating to health, safety, and the environment that was to follow in the decades ahead. The watchword has been, and still is, "Prevent the injury or damage before it happens."

Despite the philosophy underlying the Food and Drug Act, it was a very simple law compared with the complex statutes that the food and drug industries, as well as all other manufacturing industries, are required to obey today. Its definitions were few and narrow, leaving substantial omissions of products that would in later years be considered to be drugs. It prohibited adulteration and misbranding, but definitions of the acts constituting adulteration and misbranding were very limited in nature, leaving the experience of succeeding decades to result in later legislation to fill in the gaps.

Despite all its shortcomings, the Food and Drug Act was in its day a monumental piece of legislation. A favorite slogan of its advocates was "pure food and drug," although the word "pure" does not appear in its title. Three-quarters of a century later, we still refer in popular parlance to its successor law as "the pure food and drug law."

The Food and Drug Act of 1906 had teeth, but they were not very sharp. Violation of the Act was a misdemeanor, with a maximum fine of $200 for the first offense. For a subsequent offense, the Act prescribed a maximum fine of $300, or up to a year in jail, or both. Another remedial (or preventive) device of the Act was the procedure for seizure and condemnation of adulterated or misbranded articles, a practice still authorized in current food and drug legislation, as well as in other laws regulating products. Corporate officers were subject to personal liability for violations.[4]

## The Food, Drug, and Cosmetic Act of 1938

After thirty-two years, the Congress determined that experience had shown that the Food and Drug Act was inadequate. Its definitions were too narrow. The statements of prohibited acts left many loopholes. There was no procedure for ensuring the safety of new drugs coming onto the market. Cosmetics, another class of products that, like food and drugs, come into intimate contact with the human body, were unregulated. Thus was born the Food, Drug, and Cosmetic Act of 1938,[5] which superseded and repealed the 1906 Act. It was amended and strengthened during the succeeding decades, and at this writing it is undergoing a complete revision in the Congress. It will probably be replaced with an entirely new act (discussed later in this chapter), recodifying existing law to the extent that it is retained and making extensive substantive and procedural changes. Its sponsors hope that it thus will be a workable statute from the standpoint of both the government and the affected industry in the light of current knowledge.

The 1938 Act increased the penalties over those of the 1906 Act. For a first offense, the fine was raised from a $200 maximum to a $1,000 maximum, and the possibility of a jail sentence up to one year was added. For a subsequent offense, the maximum fine was raised from $300 to $10,000, and the maximum jail sentence was increased from one year to three years. The penalties prescribed for a subsequent offense were also applied to a first offense where the violation was committed with the intent to defraud or mislead.[6]

Although corporate officers were prosecuted in the district courts for violations under the 1906 Act as well as the 1938 Act, the United States Supreme Court did not determine whether there was a sound legal basis for their prosecution until 1943 in *United States v. Dotterweich*.[7] The problem was that neither the 1906 nor the 1938 Act made a specific reference to a corporate officer or agent, but referred merely to any "person" who violated the Act. In *Dotterweich*, both the corporation and its president were indicted for the introduction of adulterated and misbranded drugs into commerce. At the trial, the jury disagreed as to the liability of the corporation but convicted the president. The Court of Appeals reversed the conviction on the ground that the individual could be held personally liable only if he was operating the corporation "as his alter ego."[8] The Supreme Court reversed the Court of Appeals and reinstated the conviction. The Court emphasized that "the only way in which a corporation can act is through the individuals who act on its behalf." The nature of the product involved was foremost in the Court's mind when it stated that the Act "dispenses with the conventional requirement for criminal conduct—awareness of some wrongdoing."

Further, the Court said that the statute "puts the burden of acting at hazard upon a person otherwise innocent but standing in responsible relation to a public danger."

## The *Park* Case

Over the next three decades, a number of cases were decided in which personal criminal responsibility was imposed upon corporate managers under the authority of *Dotterweich*. These cases all involved small companies where the individual defendants were in immediate control of the corporation.[9] The question of the liability of an officer of a large corporation, one who was remote from the scene of the actual violation and operating the business through delegation to subordinate officers and other managers, had never been litigated prior to the 1970s. Thus the decision of the Supreme Court in 1975 in *United States v. John R. Park*[10] came as a shock to the corporate world in general and the food, drug, and cosmetic industries in particular—for it now appeared that a corporate officer could be convicted of a crime without having had criminal intent or having actually participated.

The *Park* case was a prosecution of Acme Markets, Inc., a national retail food chain headquartered in Philadelphia, and John R. Park, its president. Acme had approximately 36,000 employees, 874 retail outlets, 12 general warehouses, and 4 special warehouses. In 1970, the Food and Drug Administration (FDA) advised Park by letter of unsanitary conditions in Acme's Philadelphia warehouse. The next year, FDA found similar conditions at Acme's Baltimore warehouse. The FDA then advised Park by letter of the conditions at Baltimore. Some improvement was found in a 1972 inspection at Baltimore, but "there was still evidence of rodent activity . . . and some rodent-contaminated lots of food items."[11] The corporation and the president were both charged with violations of the Food, Drug, and Cosmetic Act, based upon the unsanitary conditions in the Baltimore warehouse following shipment in interstate commerce.

Acme pleaded guilty and Park pleaded not guilty. On trial, the Baltimore division vice president testified as to the steps taken to remedy the unsanitary conditions. There was also testimony that Park

> functioned by delegating "normal operating duties," including sanitation, but that he retained "the big, broad, principles of the operation of the company," and had "the responsibility of seeing that they all work together."[12]

Park, in his testimony,

> conceded that providing sanitary conditions . . . was something that he was "responsible for in the entire operation of the company," and . . . it was one of many phases of the company that he assigned to "dependable subordinates" [and] admitted that the Baltimore problem indicated the system for

handling sanitation "wasn't working perfectly" and that . . . he was responsible for "any result which occurs in our company."[13]

Motions for judgment of acquittal were denied after the presentation
of both the government's case and the defendant's case. The jury found
Park guilty on all counts and he was subsequently fined $250.

The Court of Appeals reversed the conviction and granted a new trial.
The United States Supreme Court reversed the Court of Appeals and
reinstated the conviction. In commenting upon *Dotterweich* and the cases
following it, Chief Justice Burger stated

> that in providing sanctions which reach and touch the individuals who
> execute the corporate mission—and *this is by no means necessarily confined to a
> single corporate agent or employee*—the Act imposes not only a positive duty
> to seek out and remedy violations when they occur but also, and primarily, a
> duty to implement measures that will insure that violations will not occur.
> The requirements of foresight and vigilance imposed on responsible corpo-
> rate agents are beyond question demanding, and perhaps onerous, but they
> are no more stringent than the public has a right to expect of those who
> voluntarily assume positions of authority in business enterprises whose
> services and products affect the health and well-being of the public that
> supports them.[14] [Emphasis supplied.]

The Chief Justice emphasized that guilt was not to be predicated solely
on Park's position in the corporation, but rather, on the basis of his
relation to the situation and his authority and responsibility to deal with
it. The two letters received by Park from the FDA in 1970 and 1971 were
evidence that his system of delegation was not working.[15]

The implications of the *Park* decision have been discussed by a number of writers.[16] The decision has serious implications for the corporate
manager and a number of perplexing questions occur as a result of it.
Among them are: (1) Does *Park* announce a doctrine of vicarious liability
of corporate managers? (2) At what levels in the corporate hierarchy will
managers be held liable? (3) Does *Park* extend beyond food and drug law?
(4) Can liability be avoided by extenuating circumstances?

So far as vicarious liability is concerned, the decision expressly dis-
claimed guilt based solely upon the basis of position in the corporation,
but it emphasized authority and responsibility to deal with the situation.
This is a very fine distinction that is probably of little value to corporate
managers in their day-to-day operations. Generally, authority and responsibility are inherent in the position. For all practical purposes, *Park*
means that if the act of omission is committed by a subordinate at
whatever level, high or low, all those above that subordinate in the
corporate chain of command are subject to criminal liability. Thus the
answer to our first question also answers the second question. The Chief
Justice expressly stated that the duties under the Act were "by no means
necessarily confined to a single corporate agent or employee."[17]

As to the implications of *Park* beyond the food and drug law field, one can only speculate. The Court placed great emphasis upon the public health aspects. Traditionally, concepts of liability have developed earlier in the food and drug field than they have in relation to other products and activities. This has been true both in the law of torts and in the willingness of the Congress and other legislatures to enact regulatory laws. Today, however, there is far greater attention to public health than ever before in history, and that attention is not confined solely to food and drugs. The laws relating to safety and the environment are also inextricably linked to the public health.

Some environmental considerations may be only remotely related, or perhaps unrelated, to public health, such as those concerned with aesthetics or preservation of endangered species. But it is inconceivable that so much new law could possibly have been enacted without being very much relevant to public health. Thus it is fair to assume that a court considering a prosecution of a manager under a safety or environmental statute would look to *Park* as a precedent. The same considerations are there. The alleged illegal act is not a crime in the traditional sense, such as robbery, rape, or murder. So the matter of criminal intent, a necessary element of the traditional crime that is called *malum in se,* is not present. Rather, the Congress has set up standards for public protection. A violation of these standards is best described as a regulatory crime, or, in even more legal jargon, *malum prohibitum.* Criminal intent need not be proven and the interest in protecting the public health is high.

The principle is the same, therefore, in any law regulating health, safety, or the environment, but the application may not necessarily be the same. As the offense is defined by statute, so also is the penalty prescribed by statute. The Food, Drug, and Cosmetic Act makes a distinction in its penal provisions between a mere violation and a violation with intent to defraud or mislead.[18] Some of the other statutes in the health, safety, and environmental field use such words in connection with violations as "knowing," "willful," and "negligent."[19] Their presence or absence can be crucial in a determination of whether the *Park* case will be followed. The penal provisions of these various statutes will be examined later in this chapter.

The final question, whether liability can be avoided by extenuating circumstances, can be answered yes because Chief Justice Burger said so, but the answer may very well be no in a practical circumstance. In *Park* the Chief Justice noted that "the Act, in its criminal aspect, does not require that which is objectively impossible."[20] He cited an earlier decision, *United States v. Wiesenfeld Warehouse Co.,*[21] a case involving corporate, rather than individual, liability under the Food, Drug, and Cosmetic Act, as permitting the introduction of proof that the defendant was "powerless" to prevent or correct the condition constituting a violation.

A recent attempt to show that the defendant was powerless failed in a case arising in Hawaii.[22] The defendant claimed that he could not prevent the infestation of the warehouse by birds because the necessary wire fencing had not arrived from the mainland. His defense was re-

jected because he did not order the wiring after earlier inspections had
revealed the alleged unsanitary condition, but waited until after a later
inspection. In another recent case, the manager in charge of the
warehouse was held liable even though a janitor had sabotaged his
instructions to keep field mice out of the warehouse.[23] Presumably, if a
defendant officer is only a figurehead or if a lower-echelon defendant
manager can prove that a higher-echelon manager prevented compliance, a defense of objective impossibility or powerlessness might be
successful, but it is difficult to imagine many situations where this
condition might occur.

## A Legislative Response to *Park*

The reaction in the business community to *Park* has been one of fear and
perplexity.[24] The standard of strict liability that seems to be established
by *Park* has caused concern not only among business executives and their
lawyers but also within the federal government itself. When the Carter
administration proposed an entirely new regulatory and enforcement
system for the approval, monitoring, and withdrawal from the market of
all drugs, the administration bill to accomplish this purpose, the Drug
Regulation Reform Bill of 1978,[25] contained proposed changes in the
penal provisions designed to soften the impact of the *Park* decision. This
bill was never reported out of committee and thus died with the ad-
journment of the 95th Congress.

The following year, a new bill to establish the Drug Regulation Reform
Act of 1979[26] was introduced by most of the same senators who had
sponsored the 1978 bill. This bill also would make far-reaching changes
in the substantive law of drugs but does not go so far as the 1978 bill. The
penal provisions of the 1978 and 1979 bills are, however, almost identical.
As for severity, the maximum fine for an individual would be raised from
$1,000 to $25,000 for a first offense and from $10,000 to $50,000 for a
subsequent offense. The maximum prison sentences of one year and
three years for first and subsequent offenses, respectively, would remain. For corporate offenders, the maximum fines would be $50,000 for a
first offense and $100,000 for a subsequent violation.[27]

The impact of *Park* would be ameliorated somewhat by limiting criminal sanctions to those who "negligently" violate the act. If, however, the
violation should occur "knowingly or willfully," the more severe penalties of a second violation would be imposed even though only a first
offense might be involved. The following definition of "negligently" is
provided in the bill:

[A]cting without the care, skill, prudence, or diligence, under the circumstances then prevailing, that a prudent person would use if acting in a like
capacity and familiar with the matters with which a prudent person in like
capacity would be familiar.[28]

The insertion of the negligence requirement as a basis for criminal prosecution has been praised by industry leaders as well as by the Food and Drug Administration (FDA), and the Department of Health, Education, and Welfare (which became the Department of Health and Human Services in May 1980), of which FDA is a part. It has been opposed, however, by the Federal Trade Commission, and enforcement officials in FDA field offices have not agreed with their superiors in Washington.[29]

The pending bill, as well as its 1978 predecessor, would introduce civil penalties into the Food, Drug, and Cosmetic Act for the first time. These penalties, which could be imposed by the Secretary of Health, Education, and Welfare, after "notice and opportunity for discussion" could be as high as $10,000 for an individual and $25,000 for a corporation. Each day of a continuing violation would constitute a separate violation, but the maximum penalty in any single proceeding would not exceed $500,000 for an individual or $1 million for a corporation.[30] As there is no requirement that the violation be negligent, knowing, or willful in order to establish a civil penalty, that type of penalty could be used in those cases where the government, under the authority of *Park*, might have been able to establish a criminal violation under the proposed law but would not be able to establish sufficient involvement by the individual manager.

## FDA Enforcement Policies

In the enforcement of the Food, Drug, and Cosmetic Act, the government has weapons other than criminal sanctions at its disposal. Seizure of adulterated and misbranded articles is a well-known and long-established procedure going back to the first years of the 1906 Act. Injunctions against further violations are also frequently used, with the potentiality of contempt citations if they are not obeyed. From the standpoint of personal liability of the manager, however, the criminal proceeding has the greatest impact.

Criminal proceedings under the Act are prosecuted by the Department of Justice, usually through the various United States district attorneys, after a violation has been reported by the Food and Drug Administration. This is generally preceded by what is known as a Section 305 hearing, so called because of the following requirement of Section 305 of the Act:

> Before any violation of this Chapter is reported by the Secretary to any United States attorney for institution of a criminal proceeding, the person against whom such proceeding is contemplated shall be given appropriate notice and an opportunity to present his views, either orally or in writing, with regard to such contemplated proceeding.[31]

This hearing is informal in nature. A corporation may appear through one of its officers and an individual may appear personally. They may be represented by counsel and it is probably better practice if they are, but

there is no requirement. Witnesses are not sworn and there are no rules of evidence and no transcript, although a summary of the hearing is written by the FDA Compliance Officer, subject to review by the respondents and their opportunity to state their views in the summary. Despite the seemingly mandatory language in Section 305, it has been held that the lack of a Section 305 hearing is not a bar to prosecution for violation of the Act. The failure of FDA to follow the administrative steps does not prevent a United States attorney from prosecuting for a criminal act of which he or she has knowledge.[32]

In our review of antitrust law enforcement in the preceding chapter, we noted an increasing tendency to join participating officers and other managers in criminal proceedings. In the food and drug law field, there is an even greater level of enforcement activity against managers than in the antitrust field, probably because health and safety, and not merely economic considerations, are involved.[33] The policy of the Food and Drug Administration and of the Department of Justice, as announced by high-ranking attorneys in both Justice and FDA and by FDA's Associate Commissioner for Compliance, is to bring charges against a responsible corporate manager in every case where a criminal action is brought against a corporation.[34] They believe that prosecution of the individual will have a greater deterrent effect than prosecution merely of the corporation alone. They will, therefore, seek out the individual or individuals within the corporation who had the power or authority to prevent, detect, or correct the violation.

The passage of the proposed Drug Regulation Reform Act of 1979 is not likely to change the government's policy of pursuing responsible corporate managers along with their respective corporations. It should be noted that the word "negligently" in the 1979 bill refers to both individual and corporate violators. Therefore, if the FDA recommends a criminal action against a corporation for a negligent (or knowing or willful) violation, it will also presumably recommend a like action against the manager or managers participating in, or responsible for, the violation. If the FDA cannot find a basis for a criminal violation under the Act because of its inability to establish negligence, it can, as suggested above, utilize the new civil penalty procedure against either the corporation or the responsible individual, or both.

## REGULATION OF THE ENVIRONMENT

The fastest developing field of the law during the past decade has been environmental law, especially federal regulation of the environment. Traditionally, environmental law was a matter for state concern, although the terms "environment" and "ecology" seldom, if ever, were used in statutes, court decisions, and legal literature. Matters involving pollution of water and air were resolved in private suits between landowners and between local governments and their citizens under the principles of the laws pertaining to nuisance. State statutes provided some rules governing discharges into bodies of water.[35] Generally, however, these statutes were relatively mild, were not uniformly enforced, and were, in fact, often unenforceable if an interstate waterway was involved, as there was no legal mechanism by which a state could defend itself against pollution coming from an adjoining state.

## Evolution of Federal Antipollution Laws

### THE FIRST TWO DECADES

The first comprehensive federal legislation in the field of water pollution came in 1948 with the passage of the Water Pollution Control Act.[36] That Act was primarily an appropriation for research. It did, however, contain provisions for interstate compacts and for remedies for pollution originating in one state but endangering the health or welfare of persons in another state. In the 1948 Act and its 1956 and 1961 amendments,[37] the principle of state rights and responsibilities prevailed.

Congress enacted the first federal statute on air quality in 1955.[38] Like the then-current water-quality statute, it was primarily concerned with research and with assistance to the states. In 1963, however, the Congress established grants in aid to states to establish and improve air-pollution control programs and authorized the Secretary of Health, Education, and Welfare (HEW) to take a more direct role in the abatement of interstate air pollution and to participate actively with the new states in their own abatement procedures.[39] States began enacting new legislation to take advantage of the grants in aid.[40]

Two years later, Congress enacted the Water Quality Act of 1965. It too used the carrot approach of requiring each state to establish water-quality standards for interstate waterways as a condition of receiving federal funding, but it also provided a stick by empowering the Secretary of HEW to establish such standards if the state did not.[41] In that same year, Congress passed the Solid Waste Disposal Act,[42] which followed the usual beginning pattern of research, technical assistance, and guidelines.

Then came the Federal Air Quality Act of 1967.[43] The principle of state action under federal guidance was continued, but the federal power was extended. The states were given the first opportunity to adopt air-quality standards and enforcement plans based upon federal criteria, but the federal government could move in where a state failed to act.

### THE 1970s—A DECADE OF RAPID DEVELOPMENT

With the advent of the 1970s, the federal government began to act in earnest to abate water and air pollution. There have been previous references to the Refuse Act of 1899, whose broad language was found to provide a basis for a permit system relating to discharges into navigable

waters. The Congress in 1899 was directing its attention to impediments to navigation, not to clean water per se. The Refuse Act did, however, contain convenient language, and it was first utilized to establish a permit system in 1970. That was also the year the Environmental Protection Agency was established by order of President Nixon. There were also two important acts of Congress in the environmental field in 1970. One was the National Environmental Policy Act,[44] which imposed upon all federal agencies the responsibility to make certain that environmental considerations are taken into account in connection with all major federal action. The other was the Clean Air Amendments of 1970,[45] which, among other things, authorized and directed the establishment of nationwide emission standards in certain cases, nationwide performance standards for new stationary sources, and to a large extent placed the states in a subservient position to the federal government in carrying out the multitude of all-inclusive federal requirements. The Clean Air Amendments of 1970 also contained the beginning of noise abatement and control regulation in the form of grants for research into that field.

Next, the Congress made major changes through the Federal Water Pollution Control Act Amendments of 1972.[46] Water-quality standards were retained as a measure of program effectiveness and performance, but the enforcement emphasis was shifted to adherence to effluent limits. The permit system of the Refuse Act of 1899 was superseded by a new permit system by which all permits for the discharge of effluents would be conditioned upon their being within the limits established under the authority of the 1972 Amendments. These Amendments contain many complexities involving such things as the timetable for achieving reduction of effluents, standards for toxic pollutants, provisions for recordkeeping and reports and for maintenance of monitoring systems by operators, and provisions for inspections, monitoring, and entry by governmental authority. More substantive amendments came in 1977,[47] which, among other things, made changes in the timetable for reduction of polluting effluents and also authorized more detailed regulation by the Environmental Protection Agency (EPA) of methods of plant operation.

Noise pollution came under full regulation with the passage of the Noise Control Act of 1972,[48] which stated as its goal the protection of all Americans from "noise that jeopardizes their health or welfare." It provided, among other things, for the establishment of noise standards and for regulation of noise emissions from products in commerce.

The federal government's role in control of solid-waste disposal was expanded beyond the research and guideline arena with the enactment of the Resource Conservation and Recovery Act of 1976.[49] As solid waste disposal appears to be more a matter of local, and less of interstate, concern than does control of water, air, and noise, there is more emphasis on state effort in this area. The role of the federal government is to provide standards and assistance.

Coincident with the rapid development of environmental statutes during the 1970s was the imposition of penalties of a considerably greater magnitude than had normally been associated with federal statutes governing business conduct. Under the Interstate Commerce Act, the typical maximum fine was, and still is, $5,000, and if a prison sentence is provided for, it is typically stated at a maximum of one year. Under the Sherman Act, the original penalty was a $5,000 fine and a jail sentence not exceeding one year. As stated in Chapter 5, the maximum fine was increased in 1955 to $50,000, and in 1974 it was increased to $1 million for a corporation and $100,000 for an individual, with the maximum prison sentence increased to three years. Violations of the Food, Drug, and Cosmetic Act are punishable by a fine up to $1,000 for a first offense and $10,000 for a second offense, with jail sentences of up to one year for a first offense and three years for a second.

The pollution control laws started out with more severe fines than these other laws. Fines of $25,000 for *each day* of violation and imprisonment not to exceed one year, or both, are imposed for violations of the Water Pollution Control Act, the Clean Air Act, the Noise Control Act, and the Resource Conservation and Recovery Act where such violations are willful, negligent, or knowing (the precise word varies from one statute to another) and are contrary to the terms of permits, or where they consist of activities that may not be undertaken without a permit or are in violation of standards (in other words, "the acts of polluting"). For a second or subsequent offense, the penalties are doubled.[50] There are generally somewhat less stringent penalties for false statements knowingly made in applications, reports, and records or for tampering with monitoring devices ("administrative violations rather than acts of polluting"): fines of $10,000 or imprisonment not exceeding six months, or both. The Resource Conservation and Recovery Act, however, provides for the same magnitude of penalty for an "administrative" violation as for an "act of polluting," and this is also true for certain types of "administrative" violations of the Water Pollution Control Act. It is also possible that an administrative violation may constitute a false statement to a government agency and can be prosecuted on the Criminal Code.[51]

The relative severity of the criminal sanctions in the pollution control laws can be attributed to the public reaction to pollution that has occupied much of the time and attention of public interest groups, the media, the academic world, and elected officials. Two law review articles, published in the early 1970s, express the point of view that has motivated the more severe sanctions. Iseman, writing in 1972, said:

> Ten years ago, when the dire implications of pollution were not as apparent, environmental offenders could be accurately placed in the same *malum prohibitum* category as antitrust and housing code violations. But today pollution can almost be classified as *malum in se*, something wrong in and of itself, like robbery, assault or murder.[52]

Michael K. Glenn, then the Acting Deputy Assistant Administrator for

Water Enforcement of the Environmental Protection Agency, writing in
1973, said:

> Pollution is a crime. It is apparent that it has become a more severe crime
> than it was only a few years ago . . . . There are sound reasons to believe that
> pollution is a problem that can best be solved by technically competent
> people in earnest negotiation and consideration of the use of available
> technology. The law must provide a remedy, however, when this process
> fails . . . . By virtue of the sheer magnitude of the potential liability this
> economic deterrent should dramatically increase compliance with estab-
> lished abatement requirements. If strictly enforced, the criminal sanctions
> under the 1972 Amendments can effectively serve the purpose of pollution
> abatement.[53]

The Clean Air Act and the Water Pollution Control Act make specific
reference to corporate officers by stating that for the purpose of the
criminal sanctions, the term "any person who willfully or negligently
violates" shall include "any responsible corporate officer."[54] A question
could be raised as to whether this language exempts from criminal
liability an employee who is not an officer. Looking at the general
criminal law concept of responsibility for one's own act, it would appear
that no such exemption is intended. A nonofficer employee who actively
participates in an intentional violation is probably personally liable
simply because it was his or her personal act. The singling out of officers
for special mention in the statutes is intended to establish a place in the
corporate chain of command where responsibility can be fixed if a violation occurs.[55]

RULE MAKING AND RESPONSIBILITY

Recent rule-making action by the EPA further illustrates the intent to
place personal responsibility upon officers and other high-ranking individuals within the corporation. Consolidated permit regulations
under several acts, including the Clean Water Act, the Clean Air Act,
and the Resource Conservation and Recovery Act, adopted in May 1980,
provide that all corporate permit applications, with one minor exception, be signed by a principal executive officer of at least the rank of vice
president. They also provide that all reports required by such permits or
otherwise required by the EPA be made by such officers or their duly
authorized representatives. It is further required that the duly authorized representative be the person responsible for the overall operation of the facility that originates the activity for which the permit is
issued, such as "a plant manager, operator of a well or a well field,
superintendent or person of equivalent responsibility."[56] The authorization of such a person to sign must itself be signed by a corporate
executive officer of vice-presidential or higher rank and must be on file

with the EPA. The proposed regulation further provides for the following certification on the permit application or report:

> I hereby certify under penalty of law that I have personally examined and am familiar with the information submitted in the attached document, and that based on my inquiry of those individuals immediately responsible for obtaining the information, I believe that the submitted information is true, accurate and complete. I am aware that there are significant penalties for submitting false information, including the possibility of fine and imprisonment.[57]

The language of the certification makes it abundantly evident that the manager, officer, or nonofficer who signs a permit document has an obligation to inquire and diligently seek out the truth of the statements contained therein. The signer of the document is reminded of the possibility of being fined or imprisoned if found lacking in diligence.

Nonofficer employees are mentioned specifically in special provisions in the Water Pollution Control Act pertaining to discharge of oil and other "hazardous substances" into or upon navigable waters. Those provisions require "any person in charge of a vessel or of an onshore or an offshore facility" to notify immediately the appropriate agency of the United States government of any such discharge. Failure to notify is a crime subjecting the person in charge to a fine of not more than $10,000 or imprisonment for not more than one year, or both.[58] The liability is based upon the person's immediate responsibility with regard to the operation where the discharge occurred and bears no reference whatsoever as to whether that person is or is not a corporate officer.

EMPLOYEE PROTECTION

Most of the federal pollution laws contain provisions for the protection of corporate employees who assist the government in their enforcement. Three of the four acts we have been discussing contain prohibitions against firing or discriminating against any employee for having instituted a proceeding under the act or for giving testimony in a proceeding for enforcement of that act.[59] While these prohibitions are intended primarily to protect rank-and-file employees, there is no reason why they cannot also be invoked to protect managerial employees. The provisions for reporting oil discharges carry with them an immunity from prosecution for a polluting act committed by the person in charge of the vessel or facility if the discharge is reported in the manner required by the Water Pollution Control Act.[60]

## Responsibility for Action of Subordinates

In discussing the *Park* case as a precedent for prosecutions under the antipollution statutes, we noted that the Food, Drug, and Cosmetic Act is a strict liability statute and that its penal provisions are triggered by any kind of violation, whether or not it is willful, negligent, or knowing. We have seen, however, that the four antipollution statutes each contain one or more of these adjectives in connection with "violation" (or in the adverb form in connection with "violate"). The water and air laws also have strict liability features, for, in addition to criminal penalties, they also provide for civil penalties. The civil penalties under these statutes are generally, but not always, comparable in dollar amount to the criminal fines, and it is not necessary to show that the violation is willful, negligent, or knowing.[61] Civil penalties have been likened to recovery of damages in a private civil suit. The offender is, in effect, paying for damage to the environment.[62] Thus far, civil penalties for violation of these statutes have been imposed only upon corporations and sole proprietors and not upon managerial personnel. There is, however, nothing in the statutes to preclude recovery of civil penalties from responsible corporate managers, and the Environmental Protection Agency has given no indication of its intent in this matter.[63]

Does the presence of civil penalties in two of these pollution control acts, coupled with the requirement that a criminal violation must be willful, negligent, or knowing, mean that a corporate manager cannot be prosecuted under one of these laws for the actions of subordinates? There is no ready answer. A number of circumstances must be considered. Most of these statutes provide that in connection with actions for recovery of civil penalties or the issuance of an injunction, the EPA shall give the alleged violator notice of the alleged violation and afford thirty days within which to cease, in default of which the civil action may be commenced.[64] A corporate officer receiving such a notice on behalf of the corporation may then be in a position where any continued violation is "knowing," thereby placing him or her in a position of possibly being prosecuted for a criminal violation. The officer's situation factually is not unlike that of the corporation president in the *Park* case. Being on notice that a violation is occurring, the officer's responsibility may now be to take every means to make certain that the violation is abated. The executive who does not do so may be committing a "knowing" violation.[65]

## Overview of Enforcement Against Managers

Whatever the interpretation of the pollution control statutes may ultimately be on the matter of managerial liability for corporation violations, it cannot be denied that the risk of liability is real. In Chapter 5 we saw the increased attention being given by the Department of Justice to criminal proceedings against corporate personnel for antitrust violations. By contrast with the antitrust policy, no guidelines have been yet published by the EPA or the Justice Department for jail sentences for corporate individuals violating the pollution control laws.

At the American Law Institute–American Bar Association Conference on Environmental Law held in February 1978, James W. Moorman, Assistant Attorney General in charge of the Land and Natural Resources

Division of the Department of Justice, promised vigorous enforcement of the criminal provisions of the antipollution laws. He pointed out that violations of such laws can often also be crimes under the more general and more stringent provisions of the criminal code, such as 18 U.S.C. § 1001, which covers false statements to government agencies. The usual antipollution violations are misdemeanors while the usual criminal code violations are felonies. In commenting upon enforcement against corporate managers, Moorman stated:

> It should be evident to all here that the price paid for criminal misconduct can be quite high. Many of those who have chosen to violate or who will be tempted to violate the pollution control laws are professional and business people. These are people for whom an indictment alone, not to mention conviction or imprisonment, can be a catastrophe. As a consequence, I believe a policy of vigorous criminal enforcement will be truly effective as a deterrent and will result in a high degree of pollution control.[66]

### Citizen Suits and Stockholder Derivative Suits

Another remedy provided in the antipollution laws is the citizen suit. Typically, such laws provide that if governmental authority fails to take action against an alleged violator, a private citizen may either sue the alleged violator directly or sue the governmental agency to require it to take action.[67] While it is conceivable that a corporate manager could become a defendant in such an action along with the corporation, there are as yet no precedents for such an action.

Another possible remedy in the environmental law field is the stockholders' derivative action. Such a suit would, of course, be against the directors and officers. At least one such suit has been brought.[68] The grounds can be negligent management and violation of law and public policy by the management.

## REGULATION OF PRODUCTS

### Pesticides

The Food and Drug Act of 1906 was the first act of Congress regulating activities in the manufacture and distribution of a product in the interest of public health and safety. Food and drugs, because they are consumed by humans, constituted a logical starting point for this type of regulation. Four years later, insecticides came under federal control with the passage of the Insecticide Act of 1910.[69] These products received early congressional attention because of their very close relationship to the production of food and their protection of the public health against insect infestation, accompanied by qualities that presented dangers to users and consumers if not properly used. Like the Food and Drug Act, the

Insecticide Act was rather primitive compared with the type of legislation that exists today. Its penalties, also like those of the Food and Drug
Act, were relatively mild.

**105**

*The Manager and
Health and
Safety: Product
Standards and the
Environment*

Technological development, including the development of new types
of products and increasing knowledge of the effects of their use, in 1947
brought about a more modern and comprehensive statute, known as the
Federal Insecticide, Fungicide, and Rodenticide Act (FIFRA).[70] While the
1906 Act was concerned only with adulteration and misbranding, FIFRA
not only greatly expanded the concept of what constitutes adulteration
and misbranding, but also added other products to the scope of the law
and affirmative requirements for directions for use, warnings, and safety
measures, as well as initiating a procedure for registration of products.
Coincident with the environmental movement and the enactment of the
various antipollution laws during the 1960s, FIFRA underwent amendments in 1964 to tighten governmental control over registration of products by procedures for cancellation or suspension of registration.[71] In
1972, FIFRA was completely restated and revised by the Federal Environmental Pesticide Control Act.[72] Among other things, the new Act
further tightened labeling requirements, required reregistration of all
presently registered products, revised procedures for registration and
cancellation of registration of products, and required registration of
manufacturing establishments and certification of certain types of
applicators.

Penalties for violation under the 1910 Act were fines at the $200 to $300
level, with possible one-year jail sentences for subsequent violations.
Under FIFRA, as adopted in 1947, the maximum fine was increased to
$1,000, but in case of fraudulent violations (misuse of information ac-
quired under the authority of the Act), the maximum fine was $10,000
and the maximum jail sentence was three years. The 1972 Act increased
the maximum fine to $25,000. This increase appears consistent with the
attitude toward environmental pollutors expressed in the laws then
being enacted governing air, water, and noise pollution and solid waste
disposal. Regulation of pesticides is very much an environmental law, its
only fundamental difference being that its application is limited to certain segments of industrial and agricultural activity, while the other
environmental laws regulate a broader spectrum of activity. No increase
in jail sentences was provided in the 1972 Act. The Act did, however,
introduce civil penalties of $5,000 for each violation.[73]

Unlike the Food, Drug, and Cosmetic Act, the Pesticide Act makes
specific reference to the liability of corporate managers, stating:

> [T]he act, omission, or failure of any officer, agent, or other person acting for
> or employed by any person shall in every case be also deemed to be the act,
> omission, or failure of such person as well as that of the person employed.[74]

This language evidences a clear congressional intent to hold an offending corporation and all participating employees at all responsible levels

liable for any infractions of the law that occur. Like the Food, Drug, and Cosmetic Act, however, the Pesticide Act does not premise criminal liability upon the violation being willful, negligent, or knowing. It can be expected that the principles of the *Park* case would therefore apply to a prosecution of a corporate manager under the Pesticide Act.

## Consumer Safety

Prior to 1960, the only really significant federal laws pertaining to consumer safety were the Federal Food, Drug, and Cosmetic Act and the Federal Insecticide, Fungicide, and Rodenticide Act. The few others that existed were relatively narrow in scope and were directed to specific hazards that had come to the attention of the Congress. Among these was the Caustic Poison Act of 1927, which imposed labeling requirements, including directions for use, on a dozen chemical household products.[75]

In 1953, in response to reports of children being injured or dying when their clothing caught fire, the Congress passed the Flammable Fabrics Act, which forbids the use of flammable fabrics (as defined in the Act) in children's clothing.[76] This Act, which is still in effect, provides for fines up to $5,000 and jail sentences up to one year for willful violation.

Anothar national child safety concern in the 1950s stemmed from the deaths of children who had shut themselves into discarded refrigerators. This gave rise in 1956 to the Household Refrigerators Act,[77] which requires refrigerators to be equipped with doors opening from the inside. Violations are punishable by a fine up to $1,000 or jail up to one year, or both. No specific mention is made of managers, but they are undoubtably included in the phrase "any person who violates." As this is a health and safety measure and such words as "willful," "negligent," and "knowing" are missing from the Act, it can be assumed that the principles of the *Park* decision would apply to the prosecution of a corporate manager under this legislation. There are, however, no decided cases under the Act.

The Caustic Poison Act of 1927 was repealed and superseded in 1960 by the Hazardous Substances Act,[78] which applies to chemical, mechanical, and electrical products intended for use in the household or by children. It is essentially a labeling law. Its penalties for violation are fines up to $3,000 or jail up to one year, or both. No mention is made of corporate managers, but again they are probably included in the phrase "any person who violates," and the principles of the *Park* case probably apply.

Prior to 1972, the Congress had used a product-by-product approach of enacting legislation on specific selected matters of consumer safety. In that year, however, it took a more comprehensive approach with the enactment of the Consumer Product Safety Act.[79] That Act, while not repealing any of the other consumer safety acts mentioned in this chapter, has set up a comprehensive system for the establishment of safety standards by the Consumer Product Safety Commission—standards to be applied to individual products pursuant to notice and hearing. The

Act has also set up procedures for notification to the Commission and
repair or recall of products found to contain a substantial product hazard
resulting from a defect in the product or failure to comply with an
applicable consumer product-safety rule.

The Consumer Product Safety Act imposes civil penalties for "knowingly" violating its provisions in the amount of $2,000 for each violation, with each day constituting a separate violation and with a maximum civil penalty of $500,000 for any related series of violations. The Act states:

> [T]he term "knowingly" means (1) the having of actual knowledge, or (2) the presumed having of knowledge deemed to be possessed by a reasonable man who acts in the circumstances, including knowledge obtainable upon the exercise of due care to ascertain the truth of the representations.[80]

Criminal penalties under the Consumer Product Safety Act may be invoked for a willful violation after notice of noncompliance. The penalties are fines up to $50,000 or imprisonment up to one year, or both. Specific mention is made of the criminal liability of managers in language that is unusually detailed:

> Any individual director, officer, or agent of a corporation who knowingly and willfully authorizes, orders, or performs any of the acts or practices constituting in whole or in part a violation of section 2068 of this title, and who has knowledge of notice of noncompliance received by the corporation from the Commission, shall be subject to penalties under this section without regard to any penalties to which that corporation may be subject under subsection (a) of this section.[81]

It is clear from this section that Congress intended to place a high degree of responsibility upon corporate managers. The language is strong, but it is also clear that a completely unknowing violation will not subject the individual to criminal penalties, as the individual must have "knowledge of notice of noncompliance received by the corporation." This section appears to present the fewest problems of interpretation of any of the health or environmental penal provisions discussed in this chapter.

Another example of the governmental intent to place personal responsibility upon management for compliance with the Act appears in the regulations for notifying the Commission of unanticipated defects—that is, defects in a product that appear after it has reached the consumer market. It is specifically provided that written notice must be signed by either the chief executive of the reporting corporation or by such other officer or agent as the chief executive shall have specifically authorized in a written delegation filed with the Commission.[82]

Another recent statute prescribing standards of consumer safety is the Mobile Home Construction and Safety Standards Act of 1974.[83] Violation of the safety standards imposed by this Act can result in civil penalties of

$1,000 for each violation (each home built in violation of the standards being a separate violation) up to a maximum of $1 million for any series of violations within a year. The criminal penalties, however, apply only to individuals, including directors, officers, and agents of corporations. The penalty is $1,000 or not more than one year in prison, or both, where the violation "threatens the health or safety of any purchaser" and where it occurs "knowingly and willfully."

## Regulation of the Motor Vehicle Industry

During the past fifteen years, the motor vehicle industry has become one of the most highly regulated of the manufacturing industries. The laws and regulations pertaining to it fall mainly into three categories: (1) emission control, (2) safety, and (3) fuel conservation. The subject is very complex and, while it is of great public interest, the problems of managerial liability and regulation that are the themes of this book are concentrated in the managers of only a relatively few corporations. No attempt is made, therefore, to analyze the substantive requirements of these three fields of regulation, except to note that they are there and to comment briefly upon the penalties that may be imposed upon managers for violation.

Regulation of emissions began in 1965 and is authorized under certain sections of the Clean Air Act.[84] The authority to establish emission standards is vested in the Administrator of EPA. Penalties for violation of the law and the standards are civil in nature and range from $2,500 to $10,000 for each offense, depending upon the nature of the violation. Each sale of a motor vehicle produced in violation is treated as a separate offense.

Safety standards are established by the Secretary of Transportation under the authority and the detailed requirements of the Traffic and Motor Vehicle Safety Act, originally enacted in 1966 and frequently amended.[85] There are civil penalties in the amount of $1,000 for each motor vehicle produced in violation. Originally, the Act imposed a ceiling of $400,000 for all related violations, but that ceiling was raised to $800,000 by a 1974 amendment.

There is no reference to managerial personnel in either of the foregoing laws, but in each case the penal section refers to "whoever violates," which appears broad enough to cover individual, as well as, corporate action.

In 1972 the Congress enacted the Motor Vehicle Information and Cost Saving Act.[86] While its main purpose appears to be to give consumers more information concerning the performance of motor vehicles, it does have safety aspects in the form of the kind of information that must be disclosed and in bumper standards promulgated by the Secretary of Transportation under the authority of the Act. Violation of bumper standards can result in a civil penalty of $1,000 per vehicle, with a maximum penalty of $800,000 for a related series of violations. There are also criminal penalties of a $50,000 fine or a year in prison, or both, for "knowingly and willfully" violating the Act. It is specifically provided that if a corporation has been served by the Secretary of Transportation with a notice of violation, any director, officer, or agent who knowingly and willfully ordered or performed any of the acts or practices constituting the violation and who had knowledge of the notice shall be liable for criminal penalties in addition to those imposed upon the corporation.[87]

The Motor Vehicle Information and Cost Saving Act also contains provisions forbidding any device to cause an odometer to register any but the true mileage. Criminal penalties are the same as under the bumper standards and so are the civil penalties, except that the maximum for a series of related violations is $100,000 rather than $800,000.[88]

Fuel conservation or mileage standards were legislated in 1975 by the Energy Conservation Act, Title V, Improving Automotive Efficiency.[89] Mileage standards are required to be improved each year in accordance with the goals established for certain years by the Congress and for certain other years under regulations to be promulgated by the Secretary of Transportation, based upon tests conducted under the authority of the Administrator of EPA and after consultation with the Secretary of Energy. Civil penalties are exacted for violations, based upon the degree of variance of the motor vehicles from the statutory or regulatory standards. Such penalties are, however, entirely upon the corporation, and there appears to be no personal liability of managers in this area.

## The Toxic Substances Control Act

In the context of all the discussions, hearings, lawsuits, legislation, and regulations of the 1960s and 1970s concerning the environment, chemicals were placed under considerable scrutiny. Portions of the industry had been under regulation by virtue of the Food, Drug, and Cosmetic Act and FIFRA, and now it was proposed to place the entire chemical industry and all its products under strict governmental controls. This was accomplished in 1976 by the enactment of the Toxic Substances Control Act (TSCA),[90] which in practical effect made the chemical industry a regulated industry.

Among the salient features of TSCA are provisions for required testing of a chemical substance or mixture upon a finding by the Environmental Protection Agency (EPA) of unreasonable risk to health or the environment accompanied by insufficient data as to its effect. The Act also requires premarket notification and submission of test data before manufacturing a new chemical substance or an existing chemical substance for a significant new use. TSCA authorizes regulation by EPA of the manufacture, distribution, use, or disposal of a chemical substance or mixture to prevent unreasonable risk to health or the environment, as well as seizures and injunctions in event of imminent hazard. There are also extensive recordkeeping and reporting requirements.

Criminal sanctions are imposed upon "any person who knowingly or willfully violates"; they consist of a fine of $25,000 for each day of violation or a jail sentence of up to one year, or both. Civil penalties of up to $25,000 for each day of violation are also prescribed. The statute is specific that both criminal and civil penalties may be assessed for the same violation if it is knowing or willful.[91] Nowhere in the Act is the term "person" defined, but it is presumed to include corporate managers, as has been the case in interpreting the penal provisions of other federal statutes that do not make a specific reference to managers.

The lack of definition of "person" in TSCA has given rise to a question of interpretation under Section 8(e). That subsection reads:

> Any person who manufactures, processes, or distributes in commerce a chemical substance or mixture and who obtains information which reasonably supports the conclusion that such substance or mixture presents a substantial risk of injury to health or the environment shall immediately inform the Administrator of such information unless such person has actual knowledge that the Administrator has been adequately informed of such information.[92]

In 1977, EPA issued proposed guidelines under this subsection that appeared to place the burden on individual employees to report to EPA. Members of the industry protested the proposed guidelines on the basis that an employee was not a "person who manufactures," etc., as stated in the subsection, and that because of the penal provisions, employees were being placed in an unduly risky position. The guidelines as finally issued are somewhat softer but still maintain the principle of individual employee responsibility. Such responsibility is limited, however, to "those officers and employees . . . who are capable of appreciating the significance of pertinent information."[93] The guidelines further provide that a business organization may set up and internally publicize a procedure for having employees report to a responsible company official, which, if done, fulfills the employee's obligation under the law. The procedure must, among other things, advise employees of the federal penalties for failure to report and provide a mechanism to advise officers and employees in writing of the disposition of the report. If the company decides not to submit the report to the EPA, the reporting employee must be informed of his or her right to report to the EPA directly. As is the case in the various pollution control statutes, employees are protected against discrimination in employment for having done anything to assist in enforcing or otherwise carrying out TSCA.[94] Reporting to EPA is, of course, one of those protected activities.

## CONCLUSION

This chapter is a very brief overview of the federal laws pertaining to health, consumer and public safety, and the environment, and their personal impact upon corporate managers. (Employee safety, a closely related subject, will be discussed in Chapter 7, which deals with the laws

**111**

*The Manager and
Health and
Safety: Product
Standards and the
Environment*

governing employee relations.) Obviously, these laws contain many more provisions, complexities, and qualifications than could possibly be discussed in this chapter. To the extent that historical or political background and substantive law provisions have been presented, the sole purpose of the discussion has been to give some idea of the scope and magnitude of the corporate manager's personal obligations and the risks to be encountered in noncompliance, whether intentional or unintentional.

It should be evident that the statutes discussed in this chapter (and other statutes in the field which may have been omitted because of space limitations) impose severe responsibilities upon corporate managers and severe liabilities for their noncompliance. As in the case of the antitrust laws, it is evident that the intent of Congress is that these laws are to be taken seriously by corporate managers, and the officials charged with their enforcement have stated unequivocally their intentions to carry out what they perceive to be the congressional mandate.

The potentialities for further legislation are infinite. For example, at press time a bill is pending in the Congress which would require that if a manager "discovers in the course of business as such manager a serious danger associated with" a product (or component) or business practice for which he or she has management authority, that manager shall report the danger to the appropriate federal agency and shall warn affected employees. If the report and warning are not made within thirty days after discovery of the danger, the manager shall be subject to a fine of *not less* than $50,000 or imprisonment of *not less* than two years, or both.[95] If enacted, this bill would greatly enlarge the exposure of corporate managers and would create substantial interpretative questions.

## NOTES

1. 30 Stat. 1152; 33 U.S.C. § 407. See also Executive Order 11574, Dec. 23, 1970, 35 Fed. Reg. 19627. Violation of this statute was also the basis for indictment in the well-known Kepone incident, United States v. Allied Chemical Corp., 420 F. Supp. 122 (E.D. Va. 1976).

2. The Federal Water Pollution Control Act Amendments of 1972, P.L. 92-500; 86 Stat. 816.

3. 34 Stat. 768. In this chapter, unless the context indicates otherwise, the word "safety" will refer to consumer safety or public safety as distinguished from employee safety, which will be discussed in Chapter 7.

4. An early case in which corporate officers were indicted for violation of the Food and Drug Act is United States v. Mayfield, 177 F. 765 (N.D. Ala. 1910). The alleged offense was the introduction into interstate commerce of a beverage adulterated with cocaine. The officers' defense was lack of knowledge of the shipment. Having delegated the operations to a manager, they did not know that he had shipped the beverage across state lines. In instructions to the jury, the court ruled that if the officers knew of the presence of cocaine in the beverage and had authorized the manager to

operate the plant and to sell the product without restriction, they were subject to prosecution even if they did not know of the specific illegal shipment.

5. 52 Stat. 1040. In its present form, with all amendments, this Act is compiled at 21 U.S.C. §§ 301–392.

6. 21 U.S.C. § 333.

7. 320 U.S. 277, 88 L. Ed. 48, 64 S. Ct. 134 (1943). See comments: Quigg, "Due Process—Punishment for Acts Done Without Consciousness of Wrongdoing," 42 *Mich. L. Rev.* 1103–1110 (1944); "Federal Food, Drug, and Cosmetic Act—Corporations—Criminal Liability of Officers and Agents," 12 *Geo. Wash. L. Rev.* 366–368 (1944).

8. United States v. Buffalo Pharmacal Co., 131 F.2d 500, 503 (2d Cir. 1942).

9. Best, "Criminal Law: Public Welfare Violations—Imposing Criminal Sanctions with a Strict Liability Standard," 28 *U. of Fla. L. Rev.* 596, 604 (1976); O'Keefe, "Criminal Liability: *Park* Update," 32 *Food Drug Cosm. L.J.* 392 (1977). Among the principal cases following *Dotterweich* were Golden Grain Macaroni Co. v. United States, 209 F.2d 166 (9th Cir. 1953); United States v. H. Wool & Sons, Inc., 215 F.2d 95 (2d Cir. 1954); United States v. Diamond State Poultry Co., 125 F. Supp. 617 (D. Del. 1954); United States v. Colosse Cheese & Butter Co., 133 F. Supp. 953 (N.D.N.Y. 1955); Lelles v. United States, 241 F.2d 21 (9th Cir. 1957), *cert. denied,* 353 U.S. 974 (1957), *reh. denied,* 354 U.S. 944 (1957); United States v. Calise, 217 F. Supp. 705 (S.D.N.Y. 1962); United States v. Shapiro, 491 F.2d 335 (6th Cir. 1974). In United States v. Omar Inc., 91 F. Supp. 121 (D. Neb. 1950), a corporation was found guilty of violating the Act, but its vice president and general manager was found by the court to be personally not guilty because the acts complained of were performed by agents other than him.

10. 421 U.S. 658, 44 L. Ed.2d 489, 95 S. Ct. 1903 (1975). For a comprehensive review of the state of the law when this case was pending in the Supreme Court, see O'Keefe & Shapiro, "Personal Criminal Liability Under the Federal Food, Drug, and Cosmetic Act: The *Dotterweich* Doctrine," 30 *Food Drug Cosm. L.J.* 5–78 (1975). For comment on the Supreme Court decision, see O'Keefe & Isley, "*Dotterweich* Revisited—Criminal Liability Under the Federal Food, Drug, and Cosmetic Act," 31 *Food Drug Cosm. L.J.* 69–80 (1976).

11. 421 U.S. 658, 662.

12. *Id.,* 658, 663.

13. *Id.,* 658, 664–665.

14. *Id.,* 658, 672.

15. *Id.,* 658, 677–678.

16. See articles cited in notes 9 and 10. See also Friedlander, "Prosecution of Corporate Officials Under the Federal Food, Drug, and Cosmetic Act," 37 *Ohio St. L.J.* 431–450 (1976); Pepperman, "The Standard for Criminal Responsibility Under the Federal Food, Drug, and Cosmetic Act," 13 *Am. Crim. L. Rev.* 299–316 (1975); Sethi & Katz, "The Expanding Scope of Personal Criminal Liability of Corporate Executives—Some Implications of United States v. Park," 32 *Food Drug Cosm. L.J.* 544–570 (1977); Kent, "Civil and Criminal Liability of Engineering Executives," *Chem. Eng. Prog.,* Vol. 74,

No. 3, March 1978, pp. 11–16; "The Law Closes In on Managers," *Bus. Week*, May 10, 1976, pp. 111–116 at 113–114. **113**

*The Manager and Health and Safety: Product Standards and the Environment*

17. 421 U.S. 658, 672.

18. 21 U.S.C. § 333.

19. O'Keefe & Shapiro, 30 *Food Drug Cosm. L.J.* 5–78 at 33–38 and 50–78 (1970) (language of numerous statutes in the field analyzed in detail). See also Kent, *Chem. Eng. Prog.*, March 1978, pp. 11–16 at 13–14.

20. 421 U.S. 658, 673.

21. 376 U.S. 86, 11 L. Ed.2d 536, 84 S. Ct. 559 (1964).

22. United States v. Y. Hata & Co., 535 F.2d 508 (9th Cir. 1976), *cert. denied*, 429 U.S. 828, (1976).

23. United States v. Starr, 535 F.2d 512 (9th Cir. 1976).

24. "Nothing in the modern enforcement history of the food and drug laws has stirred so widespread, so impassioned and so inconclusive, if not pointless, debate among lawyers and businessmen alike, as has the Supreme Court's decision in *United States v. Park*." Hoffman, "Enforcement Trends Under the Federal Food, Drug and Cosmetic Act—A View From Outside," 31 *Food Drug Cosm. L.J.* 338, 343 (1976).

25. S. 2755, 95th Cong., 2d Sess. (1978); H.R. 11611, 95th Cong., 2d Sess. (1978).

26. S. 1075, 96th Cong., 1st Sess. (1979). The possibilities of passage are rated very high in "A Drug Bill Congress May Buy," *Bus. Week*, Aug. 13, 1979, p. 29. In October 1979, this bill passed the Senate by a voice vote. At press time it was still pending in the House of Representatives.

27. *Id.*, § 105.

28. *Id.*

29. O'Reilly, "First the Good News: You're Not Going to Jail . . . ," 33 *Food Drug Cosm. L.J.* 482–487 (1978); "Power to Prosecute Drug Concern Aides Would Be Cut by Carter Bill, Says FTC," *Wall St. J.*, May 19, 1978, p. 13.

30. S. 1075, § 107.

31. 21 U.S.C. § 335.

32. United States v. Commercial Creamery Company, 43 F. Supp. 714 (D.C. Wash. 1942); United States v. Dotterweich, 320 U.S. 277 (1943). For a full discussion of this procedure, see Pfeifer, "Section 305 Hearings and Criminal Prosecutions," and McMurray, "Section 305 Hearings—Defense Considerations," 31 *Food Drug Cosm. L.J.* 376–385 & 386–392 (1976).

33. Hoffman, 31 *Food Drug Cosm. L.J.* 338, 343 (1976).

34. Fine, "The Philosophy of Enforcement," and McConachie, "The Role of the Department of Justice in Enforcing the Federal Food, Drug, and Cosmetic Act," 31 *Food Drug Cosm. L.J.* 324–332 & 333–337 (1976); Pfeifer, 31 *Food Drug Cosm. L.J.* 376 (1976).

35. See, for example, *N.Y. Cons. Public Laws Health Ann.*, § 1200 (McKinney) (origin, 1909); *Mich. Comp. Laws*, §§ 323.1–323.13 (origin, 1929); *Calif. Ann. Fish & Game Codes*, § 5650 (West) (origin 1933).

36. P.L. 80-845; 62 Stat. 1155. I have discussed the evolution of federal environ-

mental laws in "The CPI and the Law: 40 years back, 40 years ahead," *Chem. Eng. Prog.*, Vol. 74, No. 7, July 1978, pp. 17–20 at 18–19.

37. P.L. 84-660; 70 Stat. 498. P.L. 87-88; 75 Stat. 204.

38. P.L. 84-159; 69 Stat. 322.

39. P.L. 88-206; 77 Stat. 392.

40. See, for example, *Mich. Comp. Laws*, § 336.11–36.

41. P.L. 89-234; 79 Stat. 903.

42. P.L. 89-272; 79 Stat. 992.

43. P.L. 90-148; 81 Stat. 485.

44. P.L. 91-190; 83 Stat. 852; 42 U.S.C. §§ 4321–4361.

45. P.L. 91-604; 84 Stat. 676. The Clean Air Act in its present form is compiled at 42 U.S.C. §§ 7401–7626. Also enacted in 1970 was the Resource Recovery Act, which amended and continued the program begun under the Solid Waste Disposal Act. P.L. 91-512; 84 Stat. 1227; *extended further in* 1973, P.L. 93-14; 87 Stat. 11. For summaries of the substantive provisions of the Clean Air Act and the Solid Waste Disposal Act, see Hancock, *Executive's Guide to Business Law* (McGraw-Hill Book Co., 1979) 51-1 to 51-12 and 53-1 to 53-3.

46. P.L. 92-500; 86 Stat. 816.

47. P.L. 95-217; 91 Stat. 1567–1675. The Water Pollution Control Act in its present form is compiled at 33 U.S.C. §§ 1251–1376. It is summarized in Hancock, *Executive's Guide to Business Law* 52-1 to 52-6.

48. P.L. 92-574; 86 Stat. 1234, 42 U.S.C. §§ 4901–4918.

49. P.L. 94-580; 90 Stat. 2795; 42 U.S.C. §§ 6901–6987.

50. Water Pollution Control Act, 33 U.S.C. § 1319; Clean Air Act, 42 U.S.C. § 7413; Noise Control Act, 42 U.S.C. § 4910; Resource Conservation and Recovery Act, 42 U.S.C. § 6928.

51. Water Pollution Control Act, *id.*, Clean Air Act, *id.*; Noise Control Act, 42 U.S.C. § 4912; Resource Conservation and Recovery Act, *id.*; and Criminal Code, 18 U.S.C. § 1001.

52. Iseman, "The Criminal Responsibility of Corporate Officials for Pollution of the Environment," 37 *Albany L. Rev.* 61–96 at 67 (1972).

53. Glenn, "The Crime of Pollution: The Role of Federal Water Pollution Control Sanctions," 11 *Am. Crim. L. Rev.* 835–882 at 881–882 (1973).

54. Water Pollution Control Act, 33 U.S.C. § 1319; Clean Air Act, 42 U.S.C. § 7413.

55. See Olds, Unkovic & Lewin, "Thoughts on the Role of Penalties in the Enforcement of the Clean Air and Clean Water Acts," 17 *Duquesne L. Rev.* 1–31 at 22–24 (1978–1979), in which the authors observe that express statutory designation of corporate officers as persons subject to criminal penalties is not a prerequisite to their liability under the air and water acts. No such phrase appears in the Food, Drug, and Cosmetic Act, under which *Dotterweich* and *Park* were decided.

See also Tennille, "Criminal Prosecution of Individuals: A New Trend in Federal Environmental Enforcement?" *Environmental Law*, Spring 1978, p. 3;

also published in *Environmental Enforcement* 20–22 at 21, (American Bar Association Standing Committee on Environmental Law, 1978):

> Although this term [any responsible corporate officer] has not yet been construed under either of these statutes [Clean Water Act and Clean Air Act], it is reasonable to predict that the enforcement authorities will seek to extend that term (as has been done in the food and drug area) to those officers with managerial responsibility over the activities in connection with which the violation took place, even where those officers were not active participants in the transaction under scrutiny.

56. 45 Fed. Reg. No. 116, 33290, 33425 (May 19, 1980); 40 C.F.R. § 122.6.

57. *Id.,* at 34273.

58. 33 U.S.C. § 1321(b)(5). If the report reveals a discharge in violation of the statute, the use of the report to support a *civil,* as distinguished from a *criminal,* penalty against the person reporting does not constitute self-incrimination in violation of the Fifth Amendment. United States v. Ward, ___ U.S. ___, 65 L.Ed.2d 742, 100 S. Ct. ___ (1980). That case involved a sole proprietor, rather than a corporate manager.

59. 33 U.S.C. § 1321.

60. Water Pollution Control Act, 33 U.S.C. § 1367; Clean Air Act, 42 U.S.C. § 7622; Resource Conservation and Recovery Act, 42 U.S.C. § 6971.

61. 33 U.S.C. § 1321.

62. Water Pollution Control Act, 33 U.S.C. § 1319 ($10,000 a day); Clean Air Act, 42 U.S.C. § 7413 ($25,000 a day).

63. Marshall, "Environmental Protection and the Role of the Civil Money Penalty: Some Practical and Legal Conclusions," 4 *Environmental Affairs* 323–366 (1975). Marshall does not agree with the conclusion of some writers that pollution has reached the stage of a crime because it is morally wrong. He adheres to the view that pollution "is a crime merely because it has been declared unlawful." He concludes that the civil penalty against the corporation is the best means of abating pollution. He does not favor sanctions against individuals, as he believes there are too many problems in finding the person "ultimately responsible for the violation."

64. Olds, Unkovic & Lewin, 17 *Duquesne L. Rev.* 1–31 at 30.

65. Water Pollution Control Act, 33 U.S.C. § 1319; Clean Air Act, 42 U.S.C. § 7413; Resource Conservation and Recovery Act, 42 U.S.C. § 6928.

66. Moorman, "Criminal Enforcement of the Pollution Control Laws," *Environmental Enforcement* 25–28, American Bar Association Standing Committee on Environmental Law (American Bar Association, 1978).

Jeffrey G. Miller, Deputy Assistant Administrator for Water Enforcement of the EPA, addressing the environmental regulation course sponsored by Executive Enterprise, Inc., on September 26–28, 1978, stated that EPA and the Department of Justice are giving renewed and careful emphasis to criminal indictments in appropriate cases, particularly where responsible officers are indictable. He stated that the most likely targets are false reports, concealing information, deliberate disregard of specific regulatory requirements, and corporatewide patterns of conduct amounting to calculated disregard of regulatory requirements. Current practices in criminal enforcement of environmental laws against managers are discussed in the report of a program of the Committee on Environmental Controls, Section of Corporation, Banking & Business Law, American Bar Association, "Air and Water Enforcement Problems—A Case Study," 34 *Bus. Law.* 665–723 at 704–712 (1979).

67. Water Pollution Control Act, 33 U.S.C. § 1365; Clean Air Act, 42 U.S.C. § 7604; Noise Control Act, 42 U.S.C. § 4911, Resource Conservation and Recovery Act, 42 U.S.C. § 6972.

68. Herring v. H.M. Walker Co., 409 Pa. 126, 185 A.2d 565 (1962). See "The Shareholder's Derivative Suit—A Solution to the Pollution Problem?" 5 *Valparaiso U.L. Rev.* 149–171 (1970); also Laughran, "The Law and the Corporate Polluter: Flexibility and Adaptation in the Developing Law of the Environment," 23 *Mercer L. Rev.* 571–601 (1972).

69. 36 Stat. 331.

70. P.L. 80-104; 61 Stat. 163; in amendment and compiled form before enactment of the Pesticide Act of 1972, 7 U.S.C. § 135–135k.

71. P.L. 88-305; 78 Stat. 190.

72. P.L. 92-516, 86 Stat. 975, 7 U.S.C. § 136–136w.

73. 7 U.S.C. § 1361.

74. *Id.*

75. P.L. 69-783; 44 Stat. 1406.

76. P.L. 83-88; 67 Stat. 111; 15 U.S.C. §§ 1191–1204.

77. P.L. 84-930; 70 Stat. 953; 15 U.S.C. §§ 1211–1214.

78. P.L. 86-613; 74 Stat. 372; 15 U.S.C. §§ 1261–1274. For a detailed discussion of this Act, see Scriba, "The Federal Hazardous Substances Labeling Act," 17 *Bus. Law.* 137–156 (1961).

79. P.L. 92-573; 86 Stat. 1207; 15 U.S.C. §§ 2051–2081. This Act is summarized in Hancock, *Executive's Guide to Business Law* 44-1 to 44-19.

80. 15 U.S.C. § 2069(2)(c).

81. 15 U.S.C. § 2070(b).

82. 16 C.F.R. § 1115.13.

83. P.L. 93-383, 88 Stat. 700; 42 U.S.C. §§ 5401–5426.

84. P.L. 89-272; 79 Stat. 992. In its present amended form, the law regulating motor vehicles is compiled at 42 U.S.C. §§ 7521–7551.

85. P.L. 89-563; 80 Stat. 718. In its present amended form, the Traffic and Motor Vehicle Safety Act is compiled at 15 U.S.C. §§ 1381–1431.

86. P.L. 92-513; 86 Stat. 947. In its amended form, this Act is compiled at 15 U.S.C. §§ 1901–1991.

87. 15 U.S.C. §§ 1911–1922.

88. 15 U.S.C. §§ 1981–1991.

89. P.L. 94-163; 89 Stat. 901. In its present amended form, Title V is compiled at 15 U.S.C. §§ 2001–2012, as part of the Motor Vehicle Information and Cost Saving Act.

90. P.L. 94-469; 90 Stat. 2003; 15 U.S.C. §§ 2601–2629. For general overviews of the provisions of TSCA, see Zener, "The Toxic Substances Control Act:

Federal Regulation of Commercial Chemicals," 32 *Bus. Law.* 1685–1703 (1977); Groening, *Chem. Eng. Prog.*, Vol. 74, No. 7, pp. 17–20 at 19 (1978); Hancock, *Executive's Guide to Business Law* 54-1 to 54-6.

**91.** 15 U.S.C. § 2615.

**92.** 15 U.S.C. § 2607.

**93.** 43 Fed. Reg. 11110, (March 16, 1978).

**94.** 15 U.S.C. § 2622.

**95.** H.R. 4973, 96th Cong., 1st Sess. (1979). A similar provision appears in H.R. 7010, 96th Cong., 2nd Sess. (1980).

# CHAPTER SEVEN

# The Manager, Employee Relations, and the Law

$P$rior to 1935 the role of the federal government in the field of relations between employer and employee was relatively unimportant. There were a few exceptions, such as the Railway Labor Act of 1926,[1] which guaranteed the rights of railroad employees to organize and to bargain collectively. The union movement was on the ascendancy in the early thirties, and the hardships of the Depression gave it considerable impetus. Union leaders felt, however, that they could not be successful in their objective of collective bargaining without the protection of a law guaranteeing their equality with the employer. This need, coupled with the support that President Roosevelt and the Congress of that period received from organized labor resulted in the enactment of the National Labor Relations Act (NLRA)[2] in 1935. The federal government now assumed a major role in labor-management relations in manufacturing companies. This legislation was followed soon by federal laws pertaining to wages and hours and the employment of minors, and later, to such fields as employee safety, discrimination on account of race, sex, age, or handicap, and regulation of employee pension plans. In most of these fields, except in wages, hours, employment of minors, and the regulation of pension plans, the exposure of corporate managers to sanctions has been relatively low. The enforcement agencies have pursued more effective remedies against the corporations rather than against the individuals who manage them. There are, however, a few instances of sanctions against managers.

## THE NATIONAL LABOR RELATIONS ACT

The National Labor Relations Act was hailed as the charter of liberties for the American worker and was simultaneously damned as an unwarranted interference with the right of management to manage. It guaranteed the right of employees to organize and to join labor unions without interference from management and required employers to bargain with unions of their employees. It coincided with the beginning of the era of large industrial unions, sometimes marked with violence, often with acrimony, frequently with a polarization of positions. Finally, there came the recognition that labor and management must sit down and resolve their differences at the bargaining table. Hearings before the National Labor Relations Board (NLRB) were frequent. Few major employers escaped them. Disestablishment of company-dominated unions, back pay for workers unlawfully discharged, supervision of elections to determine the bargaining agents, and orders to bargain with such agents were the frequent experience of employers during the thirties and the forties. In the late 1940s, the pendulum began to swing and the earlier posture of the NLRA, which was definitely pro-union, was modified by the Labor Management Relations Act of 1947, popularly called the Taft-Hartley Act.[3] Taft-Hartley retained the rights of labor to organize and bargain collectively but also placed certain limits upon union activity. Naturally, many, if not all, of these limits were opposed by organized labor as being antiunion in nature, but most of them have survived the ensuing decades. While there is not unanimity of opinion on the legislation, the National Labor Relations Act, as amended by the Taft-Hartley Act, is generally regarded as providing a reasonably balanced code of law to govern the relationship between employer and labor.

Because managers, as well as the rank and file, are corporate employees, it was natural that the question should arise as to the scope of coverage of the NLRA with regard to different levels of employees. There was never any uncertainty with regard to top levels of management. They were never given any protection under the NLRA. Unionization of managerial personnel does not exist in American companies, although it is found in some European companies. A problem did arise, however, with regard to lower-ranking managerial employees, such as foremen. Often they are former hourly employees promoted to supervisor rank. In some instances, unions have permitted them to retain their union membership. This has in times of stress given rise to conflicts of interest, such as when the foreman is charged with enforcement of a company policy that is unpopular with the rank-and-file union members. This has resulted in efforts by unions to discipline foremen by exacting fines from them for action contrary to the best interests of the union. While there is very little in the line of decided cases on the subject, it is now generally accepted that a union may not discipline a foreman for carrying out company policies.[4]

Interestingly enough, the matter of coverage of managerial employees by the National Labor Relations Act was not determined by the United States Supreme Court until forty years after the passage of the Act. In making that decision in 1975 in *National Labor Relations Board v. Bell Aerospace Company,*[5] the Court stated that the Congress, in enacting the

NLRA, as well as the 1947 amendments, was concerned with protecting the welfare of the common workers and not the welfare of those representing management's interests. Although the NLRA contains no specific exclusion of managerial or supervisory employees from its definition of "employee," there had been a long history of NLRB action (often affirmed by courts of appeal) in excluding managerial employees from the scope of the Act. In 1970, however, its effort to exclude them was overruled by the Court of Appeals for the Eighth Circuit.[6] In the Supreme Court's review of the history of the question, it was pointed out that in enacting the Taft-Hartley Act, the Congress had taken note of the NLRB practice and determined that it was not necessary to amend the definition to exclude managerial or supervisory employees from the protection of the Act. The Supreme Court, looking at this early history of administrative action, combined with frequent court of appeals affirmance and congressional acquiescence (when it amended the Act in 1947 and 1959), vacated the Eighth Circuit's decision and concluded that managerial employees are not covered by the Act.

Penal sanctions against managers in the area of labor-management relations are rather rare. It is not a federal crime for a manager to interfere with the right of employees to organize or to refuse to bargain. The remedy is administrative. There is a hearing before the NLRB and the sanctions imposed by the Board, such as disestablishment of a company-dominated union, back pay, and orders to bargain, are remedial in nature. There can be sanctions against the corporation for failure to obey. The only criminal penalty is a $5,000 fine or a year in prison, or both, against any person who willfully resists, prevents, impedes, or interferes with any member of the NLRB or any of its agents in performing their duties under the Act.[7] There are no published cases of individuals having been prosecuted for such action.

While criminal penalties are rare in the case of NLRB violations, there is one aspect of labor relations where corporate managers as well as union officials have been subjected to fines and imprisonment: The Taft-Hartley Act made it unlawful for an employer or its representative to make a payment of money or any "other thing of value" to a representative of employees.[8] Under this prohibition, a nonunion contractor's general manager and its labor relations advisor were prosecuted and convicted for unlawfully paying money for bogus union cards used to enable the corporation to obtain a construction subcontract with a unionized prime contractor. The payments were made in the mistaken belief that the payee was a union representative when in fact he was not, but the conviction was upheld because the individuals intended to pay off a union representative.[9]

The question of what constitutes a "thing of value" came up a few years ago in a case where a vending machine company's president and another high-ranking supervisor arranged, and provided the funds, for a finance company to grant interest-free loans to the secretary-treasurer of the union representing the vending machine company's employees. The court held that it was a proper question for the jury to determine whether an interest-free loan was a thing of value. The jury found both corporate managers and the union officer guilty of violating the statute. They were fined an aggregate of $24,000 and all three received jail sentences varying from two to six months. Subsequent to the violation, the statute was amended specifically to cover loans.[10]

The intent of the statutory prohibition is, of course, to prevent a conflict of interest and to keep both management and labor representatives honest in their dealings with one another, thereby affording protection to the rank-and-file employee.

## WAGE AND HOUR LEGISLATION

The National Labor Relations Act was one of the most significant laws passed by the Congress during the early days of the New Deal. It was followed three years later by the Fair Labor Standards Act (FLSA),[11] which established for the first time a minimum wage for employees and required premium payments for overtime. The FLSA also placed restrictions upon the employment of minors. This Act has been amended many times, primarily to keep the minimum wage updated in tune with the declining purchasing power of the dollar.

Unlike the NLRA, the FLSA does contain strong criminal sanctions, which have been invoked on various occasions against corporate managers. The Act imposes a fine of $10,000 on any person violating its provisions. For a second or later offense, a prison sentence not to exceed six months may be imposed in lieu of, or in addition to, a fine. There is also a civil penalty of $1,000 for each child-labor violation.[12]

Although the reported cases of penalties against corporate managers are not numerous, there are enough to give a picture of how the Act is enforced against them. In an early case, a corporation, its general manager, and two other officers were indicted for violation of the minimum wage requirement. The jury acquitted the individual defendants but convicted the corporation. The corporation appealed on the ground that the verdict was inconsistent, but the conviction was upheld on the basis that there was evidence of violation by the corporation even though the jury was not satisfied that the individuals who were indicted had participated in it.[13]

In a case brought against a corporation, its division operations manager, and a branch manager, the question was presented of whether failure to pay the minimum wage or required overtime to a group of employees constituted a separate violation for each employee. The United States Supreme Court ruled that the Act forbade a "course of action" and that the District Court was correct in amending the indictment to cover only three offenses—failure to pay the minimum wage, failure to pay required overtime, and failure to keep proper records.[14]

The converse of the conviction of the corporation and acquittal of its officers was presented in a 1969 decision where a bankrupt corporation was acquitted, but the president was convicted. It was shown that he had run the corporation and its subsidiaries without particular regard for separate corporate identity and that he was, for all practical purposes, the "employer."[15]

In addition to the criminal and civil penalties for violating the FLSA, there are also provisions for injunctions against further violations. If the injunction is violated, the corporate manager causing the violation may be imprisoned for contempt of court. In *United States v. Fidanian*,[16] a corporate president claimed he could not be imprisoned for failure to pay back wages as required by a consent decree of the previous year, on the ground that the nonpayment was a first offense and imprisonment for violation of the Act was only for a second or subsequent offense. The court held, however, that he was not being imprisoned for a violation of the Act, but for contempt of court, to which the statutory requirement of second offense did not apply.

In addition to the Fair Labor Standards Act, there are state laws governing the payment of wages or contracted benefits and regulating the hours of work. For their violation, convictions of corporate managers ranging from factory superintendent to president have been upheld.[17] The imposition of prison sentences upon managers for failure to pay wages has in recent years raised constitutional questions. In Rhode Island, it was contended unsuccessfully that such a penalty was contrary to the state constitutional prohibition against imprisonment for debt. The Rhode Island Supreme Court held that the public benefit resulting from the prompt payment of labor overrode the constitutional prohibition.[18] In Virginia, however, a similar statute was held in violation of the Fourteenth Amendment guarantee of equal protection under the laws because it did not make an exception for insolvency.[19]

## EMPLOYEE SAFETY

Although the federal government was concerned from the 1930s with the rights of employees to organize and bargain collectively and with standards of wages and hours, it left the field of employee safety to state regulation until three decades later.

The first federal statutes in the employee safety field were concerned with mining, which is considered to be one of the most hazardous occupations. The Metal and Nonmetallic Mine Safety Act[20] was passed in 1966, followed by the Coal Mine Health and Safety Act[21] in 1969. The two were merged into the Mine Safety and Health Act[22] in 1977.

In 1970, the Congress, responding to what it termed "a worsening trend" in the number of disabling injuries in proportion to hours worked, enacted a comprehensive law on employee safety known as the Occupational Safety and Health Act (OSHA).[23] OSHA sets forth duties of employer and employee. For the employer, the duties are: (1) to provide a place of employment free of recognized hazards that are causing, or are likely to cause, death or serious physical harm to employees; and (2) to comply with the occupational safety and health standards promulgated under the Act. For the employee, the duty is also to comply with the standards and all rules, regulations, and orders issued under the Act that are applicable to her or his own actions and conduct.

A violation of OSHA subjects an employer to a fine of up to $10,000 and imprisonment up to six months. For a second offense, the fine is $20,000 and the prison term one year.[24] The statute says, specifically, that the penalty is upon the *employer* who violates. It does not use the word "person," as do many other federal penal provisions, nor does it specify any penalties for officers or other managers or agents of the employer. It appears, then, that the prison sentences provided in OSHA are applicable only to sole proprietors.

The impact of OSHA upon corporate managers has been discussed in only a few cases. In *Skidmore v. Travelers Insurance Co.*,[25] a civil action was brought by an injured employee against a corporate manager for injuries resulting from an alleged violation of OSHA standards. The action was dismissed on two grounds: (1) that OSHA does not create any private rights of action and (2) that Congress did not intend "to create a duty on other employees of the same employer (even though they are executives)." The ruling of the district judge was upheld by the Court of Appeals for the Fifth Circuit.

The next year, however, the same district judge in another case stated that in *Skidmore* he had overlooked the fact that Section 5(b) of the Act also placed a duty on employees, and to the extent that his decision in that case rested upon a lack of duty by employees, he was disavowing it as erroneous.[26] A year later, however, the Fifth Circuit reaffirmed the ruling of *Skidmore* that OSHA does not give a "private right by an employee against an executive officer of the employer."[27]

The few cases on the subject of executive responsibility under OSHA leave the subject slightly in the air. Since the terms of the penal sanctions apply only to the employer, and since the few decisions affirm that there is no private right of action under OSHA, it is difficult to see how a corporate manager can have any liability, criminal or civil, for violation under OSHA itself. It is conceivable, however, that there might be an instance of a manager's so dominating an operation that he or she might be considered the "employer" under the statute.

While the exact language of OSHA may preclude personal liability of a corporate manager under its terms, it does not follow that the government is without any remedy against a corporate manager in case of a willful violation by the corporation. Under the terms of the Criminal Code, a manager could be indicted as one who "aids, abets, counsels, commands, or procures" another's commission of the criminal act or as one who "willfully causes an act to be done which if directly performed by him . . . would be an offense against the United States."[28]

In contrast, the Mine Safety and Health Act, like the two preceding statutes that were merged into it, provides specifically that:

Whenever a corporate operator violates a standard or . . . order, . . . , any
director, officer or agent of such corporation who knowingly authorized,
ordered or carried out such violation . . . shall be subject to the same civil
penalties, fines and imprisonment that may be imposed upon a person
under subsections (a) and (d) of this section.[29]

The subsections mentioned above impose a $10,000 civil penalty for each
violation, as well as a fine up to $25,000 or imprisonment up to one year,
or both, for a first offense. For a subsequent offense, the maximum fine is
$50,000 and the maximum prison term is five years.[30]

The more severe penalties and harsher treatment of managers under
the Mine Safety and Health Act as compared with the Occupational
Safety and Health Act remain unexplained.

## DISCRIMINATION IN EMPLOYMENT

The two areas of greatest social concern in recent decades have been civil
rights and the environment. Both have resulted in a vast body of new
federal law and regulations. The impact of these two bodies of law upon
corporate managers has, however, been quite different. In both instances, new and important obligations have been placed upon corporations, and their managers have the duty to make certain that they comply. In the case of the environmental statutes, managers face personal
penalties for noncompliance, but in the civil rights field, the penalties
imposed upon corporate managers have been relatively light. In this
respect, the statutes resemble the National Labor Relations Act and the
Occupational Safety and Health Act. There appears to be a congressional
pattern of not imposing heavy penalties upon corporate managers in
matters relating to employee relations (except in certain special situations that have been discussed in this chapter). Rather, the Congress
provides in most situations that the remedy shall be exclusively against
the employer itself.

The concept of civil rights, as the term is used today, hinges on race
relations, the guarantees to all citizens of the rights afforded them under
the federal Constitution. Since this book is not a treatise on constitutional law, we will not attempt to examine these rights. It is sufficient to
say that concepts of civil rights have led to legislation in many areas
concerned with equality of opportunity—in education, voting, public
accommodations, employment, and other phases of life in late
twentieth-century America. In this chapter we are concerned only with
the relationship of employer and employee. Federal law now guarantees
equal employment opportunity. It prohibits discrimination in employment on account of race, sex, age, or physical handicap.[31] So we are
concerned here with eliminating discrimination in employment, a concept that originated with the civil rights movement but has gone considerably beyond it.

The civil rights activists of a decade ago really were not concerned about compulsory retirement at age sixty-five, and perhaps it is not a civil rights problem. If it is, perhaps highly paid executives are being deprived of their civil rights, for their companies are free to compel their retirement at sixty-five while keeping lower-ranking employees on the payroll until age seventy.[32]

Examination of the Equal Opportunity Employment sections of the Civil Rights Act of 1964 reveals no sanctions on corporate managers for failure to comply, although the sanctions against offending corporations themselves can be enormous.[33] The Age Discrimination in Employment Act, however, contains penalties for interfering with a duly authorized representative of the Equal Opportunity Commission in the performance of duties under the Act.[34] This provision appears to have been borrowed from the National Labor Relations Act, but the penalties are somewhat less severe. They are applicable to corporate managers, although there are no reported cases on the subject.

There are, however, some possible exposures of corporate managers to personal liability for civil rights violations. Although it is not an employment case, the directors of a community swimming pool association were held personally liable for compensatory damages and for attorneys' fees for having denied membership in the association to a black couple and guest privileges to the black guest of a white member. The action was brought under the Civil Rights Act of 1866, which guarantees all citizens the rights to purchase and hold real property.[35]

The only employment discrimination case involving corporate managers is *Great American Federal Savings & Loan Association v. Novotny*,[36] decided by the United States Supreme Court in 1979. This was not a case of a woman or a minority person suing the management, but an action by a former manager against other members of management. A corporate officer and director had a serious disagreement with his colleagues in which he accused them of intentionally denying female employees equal employment opportunity. He was dismissed from his position, and he then sued the corporation and its directors for a conspiracy to deprive him equal protection of, and equal privileges and immunities under, the Civil Rights Act of 1871.[37] The Court of Appeals held that he had standing to sue.[38] The Supreme Court held, however, that the Civil Rights Act of 1871 was purely remedial in nature and conferred no substantive rights. Substantive rights to equal opportunity employment were conferred by Title VII of the Civil Rights Act of 1964. That title contains its own plan of administrative remedies and judicial process which a complainant must follow, and the complainant was directed to seek that route.

Because the Equal Employment Opportunity Act does not provide for sanctions against managers and the Supreme Court has denied a remedy under the Civil Rights Act of 1871, it would appear that there is no risk of personal liability of corporate managers in employment discrimination cases.

Perhaps the most important piece of federal legislation in the employee relations field from the viewpoint of impact upon the liabilities of corporate managers is the Employee Retirement Income Security Act of 1974, also known as the Pension Reform Act, but popularly and conveniently identified by its acronym, ERISA.[39] This Act also has an impact upon managers in other than liability areas because of limitations placed upon their own participation in pension plans.

The federal law governing employee pension plans had its origin in the Internal Revenue Act of 1928, which provided special tax treatment for a trust to fund retirement benefits for employees. The income of such a trust would be exempt from federal income taxation, and the employer could make annual contributions and claim them as business expenses for federal income tax purposes.[40] A retirement plan had to be "qualified" under the Internal Revenue Code by filing with the Internal Revenue Service a copy of the plan, together with collateral information concerning the plan and its participants as required by the Code and the regulations thereunder. Certain requirements had to be met to make certain, among other things, that the plan did not discrimatorily favor highly compensated employees, that the funds were not diverted to purposes other than payment of benefits to the participants and their beneficiaries, and that contributions to the plan were made within established actuarial limits.

As many pension plans were the result of collective bargaining, pension funds were administered sometimes jointly by the employer and the union, sometimes by the employer alone, and sometimes by the union alone. Abuses of pension funds did occur in some instances, and in an effort to bring the operations of the funds more into the open, the Congress enacted the Welfare and Pension Plan Disclosure Act of 1958.[41] Amendments to that Act in 1962 made theft, bribery, and kickbacks associated with employee welfare and pension plans federal crimes. The management and investment of pension funds were left to state law, with the standards, of course, varying from state to state. Prohibited transactions under the federal law would result in disqualification of the plan, so that it would lose its tax-exempt status.[42]

The Welfare and Pension Plan Disclosure Act did not end all the abuses and inequities. There is, of course, a difference of opinion as to how extensive the abuses and inequities were. One writer stated in 1975:

> [T]he scores of case histories studied by Congress in the early 1970's revealed an *overwhelming tendency* to operate pension plans in an overtly unconscionable manner.[43] [Emphasis supplied.]

On the other hand, William J. Kilberg, then Solicitor of the Department of Labor, in the same year stated the problem in a more restrained manner:

We have always recognized that *most* plans are reasonably well managed, that *most* funds are prudently invested, and that *most* people involved with funds, whether managing them or dealing with them, are both honest and conscientious. And yet the number of plans is exceedingly large, over a million and three-quarters. That's a very big universe and it has its share of both cupidity and ignorance.[44] [Emphasis supplied.]

Still other writers commented upon the circumstances that led to ERISA in this manner:

The new pension legislation has been hailed as both reform and revolution. It also has elements that suggest a quality not unlike biblical atonement or revenge. Succeeding generations must now atone for the sins of a *small percentage* of fiduciaries.[45] [Emphasis supplied.]

While it might be argued that there was overkill in the enactment of ERISA, there was probably no more overkill than inheres in many other statutes enacted to remedy the faults of a few. There are always many ethical and responsible business people who find themselves confronted with troublesome rules that they believe go further than necessary to eradicate the unethical and irresponsible actions of others. Be that as it may, the Congress spent seven years laboring over the problem, devoting extensive study, hearings, and debate to the subject before ERISA was finally enacted.

ERISA is a formidable act purely on the basis of size and complexity, if no other. It contains 138 sections and is 180 pages long. It is not practical to analyze all its provisions here. A few words on its scope will give the general picture. It provides for administration of some portions by the Internal Revenue Service, the traditional department where pension plans have been overseen since 1928, but oversight and enforcement of most of the new provisions are vested in the Department of Labor. It contains extensive requirements for reporting and disclosure and imposes minimum participation standards, minimum vesting standards, and beneficiary standards. It requires compulsory termination insurance, sets up minimum funding standards, and places limits upon benefits to, and contributions based upon the earnings of, highly compensated employees. It establishes standards of fiduciary responsibility, including investment of funds, and regulation, and in some instances outright prohibition, of certain transactions by fiduciaries. It imposes special taxes and criminal penalties upon those who breach its prohibited acts.

The personal impact of ERISA upon corporate managers is found in two areas: (1) limitation of benefits and contributions and (2) fiduciary responsibility.

## Executive Limitations

Before proceeding to a discussion of the limitations on executive benefits under ERISA, we should recognize that there are two different basic types of pension plans, that they are defined in ERISA, and that recogni-

tion of the difference between them is important to an understanding of
the limitations upon executive benefits. The difference between these
two types of pension plans is also important to an understanding of the
fiduciary obligations under ERISA, which we shall discuss shortly.

The two types of plans are the "defined contribution plan" (also called
the "individual account plan") and the "defined benefit plan." In the
defined contribution plan, the employer contributes a stated amount to
the account of each employee participating in the plan, and the employee's benefits are derived solely from the amount contributed to his or
her account, plus or minus any income, expenses, gains, and losses, and
any forfeitures from the accounts of others that may be allocated to the
employee's account. A defined benefit plan is a pension plan that is not a
defined contribution plan.[46] There is no individual account of the employee, but the plan provides for a pension based upon a formula, which
is generally a composite of earnings during the period of employment (or
a stated portion of them), years of service, age at retirement, and other
relevant factors, all of which are spelled out in the plan and will vary
widely from plan to plan.

Prior to ERISA, there were no limitations on benefits to highly compensated employees except the requirement that a plan could not dis-
criminatorily favor them. ERISA has, however, placed an upper limit on
individual benefits under a defined benefit plan and an upper limit on
contributions to the account of an individual under a defined contribution plan.[47]

The basic maximum annual benefit payable to any one participant
under a defined benefit plan is the lesser of $75,000 or 100 percent of the
participant's average annual compensation for the three consecutive
calendar years in which such a person actively participated in the plan
and had his or her highest aggregate compensation from the employer.
The $75,000 limitation is adjusted annually in proportion to increases in
the cost of living above the last calendar quarter of 1974. In a situation
where the limitation of 100 percent of compensation is applicable, there
is an annual adjustment to reflect the increases in cost of living above that
of the last calendar quarter of the year before the year of the participant's
retirement. The basic maximums are also subject to adjustments downward in the event of retirement before age fifty-five or before completion
of ten years of service with the employer.

In the case of a defined contribution plan, the maximum amount that
can be credited in any one year is the lesser of $25,000 or 25 percent of
the participant's compensation for the year. There is no defined limit on
the benefits that may be paid from this contribution. The limit is, of
course, a result of the size of the annual contributions and the gains or
losses attributed to them during the period they remain in the plan's
trust for the participant's account. The $25,000 limitation is, like the
limitation on defined benefits, adjusted upward to reflect increases in
the cost of living.

As an employer may possibly have both a defined benefit plan and a defined contribution plan, ERISA has, by formula which need not be analyzed here, provided a mechanism to prevent evasion of the limits by having the two types of plans. On the other side of the coin, ERISA has made certain that the new limitations do not result in forfeiture of benefits accrued to participants and contributions made to their accounts before the enactment of ERISA. Accordingly, there is a "grandfather clause" that preserves the benefits accrued and the amounts contributed prior to the enactment of ERISA.[48]

## The Manager as a Fiduciary Under ERISA

The most important consideration motivating the Congress in enacting ERISA was preservation of the integrity of pension funds. Congress wanted to make certain that employees would actually receive the retirement benefits that were promised them by the one and three-quarter million pension plans then in existence. For this reason, they imposed vesting standards, participation standards, and beneficiary standards, and required all pension plans to be insured to protect employees against losses in the event of plan termination. That was not all, however, for Congress wanted to make certain that pension funds were properly administered; therefore ERISA established new and far-reaching rules for administration of funds. It used the words "fiduciary" and "prudent man" (with which we became acquainted in Chapter 3) and gave them new and enlarged definitions.

Corporate managers, professional trustees, investment advisors, and all others who had been associated with the establishment and management of pension plans suddenly found themselves seized with a fear of the unknown. They visualized that from now on they would proceed at their peril—that the slightest misstep would make them targets for criminal indictments and civil lawsuits, with judgments in figures that would spell personal economic ruin. The experience of six years with ERISA has, however, caused most of these fears to subside. That is not to say, however, that there are no risks of criminal or civil liability under ERISA, for indeed such risks do exist.

Careful analysis by lawyers, accountants, and other professionals working in the field has shown that there are reasonably safe ways of operating under ERISA. Certainly, close attention must be paid to all the requirements of the Act. There can be no cutting of corners. It is not a field for amateurs to dabble in. There will, no doubt, be lawsuits brought against careful, as well as careless, operators, but it is not likely that rules of absolute liability will be imposed. Over the years, court decisions will gradually spell out the boundaries, and it can be expected that those who are conscientious and competent in their duties in the pension area will prevail.[49]

We discussed fiduciary concepts in Chapter 3 in connection with the internal obligations of directors and officers—their obligations to the stockholders of the corporation. Now we look at the obligations of direc-

tors and officers (and corporate managers below the director and officer
level) in a somewhat different type of fiduciary capacity—their obligations to the employees who are participants in corporate pension plans.

There are differences, of course, in the two types of relationships. The
stockholders own the corporation. The managers are working for them.
They are administering the corporate assets, which ultimately belong to
the stockholders. This is a responsibility a person assumes by reason of
becoming a director, an officer, or other manager. The employees, on the
other hand, do not own the corporation, and so there is a different type
of relationship.

There is no legal requirement that a corporation have a pension plan,
but once it elects to have one—whether by its own unilateral action or by
collective bargaining with a labor organization—it then comes under the
requirements of ERISA. Certain assets of the corporation are set aside for
the benefit of employees in the form of contributions to a qualified
pension plan. A new fiduciary relationship comes into being at that
moment. The assets so contributed no longer belong to the corporation.
They belong to the employees who are participants in the plan. The
fiduciary relationship is to them.

There was a fiduciary relationship under pension plans before ERISA.
What ERISA did was to bring that relationship out from the sometimes
fuzzy recesses of common law, to polarize the relationship by requiring a
"named fiduciary," and to state the rules under which the fiduciary must
operate.

For the first time, a federal statute has defined the duties of a fiduciary
under a pension plan:

> [A] fiduciary shall discharge his duties with respect to a plan solely in the
> interest of the participants and beneficiaries and—
>
> A. for the exclusive purpose of: (*i*) providing benefits to participants and
>    their beneficiaries; and
>    (*ii*) defraying reasonable expenses of administering the plan;
>
> B. with the care, skill, prudence and diligence under the circumstances then
>    prevailing that a prudent man acting in like capacity and familiar with
>    such matters would use in the conduct of an enterprise of a like character
>    and with like aims;
>
> C. by diversifying the investments of the plan so as to minimize the risk of
>    large losses, unless under the circumstances it is clearly prudent not to do
>    so; and
>
> D. in accordance with the documents and instruments governing the plan
>    insofar as such documents and instruments are consistent with the
>    provisions of this title.[50]

The Act then proceeds into certain details concerning such things as
limitations on the holding of employer securities and a list of prohibited

transactions between a plan and a party in interest, followed by a list of exemptions from prohibited transactions.[51] Finally, ERISA provides that a fiduciary breaching any of the responsibilities, obligations, or duties imposed upon fiduciaries shall be personally liable to restore to the plan any losses incurred by the plan as a result of the fiduciary's breaches, as well as any profits the fiduciary may have made through use of the assets of the plan.[52]

Much of the concern about the fiduciary standards of ERISA centered on the "prudent man" paragraph (B above). As stated earlier, the administration of pension trusts before ERISA was governed by state law, with the inevitable variations that exist from state to state. Generally speaking, however, the concept of the "prudent man" has long existed in the law of trusts in all the states. It is a common-law concept that says, in effect, that a trustee has the duty to exercise such care and skill as a person of ordinary prudence would exercise in dealing with his or her own property.[53] This is a considerably lower standard than that imposed by ERISA. The common-law concept is largely subjective. A person, even a prudent person, might take more chances with his or her own funds than should be taken with the funds of others. A court of one state might interpret the standard differently from the court of another state. It is these risks that ERISA's "prudent man" definition attempts to avoid. It places the responsibility on a professional basis by the use of such phrases as "like capacity," "familiar with such matters," and "enterprise of a like character and with like aims."

ERISA not only promulgates standards of fiduciary conduct, but it also prescribes who shall be a fiduciary within the meaning of the Act. The section of ERISA entitled "Definitions" lists and defines thirty-nine different words and phrases, but "fiduciary" is not among them.[54] One must look to the sections on fiduciary responsibility where the term "fiduciary" is introduced and, while not defined, is described in such a manner as to convey the broad meaning that the Congress obviously intended to give to the term. Here is the relevant provision:

> (1) Every employee benefit plan shall be established and maintained pursuant to a written instrument. Such instrument shall provide for one or more named fiduciaries who jointly or severally shall have the authority to control and manage the operation and administration of the plan.

> (2) For purposes of this title, the term "named fiduciary" means a fiduciary who is named in the plan instrument, or who, pursuant to a procedure specified in the plan, is identified as a fiduciary (A) by a person who is an employer or employee organization with respect to the plan or (B) by such an employer and such an employee organization acting jointly.[55]

The Act then proceeds with such provisions as permitting any person or group of persons to serve in one fiduciary capacity or more, permitting a fiduciary to employ advisors with regard to the fiduciary's responsibility, and permitting a fiduciary to appoint an investment manager.[56]

ERISA requires that all the assets of a plan be held in a trust, with the
trustees named in the trust instrument or in the plan instrument or appointed by the named fiduciary. If the plan expressly provides for it, the trustees may be made subject to the direction of a named fiduciary who is not a trustee, and they shall be subject to proper directions of that fiduciary made in accordance with the terms of the plan and not contrary to ERISA.

Pension plan trustees existed before ERISA. Certainly, they were thought of as fiduciaries, which, of course, they were. Now, however, the concept of fiduciary has been broadened. There must be at least one named fiduciary, in whom shall inhere the authority to control and manage. There is a named person or group of persons to whom participants in the plan can look to determine whether their rights are being properly protected.[57]

The named fiduciary may, as the term implies and as the Act provides, be whoever the plan instrument designates as a named fiduciary. It may or may not be a corporate manager. It may or may not be a bank or trust company. It may be the employer corporation itself. The Department of Labor has announced that a corporate employer may be the named fiduciary with respect to plans for its own employees.[58] Many corporations are, in fact, following this practice. It is likely that the employer would be a fiduciary under the Act, whether or not it is the named fiduciary.

If the employer corporation is a fiduciary, it logically follows that its directors, who control the corporation, are also fiduciaries.[59] If we were to stop there, it would follow that all fiduciary responsibility inheres in the corporation or in the directors, but normally we would not stop there.

Operation of a pension plan involves a host of financial and administrative details. The board of directors would not normally make the investments for the plan. That function would be delegated to an investment committee, to a corporate trustee, or to an investment advisor. They can be vested with the responsibility for investing in accordance with the principles mandated by ERISA. The board of directors would not normally keep the accounts of the participants, determine their eligibility for benefits under the plan and the amounts thereof, and write the pension checks. These responsibilities can also be delegated—to an appropriate department manager or managers within the corporation or to an outside concern such as a trust company. In making such a delegation, however, the directors must act as prudent people in the manner prescribed by ERISA. They cannot delegate the investment function to the students in the local high school economics class and expect that assignment to be upheld as a prudent delegation. They cannot place persons known to be incompetent, inaccurate, and of questionable integrity in responsible positions for recordkeeping and the calculation and payment of benefits. Again, the Department of Labor has defined its position on this subject. It has stated that to the extent that a corporate officer or director acts in the selection of the administrative committee or the investment committee for the plan, such a person is acting as a fiduciary and is accountable for the selection and retention of the persons holding such offices, even though the officers and directors may have no other contact with the plan.[60] This implies that the directors must supervise those who perform the various investment and administrative functions. Again, they can delegate to a committee of the board or to an executive officer the responsibility of monitoring the performance of those who are assigned the various operational functions, but when they delegate, they are well advised to require periodic reports from the committee of the board or the executive officer.

Corporate officers who are not directors may also be fiduciaries. For that matter, any corporate manager, whether an officer or not, may be a fiduciary if possessing discretionary powers and duties in the administration of the plan. The end result of all these requirements is to recognize that there are indeed serious exposures of corporate managers under ERISA. The best way to minimize the exposures is to spell out in the plan instrument not only the identity of the named fiduciary but also the extent to which he or she may delegate and the manner of so doing. Every step of delegation should be carefully documented. The responsibilities of those to whom delegation is made should be stated in writing. This written statement can have the effect of limiting the fiduciary obligation of each fiduciary to those aspects of the operation as are within his or her area of responsibility (unless the fiduciary learns of a breach by another fiduciary and condones it by inaction).[61]

The exposure of a fiduciary to personal liability will, of course, vary with the financial condition of the plan, the financial condition of the employer, the nature of the breach, the area of responsibilities of the particular fiduciary to the plan, and also whether the plan is a defined benefit or a defined contribution plan.

If it is a defined benefit plan, the corporate employer is responsible for providing sufficient contributions to fund the plan. If the funds are inadequate to pay the pensions, the corporation has an obligation to supply the deficiency, whether or not there has been a breach of fiduciary obligation by the fiduciary. The liability of the defaulting fiduciary is to the plan itself, not to any one participant. A participant may, however, bring a derivative action on behalf of the plan to require a restoration of the losses to the plan or the illegal gains of the fiduciary, as the case may be.[62] This, of course, is analogous to the stockholders' derivative action against directors and officers discussed in Chapter 3. Such an action may also be brought against a fiduciary by the Secretary of Labor.

If the employer corporation is solvent, it is likely that an action to restore a depleted fund will be brought against the corporation itself, although there appears to be no reason why other fiduciaries (assuming they participated in the events constituting a breach) cannot also be joined as defendants.

If, however, the plan is a defined contribution plan and the employer corporation has made all the contributions to the plan that it is required to make, there can be no recourse against the corporation unless it has failed in its fiduciary obligations. If there is no failure on the employer's part, the Secretary of Labor or the participants must look to those fiduciaries who actually participated in the breach. If they are independent entities, such as banks or trust companies, the corporation is probably immune. If, however, those fiduciaries are directors, officers, or other managers of the corporation, presumably the corporation will be responsible for their acts as it would be for other acts of such personnel.

In either type of plan, defined benefit or defined contribution, a corporate manager who is a fiduciary under ERISA would face a serious personal exposure if the breach was attributable to the manager's own action or inaction. If the corporation were now insolvent, corporate funds would be insufficient or nonexistent to restore funds to the plan. Even if corporate funds were adequate, it is not inconceivable that the corporate manager, particularly if on the director or officer level, could be subject to a derivative action by stockholders to restore to the corporation the monies that the corporation was required to restore to the pension plan. Such a suit would not be under ERISA, which does not authorize stockholders' suits, but under ordinary and well-known principles of corporation law.

As we have noted earlier, ERISA also lists a number of prohibited transactions. A fiduciary may not engage in certain transactions with a "party in interest." A party in interest is defined to include, among others, any fiduciary (including any administrator, officer, trustee, or custodian), counsel, or employee of the plan, a person providing services to the plan, an employer whose employees are covered by the plan, a union whose members are covered by the plan, holders of 50 percent or more of the stock of corporations that are parties in interest, or an employee, officer, or director of a corporate or labor union party in interest.[63]

## Reporting Responsibilities

In addition to the fiduciary responsibilities, ERISA also places upon corporate managers responsibilities for reporting and disclosure. These include such matters as filing a plan description, a summary plan description, and an annual report with the Secretary of Labor. Also, the plan administrator must furnish to any participant upon written request a statement of the participant's status with respect to benefits under the plan, and in the case of any participant who terminates with vested deferred benefits, a statement of such deferred benefits. The keeping and retention of pertinent records are also required.[64] The plan administrator is also required to file an annual registration statement with the Internal Revenue Service.[65] This administrator may be the corporate employer, or it may be an individual or individuals designated as plan administrator in the plan instrument.

There are criminal penalties for willful violation of ERISA requirements. A corporation may be fined up to $100,000 and an individual may be fined up to $5,000. An individual may also be imprisoned up to one year, or may be sentenced to both a fine and imprisonment.[66]

It is evident from the foregoing that the complexities of ERISA are myriad and that there are real potentialities for liability, civil and criminal, for the unwary or the careless. As in the case of all federal legislation directly affecting business corporations, corporate managers must take ERISA seriously, devote sufficient time to it, and engage, either full time or on a consulting basis as the exigencies may require, an adequate number of well-informed professionals to assure compliance and to reduce exposure to liability on the part of both the corporation and its managers.

## NOTES

1. 45 Stat. 577. Constitutionality upheld, Texas & N.O.R. Co. v. Brotherhood of Railway Clerks, 281 U.S. 548, 74 L. Ed. 1064, 50 S. Ct. 427 (1930).

2. 49 Stat. 449. This Act, with all its amendments, including the Labor-Management Relations Act of 1947, is compiled at 29 U.S.C. § 151–188. It is summarized in Hancock, *Executive's Guide to Business Law* (McGraw-Hill Book Co., 1979) 30-3 to 30-45. The NLRA's significance is not limited to the field of labor law. The decision of the United States Supreme Court upholding its constitutionality is the leading case extending the boundaries of federal power to regulate business through the commerce clause. National Labor Relations Board v. Jones & Laughlin Steel Corp., 301 U.S. 1, 81 L. Ed. 893, 57 S. Ct. 615 (1937).

3. 61 Stat. 136.

4. See Brotherhood of Electrical Workers v. NLRB, 69 Lab. Cases (CCH) ¶ 13,017. Law review comments on this problem include "Labor Law—Union Discipline of Supervisor Members," 51 *N. Car. L. Rev.* 932 (1973); "Union Discipline of Supervisors: Illinois Bell Telephone Co.," 14 *Wm. & Mary L. Rev.* 674–704; "Labor Law—Supervisor Member Exempt from Union Discipline for Acting in Furtherance of Employer's Interest," 26 *Vand. L. Rev.* 837–850 (1973).

5. 416 U.S. 267, 40 L. Ed. 2d 134, 94 S. Ct. 1757 (1974); discussed in Wells, "Labor Law Organizational Rights of Managerial Employees," 53 *N. Car. L. Rev.* 809–817 (1975).

6. NLRB v. North Arkansas Electric Cooperative, Inc., 446 F.2d 602 (8th Cir. 1971).

7. 29 U.S.C. § 162.

8. *Id.*, § 186(a).

9. United States v. Ventimiglia, 145 F. Supp. 37 (D. Md. 1956).

10. United States v. Roth, 333 F.2d 450 (2d Cir. 1964). Recent indictments of, and guilty pleas by, corporations and certain of their managers for violating the antibribery section of Taft-Hartley involved Pepsi Co. Inc. and McGrath Services Corp., *Wall St. J.*, July 5, 1979, p. 19, and July 26, 1979, p. 29.

11. 52 Stat. 1060. This Act, with all its amendments, is compiled at 29 U.S.C. §§ 201–219. For a summary, see Hancock, *Executive's Guide to Business Law* 28-1 to 28-20.

12. 29 U.S.C. § 216.

13. Southern Advance Bag & Paper Co. v. United States, 133 F.2d 449 (5th Cir. 1943), *aff'g*, 46 F. Supp. 105 (W.D. La. 1942). In another early case, the branch manager of an automobile rental company was convicted, along with the company, of falsifying wage records. Both were fined. Hertz Drivurself Stations, Inc. v. United States, 150 F.2d 923 (8th Cir. 1945).

14. United States v. Universal CIT Credit Corp., 344 U.S. 218, 97 L. Ed. 260, 73 S. Ct. 227 (1952), *aff'g*, 102 F. Supp. 179 (W.D. Mo. 1952).

15. United States v. Stanley, 416 F.2d 317 (2d Cir. 1969). In United States v. Klinghoffer Realty Corp., 285 F.2d 487 (2d Cir. 1960), the president and vice president of a corporation were found guilty of intentionally violating the Act by engaging employees for a financially embarrassed affiliate on an agreement to pay overtime compensation if and when the affiliate emerged from bankruptcy.

16. 465 F.2d 755 (5th Cir. 1972), *cert. denied*, 409 U.S. 1044 (1972).

17. Riley v. Commonwealth of Massachusetts, 232 U.S. 671, 58 L. Ed. 788, 34 S. Ct. 469 (1914); People v. Trapp, 20 N.Y.2d 613, 233 N.E.2d 110 (1967). Insolvency was no defense for a corporate manager indicted under New York law for knowingly failing to pay employees' wages. He knew the financial condition of the corporation was such that the workers would probably not be paid. People v. D.H. Ahrend Co., Inc., 308 N.Y. 112, 123 N.E.2d 799 (1954), *aff'g*, 118 N.Y.S.2d 426 (1953).

18. State v. Feist, 341 A.2d 725 (R.I. 1975).

19. Makarov v. Commonwealth of Virginia, 228 S.E.2d 573 (Va. 1976).

20. P.L. 89-577; 80 Stat. 772.

21. P.L. 91-173; 83 Stat. 742.

22. P.L. 95-164; 91 Stat. 1290; 30 U.S.C. §§ 801–960.

23. P.L. 91-596; 84 Stat. 1590; 29 U.S.C. §§ 651–678. For statements on the background and purpose of OSHA, see 93 *U.S. Cong. and Adm. News,* 91st Cong., 2d Sess., 1970, pp. 5177–5181. OSHA's substantive provisions are discussed in Hancock, *Executive's Guide to Business Law* 26-1 to 26-39.

24. 29 U.S.C. § 666.

25. 356 F. Supp. 670 (E.D. La. 1973), *aff'd*, 483 F.2d 67 (5th Cir. 1973).

26. Buhler v. Marriott Hotels, Inc., 390 F. Supp. 999 (E.D. La. 1974).

27. Jeter v. St. Regis Paper Co., 507 F.2d 973, 977 (5th Cir. 1975). *Skidmore* has also been followed in Russell v. Bartley, 494 F.2d 334 (6th Cir. 1974).

28. 18 U.S.C. § 2. Such an indictment was upheld in United States v. Pinkerton-Hollar, Inc., 4 OSHA 1699 (D. Kans. 1976). That decision also held that whether a corporate vice president could be considered an "employer" under OSHA was a question for the jury. See "An OSHA Crackdown on Job-Related Deaths," *Bus. Week,* Aug. 20, 1979, p. 25.

29. 30 U.S.C. § 820(c).

30. *Id.*, § 820(a), (d).

31. Title VII of the Civil Rights Act of 1964, P.L. 88-352, 78 Stat. 253. This title, as amended, is compiled in 42 U.S.C. § 2000e–2000e.17. Age Discrimination in Employment Act of 1967, P.L. 90-202, 81 Stat. 602. This Act, as amended, is compiled at 29 U.S.C. §§ 621–634. For a general discussion of laws relating to discrimination in employment, see Hancock, *Executive's Guide to Business Law* 25-1 to 25-64.

32. P.L. 95-256; 92 Stat. 189; 29 U.S.C. § 631.

33. For a discussion of some of the multimillion-dollar settlements in employment discrimination cases, see "Firing Up the Attack on Job Bias," *Bus. Week*, June 25, 1979, pp. 64–65.

34. 29 U.S.C. § 629.

35. 14 Stat. 27, 42 U.S.C. § 1982. Tillman v. Wheaton-Haven Recreation Association, 410 U.S. 431, 35 L. Ed. 2d 403, 93 S. Ct. 1090 (1973), in which the Association was held not to be a private club exempt under § 201(e) of the Civil Rights Act of 1964, 42 U.S.C. § 2000a(e). On remand and appeal, 517 F.2d 1141 (4th Cir. 1975), the directors were held personally liable.

36. 442 U.S. 366, 60 L. Ed. 2d 957, 99 S. Ct. 2345 (1979).

37. 17 Stat. 13; 42 U.S.C. § 1985(3).

38. 584 F.2d 1235 (3d Cir. 1978).

39. P.L. 93-406; 88 Stat. 829. Most of ERISA is compiled at 29 U.S.C. §§ 1001–1381, except those portions amending the Internal Revenue Code and certain other codes; see 29 U.S.C.A. § 1001, Historical Notes, for details. For a summary of ERISA, see Hancock, *Executive's Guide to Business Law* 27-1 to 27-21.

40. 45 Stat. 802, 839.

41. P.L. 85-836; 72 Stat. 997; 29 U.S.C. §§ 301–309. Repealed, except for prior offenses, by ERISA, § 111; 29 U.S.C. § 1031.

42. See Osborne, "The Employment (sic!) Retirement Income Security Act—Fiduciary Responsibility," 12 *Willamette L.J.* 298–330 (1976).

43. Bachelder, "Who's Afraid of ERISA Wolf? Sec. 405(d) and Other Houses of Straw for Trustees Under the Employee Retirement Income Security Act of 1974," 32 *Wash. & Lee L. Rev.* 921–938 at 922 (1975).

44. Kilberg, "The Labor Department Prospective," 31 *Bus. Law.* 75–82 at 79 (1975).

45. Weis & Vobiril, "Fiduciary Standards and Investment Responsibility Under the New Pension Reform Law," 113 *Trusts & Estates* 800–803, 858–860 at 800 (1974).

46. ERISA, § 3(34), (35); 29 U.S.C. § 1002(34), (35).

47. ERISA, § 2004; 29 U.S.C. § 415. All the limitations, with the adjustments and exceptions described in this chapter, together with certain other adjustments and exceptions which are omitted here in the interest of avoiding too technical a discussion, are set forth in the foregoing section.

48. The limitations on individual benefits and contributions under ERISA are not limitations on the amount of retirement benefits a corporation may pay to

a retiring executive. Rather, they are limits on the amounts that may be provided under a qualified plan entitled to the special tax treatment afforded such plans under the Internal Revenue Code. An employer is free to make supplemental arrangements for additional retirement benefits to executives by deferred compensation agreements, supplemental nonqualified plans, and numerous other methods. For a more complete discussion of the limitations, see Wilf, "Limitations on Benefits and Contributions for Corporate Employees Under the New Pension Law," 41 *J. of Taxation* 280 (1974). For a discussion of unfunded plans, see Sollee, "How the New Pension Reform Law Affects Non-Qualified Deferred Compensation Plans," 41 *J. of Taxation* 324–327 (1974). Both articles are reprinted in *Working with the New Pension Law*, 47–60 & 66–71, respectively (The J. of Taxation, Ltd. 1975).

49. For a similar view stated during the early months of ERISA's existence, see Kilberg, 31 *Bus. Law.* 75–82 (1975).

50. ERISA, § 404(a)(1); 29 U.S.C. § 1104(a)(1).

51. ERISA, §§ 406–408; 29 U.S.C. §§ 1106–1108. See also ERISA, § 2003; 26 U.S.C. § 4975.

52. ERISA, § 409(a); 29 U.S.C. § 1109(a).

53. Sanchez, Cain & Wood, "The Pension Reform Act of 1974; Fiduciary Responsibility and Prohibited Transactions," 6 *Tax Adviser* 86–98, 148–160, at 91–92 (1975). See also Kleven, "Fiduciary Responsibility Under ERISA's Prudent Man Rule: What Are the Guideposts?" 44 *J. of Taxation* 152–156 (1976); Report of Committee on Investments by Fiduciaries, Probate, and Trust Division, American Bar Association, "Fiduciary Responsibility and the Employee Retirement Income Security Act of 1974," 12 *Real Property, Probate & Trust J.* 285–299 (1977).

54. ERISA, §3; 29 U.S.C. § 1002. The term "fiduciary" is defined, however, in that section of ERISA which taxes prohibited transactions (ERISA, § 2003; 26 U.S.C. § 4975(e)(3) discussed at note 63 to this chapter), but the definition is only for the purpose of that section. It includes, among others, any person who exercises any discretionary authority over or control of the management of a plan or disposition of its assets, or who has any discretionary authority or responsibility in the administration of the plan.

55. ERISA, § 402(a); 29 U.S.C. § 1102(a).

56. *Id.*, § 402(c); 29 U.S.C. § 1102(c).

57. House Conference Report No. 93-1280, Joint Explanatory Statement of the Committee of Conference, 3 *U.S. Cong. Code and Adm. News*, 93d Cong., 2d Sess., 1974, pp. 5038–5165 at 5078. See also Osborne, 12 *Willamette L.J.* 298–330 at 309 (1976).

58. ERISA IB 75-5, QFR-3 (6-24-75), 40 Fed. Reg. 31599 (1975). Shortly before this interpretative bulletin was issued, Steven J. Sacher, Associate Solicitor of Labor, stated that the Labor Department did not consider it good practice to designate the employer corporation as a named fiduciary, "partly for the reason stated in the Conference Report, which is that one purpose of the named fiduciary requirement was to identify an individual to whom participants can go with problems." "Fiduciary Responsibility: Questions and Answers," Panel Discussion at ABA National Institute on Fiduciary Responsibilities under the Pension Reform Act, 31 *Bus. Law.* 127 (1975).

59. See remarks of Marshall Bartlett in panel discussion "Who Are Fiduciaries?" 31 *Bus. Law.* 83, 85–86 (1975).

60. ERISA IB 75-8, D-4 (10-6-75), 40 Fed. Reg. No. 197, p. 47491 (1975). See also Gilchrist, "Issues of Scope Under the New Fiduciary Responsibility Rule Affecting Management Service Under Qualified Plans," 33 *N.Y.U. Institute on Federal Taxation* 447–475 at 461 (1975).

61. For more complete information on the desirability of, and procedures for, express delegation of fiduciary responsibilities, see Bachelder, 32 *Wash. & Lee L. Rev.* 921–938 (1975); Osborne, 12 *Willamette L.J.* 298–330 (1976); panel discussion, "Insulating the Board of Directors," 31 *Bus. Law.* 201–223 (1975); Cummings, "Fiduciary Duties of Corporate Directors Under the Pension Reform Act," 31 *Bus. Law.* 1433–1442 (1976); White, "Prudent Delegation of Trustees' Responsibilities to Professionals," 29 *Labor L.J.* 586 (1978).

62. ERISA, §§ 101–111; 29 U.S.C. §§ 1021–1031.

63. Essentially, a prohibited transaction between a fiduciary and a party in interest is one that involves the sale, exchange, or lease of property, the lending of money or extension of credit, or the furnishing of goods, services, or facilities between the plan and a party in interest. Another type of prohibited transaction is the transfer of any assets of the plan to, or use by or for the benefit of, a party in interest. Still another type of prohibited transaction is the acquisition by the plan of any employer security or employer real property above the amount permitted under the Act. There are statutory qualifications to, and exceptions from, certain transactions of the type described above, in order to make the prohibitions practicable and workable. Engaging in a prohibited transaction is, as already noted, a breach of fiduciary obligation under ERISA. ERISA, §§ 406–408; 29 U.S.C. §§ 1106–1108.

   In addition to the liability for breach of fiduciary obligation, there is another type of penalty imposed by ERISA. It is a tax equal to 5 percent of the amount involved with respect to the prohibited transaction. It is payable, not by the fiduciary of the plan who is acting as such, but by the other party, who under the taxing sections is called a "disqualified person" rather than a "party in interest." A fiduciary is liable for breach of trust only if he or she knows, or should know, that the transaction constitutes one in the prohibited category. A disqualified person, however, is subject to the 5 percent tax even if he or she did not know that it was prohibited. Once the 5 percent tax is levied, the disqualified person has ninety days after notice within which to correct the prohibited transaction. Upon failure to do so, that person is subjected to an additional tax of 100 percent of the amount involved. ERISA, § 2003; 26 U.S.C. § 4975.

64. ERISA, §§ 101–110; 29 U.S.C. §§ 1021–1030.

65. ERISA, § 1031; 26 U.S.C. § 6057.

66. ERISA, § 501; 29 U.S.C. § 1131.

# CHAPTER EIGHT

# The Securities Laws: Management in a Goldfish Bowl

Of all the federal laws regulating the activities of business, the federal securities laws have undoubtedly had the greatest effect upon the personal affairs and personal exposures of corporate managers. Other federal statutes, as we have seen, set forth standards of compliance by corporations and in most instances place upon managers the responsibility of making certain that their corporations comply. The statutes also prescribe sanctions for violation, which may be applied against the offending corporation or its responsible managers, or both. All these features are present in the federal securities laws, but in addition, affirmative obligations are placed upon corporate managers to do, or refrain from doing, certain acts, not necessarily only in their capacities as corporate managers but also in their *personal* capacities *because* they are corporate managers.

The federal securities laws, as every business person knows, were born in the early days of the New Deal. They were a response to practices in the sale and distribution of corporate stocks and bonds that were perceived by many as being inimical to the best interests of the investing public. Although most of these concerns had been articulated by Louis D. Brandeis two decades before, the writers whose views had the most influence in the principles underlying the securities laws were Adolph A. Berle and Gardiner C. Means, whose classic work, *The Modern Corporation and Private Property*, was first published in 1932, with a revised edition appearing in 1968. Berle and Means, like Brandeis before them, emphasized the need for the investing public to know what was going on in the marketplace and in the corporations in which they were investing. It was *light* that was needed. The watchword was "disclosure." Thus disclosure came to be, and still is, nearly a half-century later, the fundamental feature of the Securities Act of 1933 and the Securities Exchange Act of 1934.[1]

These two acts have different scopes, but are interrelated and complementary to each other. Both are administered by the Securities and Exchange Commission (which will frequently be referred to as the SEC), and many of the same definitions, legal principles, and enforcement policies are applied to the two statutes.[2] Frequently, in private litigation as well as in enforcement proceedings brought by the SEC, violations of both acts are alleged. The Securities Act (which will sometimes be referred to hereafter in this book as the 1933 Act) is concerned with full and fair disclosure and the prevention of fraud in the initial sale of securities. It regulates the sale of securities by the issuer or by persons in control of the issuer. The Securities Exchange Act (sometimes identified in this book as the 1934 Act) regulates securities exchanges and over-the-counter markets, and it is designed, primarily through the means of disclosure, to prevent inequitable and unfair practices on such exchanges and markets. The 1934 Act thus regulates the activities of a broad range of entities. Among the persons, both natural and corporate, whose conduct is affected by the 1934 Act are the securities exchanges themselves, brokers and dealers, and the corporations whose securities are being traded, as well as individual directors, officers, other corporate employees, large stockholders, members of their families, and certain business associates. In this chapter, we will be concerned chiefly with the officers and directors and other managerial personnel of the corporations whose stock is being issued (covered by the 1933 Act) or is being traded (covered by the 1934 Act).

## THE SECURITIES ACT OF 1933

The 1933 Act is primarily concerned with the public offering of corporate securities—in popular parlance, stocks and bonds of business corporations[3]—by the corporations themselves or by persons in "control." The statute enumerates various kinds of exempted securities and exempted transactions which need not be discussed here, as they are often technical in nature and shed little or no light on the matter of responsibility and regulation of the corporate manager. The 1933 Act is premised upon the use of the instruments of interstate commerce or of the mails in connection with the offering or sale of securities, in order to establish the necessary federal power to regulate. Its fundamental requirement is registration of the security. A corporate security may not be sold or offered for sale unless and until there is a registration statement, duly filed with the SEC, containing all the information required by, or under the authority of, the 1933 Act, and having become "effective" by order of the SEC.

The Act requires the use of a prospectus containing certain required information.[4] The prospectus forms a part of the registration statement. Under the Act, the normal effective date of a registration statement is the twentieth day after filing. There are procedures for acceleration or postponement of the effective date. The SEC may refuse to permit a registration statement to become effective (it may issue a "stop order")

if it appears "on its face incomplete or inaccurate in any material respect."[5] There has grown up an informal practice of comments by the SEC staff to registrants concerning the contents of a registration statement during the twenty-day period following its initial filing. This enables registrants to make changes required by the SEC, but in no way relieves the registrant and persons working with it on the registration statement from liability for any material omission or inaccuracy.

The 1933 Act places personal responsibility upon certain individuals within the corporation. First, there is a requirement that the registration statement be executed by the principal executive officer, the principal financial officer, the controller or principal accounting officer, and a majority of the board of directors.[6] Then Section 11 of the Act prescribes civil liabilities on account of a false registration statement. Liability is premised upon any part of an effective registration that contains "an untrue statement of a material fact" or omits "a material fact required to be stated therein or necessary to make the statements therein not misleading."[7] Such liability is imposed upon every person who signs the registration statement (the corporation itself, its principal executive officer, its principal financial officer, its principal accounting officer), every director (whether or not signing the registration statement), and every person consenting to being named in the registration statement as being or about to become a director. Liability is also imposed on "experts," such as accountants, engineers, or appraisers, who with their consent are named as having prepared or certified any part of the registration statement. Finally, liability is imposed upon every underwriter of the security.

The liability of such persons is to any person who purchased the security covered by the registration statement and who did not know of the untruth or omission at the time of purchase. It is not necessary for the purchaser to prove reliance upon the contents of the registration statement except when the purchase occurred after the corporation made generally available to its security holders an earnings statement covering operations of at least twelve months after the effective date of the registration statement. Recovery by a purchaser is based upon the difference between the amount paid and (1) the value at the time the suit is commenced, or (2) the price at which the security is resold by the purchaser in the market before the suit, or (3) the price at which it is sold after the suit but before judgment, if such a price would result in a lesser recovery than (1) or (2). At all events, recovery cannot exceed the amount at which the security was offered to the public, regardless of the amount the plaintiff may have paid.

While the liabilities imposed by Section 11 appear harrowing on first reading, a study of the various qualifications and defenses of the section reveals grounds on which a reasonably prudent person can avoid liability. This is the concept of "due diligence."

An expert is not liable for the contents of the entire registration statement but only for that portion for which he or she, with consent, has been named as an expert. The expert may be exonerated from liability by proving (1) due diligence, that is, reasonable investigation, and (2) at the time the "expertized" part became effective, reasonable ground to believe and actual belief that (*a*) the statements in such part were true and (*b*) there was no omission of a material fact required to be stated or necessary to ensure that such statements were not misleading. The expert might also be exonerated by proving that the part attributed to the expert opinion (1) did not fairly represent his or her statement as an expert or (2) was not a fair copy or extract from the expert's report or appraisal. An officer or a director is entitled to rely on the opinion of the expert if he or she has reasonable ground to believe that the statement attributed to the expert is true, does not omit a material fact, and fairly represents the expert's statement or, if purporting to be a copy or extract of the expert's report or evaluation, is a fair copy or extract.

As to those portions of the registration statement that do not purport to be made on the authority of an expert, the director or signing officer may establish due diligence and may escape liability by proving, as the expert might do in the expertized portion, that he or she (1) had made reasonable investigation and (2) had reasonable ground to believe, and did believe, that (*a*) the statements were true and (*b*) there was no omission of a material fact required to be stated or necessary to make the statements not misleading.

Section 11 establishes a definition of reasonable investigation and reasonable ground for belief as the terms are used in the two preceding paragraphs. It states that "the standard of reasonableness shall be that required of a prudent man in the management of his own property."[8]

Section 11 confers upon underwriters the same defenses with regard to reasonable investigation and reasonable ground for belief as it does upon directors and officers. The issuing corporation itself does not have such defenses but is held to absolute liability.

Section 11 also establishes a procedure whereby a director or an officer (or underwriter or expert) may disassociate from the registration statement before its effectiveness by resigning and so notifying the SEC and the corporation. It also permits disassociation after the registration statement is effective if effectiveness occurs without the person's knowledge and a prompt notice to that effect is given to the SEC and to the public.

In addition to the civil liabilities to purchasers of securities provided by Section 11, corporate directors and officers, as well as other persons, are subject to criminal penalties for making in a registration statement an untrue statement of a material fact or for omitting to state a material fact required to be stated therein or necessary to prevent the statements therein being misleading. The penalty is a fine of $10,000 or imprisonment for up to five years, or both. The same penalties apply to violations of any provisions of the 1933 Act or the rules and regulations promulgated by the SEC thereunder. The SEC may also obtain an injunction against a violation of the Act.[9]

In the early days of the Securities Act of 1933, there was considerable

concern that its rigid standards and strong statements of liability might have a deterrent effect on the business community—that honest businesspersons, afraid of the potential penalties, might refrain from engaging in legitimate business practices lest they face the hindsight application of Section 11 to transactions and statements that appeared perfectly proper and reasonable to them at the time they were made or said. This did not, however, prove to be the fact. One writer reports that only thirteen cases were brought under Section 11 during the first twenty-nine years of its existence. The reason may have been that corporations and their managers took the Act seriously because of the nature of the liabilities and the penalties, or it may have been the practice of the SEC staff to comment upon the content of the registration statement prior to its effectiveness.[10] More likely, it was a combination of both.

## THE *BARCHRIS* CASE

There had been such a long and uneventful period of living with the 1933 Act and the liabilities of Section 11 that when a major case under that section was finally decided, the reaction at first was one of disbelief. Corporate directors and officers actually were held liable for substantial amounts in a litigated case! While most landmark cases under federal laws are decided by the United States Supreme Court or at least by a United States Court of Appeals, the only decision in this case, *Escott v. BarChris Construction Corp.*,[11] was made by the United States District Court for the Southern District of New York.

BarChris Construction Corp. was a relatively small company engaged in bowling alley construction, having about 3 percent of the national market for that kind of business. The bowling alley business had grown rapidly in the 1950s and the early 1960s, and BarChris had grown with it. Both the president, Vitolo, and a vice president, Pugliese, were men of limited education and were not exercising any particular responsibility for administration of the business. Pugliese was essentially the supervisor of construction. Russo, the executive vice president, functioned as the chief executive officer and knew all the details of operation and finance. Kircher, the treasurer, was an experienced accountant and the chief financial officer. Birnbaum, the secretary and house counsel, was just four years out of law school. All five of these men were directors. There were also four outside directors—Grant, a partner in a law firm, Coleman, a partner in a brokerage and underwriting firm, Auslander, chairman of a bank, and Rose, a member of an engineering firm. Trilling, the controller, worked under Kircher's supervision and was not a director.

On March 10, 1961, the corporation filed with the SEC a registration statement covering a proposed offering of 5 ½ percent convertible subordinate debentures. At that time, Birnbaum, Auslander, and Rose were not directors of the corporation, although Birnbaum was assistant secretary. They were elected directors and Birnbaum was elected secretary on April 17, 1961. The registration statement became effective on May 16, 1961, and the debentures were sold. On October 29, 1962, BarChris filed a petition for arrangement under Chapter XI of the Bankruptcy Act. Subsequently, sixty-five purchasers of the debentures commenced an action under Section 11 against the nine directors, the controller, the underwriters, and the independent public accountants. The court went into considerable detail in analyzing the liability of each of the defendants. As we are concerned in this book with the liabilities of directors and officers and not those of underwriters or independent public accountants, the discussion here will be concerned principally with the liability of each of the directors and officers.

The court found numerous instances of false and misleading statements. There were accounting errors that the public accountants missed in their review and examination of the corporation's books. Some of these the court found to be material, others, not material. There was a statement that certain loans by officers to the corporation had been paid, but an omission of the fact that new loans had been made. There were incorrect statements concerning the proposed application of the proceeds of the offering. There were untrue statements concerning unfilled orders. Contingencies in certain material contracts were ignored.

The defendants offered defenses of reliance upon experts and diligent inquiry. The court held that the only experts involved in the registration statement were the independent public accountants. Lawyers, it stated, are not experts within the meaning of Section 11. Reliance upon the public accountants was of no avail, however, to any of the officer defendants except Birnbaum, the young lawyer who became a director in April 1961 and was not familiar with the operations for 1960 and prior years that were covered by the audit. The outside directors were also entitled to rely on the public accountants. Neither the outside directors nor Birnbaum were able, however, to establish due diligence with regard to the unexpertized portions of the registration statement, as each of them had failed to make an investigation of the truth of the statements. Birnbaum, although employed as an attorney, was engaged in routine legal work, did not have an intimate knowledge of the affairs of the company, and apparently made no effort to acquire it. Auslander signed signature pages for the first amendment to the registration statement upon request and without understanding what he was signing. A few days later, he signed signature pages for the second and final amendment and at that time saw the first amendment but did not really study it. Rose spent ten minutes reading the original registration statement and asked Vitolo and Russo whether the statements in it were true. He signed the two amendments without reading them.

The court observed that Russo, as chief executive officer, knowing all the details of the financial operation, had no due diligence defenses.

Similarly, Kircher, as chief financial officer, knew all the facts and could

not rely on the public accountants. Trilling, as controller, was chargeable with the accuracy of the figures. He could not rely on the public accountants to make them accurate. Vitolo and Pugliese probably did not read the registration statement but, in their positions as officers, directors, and members of the executive committee, must have known what was going on. The defense of due diligence was therefore denied to all these officers.

Grant came in for particularly strong criticism by the court. As outside counsel for the company, he drafted the registration statement. The court found, however, that he had failed to make the investigations necessary for such a task. He had not read the corporation's contracts, had made no investigation of unfilled orders or contingent liabilities, had not read the minutes of subsidiaries, had not asked to see the notes of a meeting of the executive committee whose minutes had not been written, had not inquired into the loans by the officers although he knew about them, had not checked the matter of application of proceeds, and had not checked the status of his own firm's fee, which was marked "paid" when it was not. He was, however, allowed to rely upon the opinion of the public accountants, but otherwise he was held not to have exercised due diligence.

Coleman, being a partner in the principal underwriting firm for the offering as well as an outside director, had apparently done a fair amount of inquiring into the business up to the end of March. After that, he relied upon Ballard, the counsel for the underwriting firm, who the court found had failed to make a proper investigation. The court held that both Coleman, as a director, and his underwriting firm were bound by Ballard's action, had accordingly not exercised due diligence, and were liable under Section 11.

In summation, the court placed the highest degree of responsibility upon the executive management. Its members could not rely on the certification of the financial statements by the independent public accountants, as they were so intimately aware of the affairs of the business that they were chargeable with knowledge that the numbers in the statements were wrong. The court included the controller, who, although not a part of executive management, was in charge of the books and therefore responsible for the errors in them.

On the other hand, the outside directors were entitled to rely on the accountants' opinion. They were not so intimately acquainted with the day-to-day operations and had the right to assume that a major accounting firm would do a proper audit. The newly elected corporate secretary, although an inside director, was also entitled to rely on the accountants, as his corporate responsibilities were not such that he could be charged with knowledge of the accuracy of the accounts. None of the officers or directors, however, could escape liability for the parts of the registration statement not covered by the accountants' opinion. All were guilty in varying degrees, but each to a degree to establish liability, of not having inquired sufficiently into the affairs of the corporation and the registration statement. None had exercised the due diligence called for by the 1933 Act.

Because it was the first decision that had gone into the defenses of reliance upon experts and exercise of due diligence, the first reaction in the business and legal communities was that *BarChris* greatly increased the personal exposures of corporate managers under the Securities Act.[12]

Upon more dispassionate reflection and discussion by the experts in the securities law field, it became evident, however, that the decision was merely saying what the statute had said for thirty-five years. As one such expert said at that time:

> The Securities Act pursuant to a great public policy has said: We would like to impose responsibility upon somebody else besides the selling company. We will impose the liability upon a larger group of persons for the purpose of seeing to it that the public is protected by a reasonable investigation by responsible persons. Those persons are listed. They are the officers, the directors, the signers of the registration statement, the experts. It was the Congress' decision that they should be responsible.[13]

*BarChris* is a dramatic illustration of the wisdom of Congress in extending liability beyond the corporation itself. In that case, the corporation was bankrupt and there was no way that the investors could recoup their losses from it. The personal liability of the directors, officers, experts, and underwriters was of immense practical value. But even in a situation where the corporation is solvent, it seems appropriate that liability should be shared by the responsible actors who have caused the violation to occur. This is consistent with the principles of managerial responsibility that we have been examining throughout this book.[14]

One reason why *BarChris* created so much concern was that it appeared to run counter to the principles of director responsibility found in many state statutes and decisions. We discussed these principles in Chapter 3 under the heading "Prudence in Management—An External Obligation," and we saw that, generally, directors were entitled in the normal situation to rely upon the representations of management. The defendants in *BarChris* relied on a New York case, *Litwin v. Allen*,[15] as authority for that proposition. It has been pointed out that in *Litwin* the directors were merely approving a transaction in which their interests were identical with the corporation itself, such as in the purchase of property. In securities offerings, however, and in other transactions subject to the securities acts, the directors must be concerned with the welfare not only of the corporation itself, but also of the investing public generally.[16] The securities laws have extended greatly the liability of directors and officers in their relations to the security holders of the corporation, far beyond the principles of the state corporation acts and the common-law decisions that we examined in Chapter 3. The

Another legal commentator has described the exposure under Section 11 in this fashion:

> The standard of responsibility imposed on a director or signing officer under Section 11 is substantially higher than the standard normally applied by the business community. One hallmark of executive skill is the ability to delegate. Directors and officers are accustomed to relying on responsible subordinates, whose work product they do little or nothing to verify by independent investigation as a routine matter. The hazards of such delegation of responsibility in the registration context should be pointed out by counsel.[17]

Since the excitement of *BarChris* died down, there have been relatively few cases interpreting the meaning of Section 11, mainly because *BarChris* said it all. The application of Section 11 and the principle of *BarChris* to inside and outside directors, respectively, was examined in *Feit v. Leasco Data Processing Equipment Corp.*[18] In that case, the court emphasized that an inside director "with intimate knowledge of corporate affairs and the particular transactions" would be expected to investigate more thoroughly and to have a more extensive knowledge of the facts than would an outside director. The investigation need not be completely independent and duplicative, the court said, but the directors were, expected to examine, at the minimum, those documents which were readily available.

## THE CONCEPT OF CONTROL

The securities laws place certain responsibilities upon persons "in control" of a corporation. For example, in case of liability under Section 11 (which we have discussed above) or under Section 12 of the 1933 Act[19] (sale or offer of sale without having an effective registration statement or by other specified prohibited means), such liability is also extended to include:

> Every person who, by or through stock ownership, agency, or otherwise, or who, pursuant to or in connection with an agreement or understanding with one or more other persons by or through stock ownership, agency, or otherwise, controls any person liable under Section 11 or 12. . . .[20]

Thus it is evident that a person in control of a corporation is subject to the same requirements as the corporation itself in selling, or offering to sell, securities of the corporation to the public. Neither the 1933 Act nor the 1934 Act, however, provides a definition of control. There is a wide range of possibilities as to who might be a controlling person. It would seem fairly obvious that one who owns an overwhelming majority of the stock of a corporation, say 85 percent, is in control. On a more practical basis, however, control usually resides in a much smaller percentage of ownership, combined with position in the corporation or the ability to influence its policies, or both. It has been suggested that there is always a controlling person or controlling group in every corporation and that, unless there is some other person or other identifiable group clearly in control, it must be presumed that all the directors and policymaking officers are members of the controlling group.[21] This, of course, is only an assumption and could be overcome by evidence to the contrary.

Control is therefore a practical problem for directors and top officers. In most situations of liability under the securities laws, it probably does not make much difference in the personal liability of the individual, as he or she will probably incur liability as a director or officer under some specific provision of the statute without having to be concerned about the corporation's violation being attributed to him or her on a theory of control. There is, however, a practical problem of ability to sell securities in the corporation personally held by the director or officer. A controlling person cannot sell without having a registration statement effective under the 1933 Act unless an exemption under the Act is available. If the block to be sold is large—with a value in the millions of dollars—filing a registration statement is not inappropriate. If, however, only a small amount is to be sold, the expense of registration may conceivably be greater than the gross proceeds of the sale. The 1933 Act empowers the SEC to exempt securities from the registration requirements where they are

> . . . not necessary in the public interest and for the protection of investors by reason of the small amount involved or the limited character of the public offering. . . .[22]

Under this authority the SEC has promulgated Regulation A,[23] which provides controlling persons with an annual exemption of $300,000 in the sale price of securities of an issuer. Any one controlling person may use up to $100,000 of the $300,000. An offering by an estate is treated separately and may total $500,000. The corporation itself has an exemption of $1,500,000 and estate offerings are chargeable against that total. Despite the exemption of Regulation A, it has often proved cumbersome because of the reporting requirements and the interrelations between the sales of all controlling persons and the corporation itself.

The problem of smaller sales by controlling persons has in recent years been solved by the promulgation of Rule 144 and the use of Form 144 required under it.[24] Under that rule, a person "in control" may sell, through a broker, dollar amounts of the security within the limits permitted by the rule after filing with the SEC a notice on Form 144 of intent to make the sale. There are limitations upon the number of shares. The amount to be sold, as reported on Form 144, may not exceed the average weekly volume of trading on all the national securities exchanges upon which it is traded during the four preceding calendar weeks, but in no event more than 1 percent of the corporation's total outstanding securities of the same class. Also, the 1 percent limitation may not be exceeded in any six-month period. There is also a requirement that there be adequate current information available about the corporation. This requirement can be satisfied by the corporation's having filed the various reports required under the provisions of the Securities Exchange Act of 1934.

There is, of course, no certainty that Rule 144 applies to all corporate directors and policymaking officers, as they may or may not be controlling persons within the meaning of the 1933 Act. Since, however, there are so many uncertainties on the subject, corporate counsel usually advise their directors and top officers to look very carefully at their positions concerning the question of control and to resolve doubts in favor of assuming that Rule 144 applies.

## THE SECURITIES EXCHANGE ACT OF 1934

Although the securities laws have an important effect upon the personal activities of corporate managers, it is not possible within the framework of a single chapter to discuss all the various matters of substantive law that have arisen under these statutes. In our discussion of the 1933 Act, we have selected certain facets of the Act that have a direct relation to the manager as an individual, namely, personal liability with respect to a registration statement and the application of the 1933 Act to the manager's own activities in selling his or her corporate securities. Similarly, in our discussion of the 1934 Act, we will be selective as to the subject matter. We will discuss the proxy rules and then direct our attention to the rules pertaining to "insider" activity with regard to corporate securities and to a limited number of cases that will illustrate the kinds of exposure faced by corporate managers under the 1934 Act.

Before discussing the proxy rules and the insider trading rules, we should first look at the basis for application of these rules to corporations and their managers. We saw that the 1933 Act was premised upon the use of the mails or the means or instrumentalities of commerce in connection with the sale or offering of a security. The 1934 Act was first premised upon the regulation of national securities exchanges. All such exchanges must be registered.[25] It is further provided that no member, broker, or dealer may trade in any security on a national securities exchange unless that security is registered in accordance with the provisions of Section 12 of the 1934 Act.[26] This is not the same kind of registration as is required under the 1933 Act. The registration under the 1934 Act is not for a block of securities to be offered, but rather, it is for all the securities of the particular class (common stock, preferred stock, debentures, etc.) issued and outstanding. Registration is upon the securities exchange, but duplicate originals of the application must also be filed with the SEC. Section 12 specifies the type of information concerning the corporation, its business, its finances, and its management that must be in the application for registration. In addition, however, to the requirement of registration on a national securities exchange that was the historical basis for SEC jurisdiction over certain types of corporate activity, the Congress expanded the regulatory scope of the SEC in 1964 by requiring also the registration with the SEC of any corporation not listed on a national securities exchange but having assets exceeding $1 million and 500 or more stockholders of record.[27]

As a result of being registered under the provisions of Section 12 of the 1934 Act, a corporation is required to file quarterly and annual reports with the SEC, to furnish annual reports to stockholders, and to offer to furnish stockholders with copies of its annual reports to the SEC. In addition, such a corporation must solicit proxies for its stockholders' meetings in accordance with the rules of the SEC, and its directors and officers are subjected to extensive requirements concerning trading in the corporation's securities.

## THE PROXY RULES

The proxy rules are important to directors and officers for two reasons: (1) They impose detailed requirements concerning their relationship and transactions with the corporation; and (2) violation of the disclosure requirements of the proxy rules can result in personal sanctions against officers and directors.[28]

The first category of required information pertains to the election of directors to be held at a stockholders meeting. Disclosure is required of each nominee's principal occupation or employment, whether with the corporation or otherwise, previous business experience, including previous service as a director of the corporation, the number of shares of stock held in the corporation, family relationship to another director or an executive officer, directorship in other corporations registered under the 1934 Act, and information concerning certain transactions between the corporation and entities in which the nominee owns more than 1 percent equity interest. Disclosure is also required of affiliation with a law firm or an investment banking firm serving the corporation.

Next, the proxy rules require information concerning compensation of directors and officers. Until the end of 1978, compensation of directors and the three highest paid officers, whether directors or not, that exceeded $40,000 in the preceding fiscal year had to be reported in the proxy statement. The rule was then revised to cover "each of the five most highly compensated executive officers or directors" receiving "cash and cash equivalent forms of remuneration" exceeding $50,000. The regulation defines an executive officer to include the following:

> [The] president, secretary, treasurer, any vice president in charge of a principal business unit, division, or function (such as sales, administration or finance), and *any other person who performs similar policy-making functions*.[29] [Emphasis supplied.]

The effect of the new rule may be to require in certain instances disclosure of compensation of major department heads or officers of subsidiaries. The rule looks to the real nature of the function performed and
not merely to the titles conferred by the corporation. Under the new
rules, three categories of compensation must be reported: (1) cash
remuneration (salary and bonuses); (2) other types of compensation
received, such as insurance premiums, excess of market value over
purchase price on exercise of a stock option, and personal benefits such
as the use of a company airplane or another company facility for other
than corporate purposes; and (3) contingent forms of remuneration for
which the corporation has allocated money, such as pension plan benefits and incentive awards that are based upon goals extending over a
period of years.

Still another requirement is the disclosure of arrangements with
persons whose remuneration must be disclosed as described above as
to future remuneration, such as employment contracts, deferred compensation, and the like. Details concerning the grants of options to such
persons and their exercise of such options are also required. Arrangements for compensation of directors must be described. Details of
indebtedness of any director or officer (and certain family members) to
the corporation in excess of $10,000 must be stated, as must any other
type of transaction, not otherwise covered by the rules, between such a
person and the corporation where that person's interest in the transaction is in excess of $40,000. The latter category also includes the interest
of the director's or officer's spouse or of any relative of such a person or
of the spouse having the same home.

The rationale for requiring disclosure of the financial relationships
and transactions between the corporation and its top executives is, of
course, consistent with the fundamental premise of the securities laws
of disclosing information that investors need in order to make intelli-
gent decisions. In the stockholders meeting context, decisions are on
whether to retain the management's slate of directors in office and
whether to support management's position on proposals submitted for
a vote at the meeting. The SEC believes that such information is useful
to the stockholder in the decision-making process. Whether or not the
purpose is being accomplished is debatable. The recent amendments
relating to executive compensation, in their efforts to lump everything
into three categories, may have served merely to confuse both management and stockholders.[30]

Stockholders meetings are, of course, not concerned solely with the
election of directors. The proxy rules permit individual stockholders to
submit proposals for consideration at the meeting. This subject has
attracted an increasing amount of attention in recent years, as stockholders have submitted numerous proposals concerning corporate conduct in various social areas. The management itself frequently submits
proposals to stockholders—adoption of option or bonus plans, changes
in authorized capital stock, mergers, and other fundamental transactions. The proxy rules contain detailed requirements as to the types of

information that must be disclosed in connection with the various types of proposals, whether offered by management or by stockholders.

Section 14 of the 1934 Act,[31] the section under which the proxy rules have been promulgated, declares that it is unlawful for any person to solicit a proxy or to permit the use of his or her name to solicit a proxy in contravention of such rules as the SEC may prescribe as "necessary or appropriate in the public interest or for the protection of investors." The SEC has promulgated Rule 14a-9, which reads as follows:

> No solicitation subject to this regulation shall be made by means of any proxy statement, form of proxy, notice of meeting or other communication, written or oral, containing any statement which, at the time and in the light of the circumstances under which it is made, is false or misleading with respect to any material fact, or which omits to state any material fact necessary in order to make the statements therein not false or misleading or necessary to correct any statement in any earlier communication with respect to the solicitation of a proxy for the same meeting or subject matter which has become false or misleading.[32]

In speaking of the concept of a false or misleading statement with regard to a material fact or the omission of a material fact necessary to make a statement not misleading, the rule incorporates principles that the reader will readily recognize as being present in the 1933 Act. Throughout both acts, the principle of disclosure relates to material facts—they cannot be omitted and they must be stated correctly and in a manner that is not misleading.

Section 14(a) and Rule 14a.9 have been the basis of damage actions against directors of a corporation by stockholders claiming to have been injured by misleading proxy statements. The United States Supreme Court established the right to bring such action in *J.I. Case Co. v. Borak*.[33] That decision was in an action brought by the stockholders of a corporation party to a merger. It was alleged that the proxy statement in connection with the stockholders meeting to approve the merger contained false and misleading statements and that the merger deprived them of their preemptive rights. While this was not a derivative action, the Court held that Section 14(a) conferred upon a stockholder the right to sue both for direct injury to the stockholder and for injury to the corporation on a derivative basis. Although Section 14(a) contains no language explicitly conferring such a right of action, the Court looked to the statutory power of the SEC to make rules thereunder "for the protection of investors." From that it concluded that judicial relief is available to achieve that protection, whether upon a suit by the SEC or by a stockholder. Relief, the Court held, could be any remedy that is available to a court, including injunction, rescission, and restitution.

While directors are liable for a misleading proxy statement by reason of permitting their names to be used in it, their liability is not absolute. As in the case of a registration statement under the 1933 Act, they may avoid liability if they can establish diligence. Liability can be grounded on knowledge of the falsity of the proxy statement or negligence in such

matters as failing to read it in draft form and to correct items which they know or should know to be erroneous or misleading.[34]

## INSIDER TRANSACTIONS—SECTION 16

There are two sections of the 1934 Act concerned with insider transactions—Section 10(b) and Section 16. Section 16 is relatively narrow in scope, in both its coverage of persons and its coverage of transactions. On the other hand, the liabilities resulting from it are absolute in nature, whether or not there was an intention to violate. Section 10(b) is very broad in scope, both in coverage of persons and in coverage of transactions. There is, however, no absolute liability. Section 10(a) raises perplexing questions of intent and negligence, as we shall see.

Looking first at Section 16, we find three distinct but interrelated provisions: (1) Section 16(a), providing a procedure for reporting by certain insiders; (2) Section 16(b), imposing liability for certain types of "short-swing" transactions by such insiders; and (3) Section 16(c), prohibiting short sales by such insiders.[35]

### Section 16(a)—Reporting

The reporting requirements come into being when a corporation's securities are first registered under the 1934 Act. They apply to a specified class of insiders, namely, each officer and director and each person who is the beneficial owner directly or indirectly of more than 10 percent of any class of stock in the corporation. Any person who subsequently becomes an officer, a director, or a beneficial owner of more than 10 percent comes under the reporting requirements upon achieving such status. The first report (on SEC Form 3) must be filed within ten days either after registration or after becoming such an insider. The report must show the number of shares of each class of stock beneficially owned by the insider, whether it be directly or indirectly held. The report is filed with the SEC and with a national securities exchange upon which the stock is listed. If, in any month, there are changes in ownership by the insider, a report (on SEC Form 4) showing such changes must be filed within the first ten days of the succeeding month.

### Section 16(b) Trading

Section 16(b) covers certain trading activities of directors, officers, and beneficial owners of more than 10 percent of any class of stock. This appears to be the same class of insiders that is obligated to report under Section 16(a), but it does not follow that everything that might be said about the coverage of 16(a) necessarily applies to 16(b) and vice versa. There are subtle differences between the two subsections, and the regulations issued by the SEC under them have in some instances resulted in still further differences. Some of these will be noted in the ensuing discussion. Specifically, Section 16(b) says that if any of such insiders should purchase and sell within the same six-month period any shares of stock of his or her corporation, any profit derived from such transactions shall belong to the corporation and may be recovered by the corporation in an action at law, or it may be recovered for the corporation by any stockholder suing on behalf of the corporation. It makes no difference whether the purchase came before the sale or the sale before the purchase. The important thing is that if a transaction of purchase and a transaction of sale occur within the same six-month period, liability under 16(b) applies automatically. The transactions described in 16(b) are often referred to as "short-swing" transactions and the profits are often called "short-swing" profits.

Section 16(b) states that the liability is imposed to prevent "the unfair use of information which may have been obtained" by the insider "by reason of his relationship" to the corporation. The corporation or the suing stockholder is not required, however, to prove that the insider made any use of inside information in entering into any of the transactions upon which liability is based. Section 16(b) does not set up a presumption of inside information that may be rebutted at trial. On the contrary, even if the insider were permitted to prove that no inside information was used, liability under Section 16(b) would still ensue. Also, it would make no difference whether the insider, in buying or selling, did or did not remember having engaged in the opposite transaction within the preceding six months. Good faith is not a defense.

## Section 16(c)—Short Selling

The practice of short selling, that is, selling stock borrowed from another expressly to sell it and then paying it back at a future date with subsequently purchased shares, is a long-recognized and sometimes controversial method of trading in the stock market. The relative merits and demerits of this type of activity are not within the scope of this book. We merely will recognize that it is a practice that has long existed, but it is denied to a director, officer, or holder of 10 percent or more of the stock of any class of the corporation. Section 16(c) states specifically that such an insider may not sell stock that he or she does not own. Moreover, any stock owned and sold by such an insider must be delivered within twenty days after sale or deposited in the mail or another usual channel of communication within five days after sale. Transactions contrary to Section 16(c) are unlawful and can trigger the criminal penalties of the 1934 Act. In this respect, they differ from the transactions described in Section 16(b), which are not declared unlawful but merely establish a basis of the insider's civil liability to the corporation.

## Who Is Covered by Section 16?

While Section 16 pertains to certain stock transactions of officers and directors, it is not always clear as to who is an officer or a director within the meaning of the section, as Congress did not define these terms in the 1934 Act. In an effort to clarify the matter, the SEC, in the early days of the Act, issued a regulation that defined an officer as including the president, a vice president, the secretary, the treasurer, the controller "and any other person who performs . . . functions corresponding to those performed by the foregoing officers."[36]

As anyone familiar with corporate managements knows, the practice of corporations with regard to titles and responsibilities varies widely. Some corporations are very lavish with the use of titles and will confer the title of vice president rather promiscuously, often to persons who really do not possess inside information and are not really performing the key managerial functions that are normally associated with such a title. Other corporations may be very stingy with titles and may have division or department heads who possess a great deal of inside information and who are performing important managerial functions but are not given vice presidential or other officer titles. Thus, it is not surprising that there has been litigation in which the plaintiff has claimed that a nontitled individual is an officer, and other litigation in which a titled individual has claimed that he or she is not an officer. To compound the problem further are the old familiar titles of assistant secretary, assistant treasurer, and assistant controller, words that by their very nature are equivocal. Then there is the problem of officers of subsidiaries. Do they ever, never, or sometimes fall within the SEC's definition?

An early case, *Colby v. Klune*,[37] demonstrated the problem and laid down tests that are still being applied. Klune was employed as a "production manager" by 20th Century Fox and was being sued for recovery of short-swing profits derived from the purchase and sale of 20th Century Fox stock. The district court looked at the bylaws of the corporation, which defined the duties of the officers, and then looked at the description of Klune's duties. It concluded that they did not fit within the duties of an officer as so defined.

That simple application of Klune's situation to the corporation's bylaws caused the court of appeals to reverse the district court and to order a trial to determine whether Klune was or was not an officer. The tests for determining whether one is or is not an officer were set forth by the court of appeals as the following: (1) the likelihood of the person's obtaining confidential information; (2) the person's responsibility for corporate policy; and (3) the person's participation in executive councils of the corporation. Thus, the court recognized that the rigid application of the title test did not rule out the possibility that a person not bearing a common officer title might nevertheless be an officer within the meaning of the 1934 Act. The court also questioned the validity of the SEC rule defining officers, but made no decision in the matter. The rule is still in effect.

The SEC some years ago issued a release stating its general counsel's opinion of the status of assistant secretaries, assistant treasurers, and assistant controllers. The release states that if the assistant's chief is so inactive that the assistant is really performing the chief's function, the assistant will be considered an officer.[38]

The status of the so-called assistant officer was litigated twice by the same corporation in Section 16(b) cases. In the first case, *Lockhead Aircraft Corp. v. Rathman*,[39] the court held that an assistant treasurer was not an officer within the meaning of the 1934 Act. The SEC rule defined the term "officer" as including one whose duties "correspond" to the duties of the treasurer, but the court stated that duties of *assisting* the treasurer did not correspond to the duties *performed* by the treasurer. In the second case, *Lockheed Aircraft Corp. v. Campbell*,[40] the defendant held the titles of assistant treasurer, assistant secretary, and manager of the finance department. He did not, however, borrow money, prepare budgets, or concern himself with financial policy. He supervised the work of about 1,700 employees who performed "the mechanics incident to the accounting and bookkeeping of a large concern." Again, the court found that the defendant's duties did not correspond to those of an officer named in the SEC rule.

The status of an officer of a subsidiary has also been litigated, and it has been held that if the officer of the subsidiary is not performing the functions of an officer of the parent corporation and no fraud or subterfuge is involved, he or she is not an officer within the meaning of the 1934 Act.[41]

The three tests suggested by the court in *Colby v. Klune* have prompted some persons bearing officer titles to deny that they were officers subject to the requirements of Section 16. In one case, a person holding an officer title but performing "mere staff functions—routine administrative chores" was held not to be within Section 16(b). In the same case, however, vice presidents having important managerial duties were held to be insiders subject to 16(b).[42]

FAMILY MEMBERS

Section 16(a) requires a director or officer subject to its provisions to report ownership of, and transactions in, stock of the corporation "of which he is the beneficial owner." The term "beneficial owner" is not defined. It obviously includes shares held in the insider's own name and without any restrictions as to his or her right to receive the dividends, vote the stock, pledge it as security for a loan, and sell it—in short, to have absolute ownership. If the shares are held in the insider's brokerage account with all the above attributes except his or her name on the certificate, beneficial ownership also exists. Another possibility is a trust of which the insider is a beneficiary. The insider cannot sell or pledge the stock, but is entitled to the dividends. That is another form of beneficial ownership.

But what if there are shares held by the insider's spouse or minor
children or other members of the household? It was not until 1966 that
the SEC issued guidelines to the effect that shares held under such
circumstances were to be included in the insider's reports to the SEC
under Section 16(a).[43] Two principles were present in the guidelines: (1)
the control that the insider might exert over such shares by virtue of the
close family relationship and (2) the possible use of the dividends in the
maintenance of the common family household. The SEC states that the
guidelines were not intended to establish new reporting rules, but were
merely a reaffirmation of its long-held position in this matter. In another release issued shortly after the guidelines, the SEC stated that the
guidelines did not necessarily imply that transactions by such household members would be imputed to the insider under Section 16(b).

As early as 1952, an insider had been held liable under Section 16(b)
for transactions by his spouse.[44] That was an easy case, however, as the
insider was exercising complete control over his wife's finances and the
transactions were financed by property acquired during their marriage.
In a 1973 decision, *Blau v. Porter*,[45] the court denied liability where an
officer sold within six months after his wife's purchases. In that case,
however, the wife had been financially independent before marriage,
kept her funds separate from his, traded without consulting him, and
did not use her funds toward maintenance of the household. Somewhere between these two extremes were the facts of *Whiting v. Dow
Chemical Company*.[46] In that case, the wife was independently wealthy
before marriage and maintained her own personal records and accounts
and there was no evidence that the husband, who was a director,
controlled her decisions in financial matters. On the other hand, the
court found that their investment accounts were managed by the same
financial advisor, that they collaborated in income tax and gift tax
matters, that they used the resources of both in maintaining "their
common prosperity," and that the husband had borrowed from the
wife the funds to exercise his option to buy the corporate stock, funds
that had been derived from her recent sales of stock of the same corporation. The court found liability under Section 16(b), and in the course of
its opinion, indicated that the financial dealings of the spouse should be
attributed to the insider "where it is shown that the insider beneficially
owns the spouse's stock for purposes of § 16(a) reports."[47] This statement appears to be contrary to the SEC's release in 1966 in which it
stated that the requirement of reporting family holdings did not imply
that Section 16(b) liability would necessarily result from transactions by
the family members.[48]

Shortly after the *Whiting* decision, another district court held an
insider liable for stock transactions by his wife, even though her property (derived from gifts by him and her gains on them) had not been
used for the support of either spouse or for paying household expenses.[49] The court found liability on the basis of *indirect* benefit to the
insider from increases in his wife's estate—the lessening of his need to

make taxable gifts to her and his potential interest in her estate in the event of her death.

Another recent decision held an insider liable by matching his sales with the purchases by his mother within the same six months' period.[50] In that case, the insider did not reside in the same household with his mother, but he held a power of attorney from her which allowed him to manage her investments and other financial affairs. He was his mother's sole heir and, by reason of his power of attorney, was able to borrow from her without being concerned with the need for repayment.

### "DEPUTY DIRECTOR" SITUATIONS

Not only can family relationships trigger complicated questions of Section 16(b) liability, but business relationships can also raise questions of that section's applicability. A frequent directorship relation is that of a partner in a brokerage firm sitting on the board of a corporation whose stock is being actively traded. May the brokerage firm trade for its own account in the stock of a corporation in which one of its partners is a director?

In *Blau v. Lehman*,[51] a partner of Lehman Brothers was a director of Tidewater Associated Oil Company. While the director, Thomas, was serving on the board, Lehman Brothers purchased 50,000 shares of Tidewater. Thomas had not been advising Lehman Brothers concerning the affairs of Tidewater, and when he learned of the purchase, he immediately notified his firm that he must be excluded from "any risk of the purchase or any profit or loss from the subsequent sale." This disclaimer was acceptable to the firm, which sold the shares within six months of purchase at a profit of $98,687. A stockholder brought a derivative suit on the theory that Lehman was the real director and that Thomas was merely Lehman's deputy. It was noted that Rule X-16A-3(b), issued under Section 16(a), had formerly required partners to report only the amount of their own holdings—not those of the partnership. This rule was amended in 1952 to require the reporting of partnership holdings, but the SEC stated at that time that this change in reporting was not intended to change the short-swing liability rule. The Supreme Court refused to go beyond the literal language of Section 16(b) and to hold that the word "director" included a partnership of which the director was a member. Had Thomas participated in the profits of Lehman's transactions in Tidewater (which he did not) he would have been liable for only his pro rata share of the profits.[52]

*Blau v. Lehman* may be contrasted with a later case in which a corporate officer was held to be the deputy of his corporation in sitting on the board of another corporation. That case did not involve any question of the officer's personal liability, as it was not alleged that he personally engaged in any short-swing transactions.[53] In that case, Martin Marietta Corporation purchased 801,300 shares of stock of Sperry Rand between December 14, 1962, and July 24, 1963. Bunker, the

chief executive officer of Martin Marietta, became a director of Sperry
Rand on April 29, 1963, following which appointment 101,300 of the
shares were purchased. Bunker customarily discussed Sperry Rand
affairs with other Martin Marietta officials and maintained a file on
Sperry Rand that was available to other Martin Marietta management
personnel. He resigned from the Sperry Rand board on August 1, 1963.
Between August 29 and September 6, 1963, Martin Marietta sold all its
shares in Sperry Rand. A stockholder of Sperry Rand sued Martin
Marietta in a derivative action to recover the profit on the 101,300 shares
purchased during Bunker's time on the board, all of which were, of
course, sold within six months of purchase. The court found that, on the
facts, Bunker was the deputy of Martin Marietta and that that corporation was liable to Sperry Rand under Section 16(b). In this case, the
officer escaped personal liability as he was not the beneficial owner, but
liability, rather, attached to the corporation of which he was found to be
the deputy.

### SOME QUESTIONS OF LITERAL INTERPRETATION

The courts have repeatedly held that Section 16(b) means precisely what
it says. Consequently, there is little opportunity for reading reasonable
qualifications into it. Two cases in 1975, one favorable and one unfavorable to the insider, illustrate the rigidity of the language.

*Lewis v Mellon Bank*[54] involved the liability of Hill, who resigned as
an officer and director of PPG Industries on September 28, 1971. On the
two days succeeding his resignation, he exercised an option, granted to
him by PPG more than six months prior, to purchase 7,282 shares of
PPG common stock. On the same two days, he sold 6,800 shares that he
had previously acquired and had held more than six months. Under the
provisions of the SEC regulations under Section 16(a),[55] these transactions had to be reported to the SEC on Form 4 because they occurred
within six months after resignation. The court stated that the purposes
of Section 16(a) and of Section 16(b) were different. Section 16(a) was
designed to place insiders' security transactions under public scrutiny.
Section 16(b), on the other hand, was designed "to prevent only a very
narrow but highly visible form of unfair dealing by corporate insiders."
The court refused to extend Section 16(b) to a situation where the
defendant was not an officer or a director at the time either of purchase
or of sale. In this respect, the case differed from *Feder v. Martin Marietta
Corporation*,[56] where an insider situation did not exist at the time of sale
but did exist at the time of purchase. The court in *Mellon Bank* recognized that there *could* be use of inside information, but Congress had
not extended the automatic liability of Section 16(b) to that kind of
situation.[57]

The same plaintiff had more success in *Lewis v. Arcara*,[58] where a
corporate vice president's attempt to settle his 16(b) liability by use of
an installment note was held to be contrary to the Act. The vice presi-

dent actually did not have any insider information and did not realize that Section 16(b) applied to him. When he was confronted by the corporation with a claim of liability, he lacked the cash to pay it. The corporation accepted his five-year installment note, but in a derivative action, the court held that "forbearance over a five-year period in the collection of the amount due does not satisfy the statutory mandate." This decision is consistent with the well-established principle that a corporation may not settle a 16(b) claim for less than the undisputed amount of the liability.[59]

## What Constitutes a Purchase or Sale?

Although the language of Section 16(b) is literally and sometimes unmercifully construed, there still are questions as to the types of transactions to which it applies. This uncertainty arises from the fact that not all stock transactions are simple exchanges of stock for money or of money for stock. So both the SEC and the courts have had to define or qualify the terms "purchase" and "sale" in the context of Section 16(b).

**Executive options**   Corporate managers often acquire stock in their corporations, not through open market purchases, but pursuant to bonus or option plans. Section 16(b) contains a provision by which the SEC may, by rules and regulations, exempt transactions "not comprehended within the purpose of this subsection." Under this grant of authority, the SEC has exempted from Section 16(b) the receipt, but not the sale, of stock acquired under a bonus plan (1) that has been approved by the stockholders, and (2) that provides for awards to be made only by the board of directors, a majority of which are disinterested, or by a disinterested committee of directors. To be "disinterested," a director or committee member must not be eligible to receive an award or must not have been so eligible during the preceding year.[60] Under this same rule, a grant of an option is also exempt if made pursuant to a plan meeting the same criteria. The exercise of such an option is not, however, exempt from the liabilities of Section 16(b), but the SEC has by rule interposed a limitation of liability in the event of a sale within six months of the exercise of an option. The liability is limited to the difference between the price realized from the sale preceding or subsequent to the exercise of the option and the lowest market price at any time within six months before or after the sale.[61] The reason for the limitation is premised on the intent in granting stock options to executives—to give then an opportunity to profit from the rise in market value of the stock between the date of granting and the date of exercise. To require such a gain to be returned to the corporation in the event of a sale within six months would defeat the corporate intent in granting the option.[62] The rule therefore limits liability to the greatest amount that the director or officer could have realized by buying and selling within the market during the same six-month period.

**Conversions and mergers**  There are two fairly common types of transactions involving stock ownership where a security holder may obtain stock, not by paying money for it (the usual concept of "purchase"), but (1) by converting a debenture or preferred stock of a corporation into common stock of the same corporation, in accordance with the provisions of the preferred stock or debenture; or (2) by exchanging stock of another corporation in accordance with the terms of a merger agreement between two or more corporations. It is, of course, possible to go through both such transactions, as by converting a convertible preferred stock into common stock and then exchanging the common stock for the stock of another corporation pursuant to a merger. The courts have had to decide whether such transactions fall within the scope of Section 16(b). In other words, is there, or is there not, a purchase or sale?

There are cases on these questions going back as far as 1947, when it was held in *Park & Tilford v. Schulte*[63] that a conversion of convertible preferred stock into common stock by a holder of a majority of the common stock constituted a purchase, and that the sale of the common stock within six months of the conversion resulted in short-swing profits within the meaning of Section 16(b). This was a literal reading of the statute, but in 1958 a different result was reached in *Ferraiolo v. Newman*.[64] That case held that the common stock was the economic equivalent of the preferred, and since the preferred was called for redemption at a price below its market value, the director who converted was being subjected to an "involuntary" conversion. The court concluded that there had not been a purchase of the common within the six-month period prior to its sale.

In 1965, a voluntary conversion by a director of preferred into common was held in *Heli-Coil v. Webster*[65] to be a purchase, although it is not clear that a different result would have been reached if it were a forced conversion. The next year, the court, in *Blau v. Lamb*[66] followed the "economic equivalent" test of *Ferraiolo* and held that a voluntary conversion was not a sale. In that case, there had been an exchange of shares of common stock of one corporation for shares of convertible preferred stock of another corporation, which exchange was held to be a purchase. It was those shares of preferred stock that were converted into common stock three months later. The defendant did not dispose of the shares of common stock after acquiring them. In its opinion, the court stated that not only were the shares of preferred stock and common stock economic equivalents, but also that, under the facts, "this conversion afforded the insiders no opportunity to realize a gain by speculative trading." In another case decided the same year, *Petteys v. Butler*,[67] the economic equivalency test of *Ferraiolo* was applied in holding that a conversion was not a purchase.

Then in 1970 the court used the "possibility-of-abuse" test that had been introduced in *Blau v. Lamb* and held that the exchange of shares by a holder of more than 10 percent pursuant to a merger constituted a sale.[68] The court did not state that there was a sale because there was possibility of abuse, but, instead, it first found that there was a possibility of abuse under the facts and then proceeded to apply the statute in its broadest terms in determining whether there was a sale.

The possibility-of-abuse test was applied by the Supreme Court in *Kern County Land Co. v. Occidental Petroleum Corp.*[69] in 1973. That case also did not involve an officer or a director but, rather, a holder of more than 10 percent of the shares. The defendant purchased its shares as a part of its tender-offer strategy, which was defeated by a subsequent defensive merger between the target company and another company within six months of its purchase. The merger was involuntary so far as the defendant was concerned. In fact, it was antagonistic to the defendant's position, and it was held not to be a sale within the meaning of Section 16(b).

A few months following the *Kern* decision, the possibility-of-abuse test was applied in *Gold v. Sloan*[70] to arrive at opposite results in the cases of different officers of the same corporation which was merged into another corporation. When their employer was merged into the acquiring corporation, they obtained shares in it in exchange for shares in their employer. All three sold within six months after the merger. The merger was held to be a purchase within the meaning of Section 16(b) in the case of one officer who possessed inside information and therefore had a possibility of abuse. It was held, however, not to be a purchase by the other two officers, whose positions were such that they did not have inside information and therefore did not possess a possibility of abuse.

While the reach of Section 16(b) purports to be automatic and absolute, without any considerations of good faith, it is evident that there are some borderline situations where the courts will look beyond the rigidities of the section to determine whether the imposition of liability on the particular facts is consistent with the congressional intent.[71] This logically leads us into a consideration of Section 10(b), which imposes insider liability in a less rigid manner but to a broader group of persons and a wider range of transactions.

### INSIDER TRANSACTIONS—SECTION 10 AND RULE 10b-5

Section 10(b) is a short statement of a broad legal principle, granting rule-making power to the SEC to fill in the details. Here it is:

> It shall be unlawful for any person, directly or indirectly, by the use of any means or instrumentality of interstate commerce or of the mails, or of any facility of any national securities exchange—
>
> (a) . . . . .
>
> (b) To use or employ, in connection with the purchase or sale of any security registered on a national securities exchange or any security not so registered, any manipulative or deceptive device or contrivance in

contravention of such rules and regulations as the Commission may

prescribe as necessary or appropriate in the public interest or for the
protection of investors.[72]

Pursuant to the authority granted it by Section 10(b), the SEC in 1942
promulgated Rule 10b-5, which reads as follows:

It shall be unlawful for any person, directly or indirectly, by the use of any
means or instrumentality of interstate commerce, or of the mails or of any
national securities exchange,

(*a*) To employ any device, scheme, or artifice to defraud,

(*b*) To make any untrue statement of a material fact or to omit to state a
material fact necessary in order to make the statements made, in the
light of the circumstances under which they were made, not misleading, or

(*c*) To engage in any act, practice, or course of business which operates or
would operate as a fraud or deceit upon any person in connection with
the purchase or sale of any security.[73]

Three fundamental differences between Section 16(b) and Section
10(b) should be noted: (1) Section 16(b) is limited to certain designated
insiders, while Section 10(b) covers *any person*, without specifying
insider status; (2) Section 16(b) is limited to an *equity security* registered
under Section 12 of the 1934 Act, while Section 10(b) covers *any security*,
equity, or debt, registered or unregistered; (3) Section 16(b) is limited to
purchases and sales within the same six-month period, while Section
10(b) is not limited to, but may include, purchases or sale or both by the
person to whom it applies, and it may also impose liability upon such a
person by reason of the sale or purchase by another person, whether or
not in league with (or even antagonistic to) the insider.

There was relatively little litigation under Section 10(b) and Rule
10b-5 during the first three decades of the 1934 Act. Two early landmark
cases were *Kardon v. National Gypsum Co.*[74] in 1946 and *Speed v. Transamerica Corp.*[75] in 1951.

*Kardon* involved a purchase by two stockholders in a closely held
corporation of the shares of two other stockholders without having
disclosed that they (the purchasing stockholders) had an agreement to
sell the corporation's assets. Section 10(b) makes certain acts "unlawful"
but does not specifically give a private right of action for their breach.
The court in *Kardon* followed the well-established principle of common
law that a violation of a statute gives rise to a tort action by persons who
have been victimized by the violation. Accordingly, the selling stockholders had a right to sue the purchasing stockholders for a violation of
Section 10(b).[76]

In *Transamerica* the controlling stockholder and owner of a major
portion of the Class B stock purchased some shares of Class A stock

pursuant to a written offer and then called for redemption of the remaining shares of Class A stock. The Class A stock was convertible into Class B. The controlling stockholder failed to disclose that the real value of the inventory of the corporation was far in excess of its book value. The amounts received by the Class A holders were considerably less than they would have been if the Class A shares had been converted into Class B, the inventory liquidated, and the assets would be distributed to the Class B holders. These steps were exactly what the controlling stockholder was planning to do. The court held that the failure to disclose constituted a violation of Rule 10b-5, indicating that the three subdivisions of Rule 10b-5 were broadly remedial and covered the implied misrepresentations of the controlling stockholders.

Neither of these cases is concerned with the personal liability of a corporate manager, but rather, each is concerned with controlling stockholders and minority stockholders, but the principles of the cases are equally applicable to corporate directors and officers and to controlling stockholders. An action against corporate directors, decided shortly after *Transamerica*, was, however, unsuccessful in establishing liability against them because of the rather narrow views (lack of privity between seller and buyer and a strict reading of Rule 10b-5) taken by the court, views that have been superseded by more recent decisions.[77]

Rule 10b-5 began to emerge as a strong enforcement device in the early 1960s. The first case to warn of the potential significance of the rule was not a court decision but a ruling in an administrative proceeding of the SEC, *In the Matter of Cady, Roberts & Co.*[78] In that case, Cowdin, a partner of Cady, Roberts & Co., a brokerage firm, who was a director of Curtiss-Wright Company, telephoned another partner, Gintel, and told him that the directors of Curtiss-Wright had just reduced its dividend. The directors had done so at 11:00 A.M. Owing to some inadvertence, Dow Jones was not given the announcement until 11:45 A.M., and it did not appear on the ticker until 11:48 A.M. The telegram required by New York Stock Exchange rules did not reach the Exchange until 12:29 P.M. In the meanwhile, Gintel placed two sell orders for Curtiss-Wright stock for certain of his discretionary accounts. These orders were executed before the news came on the ticker. Following the announcement, the Exchange suspended trading in Curtiss-Wright, and when it reopened two hours later, the stock fell about 10 percent. The SEC found that Gintel, in selling when he knew that the dividend news was not yet public, had violated the antifraud provisions of Rule 10b-5. Accordingly, it issued an administrative order against Cady, Roberts & Co. against further violations. It should be noted that the "person" who was held liable here was the broker. The director who conveyed the news of the dividend reductions presumably did not realize that the public announcement had not been made. Therefore, it was not his liability as a director that was sought or established in the SEC proceeding.

*Cady, Roberts* was the first case holding anyone liable for engaging in an impersonal transaction on a stock exchange without having made any affirmative representation or misrepresentation or without having

taken any other special action of the type ordinarily associated with fraud or deceit. All the defendant did was to act upon information that he knew would soon be public information, but he knew that somehow it had not become public. He took advantage of that information to get ahead of all others and to make sales on behalf of his clients before the market price fell, as he must certainly have known it would when the news became public. It was not his responsibility to make the news announcement. That obligation rested with Curtiss-Wright. The SEC held, however, that, being possessed of the information, he could not act upon it until it was generally known. Although not vested with the responsibility of announcing, he was not at liberty to sell to those who did not know the news, even though they were anonymous buyers whom he had never seen and had no way of identifying. His obligation was, therefore, to the investing public.

The impersonal transaction on the exchange, the silence in the face of bad news not yet disseminated, the advantageous position because of contact with an insider, the position of the seller as a broker, a member of a profession regulated by the SEC in the very business of selling securities upon the market—all these circumstances were featured in *Cady, Roberts*. If one were to look at it merely as a "broker" case, then perhaps the result would not have been surprising—but Section 10(b) and Rule 10b-5 do not use the word "broker." The word is "person." Would the implications of *Cady, Roberts* be confined to activities of brokers? The answer would come in a very few years.

## THE *Texas Gulf Sulphur* CASE

Just two years after the Commission's decision in *Cady, Roberts*, specifically on November 8, 1963, a development took place in northern Ontario that was to lead to what is probably the most celebrated case on the liability of corporate managers in the history of the securities laws—the drilling of a 655-foot core sample by Texas Gulf Sulphur Company on a site near Timmins, Ontario. The sample indicated unusually large quantities of copper and zinc, as well as silver. Texas Gulf made no announcement of its finding. The information was kept confidential among only those who had a need to know. Not even the board of directors was told. A portion of the core was sent to Salt Lake City for chemical assay. Texas Gulf commenced a program of acquiring rights to additional lands in the area. It continued its drilling activity. It wanted to make sure that the strike was remarkable as had first appeared. It wanted to be certain that its reserves were protected against the intrusions of other mining prospectors. This program of development and protection continued throughout the winter and early spring of 1963 and 1964.

During this period of official corporate silence, however, certain individuals within the corporation engaged in transactions in Texas

Gulf stock. Between November 12, 1963, and April 6, 1964, six individuals who were aware of the unusual core sample purchased an aggregate of 5,260 shares of common stock of Texas Gulf. This total included purchases by the executive vice president of an aggregate of 3,100 shares over that period. Other purchases were made by the vice president for exploration, the chief geologist, and other persons in the middle-management level. Some of them purchased calls on Texas Gulf stock, a total of 4,700 calls in all. One of the field geologists also strongly recommended Texas Gulf stock to certain friends, who purchased 2,700 shares and 6,300 calls.

On February 20, 1964, the corporation's option committee, consisting entirely of outside directors, none of whom knew of the unusual activity at Timmins, granted stock options to twenty-six officers and high-salaried employees. These included the president and the executive vice president, both of whom were also directors and were, in fact, the only directors having knowledge of the drill-hole. Other optionees included the vice president for mineral exploration and the chief geologist, both of whom were intimately involved in the Timmins activity, and the vice president and general counsel, who was aware of some activity at Timmins but did not know any of the details. The options granted to these five persons totaled 31,000 shares. None of them told the option committee of the Timmins drill-holes or its possibilities.

In the early spring of 1964, rumors of an unusual discovery by Texas Gulf began circulating in the mining press, particularly in Canada. On Saturday, April 11, the *New York Herald Tribune* and the *New York Times* published the rumor—the *Herald Tribune*, under a two-column headline, announcing "(t)he biggest ore strike in more than 60 years in Canada." The New York stories led to a decision of the president and the executive vice president to make an immediate announcement. This announcement, which was published on Monday, April 13, acknowledged recent drilling near Timmins, but asserted that sufficient work had not been done to reach definite conclusions, that "any statement as to size and grade of ore would be premature and possibly misleading," and that a later announcement would be made when the work had "progressed to the point where reasonable and logical conclusions can be made."[79]

Three days later, on April 16 at 9:00 A.M., the board of directors of Texas Gulf met and the information concerning the strike was reported to them. This was followed by a press conference at 10:00 A.M., when a major discovery of zinc, copper, and silver was announced. The release gave a lengthy detail of the official assay of the first core and disclosed estimates of reserves. Texas Gulf stock rose about 25 percent on the New York Stock Exchange that day. It had been trading at approximately 17 in November, had opened at about 30 on April 16, and closed near 37 that day. A month later, it was up to 58.

The day before the final announcement, Clayton, a Texas Gulf engineer, bought an additional 200 shares; that evening Crawford, the

corporate secretary, called his broker and placed an order for 300 shares
of Texas Gulf stock. Crawford doubled his order early the next morning. Shortly before the news became public (after having been given to the press), one of the directors, Coates, instructed his broker to purchase 2,000 shares for family trusts. The broker also made purchases of 1,500 shares for his own and other customer accounts. Another director, Lamont, who was also a bank director and officer, told another officer of his bank to watch for favorable news on Texas Gulf. The bank purchased 10,000 shares on behalf of some of its clients before the news became public. Two hours later, Lamont placed an order for 3,000 shares for himself.

One year later, the SEC filed an action in the United States District Court for the Southern District of New York against Texas Gulf and thirteen of its directors, officers, and employees, alleging violations of Section 10(b) and seeking various forms of equitable relief. The District Court decision was a partial victory for the SEC.[80] The appeal to the Second Circuit was argued before the usual three-judge panel that hears most court of appeals cases and then was considered and decided by the entire court of nine judges sitting *en banc*, without any further argument by the parties. The Court of Appeals decision, with two judges dissenting, was an almost-complete victory for the SEC's position.[81]

*Cady, Roberts,* it will be recalled, was a ruling by the SEC itself and not a court decision. Now the courts, at both the district and appeals levels, upheld the Commission's position that the prohibitions of Section 10(b) and Rule 10b-5 apply not just to directors, officers, and controlling stockholders, but also to any person who comes into possession of inside information. In *Cady, Roberts,* it was a broker. In *Texas Gulf,* it was *any employee.* The courts found that once such a person had such inside information and if it was material, he or she could not trade in the stock until the information became public. It made no difference whether the trading was in a face-to-face transaction or an impersonal transaction on the stock exchange.

The two courts differed on the question of materiality. Looking back at Rule 10b-5, we find that its second test of unlawful conduct is making an untrue statement of a material fact or omitting to state a material fact. The District Court held that the rule's application to a nondisclosure was limited to one essentially extraordinary in nature and reasonably certain to have a substantial effect on the market price of the stock if disclosed. The Court of Appeals overruled and held that a material fact is any fact which in reasonable and objective contemplation *might* affect the market value. Moreover, the test was not limited to how a prudent investor might view the matter. A fact would also be material if it might affect the market price of a stock solely because of the reactions of speculators. Thus, the court concluded, when the result of the Timmins drill-hole was first known, it became a material fact. That did not mean, however, that there was an obligation to announce it. There were good and sufficient business reasons for keeping it secret—additional land acquisition and additional exploration—but there was an obligation on the part of those who knew the secret to refrain from buying or otherwise taking a position on Texas Gulf stock.

While a corporation may remain silent until an appropriate time, assuming no insider trading, once it makes an announcement it must tell the truth and the whole truth. A corporation is not to be concerned only with the documents that it files with the SEC, such as registration statements and prospectuses, proxy statements, annual and quarterly financial reports, and interim reports of significant developments. Its statements in all those must be true, not misleading, and in accordance with the requirements of the securities laws and regulations in all respects. In addition, however, whenever a corporation issues a public announcement, such as a news release, that announcement must not be false or misleading—if it is concerned with a material fact as defined by the court. So the news release of April 13 was subject to the requirements of Rule 10b-5. The test, the court said, was whether a reasonable investor in the exercise of due care would have been misled by the release.

The Court of Appeals remanded the case to the District Court for the taking of further testimony, for a determination of whether the April 13 news release was misleading, and for a determination of the sanctions to be applied against the various defendants. The District Court, following the principles laid down by the Court of Appeals, found the April 13 news release to be misleading and ordered the injunction against further misleading news releases that the SEC had requested.[82] The court then proceeded to examine the positions of each of the thirteen individual defendants in considerable detail. The various manners in which their cases were disposed of gives us a good illustration of the consequences of Section 10(b) violations by corporate managers.

The SEC had requested four kinds of equitable injunctive relief against the individual defendants. The requested relief varied somewhat with respect to the various defendants, depending upon the differing facts of their involvement. Against all of them, however, the Commission sought an injunction against (1) buying or selling Texas Gulf stock on the basis of material information not made available to the company, its stockholders, and the public, and (2) making such inside information available to a few, select, noncorporate persons who were able to benefit therefrom.

The Commission also requested the cancellation of stock options that had been granted to five of the defendants and the return to the corporation of any profits that the optionees may have made on any options that were exercised. Stephens, the president, and Fogarty, the executive vice president, had been granted options for 12,800 shares and 7,800 shares, respectively. Fogarty had also, as noted above, purchased 3,100 shares in the market. As directors and top officers, Stephens and Fogarty were held to have had an obligation to tell the option committee of the Timmins strike at the time the options were granted. Before commencement of the suit, however, both officers had surrendered

their options and Fogarty had sold his 3,100 shares to the corporation at
his cost. The SEC nevertheless sought injunctions against them, which
the court denied, as full restitution had been made before the suit was
started and there was no evidence of any likelihood of continued or
repeated violations.

Mollison, vice president for exploration, and Holyk, chief geologist,
being at a different level from Stephens and Fogarty, were held not to
have had an obligation to disclose to the option committee what they
knew about the strike. Not being directors, they had no reason to
believe that the committee had not been informed. They were permitted to keep their options. Mollison, like Fogarty, had voluntarily
sold to the corporation at his cost the shares purchased by him and his
wife during the November to April period. Mollison, like Fogarty and
Stephens, was accordingly relieved of any further liability.

Kline, vice president and general counsel and the fifth optionee
among the defendants, was in a different position from any of the
others. At the time the options were granted, he was also the corporate
secretary and had the responsibility of drawing up the option agreements. He denied that he was top management, that he had material
inside information, and that he had any obligation to disclose to the
option committee, but the Court of Appeals held otherwise and directed the District Court to cancel his option. Before the entry of the
order of cancellation, however, Kline exercised the option to prevent its
lapse, but the corporation declined to accept the exercise until a final
determination of legality. The matter was finally disposed of in a separate remand proceeding with an order that Kline could exercise the
option if, in addition to the option price ($23 13/16 a share), he paid the
corporation the increase in value between February 20, the date of the
option grant, and April 17, the day following the public release.[83]

In its complaint, the SEC asked for an order that the individual
defendants offer rescission to each of the persons from whom they had
purchased shares or calls between November 12 and April 17. The SEC
also asked that Darke, the field geologist, and Lamont and Coates,
directors, make restitution to the sellers from whom their "tippees" had
purchased shares and calls. On the remand, as affirmed by the Court of
Appeals,[84] Holyk and Darke, as well as Clayton, a Texas Gulf geophysi-
cist, and Huntington, a Texas Gulf attorney, were ordered to pay into
court all the profits from their transactions realized as of April 17. They
were permitted to keep any profits resulting from any increase in
market value after April 17. The court would hold the amounts so paid
for a period of five years to satisfy any claims by stockholders who had
sold during that period. Any money remaining with the court after five
years was to be paid to Texas Gulf. The court emphasized that it was not
penalizing the defendants, but was merely requiring them to pay just
compensation. The residuary payment to Texas Gulf was justified on
the basis that its corporate reputation had been injured by the insiders'

actions. Darke was also ordered to make restitution for the profits of his "tippees." The court stated that that remedy was also necessary to prevent insiders from evading their duty to refrain from trading on inside information.

Lamont, the director and banker who had notified his bank of the announcement after it was given to the press but before it was fully disseminated, was originally found by the District Court not to have violated Section 10(b). He died while the appeal was pending and the SEC dismissed the appeal against him. Coates, the director who had purchased for family trusts, was also found on the initial trial not to have committed a Section 10(b) violation, and when that finding was reversed and remanded for further trial, he decided, for reasons of health, to settle, rather than to go through another trial. Shortly before the trial commenced, he paid $26,250 into court as a part of the escrow fund for selling stockholders. He died the next month.

During the course of the proceeding, Crawford, who had succeeded Kline as corporate secretary shortly before the ill-fated announcement of April 13 and who had made purchases just before the release of the announcement of April 16, sold his 600 shares to the corporation at his cost. The SEC accordingly did not seek any monetary damages against him, but it did seek and obtain from the court an injunction against further violations by using inside information concerning Texas Gulf.

The only other person against whom an injunction was issued was Clayton. He, like Crawford, had made a purchase just shortly before the April 16 news release. Darke, a Canadian, had resigned from Texas Gulf and was living in Canada. An injunction against him would be meaningless, as would an injunction against the two deceased directors. The circumstances as to the other defendants were such that it did not appear likely that future violations were apt to occur.

There were two other defendants—Murray, an office manager, whose purchases of stock were found to be a coincidence and not based upon inside information, and O'Neill, a bookkeeper, who had left the country and was probably uncollectible.

The suit by the SEC was, as might have been expected, followed by numerous actions brought by private plaintiffs who alleged that they had been damaged by the violations by Texas Gulf and the various insiders who had been defendants in the SEC suit.[85] Ultimately, all the actions were settled for a total of $2.7 million.

The Court of Appeals decision in *Texas Gulf* set up what one commentator aptly described as "shock waves" in the corporate and financial world.[86] The broad approach to materiality that the SEC had sought became the law. At the time the complaint was filed, William H. Painter, professor of law at the University of Missouri–Kansas City, anticipated the uncomfortable position in which such an extension of materiality would place corporate managers when he stated:

> [O]ne cannot help but sympathize with the dilemma of corporate officers who wish to trade their company's securities during periods of rapid

change and development. Must they disclose every possible significant
event which may take place in the foreseeable future, or must their disclosure be restricted to the merely probable? What should be the standard
with regard to the disclosure of possible or probable adverse developments?[87]

He then proceeded to answer his first question with a footnote:

The easy answer is to say that, in cases of doubt, those in possession of
potentially relevant information should not trade until the passage of time
has removed the doubts concerning their duty to disclose.[88]

It was that kind of dilemma that caused concern about, and criticism
of, the materiality test pronounced by the Court of Appeals in *Texas
Gulf*. In his dissenting opinion, Judge Moore not only disagreed with
the majority's test of materiality but commented that the issuance of the
injunctions requested by the SEC would place the company and its
executives in a position of "perpetual jeopardy." Judge Moore was most
critical of the majority's approach to the matter of the press release. He
stated in the conclusion of his opinion:

If corporations were literally to follow its implications, every press release
would have to have the same SEC clearance as a prospectus. Even this
procedure would not suffice if future events should prove the facts to have
been over or understated—or too gloomy or optimistic because the courts
will always be ready and available to substitute their judgment for that of
the business executive responsible therefor. But valuable as the news
release may be, what of the many daily developments in the Research and
Development departments of giant corporations. When and how are prom-
ising results to be disclosed? If they are not disclosed, the corporation is
concealing information; if disclosed and hoped-for results do not mate-
rialize, there will always be those with the advantage of hindsight to brand
them as false or misleading.[89]

Regardless of criticism and fears, the ruling of *Texas Gulf* stands, and
for more than a decade corporations and their executives have lived
with it. It has resulted in more high-level attention to corporate news
releases—what to release and when to release it and how to say it. It has
imbued managers with a greater sense of awareness of their responsibility to their stockholders and to the investing public generally.[90] Also,
these responsibilities do not inhere in directors and officers alone.
While only they among corporate personnel need be concerned with the
short-swing restrictions of Section 16(b), all corporate personnel, mid-
dle- and lower-level managers, accountants, engineers, researchers,
lawyers, and other professional personnel are prohibited from trading
in the corporation's stock while possessing material inside information.

RULE 10B-5 AND *Scienter*

With the expanded concept of materiality announced in *Texas Gulf* and
the judicial expansion of Rule 10b-5 to confer remedies in favor of

broader classes of plaintiffs and against broader classes of defendants, it has become increasingly important to determine the state of mind of the defendant in a Section 10(b) case. There can be little doubt of liability if the defendant has *intentionally* done one or more of the three types of acts described in Rule 10b-5. In such a case, we would say that the defendant had acted with *scienter*—the Latin for "knowingly"—or as the United States Supreme Court has defined it, "a mental state embracing intent to deceive, manipulate, or defraud."[91]

If all 10b-5 cases involved intentional wrongdoing, there would be no problem, but there are many borderline situations. The defendant's actions may be negligent. In the law of negligence, we know that there can be differing degrees of negligence—such as ordinary negligence (being just a little bit careless), gross negligence (being very careless), and willful or wanton misconduct (being extremely careless, with an utter disregard for the consequences). All these degrees of negligence, with varying shades in between, may be present in the fact situations giving rise to actions under Section 10(b) and Rule 10b-5. The extent to which negligence may be a basis for sustaining such an action is a problem that has created great confusion in the courts. The district courts and courts of appeal have differed in their statements of the law. Some have said that *scienter* is a necessary allegation to support a claim under 10(b) and 10b-5. Others have said that *scienter* is not necessary—that a showing of negligence is sufficient. The confusion in the courts' ruling has been compounded by the fact that the cases holding that *scienter* is not a necessary element generally have been those that have involved the kind of negligence that might be defined as willful or wanton misconduct. In commenting upon these cases in his dissenting opinion in *Kohn v. American Metal Climax, Inc.,*[92] Judge Arlin Adams of the Third Circuit stated in 1972:

> [I]n every case where liability was found, conduct tantamount to actual fraud existed, despite the fact that the reviewing court may have used broader language than necessary. In no case was liability affixed to nonculpable conduct regardless of the dicta.[93]

The *scienter* problem finally reached the United States Supreme Court in 1975 in *Ernst & Ernst v. Hochfelder,*[94] but only a partial answer was provided. That case was a private action against an accounting firm in which it was alleged that the firm was negligent in its auditing practices, which resulted in its not discovering that certain purported escrow accounts in a brokerage firm did not exist. The Court denied recovery to the plaintiff and, in so doing, looked carefully at the words of Section 10(b): "any manipulative or deceptive device or contrivance." In commenting upon these words, the Court stated that their use makes

> unmistakable a congressional intent to proscribe a type of conduct quite different from negligence. Use of the word "manipulative" is especially

significant. It is and was virtually a term of art when used in connection

with securities markets. It connotes intentional or wilful conduct designed to deceive or defraud investors by controlling or artificially affecting the price of securities.[95]

The Court denied recovery to the plaintiffs, but in a footnote stated:

> Since this case concerns an action for damages we also need not consider the question whether scienter is a necessary element in an action for injunctive relief under 10(b) and rule 10b-5.[96]

Thus, while the Supreme Court settled the question of *scienter* in private damage actions, it left room for disagreement in the district courts and the courts of appeal in the injunction cases brought by the SEC. The first case to deal with the subject after *Hochfelder* was *SEC v. Bausch & Lomb, Inc.*[97] This case is of immense practical interest to corporate officers and other executives whose duties include meeting and discussing with security analysts, because it presents the kind of problem that any one of them might encounter. Schuman, the board chairman of Bausch & Lomb, was interviewed for two days by security analysts. There was at that time a great deal of investor interest in Bausch & Lomb stock because of the company's activities in marketing its recently introduced soft contact lens. During the interviews, Schuman succeeded in disclosing nothing that would be considered material under the securities laws that was not already public information. Following one of the interviews, however, he received a telephone call from one of the analysts who told him that he was reducing his projection of Bausch & Lomb's first-quarter earnings from 90 cents a share to 60 cents. Schuman replied that he thought 70 to 80 cents was more likely. Later, after talking to his financial officers, he called the analyst back and changed the figures to a range of 65 to 75 cents. This occurred at 2:24 P.M. The market price of Bausch & Lomb stock closed at 125 ¼ that day, off 11 ¾ points from the previous day. Schuman received a large number of calls on his projection, most of them after the stock exchange had closed. Realizing that he had inadvertently made a material disclosure, he immediately arranged for a press release confirming his projection. On the next day, the day of publication, the New York Stock Exchange kept Bausch & Lomb off the market because of a rash of sell orders. When the market reopened on the next trading day, the stock fell an additional 20 points.

The SEC brought suit for an injunction against both Bausch & Lomb and Schuman. While the case was being tried, the Supreme Court decision in *Hochfelder* was announced. The trial judge in *Bausch & Lomb* held that, although the Supreme Court had not required *scienter* as foundation for an injunction, the same reasoning that had been used in the damage action, *Hochfelder*, compelled the conclusion that *scienter* was necessary in a suit for injunction. The judge found that Schuman had made an uncharacteristic and unintentional slip and had taken prompt steps to rectify it.There being no evidence of *scienter*, the injunction was denied.

The trial judge also observed in his opinion that the SEC had not convinced him "that absent an injunction there is reasonable likelihood that the defendants will violate the securities laws in the future."[98] On appeal, the Court of Appeals for the Second Circuit Court affirmed the District Court on the ground of unlikely reoccurrence, but declined to consider the *scienter* question.

Two other recent district court decisions agreed with the District Court in *Bausch & Lomb*. In *SEC v. American Realty Trust*,[99] the court found only one material omission by the corporation and its chief executive officer out of several that were alleged, and that one was corrected in subsequent reports. Finding that there was no "intent to deceive, manipulate or defraud," the court denied the injunction. In *SEC v. Southwest Coal & Energy Co.*[100] the officers owning two-thirds of the capital stock of a corporation were found to have been negligent in omitting material statements from offering circulars pertaining to oil and gas leases, but the court found insufficient evidence of "intent to defraud or deceive or a reckless disregard for the truth." Accordingly, an injunction against future violations of Section 10(b) and Rule 10b-5 was denied.

The District of Columbia Court of Appeals held, in an action against three companies and two officers of the three companies, that *Hochfelder* "forces the conclusion that *scienter* is an essential element of an SEC injunctive action under Section 10(b)." The court also decided that *scienter* is broad enough to include reckless behavior, although in that case the court concluded that the defendants acted neither with intent to deceive nor in a reckless fashion.[101]

Other district court and court of appeals decisions held that *scienter* is not necessary to support an injunction suit by the SEC, but then proceeded to find facts or allegations which, if not showing intentional fraudulent conduct, establish reckless action that comes very close to it.[102]

The conflict of opinions in the federal courts was finally resolved by the United States Supreme Court in June 1980 in the case of *Aaron v. SEC*.[103] In that case the SEC was seeking an injunction against Aaron, a managerial employee of a brokerage firm. Two employees working under his supervision conducted a sales campaign for common stock of Lawn-A-Mat Chemical & Equipment Corp., in which they stated to prospective investors that Lawn-A-Mat was in the process of manufacturing a new type of small car and tractor and also made projections of substantial increases in the price of stock and optimistic statements concerning the company's financial condition. All the foregoing statements and projections were without basis in fact. Lawn-A-Mat's attorney learned that these statements were being made and twice told Aaron about them. Aaron promised to stop the employees from making misrepresentations. He told one of the salesmen of the attorney's call and told him to tell the other salesmen, but took no affirmative steps to

prevent a recurrence of the false statements. He did not rebuke the salesmen nor order them to stop. The SEC charged that Aaron violated Section 17(a) of the 1933 Act, Section 10(b) of the 1934 Act, and Rule 10b-5 by failing to take adequate steps to prevent the employees under his supervision from engaging in fraudulent practices.

The District Court stated that an injunction might be based upon negligence alone, but then went further and found Aaron's violation to be intentional and thereby satisfying the test of *scienter*. The Court of Appeals for the Second Circuit upheld the injunction on the basis of negligence and declined to pass upon the question of whether Aaron's conduct constituted *scienter*.

The Supreme Court resolved the conflict among the various circuits by holding that *scienter* is required to sustain an injunction under Section 10(b) and Rule 10b-5, as well as under Section 17(a) (1) of the 1933 Act.[104] Although noting that it had reserved the question in its *Hochfelder* decision, the Court stated that the same reasoning applied in that case (quoted earlier in this chapter) led to its conclusion.

Private damage actions now seem to be centering on recklessness as establishing *scienter*. In doing so, the courts are going back to common-law concepts of fraud or deceit. It can be anticipated that in light of the *Aaron* decision, future injunction suits will follow a similar course. The Court of Appeals for the Seventh Circuit has this definition of reckless conduct:

> [R]eckless conduct may be defined as a highly unreasonable omission, involving not merely simple, or even inexcusable, negligence, but an extreme departure from the standards of ordinary care, and which presents a danger of misleading buyers or sellers that is either known to the defendant or is so obvious that the actor must have been aware of it.[105]

The Seventh Circuit has further stated that this definition is of "the kind of recklessness that is equivalent to wilful fraud."

Now that the question of *scienter* has been settled by the Supreme Court, it appears that the fears that followed in the wake of *Texas Gulf*—that legitimate businesspersons would proceed at their peril if they bought or sold stock in their own companies, if they tried to keep company secrets from leaking out, or if they talked to security analysts or reporters or didn't talk to them—have not been realized. Although there are some zealous efforts to impose sanctions for inadvertent slips, as in *Bausch & Lomb*, the courts are imposing such sanctions for only the more serious breaches of the securities laws.[106]

PERSONAL LIABILITY—NECESSITY OF PARTICIPATION

As we have reviewed the litigation under Section 10(b) and Rule 10b-5, we have seen numerous instances where directors, officers, and other corporate managerial and professional employees have been held personally liable. In these cases, there has generally been an element of active participation. Efforts have been made, however, to establish personal liability of a director on the theory that the director, although not actively participating in the transaction, is a controlling person. The 1934 Act, like the 1933 Act, provides for liabilities of controlling persons. Section 20(a) of the 1934 Act reads as follows:

> Every person who, directly or indirectly, controls any person liable under any provision of this chapter or of any rule or regulation thereunder shall also be liable jointly and severally with and to the same extent as such controlled person to any person to whom such controlled person is liable, unless the controlling person acted in good faith and did not directly or indirectly induce the act or acts constituting the violation or cause of action.[107]

The application of Section 20(a) to a cause of action under Section 10(b) came up in a sequel to the *BarChris* case, which was discussed earlier in this chapter in connection with liabilities under the 1933 Act. The sequel, *Lanza v. Drexel & Co.*,[108] involved many of the same persons as *BarChris* but a different transaction. A few months after the offering of debentures, which was the basis of *BarChris*, some of the officers negotiated an exchange of shares of BarChris stock for all the stock of Victor Billiard Co. It was not a public offering by BarChris and so no new prospectus was prepared, but the same prospectus that had been written for the debenture offering was furnished to the stockholders of Victor. In an action by the Victor stockholders for rescission and damages, the trial court imposed liability upon the treasurer as well as upon the president and the executive vice president, who were, of course, the top management. The court refused, however, to extend liability to Pugliese, the vice president for construction, a man of limited education and one of the founders of the company, but not really conversant with the company's business affairs. Pugliese had been held liable in *BarChris* because he had signed the registration statement. In the Victor transaction, however, the securities offered to Victor stockholders were not the securities covered by the registration statement and the prospectus. Therefore, the exact language of Section 11 of the 1933 Act imposing liability upon signers of a registration statement did not apply. Pugliese was exonerated from liability under Section 10(b) and Rule 10b-5 because, even though he was an officer, he did not participate in the transaction and apparently did not understand the prospectus.

The court also exonerated from liability Coleman, an outside director and partner in Drexel & Co., who had been held liable as a director in *BarChris*. This ruling was upheld by the Court of Appeals. The court held that a director has a right to assume that the officers of the corporation would make the necessary disclosures in a negotiation, unless he or she had a reason to suspect otherwise. A director, as such, is not liable

under Section 10(b) except on a secondary basis—such as an aider or
abettor, conspirator, or substantial participant in fraud. Failure to discover the misrepresentations and omissions, in order to be actionable,
must be based upon "willful, deliberate or reckless disregard for the
truth" and not mere negligence. The controlling person concept could
not be used to hold the directors liable because Section 20(a) contains an
exception for a person acting in good faith. The court so ruled without
deciding whether or not the exonerated directors were in fact controlling persons.

In a contemporaneous case in the Sixth Circuit involving two outside
directors, the court held that a director who had attended his first
meeting just twelve days before the issuance of the allegedly false proxy
statement was not a controlling person. The court also held that the
other director, a busy physician who relied on the chairman and president and the independent public accountants, was a controlling person
but acted in good faith.[109]

## Some Observations on Remedies

In our review of developments under the 1934 Act, we noted that
enforcement occurs through both governmental and private actions.
The most effective enforcement weapon of the SEC is an injunction
obtained by it in a federal court. Most of the court decisions interpreting the acts have been based upon either suits for injunctions or private
actions for rescission or damages. The SEC has extensive investigatory
powers, and persons disobeying its subpoenas may be fined up to
$1,000 and imprisoned for up to a year. The SEC may also refer viola-
tions to the Department of Justice for prosecution.[110] A willful violation
of either the 1933 Act or the 1934 Act, or of the rules or regulations
issued under either of them, subjects the violator to a fine not exceeding
$10,000 and/or imprisonment not exceeding five years.[111]

An injunction in enforcement of a statute is normally an order to
refrain from doing certain things that are violation of law. There have
been some recent moves by the SEC to extend this concept to taking
affirmative steps designed to assure compliance. The first significant
action of this nature was *SEC v. Mattel, Inc.*[112] which was settled by a
consent decree. In addition to the usual injunction against misleading
statements and false reports, the consent decree provided that Mattel
would (1) appoint to its board of directors two new individuals satisfac-
tory to the SEC; (2) establish an audit committee of four members, at
least three of whom would be directors independent of Mattel's controlling stockholders; and (3) appoint a litigation and claims committee of
three directors to determine what action should be taken with respect to
claims against officers, directors, and employees and to approve the
settlement of such claims. This is the first recorded case of the SEC's
specifying exactly who shall serve in a given capacity in a corporation. It

may be a harbinger of events to come, which will be discussed in Chapters 9 and 11.

CHANGE OF EMPLOYMENT

We have seen in our review of some of the cases how the courts have granted or denied injunctions against corporate managers on the basis of the nature of their participation in the violation and the likelihood of reoccurrence. A recent decision in the Southern District of New York shows that a court will not refrain from enjoining an individual merely because that person is no longer affiliated with the corporation in whose violation he or she participated. In *SEC v. Lums' Inc.*,[113] it was found that the corporate president had leaked to a securities salesman inside information concerning a sharp downward revision of an earnings projection previously made public. The salesman then tipped off an investor who thereupon sold his stock in the corporation. Although the president, at the time of the SEC suit, was no longer employed by the corporation, an injunction was nevertheless issued against him as he had become an officer of another corporation and was again in a position where he might acquire inside information.

REMEDIES UNDER STATE LAW

We saw in Chapter 3 that, under state law, there was no right of action against a person who traded in the market using inside information. The state law on this subject is, however, of little practical importance, as the remedies for violation of Section 10(b) have almost completely superseded actions under state law. State law on insider trading is useful only if the transaction in the security is neither executed on a securities exchange nor effected by the use of the mails or any instrumentality of commerce. This leaves under state law only those stock transactions where personal contacts are used exclusively.[114]

## 10B-5 and Mismanagement

In Chapter 3, we examined the liabilities of directors and officers for mismanagement under the various state laws. In that chapter, I deliberately avoided the impact of the federal securities laws on the subject, leaving it until the examination in this chapter of the applicable statutory provisions and some of the major court decisions under them. This has led to a point where the reader must obviously recognize that a system of federal corporation law has been superimposed upon the corporation law of the various states. The corporate manager must therefore look to both state and federal law for a delineation of managerial duties and responsibilities to stockholders.

The broad sweep of Section 10(b) and Rule 10b-5 has attracted so much attention that the liabilities of directors and officers under state

law seem at times to be almost forgotten. Stockholders often bring
actions against corporate managements under allegations of violations of the 1934 Act when actions under the relevant state law might fit better. There are a number of reasons for this. One reason is access to the federal courts. Some attorneys believe a state court is more sympathetic to the management of a corporation organized under its own state law. Criticisms have been voiced that state incorporation laws tend to be management-oriented and that state courts follow this same bias. Whether or not this is true is debatable. A second reason is that a body of federal law has been built up under the securities laws that has, as we have seen in this chapter, extended their reach to matters that were probably way beyond the contemplation of the Congress and the SEC in the early 1930s. Much of this development has been due to the SEC's own vigorous enforcement efforts during the past two decades, efforts that show no signs of slowing down. Private plaintiffs are not reluctant to build upon principles established by SEC actions—to extend them further to satisfy what the plaintiffs may perceive as wrongs done to them.

It is therefore not surprising that there are frequent unsuccessful—and occasionally moderately successful—efforts to extend the scope of the securities laws into the internal management of a corporation. One early effort was *Birnbaum v. Newport Steel Corp.*,[115] a stockholder suit for mismanagement against a corporation and its president, alleging a violation of 10(b) and 10b-5. The suit was dismissed on the ground that the plaintiffs had neither purchased nor sold securities of the corporation and had not claimed to have been defrauded in connection with any such sale, and the further ground that the acts of which they complained constituted, at the most, mismanagement and did not involve any fraud in connection with a securities transaction. This decision had the effect of deterring mere mismanagement cases under the federal securities laws for many years. The plaintiffs were relegated to their remedies under state law.

The authority of *Birnbaum* that the injury to the plaintiff must have occurred in the act of buying or selling securities was followed in decisions by numerous district courts and courts of appeals and was upheld twenty-three years later by the United States Supreme Court in *Blue Chips Stamps v. Manor Drug Stores.*[116] In that case, the plaintiffs sued a corporation, its major stockholders, and its directors, alleging that a prospectus issued by the corporation was overly pessimistic and deterred them from buying shares in the corporation. The Court, citing *Birnbaum*, denied recovery under Section 10(b) on the ground that that section proscribed certain acts "in connection with the purchase or sale of any security," a transaction to which the plaintiff had not been a party.

On the other point of *Birnbaum*, however, there was a period of erosion from the concept that Section 10(b) and Rule 10b-5 did not cover mere mismanagement and that fraud in connection with a securities transaction was an essential element. Generally, the cases arose where there was some kind of securities transaction involved, although not necessarily one in which the plaintiff was a buyer or seller. The plaintiff might be suing derivatively as a stockholder of a corporation, as in the case of a merger or issuance of stock in the plaintiff's corporation to a third party. In one such case, *Schoenbaum v. Firstbrook*,[117] a stockholder of Banff, Oil Ltd., sued the directors of Banff for having sold additional stock to Aquitaine Company of Canada, Ltd., which was already the controlling stockholder, at a price alleged to be "vastly inadequate." Three of the eight directors of Banff were representatives of Aquitaine, and they abstained from voting on the sale. The court held that a cause of action existed if Aquitaine "exercised a controlling influence over the issuance to it of treasury stock of Banff for a wholly inadequate consideration," and that approval by a majority of directors who were not Aquitaine's representatives was not a defense. *Schoenbaum* raised the possibility that mere unfairness of the transaction might be a basis for a 10b-5 action. Four years later, however, in another unfairness case, the same court, the Court of Appeals for the Second Circuit, reached an opposite conclusion. That case was *Popkin v. Bishop*,[118] in which a derivative action was brought against the directors of a merging corporation alleging that the exchange ratio in the merger was unfair to the minority stockholders. It was found, however, that all the material facts had been disclosed in the proxy statement for the stockholders meeting in which the merger was voted upon. The court stated that the mandate of the 1934 Act for full disclosure had been carried out. Therefore, the plaintiffs must seek their remedy under state law. The court distinguished its case from *Schoenbaum* by noting that in that case the court had stated that "Aquitaine and the directors of Banff were guilty of *deceiving* the stockholders of Banff (other than Aquitaine)." Thus, the fundamental feature of the securities laws—disclosure—was again the deciding factor.

The question of unfairness in a "short-form" merger under Delaware law came before the United States Supreme Court in 1977 in *Santa Fe Industries v. Green.*[119] Under the Delaware statute, a corporation holding 90 percent of the stock of another Delaware corporation may merge the subsidiary into the parent without prior notice to, or a vote of, the minority holders, whose only right is a right of appraisal if they deem the price paid to them to be inadequate.[120] In the *Santa Fe* case, the minority stockholders, rather than seek appraisal under the Delaware law, sought to rescind the merger, alleging a violation of Rule 10b-5. The District Court had found that there had been no omission or misstatement in the documents that were sent to the minority stockholders when they were notified of the merger and advised of their appraisal rights. The Supreme Court again emphasized that the fundamental purpose of the 1934 Act was full disclosure. This had been accomplished and there was no fraud, deception, or manipulation. Citing the *Hochfelder* decision, Mr. Justice White made this statement:

[T]he cases do not support the proposition . . . that a breach of fiduciary

duty . . . , without any deception, misrepresentation, or nondisclosure, violates the statute and the Rule . . . . "Manipulation" is "virtually a term of art when used in connection with securities markets." . . . The term refers generally to practices such as wash sales, matched orders, or rigged prices, that are intended to mislead investors by artificially affecting market activity. . . . [W]e do not think [Congress] would have chosen this "term of art" if it had meant to bring within the scope of § 10(b) instances of corporate mismanagement such as this, in which the essence of the complaint is that shareholders were treated unfairly by a fiduciary.[121]

In a dispute between directors, the minority directors, suing derivatively on behalf of the corporation, attempted to invoke Rule 10b-5 in *Biesenbach v. Guenther*.[122] The majority directors were making loans to the corporation at terms very favorable to themselves. The terms included repayment of portions of the loans in shares of the corporation, which, of course, increased their percentage ownership in the corporation. Other actions complained of included reduction of the board of directors from nineteen to seven members. The plaintiffs alleged fraud and deceit upon the other stockholders and upon the corporation by representing that the transactions were in their best interests. The complaint was found to allege no more than a violation of fiduciary obligation and was dismissed on the authority of *Santa Fe*. The district court held that 10b-5 can be invoked only if the conduct alleged can be fairly viewed as "manipulative or deceptive" within the meaning of the statute," quoting from the Supreme Court's description of manipulation in *Santa Fe*.

How far Section 10(b) and Rule 10b-5 can be extended into a corporate management's decisions is a question far from settled. While recent decisions, such as *Santa Fe* and *Biesenbach*, would seem to say that the limits have been reached, there is no end to the ingenuity of counsel in seeking ways to extend its scope. The current interest in corporate democracy, the expanding role of the federal government and federal laws into all phases of business activity, and the seemingly irresistible impulse to sue are bound to result in increased efforts to replace state legal remedies in the corporate field with federal remedies.[123]

## AMERICAN LAW INSTITUTE'S PROPOSED SECURITIES CODE

A major recodification of the federal securities laws, including a substantial number of substantive changes, has been proposed by the American Law Institute. Drafting of the proposed new code was begun in 1969 and completed in 1978. With Prof. Louis Loss of Harvard Law School as the reporter, consultants and advisors from law schools and the practicing bar (including several former members of the SEC) have collaborated in its preparation. In addition, a committee of the Corporation, Banking and Business Law Section of the American Bar Association acted as a further advisory group. Staff people from the SEC and appropriate congressional subcommittees also participated in meetings in the course of the preparation of the proposed code. During 1980, the proposed code was studied by the SEC to determine whether or not the Commission would support its introduction into Congress. As this book went into print, such SEC support appeared to be imminent.[125]

The proposed code, with its annotations, explanations, and appendices, is more than 800 pages in length.[124] It retains the fundamental principle of the requirement of disclosure that has been the hallmark of the securities laws since their inception. The traditional separation of the 1933 Act, concerned with the initial offering of securities, and the 1934 Act, concerned with trading in securities, has been eliminated. Concepts common to both types of activities are treated together. Where separate treatment is required because of the differing nature of the two types of activities, the differences are recognized accordingly.

So far as corporate managers are concerned, there is no diminution in the principles of personal liability, although there are some proposed limitations on the dollar amount of such liability. One such limitation would prevent an insider from having to pay damages in excess of the amount of personal gain from a transaction in violation of the code (the typical 10b-5 case under present law).[126]

The definition of an officer is expanded to include a "vice president or other employee who participates or has authority to participate . . . in major policy-making functions of a company."[127] This could have the effect of bringing a much larger number of corporate managers within the reporting requirements and the short-swing and insider trading prohibitions of the securities laws.

Other changes from existing law might be noted, but it is beyond the scope of this book to go into detail concerning a proposed code that may be changed in many respects when and if it is adopted. Discussion of such changes is left to future writers after the event of adoption.[128]

## NOTES

1. The text of the Securities Act of 1933, with all amendments, is compiled at 15 U.S.C. § 77a–77aa. The text of the Securities Exchange Act of 1934, with all amendments, is compiled at 15 U.S.C. § 78a–78jj. For a more complete discussion of the philosophy and background of the disclosure principle, see Knauss, "A Reappraisal of the Role of Disclosure," 62 *Mich. L. Rev.* 607–648 (1964). For a first-hand account of the origins of the Securities Act, see Landis, "The Legislative History of the Securities Act of 1933," 28 *Geo. Wash. L. Rev.* 29–49 (1959). The securities laws are summarized in Hancock, *Executive's Guide to Business Law* (McGraw-Hill Book Co., 1979) 38-1 to 42-4.

2. Related statutes administered by the Securities and Exchange Commission include the Public Utility Holding Company Act of 1935, 15 U.S.C. § 792–6, the Trust Indenture Act of 1939, 15 U.S.C. § 77aaa–77bbbb, and the Investment Companies and Advisors Act of 1940, 15 U.S.C. § 80a–1 to 80b–21.

3. Securities of foreign governments offered for sale within the United States

are also subject to the Securities Act of 1933, but discussion of the subject is omitted as being outside the scope of this book.

4. 1933 Act, § 10; 15 U.S.C. § 77j.

5. 1933 Act, § 8; 15 U.S.C. § 77h.

6. 1933 Act, § 6; 15 U.S.C. § 77f.

7. 1933 Act, § 11; 15 U.S.C. § 77k.

8. 1933 Act, § 11(c); 15 U.S.C. § 77k(c). This definition contrasts with the stricter use of "prudent man" in ERISA, § 404(a)(1)(b). See the discussion under "The Manager as a Fiduciary Under ERISA" and note 53 in Chapter 7.

9. 1933 Act, §§ 20 & 24; 15 U.S.C. §§ 77t, 77x. Such an injunction may not issue against a corporate officer personally in the absence of proof that the officer was personally connected with the violation. SEC v. Coffey, 493 F.2d 1304 (6th Cir. 1974), *cert. denied*, 420 U.S. 908 (1975).

10. See Comments, "BarChris: Due Diligence Refined," 68 *Colum. L. Rev.* 1411–1423 (1968), and "Escott v. BarChris Construction Corporation: Section 11 Strikes Back," 21 *Stan. L. Rev.* 171–187 (1968).

11. 283 F. Supp. 643 (S.D.N.Y. 1968).

12. As an example, a few months after the decision, the Section of Corporation, Banking and Business Law of the American Bar Association held a national institute on the subject which was attended by approximately 1,000 attorneys, accountants, and underwriters. The proceedings of the institute are reported verbatim under the title "The *BarChris* Case: Prospectus Liability," 24 *Bus. Law,* 523–720 (1969).

13. Freeman, "Liability of Counsel for Issuer," 24 *Bus. Law.* 635–640 at 635 (1969).

14. Persons held liable under Section 11 are entitled to "contribution as in cases of contract from any person who, if sued separately, would have been liable." 1933 Act, § 11(f); 15 U.S.C. § 77k(f). Rights of contribution and indemnification under the securities laws are discussed in Chapter 10, where the total subject of indemnification is examined.

15. 25 N.Y.S.2d 667 (S. Ct. N.Y. Co. 1940).

16. See Meeker, "The Outside Director—Advice to My Client," 24 *Bus. Law.* 573–583 at 581 (1969).

17. Schneider, in panel discussion, "The *BarChris* Case: Prospectus Liability," 24 *Bus. Law.* 523–720 at 557 (1969).

18. 332 F. Supp. 544 (E.D.N.Y. 1971).

19. 15 U.S.C. § 77l.

20. 1933 Act, § 15; 15 U.S.C. § 77o. Similar liability is imposed by the 1934 Act, § 20(a); 15 U.S.C. § 78t(a).

21. Sommer, "Who's 'In Control'," 21 *Bus. Law.* 559–593 at 576–577 (1966). Two more recent cases on directors as controlling persons are Mader v. Arnold, 461 F.2d 1123 (6th Cir. 1972), *cert. denied*, 409 U.S. 1023 (1972) and Holloway v. Howerdd, 536 F.2d 690 (6th Cir. 1975).

22. 1933 Act, § 3(b); 15 U.S.C. § 77c(b).

23. 17 C.F.R. § 230.251–264.

24. 17 C.F.R. § 230.144. For discussions of the rule, see Miller & Seltzer, "The SEC's New Rule 144," 27 *Bus. Law.* 1047–1071 (1972), and Lipton, Fogelson & Warnken, "Rule 144—A Summary Review After Two Years," 29 *Bus. Law.* 1183–1203 (1974).

25. 1934 Act, § 5; 15 U.S.C. § 78e.

26. 15 U.S.C. § 78l.

27. 1934 Act, § 12(g) *(added by* P.L. 88–467; 78 Stat. 565); 15 U.S.C. § 78l(g).

28. The proxy rules are Reg. 14A; 17 C.F.R. § 240.14a; promulgated under the authority of the 1934 Act, § 14; 15 U.S.C. § 78n.

29. Reg. S-K 20.4; 17 C.F.R. § 229.20.

30. See Goettinger, "Pay Disclosure Rules," Manager's Journal, *Wall St. J.,* June 25, 1979, p. 20.

31. 15 U.S.C. § 78n.

32. 17 C.F.R. § 240.14a-9.

33. 377 U.S. 426, 12 L. Ed.2d 423, 84 S. Ct. 1555 (1964). See also Mills v. Electric Auto Lite Co., 396 U.S. 375, 24 L. Ed. 2d 593, 90 S. Ct. 616 (1970).

34. Gould v. American Hawaiian Steamship Co., 351 F. Supp. 853 (D. Del. 1972). Related decisions in the same action are 319 F. Supp. 795 (1970) and 331 F. Supp. 981 (1971). This suit, as most other actions under Section 14(a), also contained allegations of violation of Section 10(b), a subject discussed later in this chapter.

35. 1934 Act, § 16; 15 U.S.C. § 78p.

36. 17 C.F.R. § 240.3b-2.

37. 178 F.2d 872 (2d Cir. 1949), *rev'g* 83 F. Supp. 159 (S.D.N.Y. 1949).

38. SEC Rel. No. 34-2687, Nov. 16, 1940; 11 Fed. Reg. 10967; *Fed. Sec. L. Rep.* (CCH) ¶ 26,058.

39. 106 F. Supp. 810 (S.D. Cal. 1952).

40. 110 F. Supp. 282 (S.D. Cal. 1953).

41. Lee National Corporation v. Segur, 281 F. Supp. 851 (E.D. Pa. 1968).

42. Gold v. Scurlock, 324 F. Supp. 1211 (E.D. Va. 1971), *aff'd in part and rev'd in part sub nom.* Gold v. Sloan, 486 F.2d 340 (4th Cir. 1973), *cert. denied,* 419 U.S. 873 (1974). See also Selas Corporation of America v. Voogd, 365 F. Supp. 1268 (E.D. Pa. 1973); Morales v. Holiday Inn, Inc., 366 F. Supp. 760 (S.D.N.Y. 1973); Hurley, "Who Is an 'Officer' for Purposes of the Securities Exchange Act of 1934—*Colby v. Klune* Revisited," 44 *Fordham L. Rev.* 489–510 (1975).

43. SEC Rel. No. 34-7793, 31 Fed. Reg. 1005 (1966); further explained in SEC Rel. No. 34-7824, 31 Fed. Reg. 3175 (1966). For a contemporaneous discussion of these releases, see Posner, "Developments in Federal Regulation of Securities," 22 *Bus. Law.* 645–680 at 662–663 (1967).

44. Jefferson Lake Sulphur Co. v. Walet, 104 F. Supp. 20 (E.D. La. 1952), *aff'd,* 202 F.2d 433 (5th Cir. 1953), *cert. denied,* 346 U.S. 820 (1953).

45. *Fed. Sec. L. Rep.* (CCH) (1973 Transfer Binder), ¶ 94,115 (S.D.N.Y. 1973).

46. 523 F.2d 680 (2d Cir. 1975), *aff'g*, 386 F. Supp. 1130 (S.D.N.Y. 1974).

47. 386 F. Supp. 1130 at 1137.

48. SEC Rel. No. 34-7824, 31 Fed. Reg. 3175 (1966). The approach of the court in *Whiting* and the cases following it in equating 16(b) liability with 16(a) reporting requirements is criticized in Lincer, " 'Beneficial Ownership' Under Section 16(b) of the Securities Exchange Act of 1934," 77 *Colum. L. Rev.* 446 (1977).

49. Altimil Corp. v. Pryor, 405 F. Supp. 1222 (S.D. Ind. 1975).

50. Whittaker v. Whittaker Corporation, *Fed. Sec. L. Rep.* (CCH) (1977–1978 Transfer Binder) ¶ 96,008 (C.D. Cal. 1977).

51. 368 U.S. 403, 7 L. Ed.2d 403, 82 S. Ct. 451 (1962).

52. The reader will recall that the concept of a director's being a deputy for his or her partnership came up in another case involving Lehman Brothers in the field of regulation of carriers. In that case, however, the court was dealing with a different statute having a different purpose, and the theory of "deputization" was upheld. See Chapter 5 under the heading "Other Statutes Pertaining to Interlocks." The deputy director concept has also arisen under Section 8 of the Clayton Act (interlocking directorates) in the *Cleveland Trust* case, but, since the matter was settled, the legal question remains unresolved. See Chapter 5 under the heading "Section 8 of the Clayton Act."

53. Feder v. Martin Marietta Corporation, 406 F.2d 260 (2d Cir. 1969).

54. 513 F.2d 921 (3d Cir. 1975).

55. 17 C.F.R. § 249.103.

56. 406 F.2d 260 (2d Cir. 1969).

57. No claim was made in *Mellon Bank* under Section 10(b) and Rule 10b-5 (discussed later in this chapter). If such a claim had been made, it would have been necessary to prove actual use of inside information.

58. 401 F. Supp. 449 (S.D.N.Y. 1975).

59. Lewis v. Wells, 325 F. Supp. 382 (S.D.N.Y. 1971).

60. Reg. 240.16b-3; 17 C.F.R. § 240.16b-3.

61. Reg. 240.16b-6; 17 C.F.R. § 240.16b-6. The validity of this limitation of liability was upheld in Kornfeld v. Eaton, 217 F. Supp. 671 (S.D.N.Y. 1963), *aff'd*, 327 F.2d 263 (2d Cir. 1964). The general rules for calculation of liability in Section 16(b) cases is discussed in Painter, "The Evolving Role of Section 16(b)," 62 *Mich. L. Rev.* 649–678 (1964).

62. It was suggested in 1965 that to require a return of such gains would have been inconsistent with the then prevailing policy of encouraging executive options by providing favorable tax treatment. Kramer, "An Examination of Section 16(b)," 21 *Bus. Law.* 183–193 at 192 (1965). Favorable tax treatment was removed by the Revenue Act of 1976. 90 Stat. 1574, 1834; 26 U.S.C. § 422.

63. 160 F.2d 984 (2d Cir. 1947), *cert. denied*, 332 U.S. 761 (1947). While this case

and some of the others cited in this chapter involve holders of 10 percent or more of the stock, rather than officers or directors, the legal principles on this subject are generally the same.

**64.** 259 F.2d 342 (6th Cir. 1958).

**65.** 352 F.2d 156 (3d Cir. 1965).

**66.** 363 F.2d 507 (2d Cir. 1966), *cert. denied,* 385 U.S. 1002 (1967).

**67.** 367 F.2d 528 (8th Cir. 1966), *cert. denied,* 385 U.S. 1006 (1967).

**68.** Newmark v. RKO General, Inc., 425 F.2d 348 (2d Cir. 1970), *cert. denied,* 400 U.S. 920 (1970).

**69.** 411 U.S. 582, 36 L. Ed.2d 503, 93 S. Ct. 1736 (1973).

**70.** 486 F.2d 340 (4th Cir. 1973), *cert. denied,* 419 U.S. 873 (1974). The district court decision in this case is cited in note 42 of this chapter as a case where the question of officer status under 16(b) was decided. Gold v. Scurlock, 324 F. Supp. 1211 (E.D. Va. 1971).

**71.** For a more complete discussion of the status of conversions and mergers under Section 16(b), see Davis, "Conversions as Purchases and Sales Under Section 16(b) of the Securities and Exchange Act of 1934," 24 *Bus. Law.* 1109–1120 (1969) and note, "Insider Liability for Short-Swing Profits: The Substance and Function of the Pragmatic Approach," 72 *Mich. L. Rev.* 592–627 (1974).

**72.** 15 U.S.C. § 78j(b).

**73.** 17 C.F.R. § 240.10b-5.

**74.** 69 F. Supp. 512 (E.D. Pa. 1946).

**75.** 99 F. Supp. 808 (D. Del. 1951), 135 F. Supp. 176 (D. Del. 1955), *aff'd,* 235 F.2d 369 (3d Cir. 1956).

**76.** Although *Kardon* was followed in numerous decisions granting a private right of action for Section 10(b) violations, the United States Supreme Court did not rule on the subject until 1975 when it held that "the existence of a private cause of action for violation of the statute and the Rule is now well established." Ernst & Ernst v. Hochfelder, 425 U.S. 185, 47 L. Ed. 2d 668, 96 S. Ct. 1375 (1976). It has been suggested that Congress, in enacting Section 10(b), and the SEC, in promulgating Rule 10b-5, probably did not intend to confer a private right of action. See note, "Proof of *Scienter* Necessary in a Private Suit Under SEC Anti-Fraud Rule 10b-5," 63 *Mich. L. Rev.* 1070–1081 (1965). Interestingly enough, the Supreme Court, as far back as 1964, held that a private right of action existed under Section 14(a) and its proxy rules. See note 33 to this chapter.

**77.** Joseph v. Farnsworth Radio & Television Corp., 99 F. Supp. 701 (S.D.N.Y. 1951), *aff'd,* 198 F.2d 883 (2d Cir. 1952).

**78.** SEC Release No. 6668, Nov. 8, 1961; *Fed. Sec. L. Rep.* (CCH) (1961–1964 Transfer Binder) ¶ 76,803.

**79.** SEC v. Texas Gulf Sulphur Co., 401 F.2d 833 at 845 (2d Cir. 1968), *cert. denied sub nom.* Coates v. SEC, Kline v. SEC, 394 U.S. 976 (1969).

**80.** SEC v. Texas Gulf Sulphur Co. 258 F. Supp. 262 (S.D.N.Y. 1966).

**81.** 401 F.2d 833 (2d Cir. 1968).

82. SEC v. Texas Gulf Sulphur Co., 312 F. Supp. 77 (S.D.N.Y. 1970).

83. *Id.*, 331 F. Supp. 671 (S.D.N.Y. 1971).

84. *Id.*, 446 F.2d 1301 (2d Cir. 1971).

85. Astor v. Texas Gulf Sulphur Co., 306 F. Supp. 1333 (S.D.N.Y. 1969); Reynolds v. Texas Gulf Sulphur Co., 309 F. Supp. 548 & 566 (D. Utah 1970); *aff'd in part and rev'd in part sub nom.* Mitchell v. Texas Gulf Sulphur Co., 446 F.2d 90 (10th Cir. 1971).

86. Posner, "Developments in Federal Securities Regulation," 24 *Bus. Law.* 1335–1367 at 1342 (1969).

87. Painter, "Inside Information: Growing Pains for the Development of Federal Corporation Law Under Rule 10b-5," 65 *Colum. L. Rev.* 1361–1393 at 1378 (1965).

88. *Id.*

89. 401 F.2d 833 at 870, 888–889. For a complete analysis of *Texas Gulf* written from a business writer's point of view, see Patrick, *Perpetual Jeopardy: The Texas Gulf Sulphur Affair: A Chronicle of Achievement and Misadventure* (MacMillan Co., 1972). For a contemporary legal analysis of *Texas Gulf*, see DeLancey, "Rule 10b-5—A Recent Profile," 25 *Bus. Law.* 1355–1379 (1970).

90. The New York Stock Exchange has published procedures for its listed companies in connection with public release of information and directors' and officers' stock transactions. See New York Stock Exchange *Company Manual*, A-24 to A-27.

91. Ernst & Ernst v. Hochfelder, 425 U.S. 185 at 193, n. 12, 47 L. Ed.2d 668, 96 S. Ct. 1375 (1976). See also *Black's Law Dictionary* 1207 (5th ed., West Publishing Co., 1979).

92. 458 F.2d 255 (3d Cir. 1972), *cert. denied*, 409 U.S. 874 (1972).

93. 458 F.2d 255 at 286. See also pp. 312–316, the appendix to the dissenting opinion, which analyzes twenty-three reported cases on the question. Some of these cases are also discussed in comment, "*Scienter* and Rule 10b-5," 69 *Colum. L. Rev.* 1057–1083 (1969). Not all these cases involve corporate directors and officers, but the principles appear to be the same regardless of the type of defendant—corporation, officer, director, accountant, broker, etc.

94. 425 U.S. 185.

95. 425 U.S. 185 at 199.

96. *Id.* at 194, n. 12.

97. 420 F. Supp. 1226 (S.D.N.Y. 1976), *aff'd on other grounds,* 565 F.2d 8 (2d Cir. 1977).

98. 420 F. Supp. 1226 at 1244.

99. 429 F. Supp. 1148 (E.D. Va. 1977).

100. 439 F. Supp. 820 (W.D. La. 1977).

101. SEC v. Wills, *Fed. Sec. L. Rep.* (CCH) (Current 1979) ¶ 96,712 (D.C. App. 1978).

102. SEC v. World Radio Mission, Inc., 544 F.2d 535 (1st Cir. 1976); SEC v. E.L.

Aaron & Co., Inc., *Fed. Sec. L. Rep.* (CCH) (1977–1978 Transfer Binder) ¶ 96,043 (S.D.N.Y. 1977) *aff'd* 605 F.2d 612 (2nd Cir. 1979), *rev'd sub nom.* Peter B. Aaron v. SEC, __ U.S. __, 64 L. Ed.2d 611, 100 S. Ct. 1945 (1980); SEC v. Hart, *Fed. Sec. L. Rep.* (CCH) (1978 Transfer Binder) ¶ 96,454 (D.D.C. 1978).

103. __ U.S. __, 64 L. Ed.2d 611 (1980).

104. 15 U.S.C., 77q(a)(1), which reads: "It shall be unlawful for any person in the offer or sale of any securities by the use of any means or instruments of transportation or communication in interstate commerce or by the use of the mails, directly or indirectly—"(1) to employ any device, scheme, or artifice to defraud(.)"

105. Sundstrand Corp. v. Sun Chemical Corp., 553 F.2d 1033 (7th Cir. 1977), adopting definition in Franke v. Midwestern Oklahoma Development Authority, 428 F. Supp. 719 (W.D. Okla. 1976). Followed in Wright v. Heizer Corp., 560 F.2d 236 (7th Cir. 1977), but sees Sanders v. John Nuveen & Co., 554 2d 790 (7th Cir. 1977), where the principle was affirmed but recklessness was found to be absent and mere negligence was not sufficient to establish a violation of 10(b). Other recent cases equating reckless behavior to *scienter* include McLean v. Alexander, 420 F. Supp. 1057 (D. Del. 1976) and Nelson v. Serwold, 576 F.2d 1332 (9th Cir. 1978). Also see SEC v. Cenco Inc., 436 F. Supp. 193 (N.D. Ill. 1977).

106. For discussions of *Hochfelder* and subsequent cases on *scienter*, see Haimoff, "Holmes Looks at Hochfelder and 10b-5," 32 *Bus. Law.* 147–175 (1976); Loss, "A Pothole on the Holmes-Hochfelder Highway," 32 *Bus. Law.* 1837–1839 (1977); Lowenfels, "*Scienter* or Negligence Required for SEC Injunctions Under Section 10(b) and Rule 10b-5: A Fascinating Paradox," 33 *Bus. Law.* 789–809 (1978); Castruccio and Hentrich, "Developments in Federal Securities Regulation—1977," 33 *Bus. Law.* 1645–1725 at 1662–1671 (1978), and "Developments in Federal Securities Regulation—1978," 34 *Bus. Law.* 1159–1227 (1979); comment, "*Scienter* and SEC Injunction Suits: *SEC v. Bausch & Lomb, Inc.*, and *SEC v. World Radio Mission, Inc.*," 90 *Harv. L. Rev.* 1018–1028 (1977). All these articles were written before the Supreme Court decision in *Aaron*.

107. 15 U.S.C. § 78t(a).

108. 479 F.2d 1277 (2d Cir. 1973).

109. Mader v. Armel, 461 F.2d 1123 (6th Cir. 1972), *cert. denied*, 409 U.S. 1023 (1972).

110. 1934 Act, § 21; 15 U.S.C. § 78u.

111. 1934 Act, § 32; 15 U.S.C. § 78ff.

112. *Fed. Sec. L. Rep.* (CCH) (1974–1975 Transfer Binder) ¶ 94,754 (D.D.C. 1974); SEC Litigation Releases Nos. 6487 and 6533 (1974).

113. 365 F. Supp. 1046 (S.D.N.Y. 1973).

114. For a complete discussion of this subject, see Ratner, "Federal and State Roles in the Regulation of Insider Trading," 31 *Bus. Law.* 946–972 (1976).

115. 193 F.2d 461 (2d Cir. 1952), *cert. denied*, 343 U.S. 956 (1952).

116. 421 U.S. 723, 44 L. Ed. 2d 539, 95 S. Ct. 1917 (1975). See 421 U.S. 723 and

732 for citations of intervening decisions following *Birnbaum*. Even though the plaintiffs may not have personally bought or sold, they may have standing to sue derivatively on behalf of the corporation that has been caused to issue the shares by its directors' action under circumstances that fall within the proscription of Rule 10b-5. See Biesenbach v. Guenther, 446 F. Supp. 98, 99 (E.D. Pa. 1978).

117. 405 F.2d 215 (2d Cir. 1968), *cert. denied*, 395 U.S. 906 (1969).

118. 464 F.2d 714 (2d Cir. 1972).

119. 430 U.S. 462, 51 L. Ed. 2d 480, 97 S. Ct. 1292 (1977).

120. *Del. Code Ann.*, Tit. 8, §§ 253, 262.

121. 430 U.S. 462, 476–477.

122. 446 F. Supp. 98 (E.D. Pa. 1978), *aff'd*, 588 F.2d 400 (3d Cir. 1978).

123. For discussions of the role of Section 10(b) and Rule 10b-5 in regulating corporate management, see Ruder, "Challenging Corporate Action Under Rule 10b-5," 25 *Bus. Law.* 75–99 (1969); note, "The Controlling Influence Standard in Rule 10b-5 Corporate Mismanagement Cases," 86 *Harv. L. Rev.* 1007–1046 (1973); Fleischer, "Federal Regulation of Internal Corporate Affairs," 29 *Bus. Law.* (Special Issue, March 1974) 179–184; Kaplan, "Fiduciary Responsibility in the Management of the Corporation," 31 *Bus. Law.* 882–927 (1976); Jacobs, "Liability for Corporate Mismanagement Under Rule 10b-5," 24 *Pract. Law.* (No. 7, Oct. 15, 1978) 13–34.

124. *Federal Securities Code, Adopted by the American Law Institute* (1980).

125. "Plan to Rewrite Federal Securities Laws Appears Close to Being Endorsed by SEC," *Wall St. J.*, July 31, 1980, p. 3.

126. *Id.*, § 1708(b)(3).

127. *Id.*, § 299.15.

128. For a discussion of the liability features of the proposed code, see "ALI Proposed Securities Code," a program of the Corporation, Banking and Business Law Section, American Bar Association, 34 *Bus. Law.* 345–393 at 380–389 (1978).

# CHAPTER NINE

# Bribery and Boycott: International Conduct and Disclosure Requirements

In our review of liabilities and regulation of managers of American corporations, we have thus far been concerned with essentially domestic activities. During the middle and latter parts of the 1970s, however, the attention of government agencies and the Congress was focused on certain activities of businesses operating abroad. The results were two significant legislative enactments that singled out American business executives from their counterparts in other nations and imposed upon them personally, as well as upon their corporations, penalties for performing certain acts abroad in the course of their businesses which their foreign competitors might be permitted to do with impunity. One of these statutes resulted also in significantly increased accounting controls affecting domestic, as well as foreign, activity. The activities leading to such enactments were overseas bribery, which resulted in the Foreign Corrupt Practices Act of 1977,[1] and cooperation with the Arab boycott of Israel, which resulted in certain prohibitions in the Export Administration Act Amendments of 1977.[2] Both activities were afforded special and, of course, unfavorable treatment in the Tax Reform Act of 1976.[3]

While neither of these activities could be classified as acceptable corporate behavior prior to the 1976 and 1977 legislation, there were relatively mild sanctions against them. With the exception of certain disallowances for bribe payments under the Revenue Act of 1958[4] and certain controls on the export of armaments, the federal law in both fields was concerned primarily with reporting.

## THE SEC AND QUESTIONABLE PAYMENTS

As almost everyone knows, the revelations of bribery and other questionable payments by certain American corporations was a by-product of Watergate. The investigations into the tactics of the Nixon presidential campaign led to the discovery that a few corporations had contributed to the campaign in violation of the Corrupt Practices Act.[5]

Then other revelations, wholly unconnected with United States political activities, began to surface. Further investigation into the activities of these corporations led to the discovery that some of them had engaged in questionable payments overseas, such as payments to officials of foreign governments to obtain government contracts or tax favors, to prevent repressive legislation, or to obtain almost any conceivable special treatment that might be imagined in a relation with a government. One of the most dramatic was the disclosure of bribery of the President of Honduras by representatives of United Brands, which was marked by the suicide of United's chief executive on February 3, 1975. By May 1976, approximately 100 corporations had either admitted to, or were being accused of, "questionable or illegal foreign and domestic payments and practices."[6] The number eventually exceeded 400.[7]

Although there were no general prohibitions in the laws of the United States against the payments of bribes to foreign government officials, there was a feeling in some United States governmental quarters that something ought to be done about this activity.[8] The Securities and Exchange Commission (SEC) quickly found "something to do." The corporations engaged in such practices were, in the opinion of the SEC, in violation of the securities laws for not having disclosed the existence of these practices. It was contended that they had, in their reports to the SEC, whether in proxy statements, annual and other periodic reports, or prospectuses, omitted to state material facts.

The subject of questionable payments was hotly debated during the mid-1970s. The dollar amount of such payments was an important consideration. If the amount of the payment was large, it might be material purely from a financial standpoint. If the amount of business attributable to the questionable payments was large even though the payments were small, that fact might also be material to a financial analysis of the soundness of the company's business. Direct involvement of top management might reflect upon the quality of management.

An assistant director of the SEC's Enforcement Division, addressing an American Bar Association national institute in the fall of 1975, stated his feeling this way:

> Such activities, in my view, are material to the investing public in a number of ways: They reflect on the integrity of management involved. They reflect on management's stewardship of the company assets. These activities reflect on the integrity of the corporate books and records themselves. Particularly in the foreign area, I think that these activities reflect on the ability of the corporation to procure business. Finally, I believe these activities significantly increase the risk that a company's earnings and assets may be adversely affected should such activities be discontinued or discovered.[9]

In many situations, however, management did not really know what was going on. That, then, raised the provocative question: Why did not top management know? The SEC recognized the complexity of the problem in its report to the Senate Banking, Housing, and Urban Affairs Committee, in which it stated:

> Investors have a right under the federal securities laws to be fully advised of facts concerning character and integrity of the officials relevant to their management of the corporation. This is particularly true when management administers significant assets in foreign states, where investors may not have the same protections as exist in the United States. Accordingly, transactions that would not otherwise be material may become so by virtue of the role played by management. Whether disclosure is required on the basis that it relates to the integrity of management is subject to a number of variations. In situations involving a pervasive pattern of encouragement, participation in or knowledge of these practices by senior management, the need for disclosure is clear. If, on the other hand, senior management neither knew nor should have known of the payments, disclosure may not be required, unless they are otherwise material.[10]

The phrase "should have known of the payments" is obviously one that is incapable of precise definition.

## The Voluntary Disclosure Program

A few months before its report to the Senate Banking, Housing, and Urban Affairs Committee, the SEC instituted a so-called voluntary disclosure program. The SEC had commenced a number of enforcement actions in the field of questionable payments, but it was lacking in staff and other resources to conduct a complete investigation of the practices of all corporations under its jurisdiction. So it invited all corporations that thought they might have a problem to conduct internal investigations and report the results to the SEC. Presumably a corporation carrying out such a program to the satisfaction of the SEC could thereby escape the possibility of enforcement action by the Commission, with the attendant risks of injunction against future activities and possible affirmative orders regulating management.[11]

The voluntary disclosure program brought forth a large number of responses. Most of the 400 disclosures mentioned earlier in this chapter were pursuant to that program. It would appear that a number of such disclosures were a result of corporate counsel's and corporate management's "leaning over backward." In numerous instances, one-time deviations from the straight and narrow were reported. Oftentimes the activities disclosed were performed by lower-level employees without the knowledge or participation of upper management. But managements were anxious to clear the record and to avoid the possibility of the SEC's independently discovering the questionable payments and accusing the management of not exercising proper supervision and control.[12]

Voluntary disclosure generally but not always also had the effect of shielding not only the reporting corporation but also its directors and officers from enforcement action by the SEC.[13] Enforcement officials of the SEC have reported fourteen actions against corporations in which from one to four corporate managers were joined as defendants; there was an aggregate of twenty-nine individuals in all, mostly chief executives, but also including vice presidents and, in one case, a regional manager.[14] The relief sought has not always been just an injunction against future violations. Following the precedent set by the *Mattel* proceeding, discussed in Chapter 8, the SEC has in some cases sought and obtained structural changes in the management of the corporation and reimbursement to the corporation of the amounts of illegal payments by the persons responsible for their authorization.[15] The SEC's legal ability to obtain such far-reaching relief may have had a doubtful legal basis, but generally neither the corporations nor their executives were inclined to contest its demands, and consent decrees became the customary practice.

## THE LEGISLATIVE RESPONSE

The efforts of the SEC to regulate the problem of questionable payments was by no means accepted as the ultimate solution. Its critics represented many different shades of thought.[16] Some considered disclosure to be an ineffective remedy, amounting to no more than a slap on the wrist. Others felt that the SEC was exceeding its powers when it sought and obtained structural changes in management. Still others contended that the program was placing American business at a disadvantage with foreign competition. The last-mentioned viewpoint did not, however, have much acceptance in Washington. The SEC itself felt that more legislation was needed. It noted that in most instances, questionable or illegal payments had been masked by falsified accounting entries. Accordingly, it recommended legislation that would

> . . . require management to establish and maintain its own system of internal accounting controls designed to provide reasonable assurances that corporate transactions are executed in accordance with management's general or specific authorization; and that such transactions as are authorized are properly reflected on the corporation's books and records in such a manner as to permit the preparation of financial statements in conformity with generally accepted accounting principles or any other criteria applicable to such statements.[17]

The Congress was not, however, content with merely legislating accounting standards. It considered bribery and other questionable payments reprehensible. Despite doubts about the wisdom of the United States' attempting to solve the problem by unilateral action rather than by international treaty, the law that finally was passed, the

Foreign Corrupt Practices Act of 1977, covered *both* the SEC's concept of prescribing accounting standards and proscribing falsification *and* its own prohibitions of bribery and other dubious payments in international transactions.[18]

## The Accounting and Controls Provisions

A cynic might observe that the Congress, in its zeal to legislate against deception, itself committed an act of deception in entitling its efforts "The Foreign Corrupt Practices Act of 1977." The title could lead those not engaged in foreign business to ignore the Act. In establishing accounting standards, however, the Act prescribes standards concerning practices that are not necessarily either foreign or corrupt. The thrust of the Act is that *all* transactions shall be properly recorded. Specifically, the Act amends Section 13(b) of the 1934 Act to provide that each corporation having securities registered under the 1934 Act and each corporation required to file reports under the 1934 Act shall

(A) make and keep books, records, and accounts, which, in reasonable detail, accurately and fairly reflect the transactions and dispositions of the assets of the issuer; and

(B) devise and maintain a system of internal accounting controls sufficient to provide reasonable assurances that—

(*i*) transactions are executed in accordance with management's general or specific authorization;

(*ii*) transactions are recorded as necessary (I) to permit preparation of financial statements in conformity with generally accepted accounting principles or any other criteria applicable to such statements, and (II) to maintain accountability for assets;

(*iii*) access to assets is permitted only in accordance with management's general or specific authorization; and

(*iv*) the recorded accountability for assets is compared with the existing assets at reasonable intervals and appropriate action is taken with respect to any difference.[19]

The statutory provision looks like a concise statement of good accounting practice, which is precisely what it is. Statements of accounting practice have not heretofore had the force of law, however, and it is this feature that is revolutionary. Some commentators have stated that this provision is "the most significant expansion of the securities laws since their passage in the New Deal era."[20]

Section 13(b) has been implemented by Rule 13B-2, adopted by the SEC effective March 23, 1979, which places responsibility for compliance squarely upon the shoulders of management. The regulation not only prohibits the falsification of any book, record, or account subject to Section 13(b), but also specifically provides that no director or officer of an issuer shall

> (a) make or cause to be made a materially false or misleading statement, or
>
> (b) omit to state, or cause another person to omit to state, any material fact necessary in order to make the statements made . . . not misleading[,] to an accountant in connection with (1) any audit or examination of the financial statements . . . or (2) the preparation or filing of any document or report required to be filed with the Commission.[21]

There is little doubt that the Congress and the SEC intend that the major responsibility for the maintenance of controls on the expenditures of funds, other utilization of assets, and the accurate recording of both activities should be placed with the directors and officers.

In further implementation of Section 13(b), the SEC in 1979 proposed adding a new item to the Standard Instructions for Filing Forms Under Securities Act of 1933 and Securities Exchange Act of 1934, requiring a statement of management on internal accounting controls. It includes such things as management's opinion whether the controls provide reasonable assurances that transactions are executed in accordance with management's authorization and are recorded to permit preparation of financial statements in accordance with generally accepted accounting practices and to maintain accountability for assets; that access to assets is permitted only in accordance with management's authorization; and that recorded accountability for assets is compared with assets at reasonable intervals and appropriate action is taken with respect to any differences.

The instructions would have further required management's description of any material weaknesses in internal accounting controls that have been communicated by the independent public accountants and not corrected. For periods subsequent to December 15, 1980, management's statement on internal accounting controls would have been examined and reported upon by the independent public accountants, with an opinion as to their consistency and reasonableness.

The proposed instructions resulted in an unprecedented number of protests from the business community because of their severity, and they were withdrawn in June 1980.[22]

Willful violation of the accounting and control requirements of Section 13(b) and Rule 13B-2 subjects the violator to the criminal penalties prescribed by Section 32 of the 1934 Act.[23] They are, as we noted in Chapter 8, a fine of $10,000, imprisonment for not more than five years, or both. Section 32 contains a qualification that no person shall be imprisoned for "violation of any rule or regulation if he proves that he had no knowledge of such rule or regulation." The SEC has given considerable publicity to both Section 13(b) and Rule 13B-2 to make certain the corporate managers know about them. It is going to be difficult for a manager successfully to defend on the grounds of "no

knowledge." By describing the duties and obligations of directors and
officers with particularity in Rule 13B-2, the SEC has given notice that it
expects close compliance. Violators can reasonably expect the SEC to
take enforcement action via the injunction route, as has been customary
in most violations of the 1934 Act of a serious nature, but where the
violation is willful, criminal indictments can be expected.

It should be noticed that Rule 13-B, in placing the *primary* responsibility upon directors and officers, is not placing the *sole* responsibility
upon them and leaving other employees free of responsibility. To the
contrary, in its statement accompanying the new rule, the SEC said:

> [E]xclusion from the express language of the new Rule of . . . low-level
> corporate employees does not indicate that those individuals may mislead
> the issuer's accountants with impunity. . . . [T]he existing antifraud provi-
> sions of the federal securities laws, and the concept of aiding and abetting,
> can be invoked, in appropriate circumstances, against those who deceive
> the auditors of a publicly held corporation.[24]

## ANOTHER CONTROL: THE AUDIT COMMITTEE

Concurrently with the congressional activity that led to enactment of
the Foreign Corrupt Practices Act of 1977, the New York Stock Exchange, at the urging of the SEC, was doing some legislating of its own
to tighten up accounting controls. During the mid-1970s, considerable
attention was being given by corporations to the establishment of audit
committees. Major corporations having such committees increased
from fewer than 50 percent in 1973 to 89 percent in 1975. Much of this
increase can be attributed to the encouragement of the SEC and its
change in its proxy rules in 1974 to require a statement as to the
composition of the audit committee in a corporation's proxy statement,
and, if no such committee exists, a statement to that effect.[25]

In 1976 the Chairman of the SEC recommended that the New York
Stock Exchange consider a revision of its listing policies to require each
company whose securities were listed on the Exchange to have an audit
committee composed of independent directors. The Exchange adopted,
and the SEC approved, such a policy in 1977.[26] The New York Stock
Exchange requirement was adopted after the Exchange circulated pre-
liminary drafts among listed companies and received their comments,
which resulted in considerable revision. Under the requirement, every
domestic listed company must have an audit committee of directors
who are independent of management. The requirement is indefinite as
to the size of the committee, which presumably could consist of only
one person, although such a committee would probably not be in
accordance with the spirit of the requirement. Officers and employees
are not eligible for committee membership, but a former officer may
qualify if the board determines that he or she will exercise independent

judgment and will materially assist in the function of the committee. Former officers may not, however, form a majority of the committee.

An interesting sidelight is that the audit committee requirement of the New York Stock Exchange indirectly constitutes a requirement that there be *some* independent directors. Nowhere in federal or state law is there a requirement concerning the composition of the board of directors. There is no prohibition against having all inside directors, but the New York Stock Exchange, through its listing requirements, has taken the first prohibitory step. The SEC proposed that the American Stock Exchange adopt a like requirement of independent audit committees. That Exchange was reluctant to do so because many of its listed companies reported that they would have difficulty finding enough outside directors to satisfy the requirement. Instead, the American Stock Exchange adopted a policy recommending, rather than requiring, a listed company to have an independent audit committee.[27]

There is a definite relationship between the audit committee development and the Foreign Corrupt Practices Act. The audit committee certainly has an important role to play in assuring that management devises the system of internal accounting controls mandated by Section 13(b), that the system is properly maintained, and that the books, records, and accounts are kept in accordance with that section. As one writer has stated, the SEC pushed hard for the establishment of audit committees and "will not be hesitant in seeing that they are active in reviewing management's compliance" with the Act.[28]

## PROHIBITION OF CORRUPT PAYMENTS

The second main feature of the Foreign Corrupt Practices Act of 1977 is more properly described by the title of the Act than are the accounting and control provisions. A new Section 30A has been added to the 1934 Act. No longer is disclosure the sole weapon of the SEC in combatting questionable foreign payments. Now there is a specific statutory provision that it is unlawful for an issuer or for any officer, director, employee, or agent of the issuer, or any stockholder acting on its behalf, to use

> . . . the mails or any means or instrumentality of interstate commerce corruptly in furtherance of an offer, payment, promise to pay, or authorization of the payment of any money, or offer, gift, promise to give, or authorization of the giving of anything of value to—
>
> (1) any foreign official for purposes of
>
> > (A) influencing any act or decision of such foreign official . . . ; or
> >
> > (B) inducing such foreign official to use his influence with a foreign government . . . in order to assist such issuer in obtaining or retaining business for or with, or directing business to, any person.[29]

There is a similar prohibition against like transactions with a foreign political party or official of such a party. Also prohibited are such transactions with any other person "while knowing, or having reason to know," that all or part of the money or thing of value will be utilized for one of the purposes prohibited to the issuer, its officers, directors, employees, agents, or stockholders.

The term "foreign official" is defined to exclude any employee "whose duties are essentially ministerial or clerical." This exception is designed to permit so-called grease, or facilitating payments, that is customary in many countries in order to get low-level government employees to perform the duties that are required of them. While such payments are removed from the category of illegality under American law, it does not necessarily follow that disclosure is not required under other provisions of the securities law if the total of such payments is large in amount or may in some other respect have a material relationship to the assets or business of the issuer.

Violations of Section 30A have been singled out for treatment separate from that accorded to other violations of the 1934 Act.[30] An issuer may be fined up to $1 million, compared with $10,000 for other types of violations. Needless to say, this is one of the most severe fines to be found anywhere in the United States Code. It equals the fine for a corporate violation of the Sherman Act as increased by the Antitrust Procedures and Penalties Act of 1974. An officer, director, or stockholder who acts on behalf of the issuer is subject to the same penalties for violation of Section 30A as for the violation of any other section of the 1934 Act—a fine of $10,000, imprisonment up to five years, or both. An employee or agent who is not an officer, director, or stockholder is given special consideration. Such a person is also subject to the same criminal sanctions—$10,000, five years, or both—as an officer, director, or stockholder, but only if the issuer is found to have violated, and the employee or agent has willfully carried out, the act or practice constituting the violation by the issuer.

An interesting sidelight is that if an employee who is not an officer or a director is a stockholder, such an employee can conceivably be indicted and found guilty of violating Section 30A even though the corporation itself is not indicted or found guilty. The size of the individual's stockholding would have nothing to do with it. The individual might be a majority stockholder or an employee holding five shares of a corporation having 500 million shares issued and outstanding. It is doubtful whether the Congress intended such a result, but that is what the statute says. This possibility should stand as a warning to middle managers who own a few shares of their corporate employers—their small stockholdings place them in the same category of duty and risk as the chief executive.

To emphasize its intent to place the highest degree of personal responsibility upon corporate managers, Section 32(b)(4) prohibits a corporation from paying, either directly or indirectly, any fine imposed upon a director, officer, stockholder, employee, or agent for violation of Section 30A. This means, of course, no disguised salary increases, bonuses, or unusual expense-account reimbursements. Presumably the act of reimbursing by the corporation may itself be a violation.

The prohibitions upon foreign corrupt practices and the penalties for violation are not limited to issuers subject to the jurisdiction of the Securities and Exchange Commission. The Act also applies the same prohibitions to "any domestic corporation" and prescribes the same penalties for violation.[31] In the case of violations by an issuer under the jurisdiction of the SEC, the usual civil remedy of an injunction upon the complaint of the SEC is available. To make the same kind of remedy available where the corporation is not an "issuer," the Act has given the Attorney General the power to seek an injunction.

Thus, the enforcement of the foreign corrupt practices prohibitions is divided between the Department of Justice and the SEC. Civil enforcement against issuers is handled by the SEC, while against other corporations it is the responsibility of the Department of Justice. Criminal proceedings are brought by the Department of Justice against all categories of defendants, but if the defendant is an issuer, or an officer, director, stockholder, agent, or employee of an issuer, the usual practice would be for the SEC to investigate the violation and then refer the matter to the Attorney General for any criminal action.

## ENFORCEMENT

The Foreign Corrupt Practices Act is still too new for any case law or for any definite enforcement pattern to have emerged. Thus far, only one criminal action has been brought—against Kenny International Corporation for providing free charter flights for officials of the ruling political party in the Cook Islands (a self-governing territory of New Zealand). Upon a guilty plea, the corporation was fined $50,000 and ordered to make restitution to the Cook Islands government and to cooperate with it in its own fraud inquiry. Other bribery investigations are underway, and there also have been a few actions for injunctive relief against corporations and officers for violating either the accounting provisions or the antibribery provisions of the Act.[32]

The experience of the questionable payments revelations of the mid-seventies, the exacting provisions and severe penalties of the 1977 Act, and the SEC publicity concerning it have apparently all combined to instill a corporate attitude favoring strong internal measures of compliance. Accounts in the business press indicate that, for the most part, corporate managers are taking strict measures to ensure compliance.[33]

## THE ARAB BOYCOTT PROBLEM

The year 1977 was significant for the passage of two important acts designed to regulate activities of American business abroad. These two acts imposed prohibitions against certain practices of businesses in international trade—in furtherance of the Congress's perception of the proper moral posture of American corporations and executives.

The Foreign Corrupt Practices Act of 1977 is probably the more far-reaching of the two acts because of the broad scope of its application to business done by Americans anywhere in the world. The Export Administration Act Amendments of 1977, designed to curb compliance with the Arab boycott of Israel, was aimed at a specific and highly emotional situation. Although, in scope, the prohibitions of the Amendments apply to any foreign boycott situation and a few others do exist, its practical application is only to the Middle East controversy.[34]

The Arab boycott began as early as 1922 when the Fifth Arab Congress called for a boycott of Jewish goods manufactured in Palestine. With the organization of the League of Arab States in 1945, an official boycott resolution was adopted. In 1950, the boycott was expanded to a secondary basis—that is, not only did it apply to Israel and Israelis but also to those who had certain business or other relationships with Israel.[35] Thus an American or European or other non-Israeli enterprise might be blacklisted by the League of Arab States if it engaged in manufacturing in Israel, used Israel as a base for Middle Eastern or international operations, licensed an Israeli enterprise under patents, trademarks, or copyrights, rendered technical assistance in Israel, or owned shares in, or represented, an Israeli firm or business. Corporations desiring to do business in or with Arab countries were generally confronted with questionnaires pertaining to the foregoing matters.[36] If the company gave the "wrong" answers, it would not be permitted to do business in or with the Arab countries. Then came the tertiary boycott, under which an entity doing certain types of business with a blacklisted company might itself be blacklisted.

During the early years of the boycott of Israel, there was no American legislation dealing with the situation. American companies could comply or not comply with the Arab demands. The choice was either not to cooperate with Israel or not to do business with Arab countries. If one's business with Israel consisted solely of exporting from the United States or another neutral country, without any technical assistance or other local activity in Israel, the boycott provisions did not apply. American companies engaging in such limited activities could answer the Arab questionnaires and could continue to do business with both sides of the controversy.

The United States Congress first expressed its opposition to foreign boycott practices in 1965 in a mild fashion by amending the Export Control Act of 1949 to (1) declare its policy of opposition to such practices and (2) require the Secretary of Commerce to issue regulations requiring domestic companies to report the receipt of requests for information or the signing of agreements having the effect of promoting restrictive trade practices or boycotts imposed by foreign countries upon other countries friendly to the United States.[37]

The statement of policy and the reporting requirements were repeated in the Export Administration Act, passed in 1969. Beginning in 1973, with the increased importance of oil from the Middle East, the strong Arab financial power, the growth of the Middle East as a market for exports and services, and the heightened international implications of the Arab-Israeli struggle, the boycott, which had attracted little previous attention, became an explosive issue. Reporting procedures were deemed by many to be ineffective in controlling the boycott. The economic preeminence of the Arab nations was such that fear arose that corporations, forced to choose between Arab and Israeli business, would select the Arab because of its greater volume and resultant profitability. It undoubtedly was a fact, however, that some large corporations were not engaging in many of the activities in Israel opposed by the Arabs, such as local manufacture, for the simple reason that the size of the market made such activities uneconomical. On the other hand, the mere fact that corporations knew about the Arabic opposition to such activities might deter others from investing in, or otherwise cooperating with, Israel, so that they could give the "right" answers to the Arab questionnaires.

## Regulation by Taxation

Congressional attention was directed to the problem in 1976, and bills both to prohibit cooperation with foreign boycotts and to impose tax penalties for cooperation were introduced. The prohibitory legislation did not pass that year, but the tax legislation did. The Tax Reform Act of 1976 required reporting of (1) participation or cooperation with an international boycott during the taxable year or (2) a request to participate. Boycott participation and cooperation were defined as agreeing, as a condition of doing business within a boycotting country or with its government or with a company or a national of that country, to refrain from doing business (a) in or with the boycotted country or with its government, companies, or nationals; (b) with any United States person engaged in trade in a boycotted country or with its government, companies, or nationals; or (c) with any company whose ownership or management included individuals of a particular nationality, race, or religion.

Boycott participation and cooperation also included agreeing to refrain from employing individuals of a particular nationality, race, or religion, or to refrain from selecting for, or to remove such individuals from, a corporate board of directors. Still another type of boycott participation was agreeing, as a condition of sale of a product, to refrain from shipping or insuring the product by use of a carrier owned, leased, or operated by a person who does not participate in, or cooperate with, an international boycott.[38]

Participation and cooperation with an international boycott would result in tax penalties by denying the deferral of federal income taxes with regard to income earned by foreign subsidiaries in the boycotting countries or by domestic international sales corporations (DISCs) with respect to sales made by such corporations in the boycotting countries. In addition, no foreign tax credit would be allowed for taxes paid to the boycotting countries.

Similar penalties were included in the Tax Reform Act for bribery and other illegal payments to foreign officials. Such payments, when made by a United States corporation, have long been nondeductible, but because of the deferral aspects of income earned by foreign subsidiaries and DISCs, it was felt that nondeductibility had very little immediate impact. These new provisions thus constituted a penalty for foreign bribery just as they constituted a penalty for cooperating with a foreign boycott.

## Regulation by Prohibition

The boycott became an issue in the 1976 presidential campaign. Sentiment for stiffer antiboycott legislation was much stronger in the Congress than in the Ford administration. President Ford, during the course of the campaign, issued an Executive order which placed in the realm of public information all reports filed by corporations under the Commerce Department's regulations. Business interests generally stayed in the background during this controversy because the issue was so explosive that any statement by a business executive would run the risk of being construed as either pro-Israeli or pro-Arab, thereby jeopardizing the corporation's objective of trying to do business with both sides without antagonizing either.

In early 1977, however, when antiboycott legislation appeared to be inevitable, the Business Roundtable negotiated with the leading American Jewish organizations to draft a statute that would meet the objectives of prohibiting cooperation with the Arab boycott without completely destroying the opportunity of American business to do business with Arab countries in competition with their European, Canadian, and Japanese counterparts. This was the basis for the statute that was finally passed by the Congress.[39]

The antiboycott provisions of the Export Administration Act Amendments of 1977 directed the President to issue rules and regulations prohibiting, in interstate and foreign commerce, the taking or agreeing to take certain actions with intent to comply with, further, or support any boycott by a foreign country against another country that is friendly to the United States. Among the principal proscribed acts are: (1) refusing to do business with or in a boycotted country or requiring another to refuse, pursuant to an agreement with, or a requirement or request from, a boycotting country; (2) refusing to employ, requiring another to refuse to employ, or otherwise discriminating against any United States person[40] because of race, religion, sex, or national origin or that of any owner, officer, director, or employee of such person; (3) or furnishing information with respect to any United States person or any such owner, officer, director, or employer; (4) furnishing information concerning any business relationship with or in the boycotted country, or any national or resident thereof, or any person known or believed to be restricted from having any business relationship with or in the boycotting country.

The 1977 Amendments state that the rules and regulations may contain certain exceptions. Among the principal ones is the permission for positively stated certificates of origin. That is, "Made in the United States" is permitted, but "Not Made in Israel" is prohibited. Another exception permits agreeing to comply with the boycotting country's prohibition of imports into that country of goods produced in the boycotted country. Also permitted is agreeing to refrain from shipping goods to a boycotting country on carriers of the boycotted country. There are various other substantive prohibitions and exceptions, not discussed here, which may be found by reference to the Amendments (and the Export Administration Act of 1979, which reenacted these provisions) and which are discussed at length in law journal articles.[41]

## Penalties

The penalties for violation of the antiboycott law are both criminal and civil in nature.[42] There is no specific mention of corporate officers or other managers in the penalty sections, but the criminal provisions apply to "whoever knowingly violates" and the civil penalties apply to "each violation." Under principles for applying sanctions for violations of federal statutes that we have seen numerous times throughout this book, it is obvious that a corporate manager who personally participates in a corporate violation can be held personally liable. The criminal sanctions are a fine of not more than $25,000 or imprisonment for not more than one year, or both, for a first offense. For a second or subsequent offense, the maximum fine is increased to 3 times the value of the exports or $50,000, whichever is greater, and the maximum jail sentence is increased to five years. The civil penalty, which may be in lieu of, or in addition to, the criminal sanctions, is not to exceed $10,000 for each violation.

Unlike the antibribery law, the antiboycott law's focus does not appear to be upon the conduct of individuals within the corporation, and there have been no governmental warnings directed at corporate managers. This is not to say, however, that corporate managers could not become personally involved in violations.

The Tax Reform Act of 1976 differs from the Export Administration Act Amendments of 1977 in its treatment of corporate managers by providing specifically that a person (within the meaning of Section 6671(b) of the Internal Revenue Code) who is required to report participation or cooperation with an international boycott and who willfully fails to do so shall be fined not more than $25,000, imprisoned for not more than one year, or both.[43] Section 6671(b) defines a "person" as including any corporate officer or employee "who as such officer or employee is under a duty to perform the act in respect of which the **207** violation occurs."

## NOTES

1. P.L. 95-213; 91 Stat. 1494; 15 U.S.C. §§ 78a, 78m, 78dd-1, 78dd-2, 78ff. This Act is discussed in Hancock, *Executive's Guide to Business Law* (McGraw-Hill Book Co., 1979), 41-1 to 41-6.

2. P.L. 95-52, Title II; 91 Stat. 244; reenacted by the Export Administration Act of 1979, P.L. 96-72, § 8, 93 Stat. 521, 50 U.S.C. App. § 2407.

3. P.L. 94-455, §§ 1061–1067; 90 Stat. 1649; 26 U.S.C. §§ 952(a), 995(b)(1), and 999.

4. Technical Amendments Act of 1958, P.L. 85-866, § 5(a), 72 Stat. 1608; formerly 26 U.S.C. § 162(c). The concept of disallowance was extended in the Tax Reform Act of 1976 to provide a tax penalty for bribery payments by foreign subsidiaries or domestic international sales corporations. 26 U.S.C. §§ 952(a), 995(b)(1). See discussion in this chapter under the heading "Regulation by Taxation." See also Cole, "Taxation: Anti-Boycott and Anti-Bribery Legislation," 18 *Harv. Int'l. L.J.* 365–373 at 367 (1977).

5. Formerly 18 U.S.C. § 610 (*repealed and replaced by the* Federal Election Campaign Act Amendments of 1976, P.L. 94-283; 90 Stat. 490; 2 U.S.C. § 441b).

6. Report of the Securities and Exchange Commission on Questionable and Illegal Corporate Payments and Practices, to the Senate Banking, Housing, and Urban Affairs Committee, May 12, 1976, p. 1. (Hereinafter called SEC Report 5-12-76.) Also published in *Sec. Reg. & L. Rep.* (BNA) No. 353, Special Supp. May 19, 1976.

7. House Comm. on Interstate and Foreign Commerce, Unlawful Corporate Payments Act of 1977, H.R. Rep. No. 640, 95th Cong., 1st Sess. (1977). There are numerous articles on the historical development of the foreign payments problem, in which some of the more outstanding or sensational cases are described. Among these are Nelson, "Bribes, Kickbacks and Political Contributions in Foreign Countries—The Nature and Scope of the Securities and Exchange Commission's Power to Regulate and Control American Corporate Behavior," 1976 *Wisc. L. Rev.* 1231–1268; and Herlihy & Levine, "Corporate Crisis: The Overseas Payment Problem," 6 *Law & Policy in Int'l Bus.* 547–629 (1976).

8. While it is true there were no general prohibitions of bribes or other questionable payments abroad, there were certain limitations on deductions for federal income tax purposes, specific laws governing shipment of arms abroad, and particular situations where the conduct might constitute a violation of the Sherman Antitrust Act or the Federal Trade Commission Act. For discussions of the possible impact of these various laws, see Herlihy & Levine, "Corporate Crisis: The Overseas Payment Problem," 8 *Law & Policy in Int'l Bus.* 547–629 at 594–608 (1976); Severaid, "The Regulation of Questionable Foreign Payments," 8 *Law & Policy in Int'l Bus.* 1055–1082 at 1056–1059 (1976); Verri, "A Look at Questionable or Illegal Payments by American Corporations to Foreign Government Officials," 8 *Case West. Res. J. of Int'l Law* 496–529 (1976); and Lewis, "Penalizing Bribery of Foreign

Officials Through the Tax Laws: A Case for Repealing Section 162(c)(1)," 11 *U. of Mich. J. of L. Ref.* 73–94 (1977).

9. Doherty, "The SEC's Management Fraud Program," 31 *Bus. Law.* 1279–1282 at 1280 (1976). A critic of this viewpoint has stated: "[T]he basic concept of the Securities laws, that disclosure is determined by materiality to the average prudent investor, appears to have been replaced in the minds of some with the concept of materiality in the eyes of the most ethical critic of the corporate activities, who may not even be an investor." Mann, "Watergate to Bananagate: What Lies Beyond?" 31 *Bus. Law.* 1663–1669 at 1668 (1976).

10. SEC Report 5-12-76, p. 30.

11. The voluntary disclosure program is described in detail in SEC Report 5-12-76, pp. 6–13. See also Stevenson, "The SEC and Foreign Bribery," 32 *Bus. Law.* 53–73 at 65–69 (1976); and Herlihy & Levine, "Corporate Crisis: The Overseas Payment Problem," 8 *Law & Policy in Int'l Bus.* 547–629 at 584–594 (1976). Herlihy & Levine, at 595–608, also disclose responses to the problem by the Internal Revenue Service and other government agencies.

12. See Freeman, "The Legality of the SEC's Management Fraud Program," 31 *Bus. Law.* 1295–1303 (1976).

13. SEC Report 5-12-76, p. 8, n. 7; Herlihy & Levine, 8 *Law & Policy in Int'l Bus.* 547–629 at 585, n. 208.

14. Herlihy & Levine, *id.* at 580, n. 188.

15. Nelson, 1976 *Wis. L. Rev.* 1231–1268 at 1260; DeMott, "Reweaving the Corporate Veil: Management Structure and the Control of Corporate Information," 41 *Law & Contemp. Prob.* (Summer 1977) 182–221 at 188–191; Stevenson, 32 *Bus. Law.* 53–73 at 64–65; Doherty, 31 *Bus. Law.* 1279–1282 at 1280–1281; and Mathews, "Recent Trends in SEC Requested Ancillary Relief in SEC Level Injunctive Actions," 31 *Bus. Law.* 1323–1352 (1976).

16. A few insights into the variety of opinion may be found in Freeman, 31 *Bus. Law.* 1295–1303; Severaid, 8 *Law & Policy in Int'l Bus.* 1055–1082; and note, "Foreign Bribes and the Securities Acts' Disclosure Requirements," 74 *Mich. L. Rev.* 1222–1242 (1976).

17. SEC Report 5-12-76, pp. 58–59.

18. The superiority of international rules, as contrasted with purely domestic legislation, is advocated by Severaid, 8 *Law & Policy in Int'l Bus.* 1055–1082; Sinkeldam, "Payments to Foreign Officials by Multinational Corporations: Bribery or Business Expense and the Effects of United States Policy," 6 *Calif. West. Int'l L.J.* 360–381; and McLaughlin, "The Criminalization of Questionable Foreign Payments by Corporations: A Comparative Legal Systems Analysis," 46 *Fordham L. Rev.* 1071–1114 (1978).

The Tax Reform Act of 1976 also attacked the problem of overseas bribery by the use of tax penalties. See note 4 to this chapter. See also discussion of the use of tax penalties against both bribery and boycotts in the section headed "Regulation by Taxation" in this chapter.

19. 15 U.S.C. § 78m.

20. See Baruch, "The Foreign Corrupt Practices Act," *Harv. Bus. Rev.*, Jan.–Feb. 1979, pp. 32–50 at 32; Maher K. White, "Corruption Control," *Wall St. J.*, August 25, 1980, p. 10. The Committee on Corporate Law and Accounting,

Corporation, Banking and Business Law Section of the American Bar Association has published "A Guide to the New Section 13(b)(2) Accounting Requirements of the Securities Exchange Act of 1934," 34 *Bus. Law.* 307–343 (1978).

21. 17 C.F.R. § 240.13b2.

22. SEC Release No. 34-15, 772 (April 30, 1979); 44 Fed. Reg. 26702; SEC release 34-16 877 (June 6, 1980); 45 Fed. Reg. 40134.

23. 15 U.S.C. § 78ff.

24. SEC Release 34-15570 (Feb. 15, 1979); 44 Fed. Reg. 10964, 10970; SEC Docket, Vol. 16, No. 17, p. 1193 (March 6, 1979).

25. SEC Release 34-11147 (Dec. 20, 1974), 40 Fed. Reg. 1010; SEC Docket, Vol. 5, No. 20, p. 767 (Jan. 6, 1975). See discussion in Leech & Mundheim, "The Outside Director of the Publicly Held Corporation," 31 *Bus. Law.* 1799–1838 at 1816 (1976).

26. SEC Release No. 34-13346 (March 9, 1977); SEC Docket, Vol. 11, No. 15, p. 1945 (March 22, 1977). For the text of the New York Stock Exchange Policy, see NYSE *Company Manual* A-29, A-30.

27. "Washington Outlook," *Bus. Week*, June 18, 1979, p. 157; *Sec. Reg. & L. Rep.* (BNA), No. 533, p. A-10, Dec. 19, 1979.

28. Baruch, *Harv. Bus. Rev.*, Jan.–Feb. 1979, pp. 32–50 at 50.

29. 15 U.S.C. § 78dd-1.

30. 1934 Act, *as amended*, § 32(c); 15 U.S.C. § 78ff(c).

31. 15 U.S.C. § 78dd-2.

32. SEC v. Page Airways, Inc., *Fed. Sec. L. Rep.* (CCH) (1978 Transfer Binder) ¶ 96,393, (1979 Transfer Binder) ¶ 96,717 (D.D.C. No. 78-656 (1980 Transfer Binder); SEC v. Katy Industries, Inc. *Sec. Reg. & L. Rep.* (BNA), No. 469, p. A-1, Sept. 13, 1978 (N.D. Ill., No. 78C-3476, ¶ 97,341 (W.D.N.Y. 1980). See also "Bribes and Business," *Wall St. J.*, Aug. 2, 1979, pp. 1 & 19; "The Great Bribe Hunt," *Wall St. J.*, Aug. 9, 1979, p. 20; and "SEC, International Systems Get Accord in Payments Case," *Wall St. J.*, Dec. 18, 1979, p. 2.

33. For detailed analyses of the Act, see Bathen, "A Congressional Response to the Problem of Questionable Corporate Payments Abroad: The Foreign Corrupt Practices Act of 1977," 10 *Law & Policy in Int'l Bus.* 1253–1304 (1978); Atkeson, "The Foreign Corrupt Practices Act of 1977: An International Application of SEC Corporate Governance Reforms," 12 *Int. Lawyer* 703–720 (1978); and Baruch, *Harv. Bus. Rev.*, Jan.–Feb. 1979, pp. 32–50. An American Bar Association panel-discussion of the Act is reported in full in "Foreign Corrupt Practices Act of 1977 and the Regulation of Questionable Payments," 34 *Bus. Law.* 623–664 (1979). For reports and opinion in the business press concerning reactions of business as well as government enforcement actions, see "The Antibribery Bill Backfires," *Bus. Week*, April 17, 1978, p. 143; "Questionable-Payments Drive Stimulates Competition, Tougher Internal Controls," *Wall St. J.*, June 23, 1978, p. 34; "Foreign-Bribery Act Imposes Tough Rules on the Bookkeeping of All Public Firms," *Wall St. J.*, July 28, 1978, p. 30; "U.S. Firms Say '77 B⌐ ⌐ on Foreign Bribes

Hurts Overseas Sales," *Wall St. J.*, Aug. 2, 1979, p. 1; "Misinterpreting the Antibribery Law," *Bus. Week*, Sept. 3, 1979, pp. 150–151; and "The Great Bribe Hunt," *Wall St. J.*, Aug. 9, 1979, p. 20.

34. There are at least ninety countries boycotting other countries. See Saltoun, "Regulation of Foreign Boycotts," 33 *Bus. Law.* 559–603 at 559 (1978); Ludwig & Smith, "The Business Effects of the Antiboycott Provisions of the Export Administration Amendments of 1977—Morality Plus Pragmatism Equals Complexity," 8 *Ga. J. Int'l & Comp. L.* 581–660 at 588, n. 21 (1978).

35. Friedman, "Confronting the Arab Boycott: A Lawyer's Baedeker," 19 *Harv. Int'l Law J.* 443–533 at 443–444 (1978).

36. Saltoun, 33 *Bus. Law.* 559–603 at 560, 603.

37. P.L. 89-63, 79 Stat. 209. See Saltoun, 33 *Bus. Law.* 559–603 at 568–569.

38. P.L. 94-455, Title X, § 1064(a); 90 Stat. 1650; 26 U.S.C. § 999. The substantive provisions of this section are discussed and analyzed in Rubenfeld, "Legal and Tax Implications of Participation in International Boycotts," 32 *Tax. L. Rev.* 613–650 (1978); Cole, 18 *Harv. Int'l L.J.* 365–373; Estes, "Federal Tax Consequences of International Boycotts," 8 *Ga. J. Int'l & Comp. L.* 685–709 (1978); Friedman, 19 *Harv. Int'l L.J.* 443–533 at 459–476; and Kaplan, "Income Taxes and the Arab Boycott," 32 *Tax Law.* 313–347 (1979).

39. P.L. 95-52, Title II; 91 Stat. 244; *reenacted by the* Export Administration Act of 1979, P.L. 96-72; 93 Stat. 52; 50 U.S.C. App. § 240/2420. The political and legislative history is discussed at length in Steiner, "Pressure and Principles—The Politics of the Antiboycott Legislation," 8 *Ga. J. Int'l & Comp. L.* 529–558 (1978). Only the United States and France have antiboycott laws. See Turck, "A Comparative Study of Non-United States Responses to the Arab Boycott," 8 *Ga. J. Int'l & Comp. L.* 711–739 (1978); and Saltoun, 33 *Bus. Law,* 559–603 at 594–595.

40. "United States person" is defined as any United States resident or national (other than an individual resident outside the United States and employed by other than a United States person), any domestic concern (including any permanent domestic establishment of any foreign concern) and any foreign subsidiary or affiliate (including any permanent foreign establishment) of any domestic concern which is controlled in fact by such domestic concern, as determined under regulations of the President;" 50 U.S.C. App. § 24/5(2).

41. The substantive prohibitions and exceptions are found at 50 U.S.C. App. § 2407. For more complete discussions of the antiboycott law, see Williams, "The New Anti-Boycott Laws," 23 *Pract. Law.*, No. 7, pp. 59–71 (1977); Saltoun, 33 *Bus. Law.* 559–603; Marcuss, "The Antiboycott Law: The Regulation of International Business Behavior," 8 *Ga. J. Int'l & Comp. L.* 559–580 (1978); Ludwig & Smith, 8 *Ga. J. Int'l & Comp. L.* 581–660; Pfeifer, "Anti-Boycott Legislation—The Export Administration Amendments of 1977," 19 *Harv. Int'l L.J.* 348–372 (1978); Friedman, 19 *Harv. Int'l L.J.* 443–533; and McCarthy & McKenzie, "Commerce Department Regulations Governing Participation by United States Persons in Foreign Boycotts," 11 *Vand. J. Transnat'l L.* 193–247 (1978). See also Hancock, *Executive's Guide to Business Law,* 67-1 to 67-17.

42. 50 U.S.C. App. § 2405.

43. 50 U.S.C. App. § 2405.

# CHAPTER TEN

# Response to Risk: Indemnification and Insurance

In the preceding chapters we have observed the development of the law in the United States as it pertains to the personal liabilities of corporate managers. We started with early common-law concepts under which corporate managers could in certain instances be held personally responsible for the torts or crimes of their respective corporations. We then looked at the corporate manager's responsibility to his or her own corporation and its stockholders, as developed by the state courts at common law and in the interpretation of the state corporation acts.

Superimposed upon the common-law principles of managerial liability are the multitudinous federal regulatory statutes. They began in 1887 with the enactment of the Interstate Commerce Act. In the beginning, the only sanctions for violation were those against individual managers, and it was not until 1903 that the Interstate Commerce Act was amended to provide sanctions against the corporations themselves. The next step was a broad statute prescribing rules for business conduct, the Sherman Antitrust Act of 1890, which imposed penalties against both corporations and their managers. The federal government took its first step in the field of health and product safety with enactment of the Food and Drug Act of 1906. There have followed decades of development of these laws in the fields of carrier regulation, antitrust, health, and product safety. It has been an evolutionary process. All the while, corporate managers faced penalties for violations, but generally the penalties were light and not too frequently invoked.

That is, until the New Deal. The federal government moved very strongly into the field of employee relations, as well as numerous other aspects of business activity. Most important of these insofar as the personal liabilities of corporate managers are concerned was the enactment of the securities laws in 1933 and 1934. In these acts more than any others, the corporate directors and officers were singled out for particular attention, with specific liabilities in connection with securities offerings by their corporations, disclosure of information at all stages of their corporations' operations, specific rules in connection with seeking stockholder votes for election or reelection to corporate boards, and various types of inhibitions in trading in securities of their respective corporations.

The past two decades have brought a wave of federal statutes governing almost every conceivable aspect of corporate operations—far surpassing the wave of the New Deal days. Laws pertaining to health and product safety burst upon business in great number and detail. Protecting the environment became the watchword of the late sixties and the seventies. Clean air, clean water, noise abatement, regulation of solid-waste disposal—all these were subjects of intricate statutes and regulations affecting practically all segments of American business—with responsibility for compliance and liability for failure to ensure this compliance being placed directly on the shoulders of corporate managers. Specific industries, such as the automotive, oil, and chemical industries, were subjected to statutory rules peculiar to their respective operations, and again their respective managers were made responsible.

In the employee relations field, the enactment of the Employee Retirement Income and Security Act (ERISA) placed additional risks upon corporate managers for the integrity of pension plans and other types of employee benefits. New statutes in the 1970s placed personal responsibility upon corporate managers for monitoring the accuracy of books of account, the prevention of questionable payments in overseas transactions, and the avoidance of actions that might further the efforts of a foreign nation or nations to impose an economic boycott of another foreign nation.

Our review of the federal statutes affecting business activity and the responsibility and liability of corporate managers has by no means exhausted the subject. For example, we have not discussed the banking laws and have mentioned only a few sections of the Internal Revenue Code. We have not attempted to deal with the numerous recent statutes enacted in an effort to alleviate the energy crisis. Many of the statutes that we have discussed contain other provisions affecting the liabilities of corporate managers, but we have limited our discussion to the more important aspects—to those situations that appear to be typical of the kinds of problems that could arise under them—some broad in nature, some more narrow, but all illustrating the kind of exposure that a corporate manager is most likely to encounter. It is evident from the examples in the preceding chapters that new federal statutes and regulations have substantially increased the personal risk of the corporate manager in the past two decades. During this same period, there has also been an increase of state laws affecting business and providing both corporate and managerial sanctions for their violation. These, too,

might have been examined, but any effort to deal with the enactments **213**
of the fifty states in this field would result in more detail than appears to *Response to Risk*
be needed.

During this same period, existing laws have been tightened by increased enforcement action against corporate managers by government authority; by the proliferation of private lawsuits by stockholders, customers, "public interest" groups and other members of the public; and by the enactment of more severe penalties by the Congress. Several government agencies have announced their intentions to become more active in proceeding against individual managers and in seeking more severe penalties for violation. These intentions have been generally carried forward into action.

## MANAGERS SEEK ASSISTANCE

With the increased attention upon corporate managers, it was only logical that they should seek some assistance from the corporations upon whose behalf they were incurring risks. As early as 1906, the Wisconsin Supreme Court upheld the right of a corporation to pay the expenses of directors in successfully defending an action brought against them in their capacity as directors.[1] The payment was approved by a stockholders' resolution after the suit was started, but the resolution does not appear to have been the basis for the decision. There seems to have been no other decision in this area until 1931 when the Ohio Court of Appeals set aside a directors' resolution to reimburse themselves for legal expenses in successfully resisting a stockholders' suit.[2] The resolution had not been submitted to the stockholders for a ratifying vote, and the Ohio court held that the payment was illegal because the corporation itself, as distinguished from the directors, had received no benefit from the expenses.

The decision that attracted the most attention, however, was *New York Dock Company Inc.* v. *McCollom*,[3] decided by the New York Supreme Court (which is not the highest court in New York but, rather, the trial court) in 1939. In that case, the directors of a corporation, sued in a stockholders' derivative action, were completely successful on the merits. When they sought reimbursement from the corporation for their expenses, the court rejected their claim on the same ground as the Ohio case eight years before—namely, that their successful defense conferred no benefit on the corporation. Professor Joseph Bishop of Yale Law School characterized the *McCollom* decision as "nonsense." He and many other writers have pointed out that the court overlooked the point

> that the benefit to the corporation comes from inducing valuable executives to serve it by promising them protection against unjustified litigation.[4]

The *McCollom* decision caused so much concern in corporate and legal circles that the New York Legislature in 1941 adopted the first state statute permitting a corporation to indemnify its directors and officers in certain situations. Delaware followed in 1943, and soon most of the states had adopted some form of indemnification statute. The New Jersey courts in 1941 refused to follow the *McCollom* decision.[5] But there was still too much uncertainty in the law, and the legislative efforts to deal with the problem in the various state corporation codes have not halted, but have, in fact, continued down to the present day.

## THE INDEMNIFICATION STATUTES

The first indemnification statutes were entirely permissive in nature and failed to cover situations where a director or an officer might have a right to indemnification because of having successfully defended an action brought against the director or officer in his or her capacity as such. This left the director or officer exposed in situations where there might have been an unfriendly change in management or where the corporation might be in financial difficulties and unwilling or legally unable to assume additional obligations.

The early statutes also failed to distinguish between expenses incurred in actions by third parties and actions by or on behalf of the corporation, and the distinctions between civil and criminal actions were fuzzy. Matters not constituting litigation in the strict sense, but related thereto, such as investigations and administrative proceedings, were not sufficiently covered. Many corporations attempted to solve some of these problems by the use of bylaws or corporate articles relating to indemnification. A number of these were inadequate. Others were of doubtful validity if adopted by directors without a stockholder vote or if possibly exceeding the permission granted by the statute. Over the next two or three decades, however, many of the uncertainties were solved by more sophisticated statutes, but in some cases new uncertainties were introduced. No effort will be made to analyze the old and now superseded statutory provisions, but we will look at some of the more significant of the current indemnification provisions and some of the proposals to change them.

Because New York and California are our most populous and most important commercial states and Delaware is the state of incorporation of the largest number of corporations listed on the New York Stock Exchange, the indemnification provisions of these three states are of the greatest practical importance in corporate affairs. There is also a close interrelation between the Delaware Corporation Law and the American Bar Association's Model Business Corporation Act, which has been followed in a substantial number of other states. The Corporation, Banking and Business Law Section of the American Bar Association is currently considering proposed amendments to the indemnification section of the Model Business Corporation Act.[6] A comparison of the principal features of the New York, California, Delaware, and Model

All these indemnification sections except New York's now apply not only to civil actions or suits in the courts, but also to criminal actions and to investigations and administrative proceedings. The scope of protection under the California, Delaware, and Model Acts includes directors, officers, employees, and agents. New York limits its coverage to directors and officers, presumably on the theory that indemnification of ordinary employees and agents is permitted and, in some cases, possibly required at common law.[7]

The distinction between actions by or in the right of the corporation (stockholders' or creditors' derivative suits) and actions by third parties is recognized in all three state laws and in the Model Act. No such distinction is made, however, if the manager has been wholly successful on the merits in the defense of the action or proceeding. In such a case, indemnification by the corporation is mandatory under all the acts. California, Delaware, and the Model Act go further and require indemnification if the manager is successful on the merits *or otherwise*. Thus, a successful procedural defense, such as the statute of limitations or lack of jurisdiction of the court, can result in mandatory indemnification, provided, of course, that the action has thereby been finally terminated.

New York, however, has not seen fit to go that far on mandatory indemnification. If the manager has been only partially successful in defending the action, mandatory indemnification is not available in New York, although it is provided for in California, Delaware, and the present Model Act "to the extent" that the manager has been successful. This obviously poses interesting questions of allocation of costs, as well as questions of when one has been "partially" successful. The proposed changes in the Model Act follow the New York pattern of requiring that the indemnitor be wholly successful in defending the action. In view of the fact that permissive indemnification is also available, the New York rule and the Model Act proposed change appear to be the better approach and less subject to abuse.

The distinction between the two types of actions or proceedings— third-party or by or in the right of the corporation—becomes important in cases where the corporate manager has *not* successfully defended, but has either litigated and lost or has settled. In such a case, if the action has been by the corporation or by a stockholder or creditor derivative suit, the judgment or settlement would require a payment to the corporation. Indemnification would defeat the purpose of the judgment or settlement, and accordingly, all three states and the Model Act deny indemnification for the amount of the judgment or the settlement. *Expenses* incurred in connection with the action or proceeding *may*, however, be reimbursed by the corporation in certain circumstances. New York limits such reimbursement to those situations where the settlement and reimbursement have both received court approval.

California, Delaware, and the Model Act permit reimbursement of such expenses if the manager acted in good faith and in a manner that the indemnitee believed (Delaware and the Model Act say "reasonably believed") to be in the best interests of the corporation.[8] (California goes a bit further and also requires "such care . . . as an ordinarily prudent person in a like position would use under similar circumstances.") If, however, there was an adjudication that the manager has "breached his duty to the corporation" (New York), was "liable for negligence or misconduct in the performance of his duty to the corporation" (Delaware and the present Model Act), or "liable to the corporation in the performance of . . . duty to the corporation" (California), the power of the corporation to indemnify is denied in New York and is permitted under the other acts only upon a court order. In California, Delaware, and the other Model Act states, indemnification is permissible if the court determines that "in view of all the circumstances of the case, such person is fairly and reasonably entitled to indemnity." In case of a settlement as distinguished from an adjudication of liability, court approval for indemnification of expenses is not required by the statute. In Delaware, however, Rule 23.1 of the Chancery Court Rules provides that a stockholders' derivative action may not be dismissed or settled without court approval. This rule gives the court supervision over the terms of the settlement, and inquiry into and approval or disapproval of indemnification is within the court's powers.

These last-mentioned provisions for indemnification upon court approval under the California, Delaware, and Model Acts appear to provide avenues for abuse. It might be possible that a sympathetic judge would subvert the intent of holding directors and officers to high standards of conduct by allowing indemnification for expenses when such standards have not been met. One writer has suggested, however, that it is "difficult to conceive of such a situation." Indemnification might be possible, he suggests, in a case where the court established a new and stricter standard than anticipated.[9] The proposed changes in the Model Act retain this concept, but the draft writers have proposed that indemnification not be permitted without court review in *any* case where the corporate manager has been found liable to the corporation, such qualifying language as "negligence or misconduct" and "duty to the corporation" being eliminated. Similarly, the proposed changes in the Model Act prohibit the corporation from indemnifying without court approval in any case where it has been adjudged that "personal benefit was improperly received by" the indemnitee.

Where the action or proceeding against the corporate manager is brought by a third party (government, customer, employee, or member of the public) and is not a stockholder or creditor derivative suit, the rules for indemnification are somewhat more liberal. The third-party action is, of course, the easiest one for which to justify indemnification. The corporate manager in such a situation is sued or proceeded against because of an act that was alleged to have been done on behalf of the corporation and that allegedly had injured a third party or had been in violation of a statute. In many such actions or proceedings, the corporation itself might also be a defendant.

Accordingly, the permissive right of a corporation to indemnify is not limited to those situations where the manager prevailed in the suit or proceeding. Indemnification not only for expenses but also for amounts paid upon judgments or fines or in settlements is permitted within certain limitations. All permit indemnification upon a determination that the indemnitee acted in the best interests of the corporation.[10] If the proceeding was a criminal one, there is a further qualification that the indemnitee had no reasonable cause to believe that his or her conduct was unlawful. Each statute also provides that termination of any action or proceeding by judgment, order, settlement, conviction, or upon a plea of *nolo contendere*, shall not, of itself, create a presumption against good faith or reasonable belief that the conduct was in the best interests of the corporation or, in a criminal proceeding, not unlawful.

As noted earlier, there are situations where the corporate manager is entitled to indemnification as a matter of right (mandatory indemnification) and others where indemnification may be made only with court approval. In between, however, lies an area where indemnification is neither mandatory upon the corporation nor limited to approval by a court. This is the field of permissive indemnification—that is where indemnification is permitted by a body other than a court. An example is the reimbursement for expenses in a situation where the action or proceeding has been settled.

Permissive indemnification by the corporation may be made by the stockholders. It may also be made by the board of directors acting by a quorum of directors who were not parties to the action or proceeding. If a disinterested quorum of the board is not available, New York, Delaware, and the Model Act permit indemnification upon the opinion in writing of "independent legal counsel." In all such cases, the deciding entity—stockholders, directors, independent legal counsel—must determine that the indemnitee has met the standards of conduct set forth in the statute.

The proposed changes in the Model Act provide another body for making the determination—a committee of two or more members of the board who were not parties to the preceeding. The interested directors would, under the proposed changes, be permitted to vote on the selection of the committee or upon the selection of independent legal counsel (called "special legal counsel" in the proposed changes) if that mechanism were the one selected for making the determination. California does not provide for the independent or special legal counsel method of approval, but it does permit the corporation or the person claiming indemnification to apply to the court in which the proceeding was brought to make a determination of the propriety of indemnification.

All these acts contain procedures for advancement of expenses by the corporation during the pendency of litigation and for their repayment upon an ultimate determination that the person to whom they were advanced is not entitled to indemnification. The purpose is to encourage the manager to attempt to defend his or her position even when lacking the financial resources to do so.

The indemnification procedures in the California and New York statutes are exclusive, and any corporate articles, bylaws, resolutions, or contracts that seek to extend the right of indemnification are void. Delaware and the Model Act, however, permit greater indemnification rights by "by-law, agreement, vote of stockholders or disinterested directors, or otherwise." How far a court would permit a corporation to subvert the standards set forth in the other subsections of the indemnification section is open to question. It is likely, for example, that a bylaw permitting a corporation to return to a defaulting executive moneys that he or she was ordered in a judgment to pay back to the corporation would be found void as against public policy. But between that extreme and the statutory standards are many borderline situations.

The flexibility of the statutory standards as they now exist or are proposed as Model Act changes are sufficient to cover almost any conceivable situation where a corporate manager might be entitled to indemnification. The New York and California requirement of exclusivity, which is also found in the indemnification sections of at least six other state corporation laws,[11] is certainly to be preferred to an open invitation to unrestrained private arrangements.

## INDEMNIFICATION AND FEDERAL STATUTES

Against the background of the large number of federal statutes regulating conduct of corporate managers and imposing liabilities, civil and criminal, for violation, it is not surprising that questions have arisen concerning the consistency of state indemnification statutes with such federal statutes.

### Indemnification and the Securities Laws

The question of consistency arose as early as 1944 in connection with a securities offering of Johnson & Johnson Co. Johnson & Johnson Co. was seeking acceleration of the twenty-day waiting period, required in connection with the so-called pricing amendment to a registration statement under the Securities Act of 1933 between the dates of filing of the pricing amendment and of the offering. The company had a charter or bylaw provision for indemnification of officers and directors. The SEC took the position that indemnification provisions for Securities Act violations for directors, officers, or controlling persons were against public policy as expressed in the Act and therefore unenforceable. The SEC, as a condition of acceleration, required the company (unless all parties waived in advance any claim for indemnification) to insert in its registration statement: (1) a summary of the SEC's position, and (2) an undertaking that unless the matter were settled by controlling precedent, it would submit any claim for indemnification for Securities Act liabilities (other than for expenses of a successful defense) to a court for adjudication of the question.

This type of undertaking, which has become known as the Johnson & Johnson formula, has been routine in connection with requests for acceleration ever since. The SEC formalized the practice by a note to its regulations in 1957.[12]

While the SEC has consistently taken a strong position against indemnification for liabilities under the 1933 Act, it has remained silent concerning the appropriateness of indemnification under the 1934 Securities Exchange Act. Cases have arisen, however, involving indemnification under both acts and a review of them is, therefore, in order.

The leading case on indemnification under both the 1933 and 1934 acts is *Globus* v. *Law Research, Inc.*,[13] decided by the Second Circuit Court of Appeals in 1969. It did not involve a claim for indemnification of a director or an officer, but rather, a claim by an underwriter. The principle, however, appears to be the same with regard to both classes of claimants.

*Globus* arose from a stock offering which was alleged to have been made through a misleading offering circular. Certain investors sued the company, its president, and the underwriters, alleging violations of both the 1933 and 1934 acts. The underwriter brought a cross-claim against the company and the president under an indemnification provision appearing in the underwriting agreement. The president was characterized by the court as the primary wrongdoer who omitted certain material facts to induce the public to invest. The underwriter, however, had knowledge of the material facts and nevertheless distributed the offering circular without revealing them.

The jury found for the underwriter on the cross-claim, apparently on the theory that the underwriter was less guilty than the corporation and the president. The District Court set aside the verdict and this action was affirmed by the Court of Appeals, holding that "one cannot insure himself against his own reckless, willful or criminal misconduct." The court also cited with approval the SEC's position that indemnification of directors, officers, and controlling persons is contrary to the policy of the 1933 Act.[14]

The principle of *Globus* has been extended to situations where the party seeking indemnification has been guilty of recklessness or negligence. *Gould v. American-Hawaiian Steamship Co.* was an action by a director seeking indemnification from liability for violation of the proxy rules. In it he alleged that the defendant directors were guilty of greater negligence than he. The court stated:

> To allow indemnity to those who have breached responsibilities squarely

placed upon them by the statute would vitiate the remedial purposes of Sec. 14(a).[15]

In the *Matter of Equity Funding Corporation of America,* a proceeding pertaining to one of the major corporate scandals of recent years, the court summarized the matter with these words:

> [T]he policy of the securities laws precludes indemnification of an unsuccessful defendant in all except extraordinary circumstances such as the indemnification of a corporation by its officers and directors who caused it to engage in conduct giving rise to the liability. . . . And this policy has been applied even where the liability of the party claiming indemnification is based on negligence.[16]

While it appears that the courts will not attempt to compare degrees of fault among defendants in securities law cases and thus to allow indemnification to those who are less at fault, it does not follow that a director or officer cannot compel others to *share* the liability with her or him. In the case of violations of both the 1933 and 1934 Acts, the statutes in certain instances provide for contribution among the various parties who are liable under the respective acts, so that one or two persons do not bear the whole burden while other responsible persons go free.[17]

The policy against indemnification under the securities laws does not prevent a corporation that has incurred liability under the 1933 Act from indemnifying outside directors who did not participate in the violation but who are required to make expenditures in defending themselves in an action by investors. That was the situation in *Goldstein v. Alodex Corp.,*[18] where the corporation settled the 1933 Act claims of the investors and then refused to indemnify the outside directors for their expenses. In an action against the corporation for indemnification, the court found that, in the course of the investors' suit, the outside directors had sustained the burden of proving that they had conducted a reasonable investigation in connection with the securities offering and had reasonable grounds to believe the accuracy of the registration statement. The court held that they were not required to contribute to the settlement and were entitled to indemnification.

## Indemnification and ERISA

Outside the securities laws, the only place where there appears to be an expressed federal government policy statement concerning indemnification is with reference to the Employees Retirement Income and Security Act. Section 410 of ERISA declares that "any provision in an agreement or instrument which purports to relieve a fiduciary from responsibility, obligation or duty under [ERISA] shall be void as against public policy."[19]

In the early months of ERISA's existence, this provision raised some question as to whether a corporation can agree to indemnify fiduciaries

of its employee benefit plans. Section 410 permits the purchase of
insurance, but is not clear whether the insurance is only for the benefit
of the plan, its members, and beneficiaries, or whether it can also
indemnify the fiduciaries. This matter was clarified by an interpretive
bulletin of the Department of Labor which stated that indemnification
from a source outside the assets of the employee benefit plan is permissible.[20] This can be accomplished by direct corporate indemnification or by insurance. The fiduciary was not relieved of responsibility to
the benefit plan. The Labor Department's bulletin was merely a recognition that the fiduciary could be reimbursed by some other source.

The Department of Labor pointed out in the bulletin, however, that
parties entering into an indemnification agreement should consider
whether it complies with the other provisions of Part 4 of Title I of
ERISA. This, then, raises the question of whether the penal provisions
of ERISA are a proper subject of indemnification. The same question
can, of course, be raised with regard to any other penal statute, and no
hard-and-fast answer can be given.


## Indemnification and Antitrust

The difficulty of trying to posit a simple and definite rule with regard to
indemnification for penalties is well illustrated by the decision for the
Ninth Circuit of the Court of Appeals in *Koster v. Warren*.[21] In that case,
Safeway Stores and its former president, Warren, and an employee,
Cliff, were indicted for violation of the antitrust laws. Warren and the
employee pleaded not guilty. In due course, the corporation attempted
to work out a settlement in order to avoid trial and exposure to possible
treble-damage suits. The government refused to accept a settlement that
did not involve the individual defendants as well as the corporation.
Accordingly, the corporation induced the individuals to join with it in
pleading *nolo contendere*. All defendants were fined. The individuals
were also given one-year prison sentences, which were suspended. The
corporation paid the fines, and this action was attacked in a stockholders' derivative suit. In deciding against the stockholders, the court
stated:

> It may well be that public policy would strike down, as lacking in quid pro
> quo, any arrangement whereby a corporate officer could with impunity
> from personal liability involve his company in antitrust violations. Such
> was not the arrangement here, however. The corporation was simply at-
> tempting to extricate itself from a troublesome situation which presented
> itself after the fact of the alleged violation. The payment of the fines was not
> made pursuant to any agreement of indemnity, but was to compensate
> Warren and Cliff for forgoing rights which if exercised could operate to the
> detriment of the corporation. If the United States has cause to object to the
> manner in which Warren and Cliff have managed to escape the conse-
> quences of their conduct, that problem is not before us.[22]

*Koster v. Warren* is a good illustration of the rationale for the statement in the indemnification statutes, examined earlier in this chapter, to the effect that termination of a proceeding by a plea of *nolo contendere* shall not, of itself, create a presumption against reasonable cause to believe that the conduct was lawful. Warren and Cliff believed themselves to be not guilty of the criminal charge and were prepared to defend it. By giving up their right to defend in favor of the corporation's desire to settle and be rid of the matter, they conferred a benefit on the corporation. The corporation received the benefit of their *nolo* pleas and they received a black mark on their records. For the corporation not to have indemnified them would have been an injustice.

Some writers have questioned whether *Koster v. Warren* is really an indemnification case, since there was no statute, article, or bylaw provision for indemnification involved. It was merely the agreement that the corporation made with the individuals to induce them to change their plea.[23] Technically speaking, the writers may be right, but nevertheless, the principle of the right of the corporation to indemnify (or to reimburse, if that is a better word in this context) is very much present and supports the policy of the state statutes.

In a New York Court of Appeals decision, a director who had pleaded *nolo contendere* to a criminal antitrust indictment under the Clayton Act claimed a right to indemnification under the mandatory provisions of the New York statute. He was denied indemnification under that statute as it had previously existed, the court holding that the statute was not intended to cover criminal proceedings.[24] Mandatory indemnification would probably still be denied under the present New York statute, as a *nolo* plea would not meet the test of being "wholly successful."

While indemnification in the case of *nolo* pleas has been criticized on the grounds of public policy, it is not likely that statutes will be revised in the near future to prohibit the practice. Indemnification upon a plea of not guilty followed by a conviction may, however, raise a different set of problems. Perhaps the real problem is not so much the principle of whether indemnification will ever be permitted, but the manner in which it will be awarded. In such a situation, indemnification without court approval raises a serious question of whether the penal provisions of the statute may have been frustrated.

## DIRECTORS' AND OFFICERS' LIABILITY INSURANCE

Indemnification statutes came into being in the 1940s and, as we have seen, have gone through an evolutionary process that has not yet ended. Traditionally, concepts of indemnification and insurance go together. One who has assumed liability as an indemnitor may become apprehensive about the exposure and thus seek to cover it by insurance.

Moreover, it has become evident that there are a number of situations where corporate indemnification is not available. There is, for example, the SEC's opinion that indemnification to officers and directors for liabilities under the 1933 Act is against public policy as expressed in the Act and therefore unenforceable. The numerous qualifications of the indemnification provisions examined earlier in this chapter indicate large areas where indemnification is not permitted.

In situations other than those where indemnification is mandatory, the corporate manager is largely at the mercy of what is hoped to be an understanding board of directors, supportive stockholders, or a court that may or may not be sympathetic. It should be recognized that not all corporate managers who are held civilly, or for that matter, even criminally, liable are necessarily scoundrels. Not all securities laws violations are deliberate. Many are based upon negligence. The enactment of civil penalties in recent federal legislation, particularly in the environmental area, presents further exposures to statutory liability without intent or willfulness. Then there are the common-law liabilities of corporate managers. Not all of them involve a breach of fiduciary relationship. There can be negligence situations. It is true that directors and officers have been generally protected by the business judgment rule, but they still may be liable to attack for not having exercised their best business judgment. Business decisions made in the heat of the competitive fray may not always look sufficiently wise when they are being litigated in a court five or six years later, and those who made them *may* be held liable for negligent mismanagement.[25] All these possible situations conjure up visions of huge liabilities for which indemnification is neither available nor appropriate. A bylaw granting greater indemnification rights, as may be permitted under the Delaware and Model acts, might not be in the best interests of the corporation. It might be void as contrary to public policy—and perhaps it should be.

Uncertainties of the type just described led to the creation of directors' and officers' liability insurance. This type of insurance first appeared in the 1950s but did not attract much attention until the 1960s. Today, the overwhelming majority of large industrial corporations carry this kind of coverage.[26]

In the early stages of development of directors' and officers' liability insurance, serious questions were raised as to the authority of corporations to purchase such insurance when that insurance would protect the directors and officers from exposures against which the corporations could not themselves provide direct indemnification. This question was solved by amendments to the indemnification sections of the various corporation laws which specifically permit the purchase of such insurance to cover liability of directors and officers, whether or not the corporation has the power to indemnify under the statute.

Delaware was the first state to enact such a statutory authorization. A similar provision was later adopted in California and also appears in the Model Business Corporation Act and in the statutes of states following the Model Act. New York has been more restrictive, and while it permits insurance in instances where the directors and officers may not otherwise be indemnified by the corporation, it requires retention (deductibles) and co-insurance, under the rules of the Commissioner of Insurance, so that the director or officer always has a certain limited measure of personal exposure. The practical side of the New York qualification is that the insurance companies who write directors' and officers' liability insurance generally, if not always, do require a deductible or retention, such as $10,000 per person, and a certain amount of co-insurance, such as 5 percent of the loss, which may not be insured elsewhere.

The broad statutory authorization of directors' and officers' insurance, as it exists in Delaware and in the Model Act, has been criticized as relieving directors and officers of all responsibility. Bishop of the Yale Law School, one of the strongest critics (who is not opposed to proper principles of indemnification as is evidenced in many of his writings), objects to the corporation's being permitted to pay all of the premium. In support of his objection, he has stated:

> It seems improbable that any court would uphold a contract of employment which provided that the executive should owe the corporation no duty of good faith or due care, especially if that contract were not disclosed to stockholders. But if such a straightforward attempt to avoid the responsibilities attached to corporate office would fail, it is difficult to see why the corporation should be allowed to achieve the same result by the device, differing only in technique, of purchasing insurance against liability for breaches of these duties.[27]

The Securities and Exchange Commission has stated its position concerning directors' and officers' liability insurance as one of neutrality. In a 1968 release, the SEC stated:

> Insurance against liabilities arising under the Act, whether the cost of such insurance is borne by the registrant, the insured or some other person, is not a bar to acceleration under Note (a) to Rule 460 and no waivers or undertakings need to be furnished with respect thereto.[28]

Criticisms of the purchase by a corporation of liability insurance covering situations that go beyond those in which they are empowered to indemnify are valid to the extent that the insurance might cover criminal penalties, illegal personal profits, dishonesty, and the like. The fact is, however, that directors' and officers' liability policies universally exclude fines and penalties from the definition of loss insured against under the policies. Also excluded are liabilities for short-swing transactions under Section 16(b) of the 1934 Act, return of illegal remuneration paid to the director or officer, any personal profit or advantage to which the director or officer was not legally entitled, and any claim "brought about or contributed to by the dishonesty" of the director or officer (where there has been a judgment of dishonesty against the director or officer).[29]

It may be argued that there is nothing to prevent the insurance companies from removing the exclusions and changing the definition of loss. While it is unlikely that insurance companies are apt to go to the lengths suggested by the critics, it might be desirable to consider amending the indemnification sections of the corporation acts to provide statutory limitations upon insurance consistent with the present practices of the insurance companies.

Perhaps the best argument in support of allowing insurance that goes beyond the power of a corporation to indemnify is that if directors or officers are covered by liability insurance, those who make successful claims against them will have the assurance that the judgments will be paid regardless of their financial condition. This, of course, is a fundamental justification for all types of liability insurance.[30]

## NOTES

1. Figge v. Bergenthal, 130 Wis. 594, 109 N.W. 581, *reh. denied*, 110 N.W. 798 (1907).

2. Griesse v. Lang, 37 Ohio App. 553, 175 N.E. 222 (1931). A Wisconsin decision disallowed reimbursement to directors who were defending, not in their capacities as directors, but rather, as stockholders. Jesse v. Four-Wheel Drive Auto Co., 177 Wis. 627, 189 N.W. 276 (1922).

3. 173 Misc. 106, 16 N.Y.S.2d 844 (Sup. Ct. 1939).

4. Bishop, "Indemnification of Corporate Directors, Officers and Employee," 20 *Bus. Law.* 833–844 at 839 (1965). See also Sebring, "Recent Legislative Changes in the Law of Indemnification of Directors, Officers and Others," 23 *Bus. Law.* 95–113 at 97 (1967).

5. Solimine v. Hollander, 129 N.J. Eq. 264, 19 A.2d 344 (1941). This case and others decided in the absence of indemnification statutes are discussed in Adkins & Plimpton, "Indemnification of Directors and Officers," 13 *Bus. Law.* 693–705 at 696–699 (1958). For a discussion of the early history of the indemnification problem, see Bishop, "Current Status of Corporate Directors' Right to Indemnification," 69 *Harv. L. Rev.* 1057–1079 (1956).

6. For a comparison of the Model Act provisions with the proposed changes, see "Changes in the Model Business Corporation Act Affecting Indemnification of Corporate Personnel," a Report of the Committee on Corporate Laws, 34 *Bus. Law.* 1595–1615 (1979). The three state statutes discussed in this chapter are *N.Y. Bus. Corp. Law* §§ 721–727 (McKinney) as amended (McKinney Supp. 1978); *Calif. Gen. Corp. Law*, § 317 (West) (as amended eff. Jan. 1, 1977); and *Del. Code* 8, § 145 (as amended 1974). For a comparative discussion of the California and Delaware provisions, see Heyler, "Indemnification of Corporate Agents," 23 *U.C.L.A. L. Rev.* 1255–1268 (1976). For a comparative discussion of the New York and Delaware provisions, see Johnston, "Corporate Indemnification and Liability Insurance for Directors and Officers," 33 *Bus. Law.* 1993–2053 (1978).

7. Johnston, 33 *Bus. Law.* 1993–2053 at 1994, 1996.

8. The Delaware and Model Acts say "in *or not opposed to* the best interests of the corporation." Del. Code 8, § 145(a); Model Business Corporation Act,

§ 5(a). Johnston suggests that the italicized phrase was probably inserted to protect an officer or a director who was sued merely because of his or her status as such and not because of any act done in the capacity of director or officer. Johnston, 33 *Bus. Law* 1993–2053 at 1997–1998. This suggestion is supported and the language is clarified in the proposed revision of the Model Act. Report of Committee on Corporate Laws, 34 *Bus. Law.* 1595–1615 at 1600, 1609.

9. Johnston, 33 *Bus. Law.* 1993–2053 at 1997.

10. The Delaware and Model Acts contain the same "or not opposed to" phrase as described in note 8 above. New York also uses the same phrase in reference to situations where a director or officer of the indemnifying corporation was acting at its request in the service of another corporation or entity.

11. See Schaeftler, *The Liabilities of Office: Indemnification and Insurance of Corporate Officers and Directors* (Little, Brown & Co., 1976) 112, n. 47.

12. C.F.R. § 230.460, n. (a).

13. 418 F.2d 1276 (2d Cir. 1969), *cert. denied,* 397 U.S. 913 (1970).

14. *Id.,* 1276, 1288.

15. 387 F. Supp. 163 at 168 (D. Del. 1974).

16. 416 F. Supp. 132 at 156 (C.D. Cal. 1975). See also Odette v. Shearson, Hammill & Co., 394 F. Supp. 946 (S.D.N.Y. 1975), where an underwriter who acted recklessly, but with no actual knowledge that certain statements were misleading, was denied indemnification. In Thomas v. Duralite Co., 386 F. Supp. 698 (D.N.J. 1974), a corporation was granted indemnification against two of its officers who had committed a Section 10(b) violation in connection with the corporation's repurchase of its own stock, where it was found that they were acting only in their personal interests, although in the name of the corporation. See also Feit v. Leasco Data Processing Equipment Corp., 332 F. Supp. 544 (E.D.N.Y. 1971).

17. 1933 Act § 11(f); 14 U.S.C. § 77K. 1934 Act, §§ 9–18b; 15 U.S.C. §§ 78(i), 79(v).

18. 409 F. Supp. 1201 (E.D. Pa. 1976).

19. ERISA, § 410(a); 29 U.S.C. § 1110.

20. Dept. of Labor Interp. Bull., § 2555.75–4, 40 Fed. Reg. 31599 (1975).

21. 297 F.2d 418 (9th Cir. 1961). See discussion in Bishop, 20 *Bus. Law.* 833–844 at 842.

22. *Id.,* 423.

23. See note, "Indemnification of Directors: The Problems Posed by Federal Securities and Antitrust Legislation," 76 *Harv. L. Rev.* 1403–1430 at 1425 (1963); Barrett, "Mandatory Indemnification of Corporate Officers and Directors," 29 *S.W.L.J.* 727–747 at 739, n. 106 (1975).

24. Schwarz v. General Aniline & Film Corp., 305 N.Y. 395, 113 N.E.2d 533 (1953).

25. Schaeftler, *The Liabilities of Office* 95–97.

26. Leech & Mundheim, "The Outside Director of the Publicly Held Corporation," 31 *Bus. Law.* 1799–1838 at 1834 (1976).

27. Bishop, "Sitting Ducks and Decoy Ducks: New Trends in the Indemnification of Corporate Directors and Officers," 77 *Yale L.J.* 1078–1103 at 1087 (1968). See also Hussey, "Indemnifying Corporate Officials for Williams Act Violations," 50 *Indiana L.J.* 826–847 at 846 (1975).

28. SEC Release 33-4936 (Dec. 9, 1968); 1 *Fed. Sec. L. Rep.* (CCH) ¶ 3806 at p. 3325.

29. The various forms of directors' and officers' liability insurance policies are reproduced in Schaeftler, *The Liabilities of Office* 253–295.

30. This argument is discussed at length in Schaeftler, *The Liabilities of Office* 88–97.

# CHAPTER ELEVEN

# Comment and Criticism: Corporate Responsibility and Corporate Governance

Criticism of corporations is nothing new. There appears to have been concern about the power of corporations from the earliest days. Incorporation by special acts of the legislatures was thought to lead to possibilities of abuse: charters were granted to those having the most political influence, it was said. So general incorporation laws were enacted to permit incorporation by anyone who could meet the statutory requirements. Incorporation by special legislative act was eventually forbidden altogether so as to avoid special favors not available under the general incorporation statutes.[1]

With the growth of corporations and their accompanying acquisition of economic strength and power, statutes were enacted to curb their alleged abuses. As we have seen, the first of these statutes—the Interstate Commerce Act—was passed in 1887. It was followed by the Sherman Antitrust Act in 1890. It is true that these statutes were not aimed solely at corporate power and abuse. Any other business form engaging in practices regulated by, or prohibited by, these acts was subject to their requirements, prohibitions, and penalties. Since the corporation was then, as now, the principal form of business organization utilized by large and medium-sized businesses, however, the net result was regulation of the corporate form of business, whatever the legal niceties of stating the scope and intention of the statutes. Thus, all subsequent laws of a business-regulatory nature, whether in the field of health, safety, environment, employee relations, securities regulation, or whatever other field the Congress might see fit to regulate, are applicable primarily to corporations. As we have seen in the preceding chapters, sanctions for violations have generally been imposed upon the corporations themselves and upon their responsible managerial personnel. In addition, the statutes have in some instances imposed duties upon managers to perform, or to refrain from performing, certain acts in the furtherance of the objectives of the particular statute.

## THE TRADITION OF FEDERAL REGULATION

The traditional method of regulation by the Congress has been to determine that certain types of conduct (for example, restraints of trade) are contrary to public policy and to prohibit them, or that certain other types of conduct (such as disclosure in securities matters) are in accordance with public policy and affirmatively to require them. Generally speaking, the approach has been to concentrate on certain fields of activity and to enact a statute applicable to each field, such as the manufacture and sale of food and drugs, or wages and hours of employment, or the use of public waters for the discharge of plant wastes.

In short, the Congress perceives a problem or a series of related problems and moves in to solve it by means of a statute. If, after experience, the Congress determines that there are inadequacies in the statute or that conditions have changed, it adopts amendments to it. On some occasions, the amendments may take the form of a complete restructuring and reenactment of the statute in order to bring it up to date. Numerous instances of such restructuring have been discussed in earlier chapters.

As we have seen, some of the major areas of governmental standards for regulation of business have had their origins in the days of the New Deal. In the aftermath of the Great Depression of the 1930s, numerous legislative solutions were sought for the ills that had preceded or accompanied the Depression. Those statutes that were enacted and that successfully survived the tests of time and of Supreme Court review followed the traditional path of addressing the problem and attempting to solve it. This was the pattern of the securities laws and of the labor laws.

During that same period, however, bills were introduced in the Congress to cover all the alleged abuses of corporations and the alleged illnesses of the economy in a single statute. These bills, upon which hearings were held from 1935 to 1939, were proposals to require large corporations to be licensed under a federal statute. The licenses would have constituted amendments to state corporation charters. They would have superimposed therein the kinds of reform in securities matters covered by the then very new securities laws, as well as such well-established principles as prohibitions on restraints of trade and unfair competition and the regulation of such matters as wages and hours of employment and child labor. All matters of corporate conduct would be governed by the federal licensing statute, with the "death penalty" of loss of the federal license and, thus, of the authority to engage in interstate commerce as the ultimate sanction for violation.

No such statute ever got beyond the hearing stage. The Fair Labor

Standards Act of 1938 covered wages and hours as well as child labor,
and followed the traditional pattern of addressing specific related problems and attempting to solve them. Federal incorporation, with all the regulatory proscriptions appended to it, was forgotten until the 1970s.[2]

The years of World War II and its postwar era followed. The Depression was behind us. As a nation, we had worked together to win the war. After the victory, we had a long period of prosperity. It was not all roses, however. We did have the Korean war and we did have recessions. But, through it all, the main thrust of the economy was upward. Business expanded and provided jobs. Although not everyone approved of everything that every business entity did, the general reputation of business (the corporations) was good.

New laws continued to be enacted placing higher standards on business, but mainly they were evolutionary in nature—a further refining and extension of the statutes of the New Deal period.

But then came the Vietnam war, an event that, more than any other in the nation's history, upset the national conscience and resulted in polarization of opinion, outright disobedience in the name of conscience, and an upheaval of values long accepted. In the same period, concern for the environment seized the public consciousness—accompanied by a belief that the then existing environmental laws were not adequate to afford the protection that many deemed necessary.

In parallel, there was the civil rights movement. Although it had begun in an earlier decade, having achieved a significant turning point in 1954 with the Supreme Court decision in *Brown v. Board of Education of Topeka*,[3] the movement accelerated in the 1960s and the 1970s.

Then, to cap it all came Watergate.

All these events had a highly emotional impact. There arose a noninstitutional, perhaps an anti-institutional, bias. Its influence was felt by leaders in government, in religion, in education. They found their values and their effectiveness questioned. While they sought solutions to the problems of the day, they were viewed by many as being part of the problem. Through all this turmoil the large business corporation often found itself the scapegoat. Some critics contended that the business corporations had wanted the Vietnam war so that they could make greater profits selling armaments; that the business corporations were the chief polluters of the environment and did not want to undertake antipollution activity because it would reduce profits; that the business corporations discriminated against blacks and other minorities in employment because of prejudice in both managerial and labor ranks; and that the business corporations made illegal political contributions in order to curry government favors at home and abroad.

The result has been a burst of new laws affecting business, far surpassing in magnitude, detail, and severity the laws of the New Deal or any other era. Regulation of business has reached the highest point in our nation's history.

The enactment of additional laws regulating so many specific aspects of business operations did not, however, satisfy the critics of the large corporate enterprises. Concern was expressed for their very size, for the alleged separation of management from ownership, for the feeling that corporations had become too impersonal, that there was really no way to pin responsibility upon anyone for corporate behavior. Such concern was most eloquently expressed by Berle and Means as early as 1932 in their classic work *The Modern Corporation and Private Property*. In their conclusion they stated:

> The rise of the modern corporation has brought a concentration of economic power which can compete on equal terms with the modern state—economic power versus political power, each strong in its own field. The state seeks in some aspects to regulate the corporation, while the corporation, steadily becoming more powerful, makes every effort to avoid such regulation. Where its own interests are concerned, it even attempts to dominate the state. The future may see the economic organism, now typified by the corporation, not only on an equal plane with the state, but possibly even superseding it as the dominant form of social organization.[4]

The writings of Berle and Means influenced much of the New Deal legislation. (Both, in fact, held positions in the Roosevelt administration.) Almost every book and article on corporate power that has been written since 1932 recognizes their work as the seminal writing in that field.

Thirty-six years later, Berle and Means, in the second edition of their book, took note of the changes in the intervening years when they stated:

> Though its outline is still obscure, the central mass of the twentieth-century American economic revolution has become discernible. Its driving forces are five: (1) immense increase in productivity; (2) massive collectivization of property devoted to production, with accompanying decline of individual decision-making and control; (3) massive dissociation of wealth from active management; (4) growing pressure for greater distribution of such passive wealth; (5) assertion of the individual's right to live and consume as the individual chooses.

> Of this revolution, the corporation has proved a vital (albeit neutral) instrument and vehicle. It has become, and now is, the dominant form of organization and production.[5]

## THE OBSERVATIONS OF MACE

While Berle and Means and those who were influenced by their views were concerned about the power of the large corporations and the apparent separation of ownership and management, another writer, Myles Mace, professor of business administration at Harvard, studied

the manner in which the management function is exercised. In 1971 he
published his conclusions that boards of directors have essentially abdicated their functions, that they are essentially subservient to the chief executives of their corporations, and that the large corporations are, for all practical purposes, controlled by their chief executives, except in the most unusual crisis situations.[6]

## TWO TYPES OF CORPORATION LAW

An additional factor in the background of corporate development since 1933 has been the dichotomy of two types of corporation law developing side by side. There has never been a federal incorporation statute for general business corporations. Corporations have come into being and have existed under the provisions of the laws of the several states.

As we know, Delaware has been the principal state of incorporation of the largest corporations. The practice of incorporating in Delaware and then doing business from headquarters offices and plants located almost everywhere except Delaware has long excited suspicion. Henry Ballantine, professor of law at the University of California, took note of this suspicion and controverted it in 1946 when he wrote:

> Corporations have not "left home" and resorted to Delaware as a general rule in order to enable them to operate as tramps, pirates or privateers and prey upon their fellow citizens, but rather because of the crudeness and backwardness of the corporation laws in the states in which their organizers resided. The adoption in various states, after careful study of modern incorporation laws with provisions very nearly as liberal in flexibility and corporate practice as those of Delaware, has not been due to "a race of laxity," but to a desire to furnish reasonable business facilities in the public interest.[7]

While corporation organizers and managers sought out the states most favorable for a place of organization, and while the laws of the state of incorporation governed the powers and internal management of corporations, those who came under the jurisdiction of the Securities and Exchange Commission found over the years that their relations with their stockholders, formerly a concern of state law, became increasingly governed by the securities laws.

In Chapter 8 we saw the evolution of the securities laws in such relations, particularly the extent to which Section 10(b) of the Securities Exchange Act has evolved into rule by "federal corporation law." We also saw, however, that court decisions have placed limits upon the extent to which Section 10(b) can apply to the management of a corporation. Section 10(b) cannot be invoked on the complaint of a stockholder if there has not been a sale or purchase of a security.

While Mace was decrying the alleged dominance of the chief executive in the major corporation, another professor, William L. Cary of Columbia Law School, a former chairman of the Securities and Ex-

change Commission, was analyzing the impact of the Delaware corporation law upon relations between management and stockholders. He
held the opinion that both the legislature and the courts of Delaware
were too much management-oriented. He found this bias in such subjects as fiduciary responsibility, business judgment, reclassifications of
securities, proxy material, relations between parent corporations and
partially owned subsidiaries, and indemnification of directors and
officers. He characterized Delaware as having won "the race to the
bottom."[8]

## THE DEBATES OF THE SEVENTIES

All the circumstances, criticisms, and points of view described in the
preceding paragraphs of this chapter converged in the mid-seventies to
promote major discussions of the role of the corporation, its place in
society, its power, its responsibility, and the manner of its management.

Perhaps the most vocal critic of the large corporations has been Ralph
Nader. Another severe critic, although not so extreme as Nader, is
Christopher Stone, professor of law at the University of Southern Cali-
fornia. Corporate defenders have included Ralph Winter, professor of
law at Yale, and Robert Hessen, professor of business administration at
Stanford. Somewhere in the middle, in addition to Cary, are Law
Professors Alfred Conard of the University of Michigan, Donald
Schwartz of Georgetown, and Detlev Vagts of Harvard, as well as
Courtney Brown, dean emeritus of business administration at Columbia, and Harold Williams, Chairman of the Securities and Exchange
Commission. Each has had something to say on the subject. Most of
them have made recommendations for changes in law or in corporate
practice. In addition, the Business Roundtable and the Corporation,
Banking and Business Law Section of the American Bar Association
have addressed themselves to the subject and have adopted official
recommendations. A brief review of the various positions and recommendations should give a little of the picture of the debate. The reader
is warned, however, that the material produced by such discussions
runs into thousands of pages, and the various points of view cannot
possibly be thoroughly digested within the framework of a single
chapter.

As we are concerned in this book chiefly with corporate managers,
our analyses will be directed primarily to those matters that pertain to
the management of corporations and corporate governance. "Corporate
governance" is a term that has come into vogue during the seventies. It
connotes the manner in which corporations are governed at the top. It is
concerned with the functions and composition of the board of directors
and the relationship of the board to the executive management of the
corporation, the stockholders, the employees, and the general public.

# The Proposal for Federal Incorporation

As we have seen, the concept of federal incorporation is not a new one. It was suggested on a limited basis by Madison in the Constitutional Convention, but never got beyond the suggestion stage. Senate bills forty-five years ago attempted to superimpose federal licensing upon state incorporation and to attach conditions of "good behavior" as the price of continued corporate life. In the 1970s, the idea was revived.

Ralph Nader, who had established a reputation for strong consumerist positions beginning with his campaign against General Motors and the Corvair a decade before, seized upon the unsettled events of the seventies to advocate a Federal Corporate Chartering Act, which would require all industrial, retail, and transportation corporations having sale or service revenues in excess of $250 million or employing more than 10,000 persons in the United States to obtain a federal as well as a state charter.[9] He estimated that this requirement would apply to approximately 700 of the largest corporations based upon 1975 sales, leaving about 15 million smaller business corporations unaffected. He proposed that each of the federally chartered corporations should have a board of nine so-called constituency directors, each of whom would devote full time to the position and would have responsibility for oversight of one of the specific aspects of the corporation's operations: employee welfare, consumer protection, environmental protection and community relations, shareholder rights, compliance with law, finances, purchasing and marketing, management efficiency, planning, and research.[10]

Under his proposal, although directors would serve full time, no member of management could be a director. All corporate interlocks would be forbidden. Not only could a corporate executive not be a director of that corporation, but he or she could not be a director of any other corporation. Likewise, a person serving as an attorney for the particular corporation or any other corporation could not serve as a director. It should be noted that the prohibitions against interlocks would not be based upon competition, real or potential, between corporations or any conflict-of-interest situation, but simply would constitute an absolute prohibition against any one having any other position in the business world from serving as a director.

Not only would Nader forbid corporate managers from serving on the board of directors; he would also prohibit their nominating anyone else to serve. Nominations for the board would be made by individual shareholders excludive of present executives or persons acting for them.[11]

Under the proposed Federal Corporate Chartering Act, indemnification of directors and officers against litigation expenses and judgments would be severely limited, and indemnification insurance would be forbidden altogether.[12]

The disclosure system that has been the hallmark of the securities laws would be greatly expanded. Critical of both those laws and the

SEC's administration of them, Nader would require considerable additional financial detail, as well as extensive public information concerning pollution problems, occupational safety and health, employment discrimination, advertising, and lobbying. The Federal Corporate Chartering Act would also contain an "employee bill of rights."[13]

Nader would also have a deconcentration provision in the Federal Corporate Chartering Act based upon a no-fault concept. A presumption of monopoly power would be created if four or fewer corporations accounted for 50 percent or more of the sales in an important line of commerce. Divestiture of assets or the splitting up of companies would be the remedy.[14]

The publication of Nader's books in 1976[15] attracted a great deal of attention—so much that in June of that year the Committee on Commerce of the United States Senate held a hearing on "Corporate Rights and Responsibilities." In his opening remarks at the hearing Senator John A. Durkin stated:

> The proposal of the Nader corporate accountability research group and the call for Federal legislation present an especially good opportunity for Congress to begin an examination into these questions.[16]

Nader, of course, was a key witness at the hearing. He continued in the same tone that has characterized his writings. In the course of his testimony he stated:

> The Federal chartering proposals rise before this background. It is against a background of a huge body of empirical information showing rampant corporate crime, an epidemic of late only because it was disclosed; showing manhandling of shareholder rights and a progressive atrophy, even in theory, of their status; showing exploitation of taxpayers, consumers, and the community; showing such gross insensitivity as to result in a refusal to inform workers of the lethal chemicals or gases that they have been working closely with on a day-to-day basis.[17]

Also appearing as witnesses at the hearing were numerous other persons of various shades of opinion who have written or lectured on corporate responsibility and corporate governance. A year later, the Subcommittee on Citizens' and Shareholders' Rights and Remedies of the Senate Judiciary Subcommittee held hearings, chaired by Senator Howard Metzenbaum, at which Nader advocated federal chartering of corporations and constituency directors. Many of the same witnesses who had appeared at the Commerce Committee hearing a year earlier were also there presenting their points of view. Although a number of witnesses were critical of various aspects of corporate conduct and corporate governance, none subscribed to the virulence of the Nader criticisms. Although some supported federal chartering, none endorsed the concept of a board of directors consisting entirely of constituency representatives.[18]

# The Proposal for Public Directorships

Christopher Stone has another approach to the question of corporate responsibility. His thesis is that the law is inadequate and cannot be made sufficiently adequate to assure that corporations will be socially responsible. So he would make them responsible not by requiring federal incorporation but by placing public directors on certain corporate boards. Such directors would be appointed by a government agency—the Securities and Exchange Commission or a new agency to be called the Federal Corporations Commission. For every $1 billion of sales or of assets, whichever is higher, a corporation would be required to have 10 percent of its directors as "general public directors."[18]

In addition to the inclusion of general public directors, which would apply only to the billion-dollar companies, he would also have "special public directors."[20] Such directors would be appointed to those corporations that have a "demonstrated delinquency situation" or a "generic industry problem." He does not define either, but offers some examples. He gives a single example of a demonstrated delinquency situation—the Holland Furnace Company, a Michigan corporation having $30 million annual sales, whose twenty-year history of fraudulent sale practices ended with the imprisonment of its president in 1966. His examples of the generic industry problem are mostly of an environmental or health nature, including asbestos companies, plastic plants, paper mills, oil refineries, nuclear power plants, and companies manufacturing consumer products, such as automobiles and television sets, which, he states, "present special consumer safety problems." He goes much further than this, however, when he includes multinationals as a class, claiming that they "present peculiar problems relating to our foreign relations and monetary stability."[21]

Special public directors, like general public directors, would be governmentally appointed. In the demonstrated delinquency situation, appointment might be by a court or a governmental agency. In the generic industry situation, the impetus for appointment of a special public director could come from the company's own general public directors or from a federal agency, such as the Occupational Safety and Health Administration (OSHA), the Environmental Protection Agency (EPA), or the proposed Federal Corporations Commission. Stone would provide for notice and hearing, with final approval of the appointment to be by a federal court. The powers of a special public director would go far beyond the powers normally associated with a single director. The public director, having a special area of authority, could have, Stone suggests, the absolute power to veto promotions, to suspend or fire an employee, or to halt production.[22] For all practical purposes, he or she would be the chief executive.

Stone would not limit management reform to the board of directors level. He would impose legal requirements that corporations have specified executives in charge of certain aspects of their operations, such as environmental affairs, quality control, safety, and the like.[23] He would define qualifications for these positions and enumerate their duties. Failure to perform satisfactorily would result in the individual's suspension. He would make that person "legally answerable to anyone who was injured by a product that passed through his control without putting the injured plaintiff to the task of proving actual negligence."[24]

The Stone proposals are based upon the premises that (1) governmentally appointed directors can do a better job than privately selected directors in assuring compliance with the law and in avoiding "problems," and (2) laws are needed to establish qualifications for certain key positions within companies in order to make certain that the incumbents possess the requisite skills and responsibility. Stone's thesis is that (1) corporations do not obey the law and (2) even if they did, such compliance would not be enough—they must also be socially responsible.[25]

## A Critique of Nader and Stone

The primary problem with the Nader and Stone proposals is that they are based upon a complete distrust of all big business and all corporate managers. While we are not about to canonize corporate managers, and human imperfections in corporate management must be admitted, the picture that Nader paints of tyrannical, grasping, exploiting pirates is a caricature. Most managers of large corporations, and this group includes directors and chief executives, are conscientious people trying their best to do a good job, to manage their companies providently, to produce and sell quality products and services, to obey the law, to keep attuned to the real social interests of the times, to maintain good employee relations, and to maintain a profitable position in both the short range and the long range.

Doing all these things is not a simple matter. Production of quality products involves sophisticated techniques that must be constantly improved and upgraded with more scientific discoveries. Similarly in the field of safety—whether employee or consumer—new and unsuspected risks are frequently found. Increasingly advanced analytical methods lead to discovery of hitherto unknown quantities of a given substance in air, water, or another product. Technological competence finds the problem and technological competence is required to find the solution. Laws are not always clear. Interpretative questions arise daily—particularly with respect to the detailed statutes and regulations of the past decade in such fields as health, safety, the environment, and employee relations.

Knowing the real social interests of the times is a mind-stretching exercise. There is the threshold question of the extent to which a corporation can properly be involved in social issues. It can probably be validly argued that a corporation should be concerned with those social issues that pertain to its own operations. But what is the right decision? The recent concern over the presence of American companies in

South Africa is a case in point. Does remaining in South Africa promote
apartheid, or does it give needed employment to South African blacks?[26]

How far can a corporation go in maintaining good employee relations? Should it give in to all union demands at the expense of customers and stockholders? Or should it resist all union demands to the hilt and risk long and expensive strikes?

One could go on indefinitely as to the types of very difficult decisions that corporate managers must make. Of course, they make some wrong decisions. Every human being makes mistakes, and corporate managers are very much human beings. Nor do I contend that corporate managers are never governed by improper motives. The human being who boasts of never having been governed by an improper motive is intellectually dishonest.

No one can successfully argue that in all respects the law is always adequate. It makes no difference whether we are speaking of the conduct of business institutions and their managers, labor unions and their leaders, government and its officials, or the conduct of just plain people in their relations with one another. All of us can find situations where we think the law is unjust or unclear or inadequate, and we wish it could be changed. The history of this country is that the legislatures, state and federal, have constantly addressed themselves to those areas where the law is unjust or unclear or inadequate, and they have taken steps to remove inequities or to clarify and fill in the gaps.

As observed at the beginning of this chapter, we have seen abundant evidence of how the Congress has pursued this policy in the regulation of business during the past century and particularly the past decade. Today federal statutes, detailed to a degree unimaginable a generation ago, prescribe standards and mechanisms for consumer protection and employee safety and health, for controlling and removing pollution of air and water, for preventing discrimination in employment, and for assuring the integrity of employee benefit programs. The antitrust laws and the securities laws have recently been amended and strengthened. The list is only partial. The important thing is that the Congress, the duly elected representative of the people, has declared certain national policies, has laid down certain rules for the implementation of those policies, and has prescribed penalties and liabilities against those persons, natural or corporate, who violate them.

Critics of corporations and of corporate management contend that the laws are violated with impunity by corporations and corporate managers. They cite examples of light penalties as licenses to pollute, to fix prices, or otherwise to flaunt the law. The fact is, however, that penalties are becoming increasingly severe. The million-dollar corporate fines under the Antitrust Procedures and Penalties Act of 1974 and the Foreign Corrupt Practices Act of 1977 are apt illustrations of the trend. Ever more drastic penalties are being legislated against corporate managers who violate federal statutes. Enforcers, particularly in such fields as antitrust, environmental law, and securities law, are speaking more loudly, acting more vigorously, and seeking and getting more severe penalties against corporate violators and their responsible managers.

Moreover, many of the laws are so new that there has scarcely been time to accommodate operations to their exacting requirements. The Congress has recognized the necessity of time to comply with its standards. For example, the Federal Water Pollution Control Act Amendments of 1972 directed the EPA to provide guidelines for effluent limitations, to be achieved in two stages. The first stage was to be achieved by July 1, 1977, by the application of the best practicable control technology currently available.[27] The effluent limitations applied to municipalities as well as to industries. Industry compliance was far ahead of municipal compliance in 1977 when the Congress had occasion to review progress under the 1972 Act. Industry compliance was 85 percent compared with municipal compliance of 33 percent. While 85 percent compliance is, of course, not perfect, it is evidence that progress is being made and that there is not a crass disregard of environmental standards, as contended by corporate critics.

It accomplishes little to argue that industry should not have polluted in the first place, or that municipalities or other governmental units, state and federal, should not have polluted. Pollution is a condition to which all have contributed, and which all have to do their best to remedy. There is an abundant body of law on the subject. Each corporation, each municipality, each individual has an obligation to comply. Corporate managers know that compliance is in their own self-interest.

Whether or not there will be laws to control or prevent pollution is no longer an issue. The laws are on the books, and there is no suggestion that they should be repealed. The same observation applies to laws concerning discrimination in employment, to laws forbidding foreign bribery, to laws providing for consumer product safety. They are here. Of course, there have been violations, but, despite what the critics say, the numbers of violations have been relatively small compared with the magnitude of corporate operations that have been in compliance with the law. If a corporation or a corporate manager violates the law, the corporation, the manager, or both should be prosecuted.[29] The fact that a few may violate does not justify placing watchdogs on the boards of all corporations over a given size or all corporations that happen to have overseas operations or all corporations that might possibly encounter safety or environmental problems in their operations.

Professor Lewis Solomon of George Washington University Law Center has this to say concerning constituency or public directors:

> [D]irectors unfamiliar with corporate finance or the company's business operations are ill-equipped to give constructive advice or to supervise management effectively. And a director who was distrusted or perceived as an obstructionist would only reduce the board's influence. . . . The pres-

ence of directors dedicated to goals incompatible with, if not antithetical to, the traditional aim of profit maximization might fragment and polarize the board.[30]

**241**
*Comment and
Criticism*

A law requiring a corporation to establish certain executive positions, with prescribed qualifications and duties, to monitor problems such as safety and the environment is an unnecessarily detailed intrusion into the corporation's method of operations. There are very few, if any, corporations needing such executives that do not already have them. Any legal requirement spelling out in detail what they must do completely overlooks the fact that it is the ultimate *performance* of the corporation that is important, its minimization and avoidance of employee accidents and work-related illnesses, and its avoidance of air and water pollution and of unsafe or defective products. The laws now tell us the *results* to be achieved. Corporate managers can best determine *how* to achieve the results. They do not need laws telling them whom they must hire or what the hiree must do to achieve the results.

The conclusion is that there is no valid reason for singling out corporate managers as a class of persons who are not to be trusted. Compelling the election of constituency directors would add nothing to the corporate enterprise except an adversarial atmosphere. Directors elected under such circumstances would be little more than a debating society, with a built-in mechanism for freezing innovation and progress. The result would be stalemate and the economic decline of America.

## Federal Corporate Standards

Earlier in this chapter we have discussed Cary's criticism of state corporation laws. His comments have attracted much attention. Nader has relied on some of Cary's comments in his attacks on state incorporation.[31] Cary does not, however, subscribe to Nader's virulent assaults on corporate America, nor does he advocate federal incorporation, with or without constituent directors.[32] Believing, however, that state corporation codes do not provide sufficient safeguards for stockholder protection and against management abuse, he has recommended a Federal Corporate Uniformity Act applying to all corporations having more than $1 million of assets and 300 stockholders. Such corporations would continue to be incorporated under state law but would be subject to the jurisdiction of federal courts under certain general standards. These standards would include:

(1) federal fiduciary standards with respect to directors and officers and controlling shareholders; (2) an "interested directors" provision prescribing fairness as a prerequisite to any transaction; (3) a requirement of certain uniform provisions to be incorporated in the certificate of incorporation: for example, authority to amend by-laws, initiate corporate action, or draw up the agenda of the shareholders' meetings shall not be vested exclusively

in management; (4) a more frequent requirement of shareholder approval of corporate transactions with limits placed upon the number of shares authorized at any one time; (5) abolition of nonvoting shares; (6) the scope of indemnification of directors specifically prescribed and made exclusive; (7) adoption of a long-arm provision comparable to § 27 of the Securities Exchange Act to apply to all transactions within the corporate structure involving shareholders, directors, and officers.[33]

Cary does not suggest his standards as a complete model. He anticipates that others might be added and some taken away in the legislative process. He has emphasized that his proposals require no federal bureaucratic intervention. No additional duties or authority would be vested in the Securities and Exchange Commission nor would any other federal agency be created. Enforcement of the standards would be solely a matter between the parties to the corporate enterprise itself—stockholders, directors, and officers.

As one who has practiced corporate law for over forty years, I have little fault to find with the general concept that standards of relationship of the management to stockholders should be uniform. We have lived with uniform federal rules concerning securities for nearly a half-century, and while there have been problems of compliance and surprises at unexpected interpretations, corporate managers and corporate counsel have generally been able to adapt their thinking and their operations to the developments that have occurred under these laws.

It would not be too difficult to adapt to federal standards in certain limited aspects of the intracorporate relationships. But there are some risks. Once the concept of federal standards has been adopted, it would be very easy to go to the next step and adopt some of the more far-reaching proposals, such as those calling for constituency directors or government-appointed directors. It could be argued that this is a *non sequitur;* just because certain federal standards are adopted additional requirements will not necessarily follow. Such an argument flies in the face of legislative history. This book is replete with examples of federal statutes that began as relatively simple and seemingly innocuous measures and then, by successive amendments, were expanded to become ever more encompassing of the business or activity that they sought to regulate.

Cary's proposals have drawn some support as well as opposition. Samuel Arsht of the Delaware bar has taken vigorous exception to his criticism of Delaware's standards and argues that they are higher than Cary has described them. He feels that many of Cary's proposed standards are too vague—that, for example, he has given no specifics on the fiduciary standards that he would like to see in a federal law. Arsht is also concerned that Cary's proposal to restate indemnification provisions may be masking an effort to outlaw indemnification insurance.[34]

On the other hand, there are advocates of federal incorporation who do not feel that Cary's proposals go far enough. Schwartz is concerned that cooperative federalism, that is, keeping state incorporation but making it subject to federal standards, would allow "considerable opportunity for undermining the federal goals."[35] He would, therefore, go all the way and require federal incorporation of the 1,000 largest companies. He would not, however, attempt to use the federal charter as a means of accomplishing such objectives as deconcentration of large enterprises, a task that he describes as "too difficult and too divisive . . . for a general chartering law."[36] While Schwartz states that the detailed provisions of a federal chartering act require intensive effort and study, he does offer opinions of certain key features that directly impact upon the position of corporate managers. He would limit the number of directors on a board, probably in relation to the size of the corporation. A majority of the directors would be required to be outsiders. There would be a limit to the number of directorships that an individual might hold. An audit committee and a public policy committee would be required. He also advocates giving "serious consideration to the idea of creating a cadre of professional directors and requiring their inclusion on the board."[37]

While Cary's proposals are relatively low-keyed and might have some validity, I have expressed reservations about the precedent that would be set; the federal law would then resemble the proverbial camel with his nose in the tent. Any reservations that I have about the Cary proposal apply with greater force to the Schwartz proposals. Under federal incorporation, a company would become a creature of the federal government. There is no limit to the onerous requirements that could be attached as a condition of continuing corporate life.

Even the seemingly innocuous conditions concerning composition of the board of directors and the requirements of board committees constitute undue interference. While a given composition of the board membership or board committees may be a good thing for one corporation, it does not necessarily follow that it is a good thing for all corporations. Corporations need freedom to innovate. Each corporation has its own individual personality resulting from the nature of its business, the composition of its management, and its traditions. Legislating such detail would do more harm than good.

## The Debate on Corporate Governance

There are, indeed, a few critics who, distrusting large corporations and contending that they are lawless and lacking in social responsibility, advocate a radical reform of corporate governance by the interposition of constituency directors or governmentally appointed directors. But there are a considerably larger number of thoughtful critics, generally favorable to large business corporations and representing government, academia, the practicing bar, and business itself, who have given a great deal of study and thought to corporate governance and voluntary steps to improve it and who have published their observations and views.

Much has been said and written about the role and functions of the board of directors. It is generally accepted that despite the language of most corporation statutes, the directors of a large corporation generally do not manage the corporation. The more modern language of the Delaware Corporation Law and the Model Corporation Act (described in Chapter 3) is recognized as being more in line with corporate realities—that is, that a corporation shall be managed *under the direction* of a board of directors, with the actual job of managing being left to the chief executive and his or her subordinates. The role and functions of the board have been variously described, as can be seen from some of the following examples.

Conard sees three reasons for a board, stating:

> The most fundamental need of a board is created by the need of every supreme commander for a plurality of minds to identify and applaud his successes and to detect and criticize his failures. . . .

> A second reason for a board is to distinguish the interest of shareholders and other constituents from those of the executive corps. . . .

> A third reason for a board—which will not appeal to all readers—is to represent the interests of constituents other than the shareholders.[38]

Melvin Eisenberg, professor of law at the University of California, Berkeley, lists four principal functions: (1) to provide advice and counsel to the chief executive; (2) to authorize major corporate actions; (3) to provide a means for classes of persons other than the executives to influence or control corporate action; and (4) to provide a means for selection, monitoring, and removal of the chief executive.[39]

There is a great deal of debate as to whether corporate directors are really doing their job and what can be done to make them do it more efficiently. The composition of boards has been frequently criticized. The placement of insiders, that is, of executives of the corporation other than the chief executive, upon the corporate board has come in for particularly heavy criticism. One of the most vocal and certainly most influential of such critics is Harold M. Williams. As Chairman of the Securities and Exchange Commission, he has on numerous occasions spoken out on his thesis that the only inside director should be the chief executive and that all others should be "outsiders." His definition of outside directors is such, however, as to exclude anyone having any other connection with the corporation. Thus, a retired executive, an investment banker, or a commercial banker whose firm provides services to the corporation would all fall into the category of inside directors and would be excluded from board memberships. He would also separate the positions of chief executive and board chairman. The latter, he proposes, would be an outside director.[40]

Rather than recommend legislation on corporate governance or corporate accountability, Williams asks that corporations voluntarily constitute their boards in the manner he has suggested as a step toward

fending off legislative proposals. Addressing the American Bar Associa-    **245**
tion in 1978, he stated:    *Comment and
Criticism*

> As I have suggested in the past, in my view, the best antidote for such
> legislation is for corporations to take steps to assure the public that they are
> capable of discipline which is consistent with the realities of the market-
> place and the noneconomic aspects of the public interest.[41]

While Williams has not proposed legal requirements as to board
composition, recent SEC proposals for amendment of the proxy rules
would have required corporations in their proxy statements to classify
directors as "management," "affiliated," "nonmanagement," and "independent." The proposal created so much controversy and so many
questions of definition arose that it was finally abandoned.[42]

The use of chief executives of other corporations as members of the
corporate board is sometimes criticized as being too "clubby." It is
asserted that too often a chief executive, by virtue of her or his position
as a kindred spirit, is apt to be unduly sympathetic to the wishes and
views of the chief executive on whose board she or he sits and therefore
will not perform the function of monitoring the performance of the chief
executive. Much of this viewpoint comes from the writings of Mace and
has been espoused by other critics.[43] Despite the criticism, chief executives continue to be a prime source of talent for the boards of other
companies.

Somewhere between the outside director and the inside director is
the "working director," espoused by Courtney Brown, or the "officer of
the board," as practiced by a few corporations.[44] Such persons would
be engaged full time or substantially full time in the affairs of the
corporation. They would, however, be directors only and would not
have executive or line functions within the corporation and would not
be accountable to, or under the supervision of, the chief executive.
Although these concepts are interesting and certainly worthy of study,
corporations have not rushed to adopt them.

## SOME VOLUNTARY MOVES TO DIVERSIFY BOARDS

Although the proposals of Nader and Stone for the compulsory placement of constituency representatives, public interest representatives or
governmentally appointed directors have received little support, some
large corporations have made a few voluntary moves to place on their
boards persons who might present a constituency point of view. The
first such incident of note occurred in 1971 when Leon Sullivan was
elected to the board of General Motors so that the viewpoint of the black
community might be brought more intimately to the corporation. Since
that time, a number of other corporations have added blacks, other
minorities, and women to their boards.

A survey of the composition of the boards of directors conducted by
Korn/Ferry International in 1977 showed that 13.6 percent of them

included "ethnic minority representatives," compared with 10.7 percent in 1974. The same corporations reported that 24.4 percent had women on their boards in 1977, in contrast to 11.4 percent in 1974.[45] There is little evidence, however, that the intention is to elect them to represent a constituency point of view. Generally, such persons have brought to the boards their own experience as business executives, lawyers, university officers or professors, and former government officials—the same types of occupational background as those of the traditional white male directors. During this same period, corporations have been increasing their employment of women and minorities in managerial and professional positions, and the higher number of such persons on corporate boards can just as easily be attributed to the desire to be consistent with policies of nondiscrimination in employment as to the wish to bring a constituency point of view to the board.

The Korn/Ferry study reveals two other possible constituencies on some of the corporate boards. "Consumer group representatives" were reported to be on 1.8 percent of the boards in 1977, compared with 4.6 percent in 1974—a trend downward. On the other hand, 2 percent reported having "employee representatives" in 1977, compared with none in 1974. It is not indicated by the report whether the employee representatives come from union or nonunion ranks. The question of employee representation on boards has been a subject of discussion in recent years because of the practice, in fact the requirement, in several European nations, such as Germany, the Netherlands, and the Scandinavian countries, for employee representation. Conard suggests that the largest corporations should move experimentally in the direction of both employee and consumer representation.[46] A number of others who have studied the European model, including Detlev Vagts, disagree with Conard. It is their view that the strength and tradition of collective bargaining between union and management in the United States is such that labor feels better served by not participating in the management of the corporation.[47]

In late 1979, however, an event occurred that may or may not be a prelude to a different approach. The financial troubles of Chrysler Corporation resulted in the company's requesting, and the United Auto Workers Union's agreeing to, a smaller package of economic benefits for union members in the 1979 bargaining then the union was willing to accept from the other automobile manufacturers. The price of the settlement was that the union demanded and received from the company a nomination of the union's national president for a seat on the company's board of directors. This development has not been received with enthusiasm by the business community and has, in fact, been denounced by the chairman of General Motors Corporation as a conflict of interest. He is concerned about the implications of one automobile manufacturer's having to negotiate economic and other labor matters with a director of a competitor.[48] At this stage, it is, of course, too early to determine whether Chrysler's nomination of a labor representative to its board will have any precedential impact. The unusual financial situation at Chrysler in late 1979 was such that scarcely any action taken to alleviate it can be regarded as a precedent for anything other than a crisis of similar magnitude.[48.1]

## GUIDELINES FROM EXECUTIVES AND COUNSEL

While consumerists, academics, and governmental officials have been debating corporate governance, those who have had first-hand experience with the management of and services to corporations have also been studying the subject intently, applying their own practical working knowledge and consulting also with members of the academic community. The result has been two publications by prestigious organizations. The first of these is the *Corporate Director's Guidebook*,[49] prepared by the Committee on Corporate Laws, Section of Corporation, Banking and Business Law, of the American Bar Association, and approved by the council of that section in January 1978. The second is "The Role and Composition of the Board of Directors of the Large Publicly Owned Corporation,"[50] Statement of the Business Roundtable, a group of the chief executives of 180 of the largest corporations, also published in January 1978.

The two statements, prepared and adopted separately, are nevertheless complementary to each other. Both documents are concerned with the responsibilities, duties, and functions, as well as with the composition, of the board. They are documents that every corporate director and every corporate counsel should read, understand, and seriously consider. A few pages devoted to some of their salient features will give the reader some idea of their content and spirit.

At the outset, it should be noted that neither document espouses the thesis that corporate directors should be concerned *solely* with profits. The *Corporate Director's Guidebook* (which in this chapter will sometimes be called merely the *Guidebook*) states that the fundamental responsibility of the corporate director "is to represent the interests of the shareholders as a group . . . in directing the business and affairs of the corporation within the law."[51] The *Guidebook* proceeds, however, to state that while economic objectives will play the primary role:

> Nevertheless, the director should be concerned that the corporation conducts its affairs with due appreciation of public expectations, not only by compliance with existing laws but also through alert recognition of trends in the law and social norms which may affect the corporation's activities in the future.[52]

In similar vein the Business Roundtable statement emphasizes that the board has a responsibility "to direct the enterprise in the interest of the owners, subject to the constraints imposed by law."[53] It warns, however, that there are limits to the extent that the corporation can pursue social objectives. It places the matter in perspective with these words:

> [J]ust as the board cannot review every particular aspect of business opera-
> tions, it cannot be expected to consider every question no matter how
> minor as to the social or public effect of those operations. However, major
> environmental impacts, equal employment opportunity, important rela-
> tionships with communities or governmental authorities, issues such as
> foreign trade or investment activities affecting this country's international
> relations, and matters of comparable magnitude are part of the operation of
> a business and proper for board consideration.[54]

Both the *Guidebook* and the Business Roundtable emphasize the responsibility of the board to function in the selection of the chief executive officer and other senior executives, to monitor their perfor-mance, and to remove those who have not met their responsibility—whether for business performance or for lawful and ethical behavior.[55] Both place high priority on checking financial results and reviewing and approving capital investment programs.[56] Both emphasize the necessity for the board to establish policies and procedures for compliance with the law.[57] The *Guidebook* goes into considerable detail on this matter, and devotes several pages to the director's legal duties of loyalty and care.[58]

The matter of composition of the board of directors is covered in both the *Guidebook* and the Business Roundtable statement. Both strongly reject the concept of the constituency director. The Business Roundtable statement says this about constituency directors:

> Individual directors responsible to particular claimant groups would intro-
> duce into the board a divisive and adversary atmosphere which would
> obstruct the effective performance of the enterprise. Moreover, the notion
> that the board as a whole has a direct responsibility to groups other than
> share owners would mean that there was no clear measure of board perfor-
> mance.[59]

On the question of insiders and outsiders on the board, both the *Guidebook* and the Business Roundtable statement recommend that there be a sufficient number of outside directors to staff such board committees as audit, compensation, and nominating.[60] The Business Roundtable endorses the tendency "to move toward a board structure based on a majority of non-management directors."[61] On the other hand, it rejects the proposals to exclude all inside directors except the chief executive, stating

> [W]e know of no evidence that either consciousness of fiduciary obligation
> or independence is a quality to be equated with "outsideness."[62]

Both the American Bar Association and the Business Roundtable

have contributed substantially to forward thinking in the matter of
corporate governance. If all directors would follow their recommendations, the critics of corporate behavior would soon run out of examples
upon which to base their claims of corporate irresponsibility. We do
not, however, live in an ideal world, and, while improvements are
continually being made, it is too much to expect total compliance with
either legal requirements or voluntary guidelines. Nevertheless, steps
have been taken in the right direction.[63]

## NOTES

1. Ballantine, *Corporations* (rev. ed. Callaghan & Co., 1946) 35–39; Henn,
   *Handbook of the Law of Corporations* (2d ed., West Publishing Co., 1970),
   17–19.

2. Ballantine, *Corporations* 47–48; Nader, Green & Seligman, *Taming the Giant
   Corporation* (W.W. Norton & Co. 1976) 69–70.

3. 347 U.S. 483, 98 L. Ed. 873, 74 S. Ct. 686; supplementary opinion, 349 U.S.
   294, 99 L. Ed. 1083, 75 S. Ct. 753 (1955).

4. Berle & Means (rev. ed., Harcourt Brace & World, 1968) 313. This quotation
   is part of the original text of the first edition and is reprinted in the revised
   edition.

5. *Id., The Modern Corporation and Private Property* xxv–xxvi.

6. Mace, *Directors: Myth and Reality* (Harvard University Graduate School of
   Business Administration, 1971).

7. Ballantine, *Corporations* 46.

8. Cary, "Federalism and Corporate Law: Reflections Upon Delaware," 83 *Yale
   L.J.* 663–703 (1974); Cary, "A Proposed Federal Corporate Minimum Standards Act," 29 *Bus. Law.* 1101–1116 (1974). Ernest L. Folk, professor of law at
   the University of Virginia, joins with Cary in denouncing state corporation
   laws as "largely irrelevant to many of the most seriously destructive practices of corporate managements." Folk, "State Statutes: Their Role in Prescribing Norms of Responsible Management Conduct," 31 *Bus. Law.* 1031–
   1080 at 1035 (1976).

9. Nader, Green & Seligman, *Taming the Giant Corporation* 240.

10. *Id.,* 125.

11. *Id.,* 127.

12. *Id.,* 107–108.

13. *Id.,* 132–197.

14. *Id.,* 233–236. Such a remedy was proposed by the late Senator Philip Hart in
    1972 for seven specified industries, but none of his bills to accomplish this
    purpose ever advanced beyond the committee stage.

15. In addition to *Taming the Giant Corporation,* Nader, Green & Seligman
    published *Constitutionalizing the Corporation: The Case for Federal Chartering
    of Giant Corporations* (The Corporate Accountability Research Group, 1976).

16. *Corporate Rights and Responsibilities,* Hearings before the Committee on

Commerce, United States Senate, Serial No. 94–95 (Government Printing Office, 1976) 2.

**17.** *Id.*, 201.

**18.** Late in 1979 Nader organized a coalition of consumer groups and labor unions to lobby for legislation to enact his proposals into law. "Nader-Led Coalition Seeks Federal Charters for Large Companies," *Wall St. J.*, Dec. 13, 1979, p. 40; "Antibusiness Forces Aim at Corporations," *Bus. Week*, Feb. 11, 1980, p. 42. A bill introduced in Congress in April 1980 incorporated many of the coalition's proposals for more intense governmental regulation of large corporations, but it omitted requirements for federal incorporation and constituency directors. It did, however, provide that a majority of directors must be independent and no person may serve as a director or officer of two or more corporations subject to the proposed act. H.R. 7010, 96th Cong., 2d Sess. (1980). A majority of independent directors would also be required by another bill introduced in the same month. S. 2657, 96th Cong., 2d Sess. (1980).

**19.** Stone, *Where the Law Ends: The Social Control of Corporate Behavior* (Harper & Row, 1975) 158–159.

**20.** *Id.*, 174–178.

**21.** *Id.*, 178.

**22.** *Id.*, 182–183.

**23.** *Id.*, 184–192.

**24.** *Id.*, 191.

**25.** *Id.*, 184–192.

**26.** Melloan, "The Pressures on Apartheid," *Wall St. J.*, Oct. 29, 1979, p. 22.

**27.** P.L. 92-500.

**28.** Phillips, "Water Pollution: A Case Study in the Act of Compromise," *Bus. Week*, Dec. 12, 1977, pp. 134, 138.

**29.** "[W]ith respect to some industries, [environmentalists] wish to see nothing but contraction or even extinction. Consequently, environmental interests are difficult to reflect through participation in governance; they are more effectively imposed by external government pressures." Conard, *Corporations in Perspective* (The Foundation Press, 1976) 358. In an address given on October 22, 1979, John Hanley, chairman and president of Monsanto Co., stated that corporate managers who willfully endanger the lives of others should be sent to jail. *Occ. Safety & Health Rep.* (BNA), Vol. 9, No. 23, p. 542, Nov. 8, 1979.

**30.** Solomon, "Restructuring the Corporate Board of Directors: Fond Hope—Faint Promise?" 76 *Mich. L. Rev.* 581–610 at 601 (1978). Law Professor Ralph K. Winter of Yale sees constituency directors as destroying fiduciary responsibility to stockholders. Winter, *Government and the Corporation* (American Enterprise Institute, 1978) 50. For a critical analysis of the Nader criticisms and proposals, see Hessen, *In Defense of the Corporation* (Hoover Institution Press, 1979).

**31.** Nader, Green & Seligman, *Taming the Giant Corporation* 59–60.

32. Cary, "Summary of Article on Federalism and Corporate Law," 31 *Bus. Law.* 1105–1112 at 1110–1111 (1976).

33. Cary, 83 *Yale L.J.* 663–705 at 702, and 29 *Bus. Law.* 1101–1116 at 1115.

34. Arsht, "Reply to Professor Cary," 31 *Bus. Law.* 1113–1123 (1976). For support of the Cary proposals, see Folk, 31 *Bus. Law.* 1031–1080 at 1080.

35. Schwartz, "A Case for Federal Chartering of Corporations," 31 *Bus. Law.* 1125–1159 at 1136–1137 (1976).

36. *Id.*, 1125–1159 at 1141.

37. *Id.*, 1125–1159 at 1151.

38. Conard, *Corporations in Perspective* 367.

39. Eisenberg, *The Structure and Governance of the Corporation* (Little, Brown & Co., 1976) 156–168.

40. Williams, "To Create Public Trust, Make Boards Freer, Stronger," *Financier*, Vol. 2, No. 2, pp. 36–40 (Feb. 1978); Williams, "Amplifying the Importance of the Outside Director," *Financier*, Vol. 2, No. 7, pp. 29–33 (July 1978); Williams, "Corporate Accountability and the Lawyer's Role," 34 *Bus. Law.* 7–17 (1978); and Smith, "The Boardroom Is Becoming a Different Scene," 97 *Fortune* 151 *et seq.* at 153 (May 8, 1978).

41. Williams, 34 *Bus. Law.* 7–17 at 9.

42. For the proposed rule, see SEC Release No. 34–1470; 43 Fed. Reg. 31945, 31948, & 31952 (July 24, 1978). For SEC comments on abandonment, see SEC Release No. 34–15384; 43 Fed. Reg. 58522 at 58523–58524 (Dec. 14, 1978).

43. Mace, *Directors: Myth and Reality* 106–110; Nader, Green & Seligman, *Taming the Giant Corporation* 96–98.

44. See Brown, *Putting the Corporate Board to Work* (Macmillan Co., 1976); also Statement of Bryan F. Smith in *Corporate Rights and Responsibilities*, Hearings Before the Committee on Commerce, United States Senate, June 1976, pp. 408–418.

45. Korn/Ferry International, *Board of Directors Fifth Annual Study* 10 (Feb. 1978).

46. Conard, *Corporations in Perspective* 365–366.

47. Vagts, "European Perspectives: A Foreword," 30 *Hastings L.J.* 1413–1417 at 1414 (1979). See also Schmitthoff, "Social Responsibility in European Company Law," 30 *Hastings L.J.* 1419–1432 at 1429–1431 (1979); Roth & Fintz, "Corporate Social Responsibility: European Models," 30 *Hastings L.J.* 1433–1462 at 1450–1453 (1979); Furlong, *Labor in the Boardroom: The Peaceful Revolution* (Dow Jones & Co. 1977); Eisenberg, *The Structure and Governance of the Corporation* 2–24; "Germany's Requiring of Workers on Boards Causes Many Problems," *Wall St. J.*, Dec. 10, 1979, p. 1.

48. *Wall St. J.*, Nov. 8, 1979, p. 22. See also the editorial, "The Union Moves In," *Bus. Week*, Nov. 12, 1979, p. 148:

    As a member of the board, Fraser will assume legal responsibility for acting in the interests of the corporation in general and of the stockholders in particular. But as

    See also "The Risk in Putting a Union Chief on the Board," *Bus. Week*, May 18, 1980, p. 199.

an officer of the union, he will be obliged to put labor's demands ahead of everything else. The conflict of interest is obvious.

**48.1** In September 1980, American Motors Corporation, which had been sustaining heavy losses, agreed in strike-settlement negotiations, subject to resolving conflict-of-interest problems, to place a union representative on its board. *Wall St. J.*, September 17, 1980, p. 4.

**49.** Booklet published by the American Bar Association (Rev. ed. 1978), reprinted from 33 *Bus. Law.* 1591–1644 (1978).

**50.** Booklet published by the Business Roundtable (1978), reprinted in 33 *Bus. Law.* 2083–2113 (1978).

**51.** 33 *Bus. Law.* 1606.

**52.** *Id.*

**53.** *Id.*, 2099.

**54.** *Id.*, 2101.

**55.** *Id.*, 1607 & 2098–2099.

**56.** *Id.*, 1608–1610 & 2098–2099.

**57.** *Id.*, 1610 & 2101–2102.

**58.** *Id.*, 1599–1604 & 1611–1618.

**59.** *Id.*, 2106. On this same subject, see the *Guidebook* statement at 33 *Bus. Law.* 1621.

**60.** *Id.*, 1622 & 2108. The Committee on Corporate Laws, Section of Corporation, Banking and Business Law, of the American Bar Association, has published a report, "The Overview Committees of the Board of Directors," 35 *Bus. Law.* 1335–1364 (1980). This report deals with the structure, functions, and responsibilities of the nominating, compensation, and audit committees.

**61.** *Id.*, 2108.

**62.** *Id.*, 2107. In commenting upon an earlier draft of the *Guidebook*, the American Society of Corporate Secretaries stated: "There are fine companies by any standard whose boards are made up principally of employee management personnel." "*Corporate Director's Guidebook:* Comments Submitted by the American Society of Corporate Secretaries," 33 *Bus. Law.* 321–334 at 322 (1977). Vagts has commented: "Inside boards may be more attentive to the business and more ready to take action against a faltering chief executive officer than an outside board chosen by that chief executive officer with an eye to their potential for inactivity." Vagts, "The Governance of the Corporation: The Options Available and the Power to Prescribe," 31 *Bus. Law.* 929–938 (1976).

**63.** All shades of opinion on the subject of this chapter are found in the sixty papers published in *Commentaries on Corporate Structure and Governance: The ALI-ABA Symposiums 1977–1978* (American Law Institute–American Bar Association 1979).

# CHAPTER TWELVE

# Self-Regulation by Managers: Compliance, Circumspection, and Cognizance

With the array of laws and regulations that confronts the corporate manager in the operation of the enterprise, one is moved to ask: "What next? Have we reached the zenith of government regulation of our business? Or is there more to come? And what about my personal exposure? Can I afford to be a corporate manager? Hasn't the Congress made corporate management a hazardous occupation? What can I do about it?"

In all frankness, we must admit that we have not reached the highest possible point of regulation of business or of personal exposure of corporate managers to civil or criminal liability. We need merely look at the past as we have explored it in this book—not just the past of long ago, but also the immediate past of the 1970s.

During that decade we saw more new federal statutes and more amendments of older statutes governing business activities, and more vigorous enforcement action against corporations and their managers, than in any other decade of history. Large numbers of speeches were made, congressional hearings conducted, books and articles written, television documentaries produced, all concerned with the wrongdoings—true or imagined—of American corporations and their executives.

American business has been placed on the defensive. As the decade of the 1970s closed, many segments of business were under fire. Government officials, news commentators and columnists, and consumer activists all were denouncing the oil companies and their profits. The chemical industry was being criticized for producing toxic substances in general and carcinogens in particular. Automobile manufacturers were still being accused of indifference to safety and to fuel economy. The electrical utilities were facing enormous battles: to convince the public of the safety of nuclear plants; to convince the public of the necessity of burning coal over the objections of the environmentalists; to convince the regulatory authorities of the need to increase rates to pay for the higher cost of oil.

The list is endless. The food industry, the drug industry, the steel industry, and others have problems peculiar to their own products and operations, as well as other problems that they share with industry in general. There is no evidence of the clamors dying down in the nineteen-eighties. There is sentiment for more new laws, for new amendments of existing laws, and for more vigorous enforcement. Although numerous problems exist, there is room for optimism. Corporate managers by their own conduct can accomplish much to slow, and perhaps reverse, the trend to overregulation. They cannot accomplish this, however, by maintaining a "business-as-usual" posture. They must give increasing attention to compliance with the law and the place of the corporation in society. They can do so without losing sight of the corporation's profit-making objective. That appears to be the temper of the times.

## COMPLIANCE WITH THE LAW

Despite the complications and penalties of the law, being a corporate manager does not necessarily mean that one is engaged in a hazardous occupation. The laws are on the books, and someone is going to be caught violating them—and will be fined or imprisoned. The Justice Department has promised that. Other managers are going to be subjected to civil liabilities. But if the corporate manager works diligently at compliance with the law, and exercises due circumspection and cognizance of the trends of the time, the risk of liability can be reduced.

To reduce risk it is necessary to work at it. It is not enough to learn about the law after a violation, however unknowing or inadvertent it might be, has occurred. It is then too late. There is a legal aphorism: "Ignorance of the law is no excuse." It thus behooves corporate managers at all levels to be conscious of the many laws that pertain to their respective businesses. This does not mean that every manager need know every nuance of every statute pertaining to the business. It does mean, however, that there must be an appropriate framework wherein the manager knows the general nature and scope of the applicable statutes. This framework will exist where a spirit of respect for the law and an attitude of compliance permeate the organization, where the manager is able to recognize a possible legal problem when it appears, where the manager has ready access to legal counsel who can render prompt and competent advice and can work with the manager in solution of problems, where the manager is encouraged and, in fact, directed to seek the advice and assistance of counsel.

Such a framework must begin at the top. There must be a corporate commitment. The board of directors and the chief executive officer must

the entire corporate organization their respect for the law and their
determination to observe both its letter and its spirit. The *Corporate Director's Guidebook* of the American Bar Association's Section of Corporation, Banking, and Business Law, examined in Chapter 11, makes this statement concerning such a framework:

> The corporate director should be concerned that the corporation has programs looking toward compliance with applicable laws and regulations, both foreign and domestic, that it circulates (as appropriate) policy statements to this effect to its employees, and that it maintains procedures for monitoring such compliance.[1]

But it is not just the lawyers who say that. Here is what the Business Roundtable thinks on the subject:

> Directors and top managers cannot be the guarantors of the lawful conduct of every employee or manager in a large organization—particularly in view of the fact that legal and regulatory requirements are so numerous, so wide-ranging, so obscure and complex. On the other hand, some recent lapses in corporate behavior have emphasized the need for policies and implementing procedures on corporate law compliance. These policies and procedures should be designed to promote such compliance on a sustained and systematic basis by all levels of operating management.[2]

The Business Roundtable statement compresses into a few words the problems of compliance with the law, the absolute necessity of complying, and some of the techniques to be used in helping to assure compliance. The problems are indeed great. The characterization of legal and regulatory requirements as "numerous, . . . wide-ranging, . . . obscure, and complex" is illustrated in the preceding chapters of this book. While I have touched only briefly on the substantive and procedural requirements of the vast body of law regulating corporate operations and have emphasized mainly the liabilities of corporate managers and those portions of the law that pertain particularly to them, it has been evident that there are many borderline situations that the manager encounters almost daily, in which his or her conduct may or may not be consonant with the law.

## INTERNAL DIALOGUE

In order properly to understand these situations, there must be continuous dialogue between managers and corporate counsel. Dialogue that occurs only at the board of directors and chief executive levels is not enough, although at that level, it is most essential. Every decision-making manager in a corporate organization should have access to an attorney (in the corporate legal department or, if there is no such department, then in an outside law firm designated by top management) who can advise competently on the problem involved. It is simply impractical for all legal problems of a corporation to be sent to the chief executive for consultation with the general counsel.

If corporate managers are to seek legal advice at the proper times, they must be able to recognize a legal problem when they see it. This is a principal reason that written policy statements concerning compliance with the law are so important. A properly worded policy statement can give some brief idea of the particular law with which the corporation is concerned. Merely publishing a statement, however, is not sufficient. Many corporations issue manuals in which they go into detail concerning the nature and ramifications of one or more laws that may be considered particularly important for managerial personnel to know and understand. Some utilize staff meetings, internal seminars, and other types of meetings for company lawyers to explain to managerial and professional personnel certain relevant laws, such as those pertaining to antitrust, product or environmental standards, and employee relations.

Such meetings provide an opportunity for questioning and interchange of ideas. They also bring the subject "alive." It is not the cold words of a printed page, a carefully constructed statement of policy, but a live person who can best tell of the ramifications, the prohibitions, and the consequences, generally from the standpoint of great familiarity with the subject. Personal discussion can also help get across the corporate commitment to comply—particularly if the top managerial persons at the meeting participate in the presentation and the discussion. A written message from the chief executive, read at the meeting (if he or she is not personally present), can also be very effective in helping to convince the audience of top management's dedication to compliance with the law. Compliance is, in effect, a partnership. The attorney cannot accomplish it alone, and the manager cannot accomplish it without legal advice. Best results are achieved when they work together.[3]

The logical conclusion, of course, is that corporations should not limit themselves to any one method of communicating their policies and instructions on compliance with the law, whether the medium be oral, written, or in the form of brief policy statements or expanded pamphlets or manuals. Each has its purpose. One can supplement the other.

The important thing is to keep working at the subject of compliance. A corporation cannot have a blitz campaign to tell everyone to comply with the law and then drop the matter for several years. There must be a continuous program of education.

While the teachers of the requirements of the law should normally be the company's lawyers, the major executives of the company must play an important part. They must lend their names to written statements, actively and continually endorse the programs in their communications, whether written or oral, throughout the organization. And most

of all, they must provide the best example. A corporate officer who has **257**
personally engaged in price fixing is in no position to tell subordinate *Self-Regulation*
managers that price fixing is both illegal and against company policy. *by Managers*

High-level policy statements, explanatory brochures, videotaped lectures, group meetings, and seminars—none of these will suffice to keep the corporation and its managers away from liability for violations of the law unless all persons concerned, including directors, chief executives, other officers, corporate counsel, and managers at all levels, take the subject seriously. They must understand the *spirit* of the law—they must recognize that the law was enacted by the representatives of the people and that obeying it is essential.

That is not to say that a corporation and its managers should not raise proper questions of interpretation, or that at administrative hearings they may not argue that a proposed rule is unreasonable or is not authorized by the enabling statute. They need not contend that all ambiguities in the law should be resolved by the corporate counsel and the corporate manager against the corporation, or that the corporation and its managers should not lobby for the repeal or modification of statutes that they consider to be unnecessary or oppressive or ininimical to their own perceptions of the public interest. Lawmakers and administrators are not infallible. They do make mistakes. They do create ambiguities. Corporations and their managers must contend with such mistakes and ambiguities.

The important thing here, however, is good faith. Corporate managers and their counsel must approach questions of this nature in the broad context of trying to understand the legislative intent, of attempting to carry out that intent in a reasonable manner for the best interests of the corporation itself, its stockholders, its employees, and the general public. In their day-to-day activities, managers will continue to face problems of corporate compliance. If they remain alert, if they work with their counsel, if they avoid cutting corners but act in good faith, they should be able, in most situations, to avoid legal liability.[4]

Concurrent with their obligation to comply with the law, corporations and their managers also have an obligation to keep abreast of pending legislation and to make their views known. Much of modern legislation is a result of overreaction to the misdeeds of a few. For example, whatever may have been the laudable intentions of the framers of the Employees Retirement Income Security Act and the numerous statutes pertaining to safety and the environment, there is abundant evidence of requirements far exceeding the needs for curing the alleged evils to which the statutes were addressed. If the law has gone too far in imposing unreasonable or impossible compliance problems, this finding should be communicated to Congress. Even in the highly charged, confusing political atmosphere of Washington, it is possible to obtain amendments to statutes to remove elements of unreasonableness. Efforts to do so will not always succeed, but a well-prepared, properly documented, and well-organized presentation of the faults of a statute has a reasonable chance of obtaining at least some support and, with due persistence, ultimately resulting in the passage of corrective legislation.

These same observations apply to new legislation proposed by others, legislation that may be adverse to the corporations' best interests. Corporate managers should take positions on legislation that pertains to them and their businesses. They have as much right as any other citizens to attempt to influence legislation. Corporate lobbying should be conducted on a high plane. Members of Congress are interested in learning the facts concerning matters upon which they are legislating. Corporate managers who have the facts can be of significant help in securing the passage of reasonable legislation and of preventing the passage of unreasonable legislation.

## THE CORPORATION AND SOCIETY

I make no pretension of being a sociologist or a social philosopher. More words have been written on the social responsibilities of corporations in the past decade than it is possible to count. At one extreme are the avid critics who contend that the primary mission of the large corporations should be to accomplish social reform—that is, reform in the direction that the critics would like to see it go. At the other extreme are those who see no need for the corporations ever to be concerned with anything except obeying the law and making profits.[5] Both extremes, in my opinion, are wrong.

The business corporation never was intended to be a vehicle for social reform. Its purpose is to manufacture and sell goods or to render services and, in so doing, to make a profit for its stockholders. That is the fundamental principle that should not be subverted or subordinated to any other concern. That simple statement does not, however, tell the whole story. Implicit in the fundamental obligation to make a profit for the stockholders is the obligation to make such a profit in a legal and ethical manner. The proposition that a corporation should obey the law is so axiomatic that one wonders why it need be mentioned at all. Yet the fact remains that corporations and corporate managers do sometimes break the law and they must be prosecuted.

So let us assume that the corporation has adopted mechanisms to help in compliance with the law in this day of multitudinous laws affecting every phase of its operations. What more, then, must it do? What do we mean when we say that a corporation must also operate in an ethical manner? Is that an obligation that goes beyond the law? Aren't ethical requirements satisfied by complying with the law? Should a corporation and its managers anticipate the law and take steps that they deem ethically sound and which may cost money, even though the law does not require them to do so? The answer, in my opinion, is that they should. There are frequent examples of corporations that have done just that.

Such an example is that of certain major chemical manufacturers who for many decades have been concerned about the physiological effects of exposure to their products. Toxicological and industrial hygiene laboratories were established by a number of these companies thirty and forty years before the enactment of the Occupational Safety and Health Act (OSHA).

Stone refers to the discovery of the cancer risks of vinyl chloride and asks if this risk might not have been found sooner if the producers had had to prepare impact statements.[6] What he does not state is that the largest United States manufacturer of vinyl chloride had carried out extensive research on the effects of inhaled vinyl chloride, and in 1961 published its findings that slight liver damage appeared in animals following prolonged exposure to concentrations as low as 100 parts per million. At that time, there existed a threshold limit value of 500 parts per million for vinyl chloride in the atmosphere of the workplace. This had been recommended by the American Conference of Governmental Industrial Hygienists (not an official agency but an organization of government officials whose recommendations were often incorporated into state or local codes). This producer recommended downward revision of the standard to 100 parts per million for short exposures, with 50 parts per million as a maximum time-weighted average. The Conference responded by adopting a 500-part per million *ceiling* in 1962. It was not until 1972 that a real effort to reduce the time-weighted average was made by the Conference, at which time it was set at 200 parts per million, 4 times higher than the limit recommended by the largest producer ten years before. OSHA, which came into being in 1970, gave the 500 parts per million ceiling the force of law in 1971, but did not respond to the producer's recommendation of 50 parts per million time-weighted average until 1974.[7] (The OSHA standard was reduced to a still lower ratio in 1975.)

While this is a single instance, it is an example of many that illustrate corporate concern for safety and the willingness to spend large sums of money for research to determine the physiological effects of products and to take steps to make their use more safe. It also shows that industry has published much toxicological data and is capable of getting ahead of governmental authority in the pursuit of safety. Concern for human welfare is not limited to the government or to consumer organizations or to environmental advocates. Corporations also have a real interest in the subject. In the interest of furthering the long-range profit objectives of the enterprise, corporate managers must be, and are, alert to the social impacts of their decisions.

The Business Roundtable, in commenting upon corporate social responsibility, has observed:

> [T]he interest of share owners cannot be conceived solely in terms of short-range profit maximization. The owners have an interest in balancing short-range and long-term profitability, in considering the social and polit-

ical viability of the enterprise over time and in adjusting to the global environment in which it operates. Moreover, share owners and directors alike have an interest in assuring that entities with which they are identified behave ethically and as good citizens. It is the board's duty to consider the overall impact of the activities of the corporation on (1) the society of which it is a part, and on (2) the interests and views of groups other than those immediately identified with the corporation. This obligation arises out of the responsibility to act primarily in the interest of the share owners—particularly their long-range interest.[8]

The Business Roundtable statement places corporate social responsibility in the proper perspective. It does not call for corporate managers to go out and right all the wrongs of the world—or even to try to decide what is right and what is wrong in the world. It does call upon them, however, to give careful consideration to the social impacts of their actions.

Many large corporations have established committees of their boards of directors, denominated "Public Policy," "Public Interest," or some similar name, to monitor on a regular basis the social, environmental, community, and overall public interest aspects of their operations. Such a committee customarily has the assistance of staff people within the corporation who concentrate on one or more of the fields of interest to the committee so that it may be kept up to date on the problems and the progress in these areas as perceived by the management. Just as boards of directors and chief executive officers are admonished to set up intracorporate mechanisms for compliance with the law, so they will also find it advisable to provide mechanisms constantly to appraise their social performance, and those mechanisms should exist at both the board of directors level and within the management structure. The concern of the board or of a board committee will be of little use if there are not people within the corporation who can make studies for, and prepare reports to, the board or the committee and who can assist the chief executive in implementing the decisions.

At the expense of reiteration, I must caution that I am not advocating that a corporation's public interest or public policy committee should lead it to efforts to reform the nation or the world along the lines advocated by an activist group just to keep the group away from demonstrating at its next annual meeting. Not all causes advocated by such groups are either necessarily just or in accordance with the views of a thinking majority. In environmental situations, for example, there may be hard decisions. Remove the last part per million of the pollutant at a cost that throws the plant into a perpetual operating loss; close the plant down to prevent further pollution; or seek a waiver from governmental authority if such a thing is available. Each of the three possible decisions will be unpopular with someone—the stockholders, the employees, or the environmental activists.

This is only one example of the many social problems that can arise, and in which, no matter what decision is made, there can be both good

and bad social consequences. There are no set rules to guide corporate
boards and managements in these areas. Careful study, consideration of the conflicting interests, and ultimately a determination of what is best for the long-range interests of the corporation must sometimes result in a vote for the lesser of two evils, and perhaps no one will be really satisfied. The fact remains, however, that corporate managers have to live in the world and must face problems of this nature. They should structure their corporations so that they are in a position to deal with them objectively when they arise.

## CODES OF CONDUCT

In order to demonstrate their commitment to legal and social responsibility and to define the norms of such responsibility that they expect from their employees, corporations have increasingly come to adopt codes of conduct or statements of business principles and to disseminate them both within the corporation and outside. These codes and statements take many different forms. Some are very comprehensive and detailed, setting up rules for specific situations. Others are simply statements of principles covering a few pages. The shorter statements are often supplemented with separate documents covering specific subjects, such as the environment, a conflict of interest, or the antitrust laws.

All such codes and statements appear, however, to have one thing in common—the corporations are concerned not only with obedience to the law but with recognition of responsibility to the stockholders and to the public, and their statements express this concern. A few excerpts from some of the statements give some idea of the various ways in which corporations have addressed their concern.

Oscar Mayer & Co. says it this way:

> The Company values its reputation for integrity. We intend that our business practices be compatible with the economic and social priorities of the locale in which we operate, but we believe that honesty is not subject to criticism in any culture. Accordingly, even though customs may vary from country to country and standards of ethics may vary in different business environments, honesty and integrity characterize our business activity. Management members will not be permitted to achieve results at the cost of violation of laws or regulations or through corrupt or unscrupulous dealings.[9]

Another corporation begins its statement of international business principles in this manner:

> The Dow Chemical Company operates in pursuit of maximum long-term growth in profits through superior performance. The company enters into commercial activities in any nation fully aware of its social responsibilities to that nation.

. . . . .

We comply with the laws and regulations of those countries in which we operate, and we seek to conform to the policies and objectives of host countries.[10]

Caterpillar Tractor Co., one of the first companies to publish a comprehensive code of conduct, makes the following statements concerning law, ethics, and social responsibility:

> We affirm that Caterpillar investment must be compatible with social and economic priorities of host countries and with local customs, tradition and sovereignty.
>
> . . . . .
>
> The law is a floor. Ethical business conduct should normally exist at a level well above the minimum required by law.[11]

It is unlikely that many major corporations remain that have not adopted codes of conduct or statements of business principles. Certainly it is a practice to be recommended to any and all corporations— not only the very large ones, but to those of medium size as well—that face problems of complicated laws governing their operations or relations with the various publics. It is not enough, however, simply to write a code and then forget it. The code should be reemphasized, from time to time, in written and oral communications from top management and in group meetings like those recommended for education on law compliance. Codes of conduct and programs for law compliance are very much intertwined. In the more comprehensive codes, a corporation may include a summary statement of the principal provisions of one or more statutes that are particularly important to it. Thus, meetings can cover both the subject of law compliance and the broader subject of the code of conduct. This approach provides an excellent opportunity to discuss law, ethics, and social responsibility all in the same forum and to interrelate them to the problems peculiar to the particular corporation and the industry of which it is a part.[12]

## CONCLUSION

I was a member of a corporate team for more than forty years. Although I am retired, I still consider myself a part of the corporate establishment. I have known hundreds of corporate managers over those years, not only in the corporations in which I have served as counsel, officer, or director, but in those with whom I have done business or have known through professional associations or social contacts. By and large, with very few exceptions, I have known them to be honest, trustworthy, and responsible.

I have seen mistakes made in business. I have seen losses incurred, penalties and civil liabilities inflicted, adverse public reaction to corporate policy. I know that the law is complex and sometimes confusing. I

know that people with the best of intentions can go awry. I know that public reaction cannot always be prophesied. Almost any corporate manager will acknowledge mistakes—a few things that he or she has done in the past and would like to be able to do over again and "do them right."

Commenting on the position of the corporation in society, Henry Ford II acknowledged some of the failures of corporate managers, including himself, when he said:

> In recent decades we businessmen have neglected many genuine problems and turned a blind eye to conditions that should have caught our attention. Often we have simply been stupid. We have refused to confront some of the crucial issues of our time, and as a result we have played directly into the hands of our critics and helped to make matters worse.
>
> . . . . .
>
> Today the great majority of capitalism's problems reflect the failure of businessmen to take politics and new social movements as seriously as they should have. Often, businessmen have refused to respond to what's valid in the critics' cases. . . . At the same time, many businessmen have also been inept in dealing with those charges and criticisms that aren't valid—and there are many of these. We capitalists were smart enough to make America the richest and most powerful nation the world has ever known, but in responding to our critics we have often preferred bombast to serious public policy analysis.[13]

Ford's criticism of himself and his fellow corporate managers is one of the strongest by a corporate chief executive that can be found. It goes directly, however, to the root of the problem. Corporations are not perfect. Corporate managers are not perfect. Corporate critics are not perfect. Government officials are not perfect. No one is perfect. But our not being perfect does not give us license to wallow in our own imperfections. As corporate managers and as citizens, we have an obligation to our corporations and to our country to be ever alert to the requirements of the law, to the changing social scene, to the demands of society. We must try to anticipate, as best we can, the changes in society and their impact upon our operations. We must adjust our attitudes so that we can calmly and objectively consider such changes and evaluate them to determine their impact upon our operations—and, if necessary, adjust to accommodate. We must do this not in the spirit of surrender to forces we do not believe in, but in the spirit of understanding the complexity of society and of understanding that those who recognize and can adjust to change are those who will be best able to survive and prosper.

Innumerable laws dealing with social issues have imposed severe obligations upon corporations and their managers. As the Congress addresses other situations, it is not unreasonable to expect that bills will be introduced and perhaps passed to rectify whatever wrong the Congress may define. Or, if a law already exists but the Congress determines it is not being properly obeyed, it may amend the legislation to tighten the procedures for enforcement or to increase the penalties, as it did in the case of the antitrust laws in 1974.[14]

Every regulatory statute that the Congress has passed has been in response to a reaction that there is an evil that needs to be corrected. The actions of corporate managers who have somehow failed to realize their responsibility for customer or employee safety, for responsible labor relations, for open and free competition, for many other questionable business practices, have caused the enactment of laws that have not only sought to remedy the alleged evils but all too frequently have gone too far and have placed unreasonable burdens upon business. Corporate managers must therefore be conscious of their performance in the public sector. It is not sufficient that they merely seek the most profitable opportunities, although they should not forget that profit is a prime objective. They must also try to anticipate what the public expects of them. This does not mean that they should surrender to every suggestion that comes from every far-out activist, but they must try to understand what substantial segments of the public expect of them.

The very minimum that a corporate manager can do to demonstrate social responsibility is to make reasonable efforts to comply with the law. Corporate managers cannot expect to prevent additional and more repressive laws if they are unwilling to comply with existing law. To the extent that corporate managers are diligent in the matter of compliance with the law and recognize and attempt to deal with problems that may invite new laws for solution, the steady march of increasing governmental regulation can be slowed. There is no guarantee that such a result will necessarily follow, but at least it will be worth the effort.

Corporate managers are among the finest people I know. They work hard. They are imaginative and innovative. They want to do the right thing. While the pitfalls are many, there are many ways to guard against them. I am an incurable optimist. I believe that most corporate managers are conscious of the risks and of their responsibilities and that they will survive and lead America to greater heights of well-being in the future.

### NOTES

1. *"Corporate Director's Guidebook,"* 33 *Bus. Law.* 1591–1644 at 1610 (1978).

2. "The Role and Composition of the Board of Directors of the Large Publicly Owned Corporation," Statement of the Business Roundtable, 33 *Bus. Law.* 2083–2113 at 2101 (1978).

3. Some corporations have effectively used closed-circuit television and videotapes as a means of communicating their messages on compliance. Such messages can be shown to numerous audiences in a considerably more efficient manner than multiple personal appearances can be arranged. These presentations avoid the necessity of travel when the audiences are

located in several cities. The audiences can receive the messages more

quickly than if they had to wait for the speaker to make travel rounds, and the messages can be replayed for those who missed an earlier presentation. The videotape is, however, merely an extension of the printed word. While the speaker is seen and heard on the tape, the opportunity for open discussion between speaker and audience is not there. Some of the disadvantages of videotape communication may be avoided by use of the newly emerging technology *videodisco*. See "Videodisco, a Three-Way Race for a Billion-Dollar Jackpot," *Bus. Week,* July 7, 1980, pp. 72–81 at 77.

4. In the field of antitrust law, there are a number of articles on corporate programs for antitrust compliance. See, for example, Freedman, "Antitrust: The Education of a Client," 17 *Bus. Law.* 321–331 (1962); Withrow, "Making Compliance Programs Work," 17 *Bus. Law.* 877–887 (1962); Anderson, "Effective Antitrust Compliance Programs and Procedures," 18 *Bus. Law.* 739–754 (1963). A recent manual on the subject is Garrett, *Antitrust Compliance: A Legal and Business Guide* (Practicing Law Institute, 1978). The principles of an antitrust compliance program could in some cases be adjusted to fit the tasks of complying with some of the newer federal regulatory statutes. For recommendations as to compliance programs under various laws, see Hancock, *Executive's Guide to Business Law* (McGraw-Hill Book Co., 1979) 24-1 to 24-18 (antitrust laws), 41-5 to 41-6 (Foreign Corrupt Practices Act), 51-1 to 55-6 (environmental laws), 67-11 to 67-17 (antiboycott laws).

5. See statement of Henry G. Manne, Hearings before the Committee on Commerce, United States Senate, June 1976, p. 235.

6. Stone, *Where the Law Ends: The Social Control of Corporate Behavior* (Harper & Row, 1975) 226.

7. Torkelson, Oyen & Rowe, "The Toxicity of Vinyl Chloride as Determined by Repeated Exposures of Laboratory Animals," 22 *Am. Ind. Hyg. Ass'n J.* 354–361 (1961); Kramer, "Vinyl Chloride Risks Were Known by Many Before First Deaths," *Wall St. J.,* Oct. 2, 1974, pp. 1, 22.

8. Statement of the Business Roundtable, 33 *Bus. Law.* 2083–2113 at 2099–2100 (1978).

9. From Oscar Mayer & Co. *Management Manual.* Quoted with permission.

10. From *International Business Principles, The Dow Chemical Company* (1976).

11. "A Code of Worldwide Business Conduct," issued by the Caterpillar Tractor Co., published in *Corporate External Affairs: Blueprint for Survival* (Business International, S.A. 1975).

12. For a comprehensive discussion of corporate codes of conduct, including a suggested model, see Harris, "Structuring a Workable Business Code of Ethics," 30 *U. of Fla. L. Rev.* 310–382 (1978).

13. Ford, "Where Capitalism Falls Short," remarks at the University of Chicago Business School Management Conference, April 26, 1979.

14. The proposed Criminal Code Reform Act, which has been pending in Congress in various forms since 1966, contained until 1979 a provision that would have made a corporate supervisor criminally liable for an offense committed by the corporation merely on the basis of "his reckless failure to supervise adequately." S. 1437 and H.R. 6869, 95th Cong., 1st Sess., § 403(c)

(1977). This provision was severely criticized as placing too high a degree of vicarious responsibility and of discouraging "much delegation of authority needed for the legitimate and efficient operation of any large-scale organization." Miller & Minsker, "Criminal Code Revision Would Place Corporate Officers in New Liability Situations," *Legal Times of Washington*, Aug. 7, 1978, pp. 20–22. It was omitted from the version pending in the Congress late in 1980. S. 1722, 96th Cong., 1st Sess. (1979).

# Index